Becoming Utopian

Becoming Utopian

The Culture and Politics of Radical Transformation

Tom Moylan
Foreword by Ruth Levitas
Afterword by Phillip E. Wegner

BLOOMSBURY ACADEMIC
LONDON • NEW YORK • OXFORD • NEW DELHI • SYDNEY

BLOOMSBURY ACADEMIC
Bloomsbury Publishing Plc
50 Bedford Square, London, WC1B 3DP, UK
1385 Broadway, New York, NY 10018, USA

BLOOMSBURY, BLOOMSBURY ACADEMIC and the Diana logo
are trademarks of Bloomsbury Publishing Plc

First published in Great Britain 2021

Cover design: Eleanor Rose
Cover image © Sarah Browne / IVARO

A catalogue record for this book is available from the British Library.

A catalog record for this book is available from the Library of Congress.

ISBN: HB: 978-1-3501-3333-4
       ePDF: 978-1-3501-3334-1
       eBook: 978-1-3501-3335-8

Typeset by Integra Software Solutions Pvt. Ltd.

To find out more about our authors and books visit www.bloomsbury.com
and sign up for our newsletters.

Contents

Foreword

Tom Moylan has been my friend, colleague, and constant interlocutor since the 1980s, so it is a pleasure to be invited to write a Foreword to *Becoming Utopian*.

Moylan is best known for his two sole-authored books. The first of these, *Demand the Impossible*, was published in 1986 and immediately became a landmark text. It was impossible to work in the field of twentieth-century utopian literature without reference to Moylan's argument, which identified a transformation in the utopian genre. Moylan argued that science fiction writers from the 1970s (notably, Marge Piercy, Ursula K. Le Guin, Joanna Russ, and Samuel R. Delany) had radically adapted the form of utopian fiction, rendering it less didactic and more critical—and thus he coined the term "the critical utopia" to describe this new turn. This was a statement both about content and about literary form. These utopias were less confident than those of the fin-de-siècle by writers such as William Morris, Edward Bellamy, and Charlotte Perkins Gilman. They focused on the action of the stories' protagonists, as well as on description of the alternative society. Criticism and interrogation of the possible future were brought within the text. The protagonists themselves were less typically privileged white males, more often female, gay, or from non-white ethnic groups; and they operated collectively. Even so, the transition to the new society was uncertain and provisional. Even at that time, Moylan was interested in the way utopian writing was arising out of and speaking to radical political activity of the time. While *Demand the Impossible* remains widely cited and the term "critical utopia" has become part of the vernacular of utopian studies, it has been predominantly used to discuss what happens in texts. Chapter 1 of this volume draws on the less-remarked theme of this early work to show how central the relation between political activism, self-construction, and utopian scholarship runs as braided themes throughout all Moylan's work.

It was to be nearly a quarter of a century before Moylan's second monograph appeared in 2002, this time addressing dystopia and science fiction, *Scraps of the Untainted Sky*. The mysterious and resonant title represents the last five words of E. M. Forster's 1909 short story "The Machine Stops," a dystopian vision emerging in a predominantly utopian field. But that was to change. Moylan observed that the late twentieth century was (at least in the Anglophone world) dominated by dystopian rather than utopian writing. Against the prevailing orthodoxy (in collaboration with Raffaella Baccolini of Bologna University), he argued that the dystopian imagination was not necessarily anti-utopian but in many, especially more recent, cases open-ended—thus allowing the possibility of a route out of dystopia or even posing the challenge to find one. Whilst there was initial resistance to the term "critical dystopia," this was the formulation that quickly took root. Again, it became very difficult for scholars working in the field of dystopian literature not to engage with this interpretation.

These two books together constitute a significant, even indispensable, contribution to utopian scholarship. Yet Moylan's work, as this new volume shows, was wider and deeper. There were literary and editorial collaborations, including several special issues of *Utopian Studies* and volumes of essays co-edited with Baccolini, with Jamie Owen Daniels, with Michael J. Griffin. Moylan was in demand as a keynote lecturer at utopian conferences across the globe, and some of the chapters in this volume started out in that form. Those conferences were also opportunities to engage with and support younger scholars, as was his role as a rigorous yet sympathetic PhD examiner. His greatest institutional contribution, however, was establishing the Ralahine Centre for Utopian Studies at the University of Limerick, formally inaugurated in 2003 shortly after his appointment as Glucksman Professor of Contemporary Literature. The Ralahine Centre became a focal point for utopian scholars through its program of day conferences, longer conferences, and events hosting visiting scholars. One such event with the visiting sociologist Erik Olin Wright in 2013 incorporated an audience with the President of Ireland Michael D. Higgins, who has taken a sympathetic interest in the Centre's work.

The Ralahine Centre also established a book series, published by Peter Lang, both issuing new work and re-issuing works that were out of print (including my own *The Concept of Utopia*, originally published in 1990). The first volume in that series, edited by Moylan and Baccolini and issued in 2007, was *Utopia Method Vision: The Use Value of Social Dreaming*. But the origins of that book illustrate Moylan's capacity for initiating projects and fostering collaboration, and thus his deeper and less visible contribution to the work of utopian studies as a field. In 2002, he invited a series of scholars to reflect on how we had used utopianism in our own work, giving papers first in Limerick and then in Galway. I was, I recall, the first speaker, and my paper (and subsequently the published essay) was titled "The Imaginary Reconstitution of Society: Utopia as Method." It was the question posed by Moylan and his ongoing and sympathetic conversation that led me to pursue the issue of utopia as method in my own later work.

The chapters in the second half of *Becoming Utopian* reflect Moylan's own ongoing preoccupation with utopian method. What does this mean? How can we use it, if our project is to transform the world, and, in these dark times to prevent what Bloch called "devastatingly, possible fascist Nothing"? In these chapters, there is the constant reprise of the political necessity of utopia alongside the question of what is to be done? There is also a return to questions of the formation of the subject that were to the fore in some of the chapters earlier in the book that focus on Ernst Bloch, on Jűrgen Moltmann, and on Gustavo Gutiérrez and liberation theology. These questions do not sit easily in academia, where the tension with political activism is always something that must be negotiated. However, the question of how to be in the world presses more heavily, perhaps, not just because of the darkness of the times, but because of our age. I went to see Moylan in 2011 when I was wrestling with related questions of ontology and the quest for utopia. We both found ourselves returning to themes and writers from our early careers, unwittingly obeying Richard Buckminster Fuller's exhortation to go back to what we were thinking about before we were interrupted by the need to earn a living.

Tom Moylan, however, has never stopped wrestling with the politics of utopia, either as text or as project. The chapters in this book, taken with the other published writings, do much to make sense of his intellectual biography. They also show a subtle mind at work, coupled with an indefatigable commitment to using utopianism to make the world a better place.

Ruth Levitas
Bristol, 2019

Acknowledgments

I will always begin by recognizing and thanking my students (at the University of Wisconsin-Waukesha, George Mason University, John Moores University, the University of Limerick, and the Summer School of the Centre for the Study of the Moral Foundations of Economy & Society at University College Cork, as well as many international correspondents). I am grateful to my friends and colleagues at UL's Ralahine Centre for Utopian Studies (including Aileen Dillane, Joachim Fischer, Michael J. Griffin, Michael G. Kelly, Mariano Paz, Jack Fennell, Cathal MacMahon, Deirdre Ní Chuanacháin, and Míchéal Ó'Súilleabháin [RIP]), at the School of Architecture (including Merritt Bucholz, Peter Carroll, Jan Frohberg, Anna Ryan, and Grainne Hassett), and many others in the European Utopian Studies Society and the North American Society for Utopian Studies. Particular individuals who helped along the way include Siân Adiseshiah, Raffaella Baccolini, Antonis Balasopoulos, Ildney Cavalcanti, Nathaniel Coleman, Michael Cummings, Laurence Davis, Jamie Owen Daniel, Caroline Edwards, Peter Fitting, Tadhg Foley, Vincent Geoghegan, Fredric Jameson, Raphael Kabo, Kieran Keohane, Carmen Kuhling, Patricia McManus, Andrew Milner, Angus Mitchell, Caoilfhionn Ní Bheacháin, Patrick Parrinder, Kenneth Roemer, Peter Sands, Lyman Tower Sargent, Lucy Sargisson, Christabel Scaife, Eric Smith, Edson de Sousa, Elida Tessler, Pavla Veselá, Jennifer Wagner-Lawlor, Tim Waterman, Darren Webb, Kathi Weeks, and Hoda Zaki. I want especially to note the support of Michael D. Higgins, President of Ireland/Uachtarán na hÉireann, whose own personal and political journey is one of the inspirations for this project on becoming utopian.

I greatly appreciate the contributions of Ruth Levitas for her Foreword, Phillip E. Wegner for his Afterword, and Hugh O'Connell for the interview that comprises the closing chapter. I deeply value the collaboration with Sarah Browne, whose cover image (and appended text) so powerfully carries these utopian reflections in another medium; and I appreciate the work of Eleanor Rose, the Bloomsbury designer who produced the entire cover. Finally, I am deeply grateful for the excellent and patient help with editing, permissions, and indexing by Kathleen Eull and Jack Fennell; for the careful copyediting and formatting by Lawrence Cleary and Karthiga Sithanandam and the Integra team; and for the enthusiastic support and advice from my Bloomsbury editors, David Avital, Lucy Brown, and Ben Doyle. Always, I value the friendship and solidarity of Jack Zipes and Darko Suvin. Finally, I dedicate this book to my parents, Hannah Fenton and Tom Moylan, whose nurturing helped me become utopian; my daughters, Katie Moylan and Sarah Moylan, who have carried the spirit of this work into their own lives; and to my wife, Kathleen Eull, who continues to teach me cooperation and compassion.

Permissions

Introduction: Becoming Utopian

Dystopian Time, Utopian Turn

It's not yet the worst of times, but things are worse every day. It's far from the best of times. Harm abounds everywhere. The interrelated crises that have been with all of us for a good while are nearing conjunctural explosion. Ecologically, planetary nature (including humanity) is facing a downward spiral of near-total destruction. Economically, the global intensification of capitalism (in its latest neoliberal version) is producing the alienation and exploitation of all aspects of everyone's lives. Politically, the overdetermined matrix of corporate power, superpower aggression, and the inability of democratic politics to uphold modernity's utopian potential of justice, peace, and freedom increasingly privilege the super-rich and super-powerful even as it subjects the great majority of people around the world to intensifying vulnerability; and the consequent surge of war, disease, starvation, and immiseration combined with the normalization of enslaved and precarious work is destroying the vitality and complexity of everyday life. Legally, culturally, and existentially—accelerated by these sociopolitical depredations—a virulent xenophobia is steadily attacking humanity on grounds of race, ethnicity, gender, sexuality, age, bodily form, or other modes of perceived difference—even as fascistic politicians, regimes, and mass movements are gaining ground and feeding official and individual rage as they rise from the fetid swamp of that hatred.

In the face of this dark totality, for those of us (in all our intersectional situations and endeavors) who seek to challenge and transform this current order in the spirit of a just, equal, and ecologically healthy existence for all of human and non-human nature, it is clearly time for the political exercise of the insurgent hope of the utopian impulse with its transformative capacity. In this regard, I refer specifically to a utopianism of the Left, broadly and inclusively conceived and practiced. However, even as we embrace and engage the utopian problematic and praxis, we must be wise to recognize the ways in which capitalism's retrieval mechanism "subsumes and consumes" (Fisher 2009) the radical potential of utopianism: on one hand by condemnation, on the other by cooptation.

One stream of this simultaneous erasure and enclosure of the utopian proclivity can be located in the upsurge of dystopian expression (in literature, film and television, music, visual and performance art) in the last few decades. This output of dark narratives (especially in film/television and print) has too often coalesced in a "dystopia porn" (as sf writer Vandana Singh terms it) that feeds a fatalist, anti-utopian, pessimism rather than provoking the prophetic awakening of which the dystopian imagination is capable (Singh 2018).[1] As opposed to the recognized capacity of dystopian narrative not only to warn but also to stimulate transformative political action, this neoliberal dystopian structure of feeling functions as an ethical and political inoculation that normalizes a passive indulgence in our terrifying reality, thereby paralyzing radical challenges to its terms and conditions.[2] As Franco Berardi observes, in *Futurability: The Age of Impotence and the Horizon of Possibility*, a "mutation" has occurred in the collective cultural imagination that now generates a sense of "impotence" that leads us "to think that our own suffering cannot be relieved by political projects" (Berardi 2019: 43, 44). In his assessment of the reception of the film version of *The Hunger Games*, for example, Berardi argues that such a dystopian portrayal no longer stimulates anger and rebellion but rather delivers the message that the world portrayed is the world that is given, and unchangeable. Indeed, the acceptable message is embedded within the social imperative of the film's competitive society: "In this new world, only the winner can survive, and if one wants to win she must eliminate all the others, friends and foes" (Berardi 45).

While this compliant erasure is being encouraged on the shady side of the neoliberal street, a concomitant enclosure of the "eutopian" sensibility is restricting utopia's anticipatory energies in the false dawn of managed innovations that reinforce rather than revolutionize the present reality. As these maneuvers effect the shrinkage of the utopian impulse within the terms and conditions of a passive "dystopian" structure of feeling, the utopian project itself is coopted and compromised by way of sanctioned practices of inspirational self-improvement within the existing order of things (see Webb 2016). In Mark Fisher's terms, the seamless dynamics of capitalist realism restrict utopianism to the functioning of market logic; and in this way, utopian vision and agency are limited to and judged by their viability within the present system. "What we are witnessing," Darren Webb argues, "is the domestication and recuperation of utopia. The subversive, counter-hegemonic thrust of utopia has been tamed and rendered fit" for its instrumental use in the present order, and none other (Webb 2016: 440). In these times, therefore, the radical holistic analysis and capacity for realization that are implicit in utopia's revolutionary potential are being destroyed by its entrapment within pleasurable cynicism even as it is recouped in an instrumental form of a creative "openness" that plays no part in a dialectic of critical and transformative intervention.[3] Against this toxic resignation and complicity, what is needed is not a one-dimensional black mirror that turns in on itself but rather a prismatic utopian optic that can break through this provincial temporality and open people to a range of possibilities out of which critical and transformative visions and practices can emerge. As Singh puts it, we need to "free our imaginations beyond dystopia-porn, the easy techno-fix, or the escape–to–another–planet so that we might once more learn what it means to belong" (Singh 430). If, therefore, we choose to change this oppressive maneuver, then it's time to throw off the shackles of dystopian despair and exercise what Rebecca Solnit describes as "hope in the dark" (Solnit 2016) and embrace what Sara Ahmed describes as hopeful "acts of refusal and rebellion as well as the quiet ways we might have of not holding onto things that diminish us" (Ahmed 2017: 1).

Since we are already living in this "concrete dystopia" (Varsam 2003), if we are seriously to work with a utopian proclivity that aims to change this order of things, then we need to be aware of these vampiric practices as they suck the radical energy out of all life on this planet.[4] Recalling Fredric Jameson's koan, we need to remember that the "deepest vocation" of utopia is to remind us of "our constitutional inability to imagine Utopia itself: and this, not owing to any individual failure of imagination but as a result of the systemic, cultural and ideological closure of which we are all in one way or another prisoners" (Jameson 1982: 157). Therefore, we need to remember that the first move in the utopian process must be one that refuses this totalizing closure; in other words, the first step is that of negation, or, as Marx put it, of the "ruthless critique of all that exists" (1975). Only from this negative standpoint, only by deploying a transformative interpretive critique, can we begin to articulate the negation of the negation, generating and creating prefigurative scenarios and actions that enact the better world toward which we are struggling. In the spirit of the science fictional imagination of Ursula K. Le Guin and the liberation theology of Gustavo Gutiérrez, we must therefore engage in a simultaneous yet sequential practice of denunciation and annunciation in order to work within the capitalist present in such a way that we produce the next steps on the path toward a better horizon that is anticipated by push and pull of utopian praxis.[5]

A key question, then, is just what "we" (especially those of us, in all our diversity, who self-identify as radical utopians) are to do? This existential and political question is one that I explore through several facets in the prismatic reflections that I offer in this book. However, before I move into brief overviews of my chapters, I want to reflect on the nature of the progressive utopian process itself. Of course, much has already been done in this regard: particularly, studies that build on that of Ernst Bloch, as in the long-term contributions of Fredric Jameson and Ruth Levitas. Indeed, the roots of my own utopian framework can also be traced back to Bloch (and I engage with the work of all three in the following chapters, especially Bloch's utopian hermeneutic retrieval of the traces of hope throughout history, Jameson's articulation of the primary drive of impulse and its development in program, and Levitas's elaboration of utopia as method).[6] In his life's work, Bloch significantly shifted the intellectual focus on utopia from a scholarly study of objects and practices to an engaged examination of the revolutionary charge that grows out of humanity's deep and pervasive impulse of hope for a better world that is Not Yet Become but which could guide humanity toward the novum of that better world.[7] As he extensively demonstrates, the movement toward a utopian horizon, throughout the centuries and around the world, has achieved significant instances of realization, each of which carries a utopian surplus of lessons learned and dreams actualized that can be drawn on again and again as available traces of hope in present-day struggles.

For Bloch, the world is unfinished. He works from a hopeful standpoint ready for an engagement within history; but the successful outcome of that historical engagement requires, as Jameson reminds us, both the utopian impulse and the political programs that it shapes and catalyzes.[8] In Ruth Levitas's formulation, the utopian method has three dimensions: an archaeological mode that involves "piecing together the images of the good society that are embedded in political programs in social and economic policies," leading on to an architectural mode which consists of the "imagination of potential alternative scenarios for the future" (2013: 153). However, these interpretive and political practices must also be accompanied by an ontological mode, "which addresses the question of what kind of people particular societies develop and encourage" (2013). It is this third mode that I especially consider in these introductory comments, as I work from Levitas's recognition of the graceful quality of "human flourishing" implicit in the utopian persuasion in order to consider the process of the formation of the individual utopian subject (2013).[9] As Vincent Geoghegan describes it, the emergent utopian person increasingly abandons her or his subjugated position and assumes the metaphoric stature of an unalienated "upright carriage" (Bloch) that no longer accepts "the bent-low gait of humanity" enforced by hegemonic society (Geoghegan 1996: 40).[10] Needless to say, however, this utopian project must necessarily be collective; for it involves the totalizing transformation of social reality, by all of us, for all of us. Settling for utopia in one person results in nothing but a tantalizing indulgence that is all too easily available for the capitalist disciplinary imagination. Fantasizing about lotto victories, trying to live one's own life in a bubble of happy satisfaction, or even acting in a narrowly "political" manner are not in themselves utopian; for these manifestations are but alienated abstractions of a deeper utopian impulse. No, the fully utopian unit is, must be, a collective engaged in concrete conditions and possibilities that seeks fulfillment in a radically transformed social context that has not yet been achieved. However, such collectivities are made up of individuals, and it is the individual that I now want to address. Simply put, the growth of a collective utopian movement is located in each person who comprises it; but for that person effectively to contribute to the movement, she or he must *become* utopian, and indeed *continue* to become utopian. This becoming requires the individual to break from the ideological formation (or *habitus* as Pierre Bourdieu puts it) within which she or he has been constructed and to tear through its sutured confines so as to be able to acknowledge that the existing world order is no longer sufficient, to see that something is missing and that something better can be achieved for all (Bourdieu 1977: 86).[11]

Of course, this *break* or utopian turn is not a simple binary maneuver, not a before and after gravitational flip on a voyage to a fixed telos. Despite Karl Mannheim's useful counter-pointing of *Ideology and Utopia*, the interplay between the two is more complex and ongoing than he allows. Jameson's observation in *The Political Unconscious* that the "effectively ideological is also, at the same time, necessarily utopian" provides us with a more nuanced reminder that utopia and ideology are dialectically imbricated within the general structure of social representation and socialization (Jameson 1981: 286). Therefore, the emergence of the utopian impulse occurs within the ideological milieu in which an individual exists, but the impulse manifests itself as a deep change that sees the person turn against and beyond the present world system and its formative structures. Whether working from direct suffering or the knowledge of that of others or with an exercise of fantastic imagination of a better life-world or in the intensity of political struggle (with its failures and victories) or, as is often the case, in a complex amalgam of all the above, this utopian turn may occasionally occur at a particular moment (often when historical conditions intensify) or it emerges over a series of incremental steps.[12]

My sense of this *turn* at the social psychological level resonates with the analysis developed by Fritz Perls, Ralph Hefferline, and Paul Goodman in *Gestalt Therapy* (1951). Publishing their work in the United States within the sphere of postwar radical culture that preceded the Long Sixties, the anarchist intellectual Goodman and dissident psychotherapists Perls and Hefferline brought the problematic of psychoanalysis to bear on the juncture of the social and the personal in an intervention that critically recognized the destructive psychological mechanisms of the postwar economic expansion that was extending capitalist exploitation into the realm of everyday life (including human consciousness and embodiment) and teased out the dialectical possibilities for a creative self-fulfillment that could move against and beyond it. In their project, which proceeds as both social/psychological theory and therapeutic practice, they detail the ways in which the dynamics of Western industrial society in particular and modern civilization in general desensitize and inhibit the human self (in an analysis compatible with the work of the Frankfurt School, especially Herbert Marcuse's accounts of "repressive desublimation" and the "totally administered society").[13] With an historical diagnosis that recognizes the embodiment of the self within the machinery of the social, they identify the ways in which postwar capitalism achieved the "unnecessarily tight adjustment to dubiously valuable workaday society" in which individuals are "regimented to pay ... debts and duties" (348). Consequently, they argue, "the average adult finds himself [*sic*] caught in responsibility toward things in which he is not deeply interested" (355). Thus, the ideal subject for this social regime is produced as "comparatively enslaved, not to the reality but to a neurotically fixed abstraction of it," with the outcome being imbued with "habitual deliberateness, factuality, non-commitment, and excessive responsibility" (353, 356).[14]

Against this disciplinary regime of desensitization and inhibition that induces the compliant self to accept current reality as tolerable, Perls, Hefferline, and Goodman offer a therapeutic approach that addresses the "chronic emergency" and "terrible actuality" that aims to generate a growth process in which the self achieves a "creative adjustment" that re-situates the person in a radical relationship with the enclosing regime in such a way that she or he can break through its barriers and emerge as an integral and actualizing person (299). This therapeutic process turns on the achievement of a "gestalt shift" in which the emergent self reconfigures a new relationship to lived experience. By assisting a client in the achievement of "the 'Aha' of recognition," the therapist facilitates the process of achieving an individuated wholeness that produces a new personal figure operating on, against, and beyond the ground of the established social environment (279). Clearly, the authors recognize that this intervention is not indifferent or neutral in regard to present-day society but is indeed a radical intervention, one that generates "deliberate awareness" in the pursuit of a freer and more fulfilled existence (282). In this way, the future, for the individual self and the society, is unblocked and held open to new possibilities. In language that resonates with Bloch's, they evoke the radically reconfigured person as one who is highly aware, embodying an erect posture, experiencing psycho-sexual freedom, and living a life that stands up to advanced industrial alienation in a healthy mixture of pleasure and work that can continue along a path of actualization.[15]

·While the problematic and practice of gestalt therapy in the hands of these 1950s radical intellectuals and therapists constituted a radical analysis of and intervention in the contemporary socioeconomic reality, there is no doubt that the proffered methods of treatment were recaptured within the therapy industry of postfordist capitalism and redeployed as a mechanism for fine-tuning human "potential" within its disciplinary regime (leading in time into the production of what became the neoliberal subject). Nevertheless, as a product of that postwar interrogation of consumerist economy and culture, *Gestalt Therapy* was an important part of the anti-capitalist movement that intervened at both the individual and the societal levels to expose an alienated and exploited existence and, in doing so, contributed to the emergent critical utopian problematic and practice that has been regenerating since then.

I argue, therefore, that a progressive understanding of the individual utopian turn from the "well-adjusted" subject to the radically free, self-actualizing, agent can be enriched by this approach to the psychology of the gestalt shift. However, I further suggest that the later political articulation of this turn by Alain Badiou offers a sharper-edged analysis that aims to disable the mechanisms of the current social system that offer a minimal "freedom" limited to existing terms and conditions. Shifting from a pre-1968 to a post-1968 moment, and working not only within an anti-capitalist framework but from an overtly communist standpoint, Badiou nominates the "break" as a key element in the *revolutionary* (as opposed to alternative or reformist) process of the formation of a subject who refuses to submit to the current order of things.[16] Badiou's elaboration of the break is, for me, most acutely presented in *St Paul: The Foundation of Universalism*. Herein, he evokes that historical person as neither revered saint nor authoritarian enforcer but rather as a "militant figure" whose life most effectively exemplifies the process of an "overturning" that takes place at the punctual moment of an "Event" that opens the way to the "transformation of relations between the possible and the impossible," between the world as it is and as it could be (Badiou 2003: 2, 45).

Badiou explains the *Event* as a "rupture in the normal order of bodies and languages as it exists for any particular situation" (2010: 242, see also 227), and he cites the Paris Commune, the October Revolution, May 68, and the Arab Spring as examples of such ruptural moments (which can also occur in the realms of science and love).[17] In his interpretation of Paul's Damascene turn, he creates a narrative of the formation of a new militant subject that makes this radicalizing problematic available at a universal register: the lesson of Paul becomes a general lesson for all radical agency. Generally occurring as part of a given historical moment replete with political contradiction and movement, the Event is not itself the realization of a revolutionary possibility but rather is the fruitful instance that occasions "the creation of new possibilities" (2010: 242). Therefore (in an articulation that resonates with Jameson's koan), it "paves the way" for that which is "impossible" in the present order of things; or (resonant with Bloch's formulation), it is "the occurrence of the real as its own future possibility" (243). Consequently, an individual deeply attuned to and affected (indeed, *effected*) by an Event encounters a previously "unheard-of possibility," one dependent on what Badiou calls the "grace" of this radical moment (2003: 45).[18] In this moment, she or he experiences a "breakdown" in previously secure knowledge, whether empirical and conceptual, and in turn stands open to the radically new—especially as that standpoint is developed in fidelity to the conditions of that Event (2003).[19] In this breakthrough moment then, a new subjectivity and a new way of being in the world are enabled.

Thus, for the likes of Paul, or any of us, the journey away from our construction as a sutured subject leads through a process of "ontological subversion" into the creation of the "militant" (or what I would term a radical *utopian*) subject (Badiou 2003: 47). At this point, however, it is important to consider just how the newly subverted individual can grow. Attaining a catalyzing combination of estrangement and desire for a better world is one thing, but becoming a person who has a holistic apprehension of existing society and an anticipation of one that is progressively better calls for the further nurturing of that initial desire, or impulse. In order to develop the double consciousness of knowing one's own existence in the present but also of grasping the possibilities for a future that does not yet exist, the new subjective capacity must be brought forward (*educare*) into a fuller self-awareness of the historical and political context so that it can be actualized as agency (at best, in movements comprised many such individuals). Therefore, aided by *Gestalt Therapy*'s social psychological understanding of the process of the gestalt shift and Badiou's political articulation of the evental break, I believe we can better understand the deep transformation that occurs in the formation of an individual as a utopian. While many individuals who consequently become utopian no doubt do so through a titrating series of shifts or breaks, there are indeed those moments of crisis, as figured by Paul, in which the change is instantly crystallized; but in all cases, the transformation is a form of radicalization.[20] This, then, is a process that reaches into the structural and existential depths of the social order that permeates the normative subject and effects a gestalt shift wherein the individual's holistic perception of reality alters, doing so in an estranging break from that order that can then lead to a desire for a better world.

Well before *Utopia as Method*, Levitas presented her thinking about this constructive entry into sociopolitical praxis in her 1997 chapter, "Educated Hope: Ernst Bloch on Abstract and Concrete Utopia." A central argument in this chapter is that in order for the utopian impulse to be effective it must develop into a self-aware commitment and contribution to radical transformation. It is not sufficient for utopianism to stimulate wishful thinking about a better way of being; it is crucial that it engages in *creating* it. Levitas therefore draws on Bloch's concept of "educated hope" (*docta spes*) and then turns to the work of E. P. Thompson and Miguel Abensour on the "education of desire." While Bloch acknowledges, indeed celebrates, the plethora of utopian wishing in human history, Levitas reminds us that he is critical of much of the idealized content of these wishes; and in this regard, his opposition of "abstract" versus "concrete" utopia enables him to distinguish between a compensatory wish that has no purchase on historical, material change and an anticipatory understanding and action aimed at actually creating a better future for all (in making this distinction, Bloch refers to Lenin's assertion that dreams and life must be connected for change to be realized). As Levitas puts it, he argues that the "process of extracting concrete utopia from its abstract trappings" can be understood as the activity of an "educated hope" that can enable the aspiring utopian individual to distinguish between the (re)captured images of a better world abstractly tolerated by the present order of things and its materially and politically available tendencies and latencies that can be pulled forward into a transformed future (1997: 70). Thus, she concludes: "Educated hope, *docta spes*, is born out of and articulates this relationship between ends and means, passion and reason, aspiration and possibility. It represents the transformation of wishful thinking into wish-full and effective acting, the move from the dream to the dream come true" (73). Consequently, the "distinction between abstract and concrete utopia is a necessary one if Bloch as to rehabilitate utopia as a transformative category and a category within Marxism, rather than as a repository of desire" (1997).

To further her argument for the concrete, active quality of the development of the utopian subject and the utopian project, Levitas adopts the phrase "education of desire," as it was used by Thompson in his studies of William Morris and further developed by Raymond Williams, with both drawing on the work of Abensour.[21] What is crucial for Thompson in his reading of Morris's groundbreaking utopian novel, *News from Nowhere*, is his argument that the narrative should be read not simply as a satisfying dream but as an achievable vision; for in this way, the fictive project can educate a desire for a better world by teaching us not just to desire, but to desire more and in a different way than that allowed by the present order. However, Levitas reminds us that Thompson insists that such an educated desire requires the crucial activity of *judgment* "between good and bad, or at least better and worse, utopia" (1997: 77). Thus, with the education of desire, "the disruption of the taken-for-granted is implicitly directed to a further end, that of transformation" (1997).[22] Also working from Thompson, Williams argues that the consequent activity of "willed transformation in which a new kind of life has been achieved by human effort" must always be at the core of the "crucial vector of desire" that constitutes an authentic utopianism, which he then goes on to describe as the "moment of longing for communism, the longing for rest and the commitment to urgent, complex, vigorous activity" (Williams 1978: 203, 206, 209). Thus, the individual gestalt shift or break must not only open into a desire for a better world but, through the process of a utopian education, must engage also in value-based choices within the hard work of radically making a world that has not yet been achieved.

With the individual utopian turn, however, the journey only begins; for the ongoing journey in the education of desire involves not only learning but affiliating and working with others in this transformative vocation: that is, in working as a member of a community or collective. In his *Short Organon for the Theatre*, Bertolt Brecht recalls a theatrical commonplace that has political resonance: namely, that "the smallest social unit is not the single person but two people ... [for in] life too we develop one another"; therefore, if we are to usefully grow from our own radicalized subjectivity into overt political action, we must come together, we must act collectively (1957: §58, 197).[23] Again, Williams provides a schema for tracking this process. Hovering between the idiosyncratically personal and the new sociability, the emerging utopian person experiences the unfolding of her or his existential and political maturation into an active agent. In moving from the break, or a series of breaks, through encounters with others (including politically committed change agents such as therapists, teachers, organizers, artists, as well as peers), the individual enters into a new structure of feeling, as Williams terms it. In this process, a "practical consciousness" is enriched by new insights and social relationships that are "in solution," in a mix of thought and feeling that are still in the process of growing into a more developed comprehension of the concrete situation and what can be done within and beyond it (Williams 1977: 128–35). Working within new structures of feeling, newly radicalized individuals can come together (through learning and action) and share in a stronger collective praxis.[24] Williams identifies this next stage as one of entering into "formations," which he describes as "conscious movements and tendencies" in social and cultural reality (1977: 119). From this new matrix of collective experience, those who have been radicalized, who have been liberated from the dominant sutured reality, can enter into overt sociopolitical activity aimed at a utopian horizon.

What shape that activity takes is of course a key political question in any given historical moment. Minimally, it can begin with singular participation as a concerned human being but then develop into more organized activism in once-off protests, targeted campaigns, sustained mass mobilizations—and in so doing may take the form of a party, para-party, or grassroots formation. Whatever way this change develops, in Badiou's terminology, it involves an operation of "subjectification" that moves from the singularity of the individual break into an "incorporation" within a "synthesis of politics, history, and ideology" that leads into a combination of "subjective capacity and organization" (Badiou 2010: 236–7, 227). In this process, the subjectification implicit in becoming a "communist" (which—in its evocation of a new subjectivity in a social reality that has been totally transformed beyond the realms of capitalism and socialism—I take as equivalent to *utopian*) constitutes "the link between the local belonging to a political procedure and the huge symbolic domain of humanity's forward march toward its collective emancipation," or, putting it succinctly, to "give out a leaflet in the marketplace was also to mount the stage of History" (236). Therefore, the individual who has undergone a break or gestalt shift and who realizes that he or she is not "doomed to lives programmed by the constraints of the State [and I would add Market]" becomes "authorized" within their own self to become part of the larger movement to force "the impossible into the possible" (252–3, 256).

In her discussion of what I would understand as utopian subjectivity, Jodi Dean invokes the figure of the "comrade" as her preferred term, over "communist," as a more precise interpellation of the radical person who works "in the world for something better" (Dean 35). Tracing its meaning through Left history, Dean describes the comrade as "a carrier of utopian longings" who works collectively to "alter our connection to the present" (Dean 10). Working with Kathi Weeks' utopian interpretation, she identifies a dual function for the comrade (in a formulation that runs throughout this book): one is to "alter our connection to the present, while the other is to shift our relationship to the future" (Dean 10). As Weeks puts it, the first work of estrangement "mobilizes the negativity of disidentification and disinvestment" while the second step of hope redirects "our attention and energies toward an open future ... Providing a vision or glimmer of a better world" (quoted in Dean 11).[25] Importantly, for our time especially, Dean sees the comrade as egalitarian and utopian but, significantly, as relational and generic, not affiliated with any given identity. Thus, comrades work together to "cut through the determinations of the everyday (which is another way of saying capitalist social relationships)" by moving with and beyond allied identity formations and politics into a complexly unified movement working for the "common horizon" of total social transformation (Dean 22, 27, 11, and see 11–23).

For Dean, the comrade is a "figure of political belonging," "a figure for the political relation between those on the same side"; and she consequently argues that the optimal organizational form for this collective agency is still that of a communist party, which she regards as the most effective form for the "emancipated egalitarian organization of collective life" (Dean 43, 35, 6). Recognizing the concerns about the history of party formations as reflected upon by other communist philosophers such as Antonio Negri and Badiou, she nevertheless holds out for the party as the ideal base for mobilizing commitment and struggle against "patriarchal racial capitalism" (Dean 25, and see 5–6). Of course, she recognizes the previous shortcomings and failures of the party structure, especially in its authoritarian theory and practice; yet, invoking the "courage, enthusiasm, and achievements of millions of party members for over a century," she argues for the party formation as one that can be refunctioned and re-energized (Dean 6). Thus, she values the party's potential for mobilizing and delivering an "organized response" that can effectively move forward with "growth, direction, equality, and density" (Dean 90). The party can therefore bring together diverse struggles in a unity of action that is emancipatory and egalitarian. As an organization, it can facilitate the dual function spoken of above: namely, the "disruptive negativity" opposing the present system and the relational unity generating "new values, intensities, and possibilities" (Dean 96).

As noted, for his part, Badiou sees such a party formation as no longer tenable; and he suggests other possible models, such as those found in the Event of May 68 or in emergent movements such as *L'Organisation Politique* in France.[26] As he puts it:

> The party in Lenin's sense ... was ultimately subordinated to constraints of State. Today's task, being undertaken notably by *Organisation Politique*, as to support the creation of such a discipline subtracted from the grip of the state, the creation of a thoroughly political discipline. (228)

For myself, I accept Dean's argument for the necessity of a unified political organization that is capable of standing up to the systemic power of the global patriarchal, racist capitalist order (for me, best exemplified historically in the work of the Popular Front). However, at this moment such an organization remains at the horizon of a more developed political moment; though assuredly (in Bloch's sense of a utopian surplus that can once again be available), it is necessary. Thus, I share the assessments of the likes of Negri and Badiou, and I therefore find the intermediate organizational form adopted by *L'Organisation Politique* or groups such as the Wisconsin Alliance (which was active in the 1970s across sectors throughout that US state, from the university to factory to neighborhood, in urban and rural locations, and was involved in the class and identity politics of the time) to be indicative of an effective political formation for our time. In a policy document developed by Alliance members in the mid-1970s, this form was identified as that of a "mass socialist organization" (MSO) that mediated between grassroots activity and the organizational discipline of a party structure (Peterson 1975).[27] While spontaneous uprisings, temporary occupations, and identity-based formations are crucially needed, and effective in their own right, it is necessary to move with and beyond sectoral struggles and to develop a movement with a unified organizational leadership structure (albeit one that is radically intersectional and democratic and governed by practices of criticism/self-criticism) in order to sustain a political movement that can work against the global neoliberal/superpower order while reaching for a utopian horizon by building new political, social, and cultural spaces, formations within what Fisher calls "the remorseless meat-grinder of Capital" (15).

Becoming utopian consequently names the trajectory of social subjects who break with their compliant formation (having come to re-learn the world and to imagine that it could be radically other). In this development, each newly radicalized individual, imbued with utopian desire, can, with others, engage in an education of that desire and enter into a radical utopian structure of feeling that nurtures collective solidarity and action in anticipatory harmony with all humanity and all of nature. In this sense, the utopian process is not a matter of a top-down imposition of a plan or blueprint by a designing authority but rather a dynamic amalgam of experiences by which many break with the existing world (now as strangers in what has become an unfamiliar land) and work together toward a utopian horizon. This collective movement rises out of each person and is informed by each, even as they are formed by that movement. Furthermore, this self-conscious and self-reflective dialectical process of individual and collective formation can be enhanced, indeed preserved and strengthened, by maintaining the self-reflexive and self-critical capacity of the utopian impulse to work against the grain of what is, in the name of what could be better, even within the movement, even within a realized victory.

Effectively engaging with this process therefore requires that we consider questions of psychological and political development, as well as organizational possibilities. It requires that we become aware of the process in order more effectively to embark on this path. In the specific context of our own time of "Trouble" (as Donna Haraway names it), as we are armed with this understanding and informed by this commitment to contribute to the general activity of becoming utopian, we need to "stay with the trouble" and act within this darkness (Haraway 2016). We cannot afford to indulge in nostalgia for former identities or politics; nor can we afford abstractly to wish that a transformed future will one day arrive on our doorstep. We certainly cannot give up or submit. No, we must take on the apparently impossible work of achieving the end of capitalist and superpower rule and joining the long march of building those new spaces, creating those new possibilities. Again, Fisher's words are inspirational:

> The long dark night of the end of history has to be grasped as an enormous opportunity. The very oppressive pervasiveness of capitalist realism means that even glimmers of alternative political and economic possibilities can have a disproportionately great effect. The tiniest event can tear a hole in the great curtain of reaction which has marked the horizons of possibility under capitalist realism. From a situation in which nothing can happen, suddenly anything is possible again. (Fisher 2009: 80–1)

For her part, in *Staying with the Trouble*, Haraway has issued yet another timely manifesto that resonates with this declaration and with the educated desire of many of us who see ourselves as utopians. Here and now, we must work from where we are, in a manner that is compassionate and cooperative, doing so with each other and with all of nature:

Our task is to make trouble, to stir up potent response to devastating events, as well as to settle troubled waters and rebuild quiet places. In urgent times, many of us are tempted to address trouble in terms of making an imagined future safe, of stopping something from happening that looms in the future, of clearing away the present and the past in order to make features for coming generations. Staying with the trouble does not require such a relationship to times called the future. In fact, staying with the trouble requires learning to be truly present, that is a vanishing pivot between awful or edenic pasts and apocalyptic or salvific futures, but as moral critters entwined in myriad unfinished configurations of places, times, matters, meanings. (Haraway 2016: 1)

To be utopian in our time is to refuse to give up, to refuse to be instrumentally "realistic" and thereby no longer acting as well-behaved and respectable subjects within the current terms and conditions of the present society.[28] To be utopian is to become a radical change agent. Working collectively in comradely solidarity, those who consciously desire that better world have to find ways to tease out the tendencies and latencies that will enable all of humanity to build it, here and now, in the shell of the old.

Strong Thoughts

In this book, I reflect on this overarching relationship between the utopian problematic and political agency, on the process of "becoming utopian." Written (and presented and published in various versions) between 1987 and the present, my chapters explore questions of utopian theory, method, and practice, some doing so in terms of specific political practices. Taken together, they add up to a contemporary articulation that resonates with the above discussion of the emergence of the utopian subject and her or his entry into political praxis. The final versions presented in this volume are substantially the same as the originals, although they have been variously revised and expanded to minimize repetition and to maintain the overall thread of the book's exploration of becoming utopian.

In the opening chapter, "Strong Thought in Hard Times: Utopia, Pedagogy, and Agency," I review my own utopian turn and the subsequent development of my utopian vocation and method in the personal, political, and professional dimensions of my life. In the spirit of the education of desire, I discuss the activity of reading in terms of its relationship to political activism (itself an iteration of the dialectic of utopian impulse and program). I then recount the unfolding of my lifelong utopian project: in my studies of science and utopian fiction, liberation theology, political theory and activism, and my recent work on utopia as method and agency. In the spirit of Bloch, I end with a discussion of utopia's temporal dynamics and reflect on the pedagogical and political impact of the apparently ephemeral yet long-lasting quality of the utopian persuasion, especially as it moves through various half-lives, constantly exceeding previous limits and subsequently finding new forms of expression and activity.

This chapter began as my own contribution to the seminar series "Utopia Method Vision," that launched the Ralahine Centre for Utopian Studies, which I founded upon my arrival at the University of Limerick in 2002. Beginning in 2003, my colleagues and I invited twelve scholars in utopian studies (from Canada, England, Ireland, Italy, and the United States) to participate in a two-year series of presentations in which each participant addressed the ways in which she or he entered the utopian sphere and engaged in their study of the objects and practices of utopianism (understood as social anticipations and visions produced through texts, social experiments, and political action) and how, in turn, those objects and practices shaped their intellectual life in general and their research agenda in particular. In 2007, Raffaella Baccolini and I edited and published these presentations in the first volume of the Ralahine Utopian Studies Book Series, *Utopia Method Vision: The Use Value of Social Dreaming* (this included the first version of this chapter, "Realizing Better Futures: Strong Thought for Hard Times"). Rooted in my long-term conviction that a viable left utopianism in our time must be both critical and constructive (and self-reflexive), the entire project constituted an intervention that has fostered a more self-aware engagement in utopian research and practice, especially as it helped to generate the ongoing investigation of utopia as method (seen most fully in Ruth Levitas's published work, which began to develop in her contribution to the seminar series).

The next three chapters grew out of my further explorations of utopian standpoint and method after completing my 1986 book on the critical utopian science fiction of the 1970s, *Demand the Impossible: Science Fiction and the Utopian Imagination*. This new work was prompted in general by the political crisis faced by the global Left in the 1980s and in particular by my rediscovery of progressive political theology while on sabbatical in Ireland (as I developed a renewed appreciation for its potential as a transformative discourse that offered a radical alternative to the instrumental rationality of late capitalism). For several years, I read post–Second World War political theology (especially as inspired by the French Marxist-Christian dialogue and Bloch's utopian Marxism, most notably during his time at the University of Tübingen). In pursuing this research, I was not lapsing back into a faith-driven theology, but rather bringing a utopian hermeneutic to the postsecular interpretive work of locating the traces of a utopian surplus in contemporary theological thought (in the spirit of other such interventions such as those by Charles Taylor, Joel Kovel, Slavoj Žižek, Geoghegan, and Badiou).

In Chapter 2, "Bloch Against Bloch: Liberating Utopia," I examine the way in which Bloch influenced progressive political theology even as he dialectically re-functioned its critical and anticipatory methods in such a way that severed its imbrication with a transcendental deity while retaining its historically privileged evocation of immanent awe and mystery so that a postsecular theological discourse could contribute to the project of a human anticipation that is held open to a better world on earth. In addition— influenced by my study of the critical utopia—I trace how the Bloch's utopian hermeneutic negated his own ideological tendency to hypostasize the fixed telos of orthodox Marxism, thus making a re-functioned utopian Marxist project available for emergent historical moments. My initial presentation of this work was given in 1987 at the end of my year as a Fellow at the Center for Twentieth Century Studies at the University of Wisconsin-Milwaukee (published as a Center Working Paper, "Rereading Religion: Ernst Bloch, Gustavo Gutiérrez and the Post-Modern Strategy of Liberation Theology"), and my second presentation of this work ("From Exodus to History: Religion and Utopia in Ernst Bloch's *Principle of Hope*") occurred in 1989 at the annual North American Society for Utopian Studies conference. Ruth Levitas, Vince Geoghegan, and I then included a revised version in a co-edited special issue on Ernst Bloch in *Utopian Studies* in 1990, and finally Jamie Owen Daniel and I published its present form in an expanded collection on Bloch in our 1997 book, *Not Yet: Reconsidering Ernst Bloch*.

Following from this, in "Denunciation/Annunciation: Utopian Method," I focus on Latin American liberation theology. Reading this discourse as a utopian synergy of theology and historical materialism, I situate it as a self-conscious effort to develop a method and agenda for radical change within the conditions of Latin American oppression and revolution, but I also emphasize its broader global value as a fully utopian, critical and transformative, discourse and practice. At the core of this chapter, in a formative methodological move for my ongoing work, I discuss the methodology of liberation theology: as it conjoins a negative hermeneutics of suspicion (denunciation) with a positive hermeneutics of recovery (annunciation), in an articulation closely resonant with the utopian hermeneutics of Bloch and Jameson. The chapter grew out of presentations at the Society for Utopian Studies conference in 1987 and the Northeastern Modern Languages Association conference in 1989; earlier published versions appeared as "Mission Impossible: Liberation Theology and Utopian Praxis" in 1990 and as "Denunciation/Annunciation: The Radical Methodology of Liberation Theology" in 1991.

In the next chapter, "Look into the Dark: Dystopia and the Novum," I move from theological discourse into what would become my longer-term investigation of utopian method and practice and of the, related, nature and politics of the dystopian mode. Beginning with a review of Bloch's interpretive method, I adduce its transformative potential by way of a review of Darko Suvin's critical corpus, especially as it leads into his refunctioning of Bloch's category of the novum: thus, I trace the way in which a social or textual novum can enable the forward-pulling potential of an asymptotic utopian telos that is no longer guaranteed or encapsulated within an orthodox blueprint or telos but rather held open by the potential of that which is radically new. From this analysis, I develop my first formal study of the dystopian mode. I conclude with a close reading of Suvin's poem, "Growing Old Without Yugoslavia," which teases out the author's own utopian methodology of denunciation and annunciation in his evocation of the novum of hope rooted in the history of Yugoslavia's progressive achievement at the very moment of its dystopian destruction. I initially presented my thoughts in this direction in my keynote for the 1996 University of Luton Conference on "Envisioning Alternatives: The Literature of Science Fiction," and I then brought this work into a reading of the dystopian cultural shift in the period of rising neoliberal power in the 1990s when I wrote a slightly shorter version of this chapter as my contribution to the conference volume, *Learning from Other Worlds* (2000), in which I recognized Suvin's intellectual and political contributions (as well as shaping the core argument of my study of the critical dystopia in *Scraps of the Untainted Sky*).

The next two chapters return to the critical potential of the science fictional imaginary as a radical diagnostic and anticipatory cultural form as I continued to develop my analysis after my studies of critical utopian and critical dystopian sf and political agency in the 1990s: see *Scraps of the Untainted Sky: Science Fiction, Utopia, Dystopia* (2000c).

"On the Vocation of Utopian Science Fiction" stands at the core of this book's focus on the relationship between the utopian impulse, political agency, and the formation of the radical utopian subject. This work began as a keynote lecture for Monash University's Centre for Comparative Literature and Cultural Studies 2007 conference on "Demanding the Impossible: Utopia, Dystopia, and Science Fiction," and an early version was published in the journal *Arena* in 2008. Beginning with a discussion of the sf reading protocol of "worldbuilding" through a close reading of Ken MacLeod's *Learning the World*, I reprise my argument that utopian interrogation is a form of "strong thought" that aims to transform, not just critique, the contemporary world. Accepting Jameson's argument for the primacy of the negative in the utopian project, I nevertheless call for the complementary positive anticipations of political movements and the transformed horizon toward which they struggle. I then trace a line of utopian thought that stresses the positive alternatives and trajectories made possible by the utopian problematic. From this, I carry my discussion into close readings of selected sf texts of Kim Stanley Robinson and China Miéville, ending with an interpretive loop that pulls their radical imagination (and especially their treatment of the process of revolutionary change itself) back into the spirit of William Morris's *News from Nowhere*. Overall, I reaffirm the importance of the positive utopian hermeneutic, consider the ways in which readers might open a text's figuration to productive speculation on how its provisional content as well as its estranging form can disrupt the present hegemonic order, and explore what might be done to change it—not to lock in immediate, practical answers but to enlighten and enliven the articulation of a transformative agenda and agency.

I continue this line of argument in Chapter 6, "N-H-N': Robinson's Dialectics of Ecology" (the first version of which was given as a keynote at the Conference on "Changing the Climate: Imagining Catastrophe" at Monash University in 2010 and published in *Arena* in 2011). In this expanded chapter, I focus on the global environmental crisis (climate destruction, but also all other forms of human-produced toxicity and disaster in this increasingly apocalyptic moment) and the oppositional theory and practice afforded by an ecological problematic. After reviewing liberal and revolutionary ecological standpoints, I return to sf's critical and anticipatory capacity to generate formative thought experiments, and I engage in an extended reading of Robinson's ecological imagination and engagement in his major novels—tracing his utopian project as it generates a critical and visionary intervention that is radically pragmatic and utopian.

Moving toward my conclusion, I continue my articulation of the relationship between utopian method and political agency in two final chapters on political practices (i.e., revolutionary nonviolence, radical pedagogy, and radical organizing).

"On the Utopian Standpoint of Nonviolence" focuses on the utopian core of the theory and practice of revolutionary nonviolence. This work began as a keynote lecture for the Utopian Studies Society annual conference in Prague in 2014, and a shorter version was presented at the Society for Utopian Studies in Montreal later that year. The keynote was then published in *Utopian Studies* in 2015, and a revision of that essay appears here. Like utopianism itself, nonviolence is frequently feared, misunderstood, and/or underestimated. Rather than being the passive, and abstract, stance that many attribute to it, nonviolence evinces a robust concrete utopian agency that speaks truth to power in the service of a radically transformed future. Drawing on my research as well as my direct experience as a nonviolent activist, I reflect on the utopian qualities of nonviolence: first in terms of its general characteristics (as political agency expressed as witness, intervention, and a way of life) and then in light of the specific lineage that developed in the United States (closing in on post–Second World War revolutionary nonviolence as it was conceived and practiced in the US civil rights and anti-war/anti-draft movements).

In Chapter 8, "Next Steps: Tracking the Utopian Method," I develop a more extended engagement with the work of Jameson and Levitas on utopia and political agency. I reaffirm Jameson's argument for utopian unrealizability and his imperative to focus on the break from the present, and I hold this as a backbeat to my argument for the persistence of the utopian within the political sphere. By deploying the concept of *horizon* (cf., Suvin), I call for a continuum that re-calibrates Jameson's categories of utopian impulse and program in a relational matter rather than allowing them to collapse into a binary. I then turn to Levitas to reassert the importance of not only critique and anticipation but also the existential and political judgment that must be implicit in utopian agency. While Jameson emphasizes utopia's capacity for neutralizing the present and generating the logical preconditions for transformation (thereby protecting against containment or cooptation), Levitas brings a sharper focus to the persistent functioning of impulse precisely in those movements and programs that break through those suturing mechanisms. Working from this methodological platform, I then consider two examples of how utopian method can sustain an uncompromising vitality along this continuum from impulse to horizon: namely, American radical Saul Alinsky's community organizing and Brazilian educator Paulo Freire's pedagogy of the oppressed. In my readings of these powerful interventions, I identify practices that produce not utopian space as such but rather processes that create utopian subjects capable of fighting for and building that space. First presented as a keynote lecture ("Absent Next Steps: Utopia as Structure of Feeling") at the 2011 Utopian Studies Society annual conference in Cyprus, a short essay version was published in *the minnesota review* in 2016 and then fully revised for this chapter.

My Coda ("'68 and the Critical Utopian Imagination") grows out of the fiftieth anniversary commemorations of the concrete utopian moment of May 1968. In this original interview (conducted by Hugh O'Connell), I again recall my own utopian turn and trace its impact on my personal, political, and intellectual formation in a manner that resonates with the larger theoretical and political analysis and intervention of this volume. As I look forward at the end, I return to my beginning and the core focus of this entire reflection on the formation of the utopian subject and utopian agency, again reaffirming the radical nature of both.

Working as a theoretical and political intervention, *Becoming Utopian* offers my articulation of the utopian process, from the formation of the utopian subject to the exercise of utopian program (itself mediated by an initial utopian impulse and the leading edge of a utopian horizon). Working as an intellectual memoir, it offers my narrative of personal formation as one metonym for that holistic process. I hope this entire project will speak to those who are experiencing an initial utopian break and seeking to locate themselves on the longer path as well as to those working to contextualize their own development beyond that utopian turn.

Strong Thought: Utopia, Pedagogy, Agency

Searching

It seems I have always lived between worlds, looking from one to another, finding ways to cut through the reality around me to see that other place that seemed to make more sense or at least be more interesting and maybe even satisfying. In that way, the method of utopia, with its double move of negation and anticipation, has been with me for a very long time.

I grew up finding my way across different cultures, different worlds. Son of Irish parents in Chicago, I lived between the Irish culture of my family and the new society of American promise in the postwar years of the 1940s and 1950s, happy in a nurturing home life yet often feeling it to be "old fashioned" when I went out and about in the city. Roman Catholic, in an Irish immigrant way, I found a set of values and discipline (and repression) that gave me an alternative to an increasingly consumerist culture, even as that larger sphere offered enticements not allowed by my parochial life. Working class, I found little in the sphere of the "rich" to interest me, and in fact I developed a nascent class antagonism as I saw my father patronized by his boss on the truck docks and stood there as the poor visitor as my dynamic and independent aunt was treated as a lesser servant by the North Shore couple whose children she cared for. Generally, my formation within the scope of my ethnicity, religion, and class gave me a secure sense of my self, and this was especially strengthened by my mother's independent and courageous attitude, as she honored but questioned the authority of the Church and encouraged me to explore the larger society beyond our neighborhood and parish. I consequently looked outward to those other worlds as I found them to exceed all that I knew, thereby moving me to explore their ways, to consider their possibilities alongside the ones I knew so well. I came to see stimulating differences in each of my parallel worlds, realizing that each opened up the other for me, that each brought me to a world more intriguing or disturbing than the other.

This cultural tension gradually became more confrontational. That sense of committed difference that Catholicism gave me, that (still unformed) class anger I discovered, and that more distant sense of being of a people whose history had been one of occupation and dispossession segued into a more direct experience of assertion and contestation as I ventured out to the streets (as a child and then that creature called a "teenager"). In city parks, pizza parlors, and downtown avenues, I entered a newly named youth culture that rejected the mainstream conformist culture of the 1950s. In our all-too-innocent street gang baiting of the local police, in our clothing choice of blue jeans, combat boots, and black jackets, we stood for each other and against those who tried to tell us what to do. For me, especially, in what was becoming "our" own popular culture—of B-movies, comic books, and race, then rock, music—I discovered a standpoint from which I garnered a strength to be my "self" as I negotiated that mixture of old and new worlds (including throwing off my own subjection to childhood bullying, thus developing a deep hatred of and opposition to personal abuse and violence that have shaped my personal and political life ever since). And yet, mainstream society also issued its own call to an inspiring loyalty and commitment as the official culture of anti-communism took hold. In the heroism proffered by re-run Second World War movies, new TV programming (with series such as *I Led Three Lives*, featuring Herbert Philbrick, who was a "communist," an FBI spy, and an "ordinary guy"), and public service ads extolling the norm of democracy and liberty, my Catholic call to witness, and thus to take a moral stand in a valueless world, was given a very different invitation to a social, if not yet political, imperative to work for liberty and against oppression.

What enriched these various appeals to my knowledge and commitment was my proclivity to read. Growing up in a loving home but without books, I soaked up the book culture of Catholicism once I went to school, becoming both a "devout" Catholic, as I read my way through liturgies and saints' lives, and a "good" student, as I eagerly entered the world of learning. Not able to afford books, and as a child of my time, I bought hundreds of cheap comic books and immersed myself in the exploits of superheroes, the gore of horror, and the edginess of crime. And I remember how, in an early visit to the wondrous space of the library, I picked my first volume of Robert Heinlein off the shelf, and so had my mind turned forever by the usefully escapist literature of science fiction (sf). But my reading life took another turn when I was eleven years old. My Uncle John Stack died, and my Aunt Catherine thought that I, as the studious lad, should be given his desk and books. As it happened, John was the only overtly political person in the family: a member of an elevator operator's union, he also attended what I later realized was a Trotskyist reading group, and what came down to me was his place of learning and his library. So, to my reading of saints' lives and sf, I added books such as Leon Trotsky's *History of the Russian Revolution* and Henry George's *Progress and Poverty*, along with an eight-volume atlas of the world. This infusion of history, political economy, and geography gave shape and depth to my ability to negotiate alternative, and oppositional, worlds.

For me, reading became a "subtle knife," that mysterious tool given to us in volume two of Philip Pullman's *Dark Materials* Trilogy. Reading gave me a means to cut through the barriers between worlds and to step inside other places, and move back and forth as needed, emotionally or strategically. Devouring both religious and secular texts, I began to value a life of commitment, whether articulated in the religious language of vocation, the existential (popularly beatnik) language of freedom, or, eventually, the political language of activism. That this early understanding of such a life was for me wrapped up in Catholicism, anti-communism, a slightly more removed commitment to Irish freedom, and seasoned with the frisson of life in the city was but the throw of historical dice. That this amalgam led eventually to a secularity that embraced a materialist spirituality, a generous communism, and an advocacy for freedom won by all oppressed people was but the result of a series of subsequent steps.

By high school in the late 1950s, I had, through the Young Christian Students movement, grown from an abstract anti-communist stance into the concrete anti-racist commitment of Chicago's Catholic Interracial Council, with its adult leaders who were already connected with the young Martin Luther King and the Southern Christian Leadership Conference, and shortly thereafter to the young activists in the Student Nonviolent Coordinating Committee. All this prepared me for work in my college years in the civil rights movement. From there, as a borderline member of the baby-boom and the 1960s generations, I entered the anti-war movement and then (as an eighteen-year-old who had to make pressing decisions in what I would now call "choice" or "body politics") the anti-draft movement, becoming a conscientious objector to the US imperialist war as well as a radical activist involved in both legal and extralegal campaigns. Leaving conservative and then progressive Catholicism behind, and rejecting my own white and male privilege in my personal and political life, I affiliated with the New Left and with socialist feminism, thereby joining with people who carried their activist commitment and sensibility into all dimensions of their personal and working lives. From 1957, I moved from spontaneous civil rights and anti-war/anti-draft work into organized groups such as the Students for Democratic Society and the Milwaukee Communist Party (until the Soviet tanks rolled into Prague in 1968), on to the Wisconsin Alliance, and then the Democratic Socialists of America. Along the way, I engaged not only in the above campaigns but also in urban community organizing, alternative school development, and work in the emergent ecology movement (and was a member of my local socialist-feminist men's group throughout the 1970s). As well, I continued my studies in graduate school (with an MA in English, and additional graduate study in theology) but then stepped out of the academy to teach in a community college, and only gradually returned to part-time doctoral studies. If reading was an engine of change on a personal level, my newly informed values and activism (which by the 1960s can be named as political) led me to embrace the vocation of teaching as a vehicle of sociopolitical challenge and transformation.

My purpose in recalling this trajectory in this opening chapter on utopian vision and method is to offer a reflection that revisits my upbringing in terms of what I now would call a utopian imaginary and a utopian turn, as I wandered, curiously and critically, between worlds—like a character in Pullman or like Shevek, the political activist and physicist in Ursula K. Le Guin's *The Dispossessed*. National aspiration, spiritual witness, class anger, youthful action, intellectual hunger, and racial and gender solidarity fed what grew into a utopian proclivity and no doubt set me up for life as a member of what Fredric Jameson has named the "Party of Utopia," that long red line of those who will not settle for less than justice and freedom for everyone on an ecologically healthy earth, not via American imperialism or global capitalism but through the work of a collectively transformed and transforming humanity (*Archaeologies* epigraph). However, the more pressing question for this chapter is how this proclivity grew into a developed problematic and a method, one that shaped my studies, my teaching, and my writing, as well as my life as a citizen, an intellectual, and activist.

Reading

In his essay on the early days of the Birmingham cultural studies project, Stuart Hall described how he and his faculty colleagues would work with potential postgraduate students. As he put it:

It was not possible to present the work of cultural studies as if it had no political consequences and no form of political engagement, because what we were inviting students to do was to do what we ourselves had done: to engage with some real problem out there in the dirty world, and to use the enormous advantage given to a tiny handful of us […] who had the opportunity to go into universities and reflect on those problems, to spend that time usefully to try to understand how the world worked. […] So, from the start we said: What are you interested in? What really bugs you about questions of culture and society now? What do you really think is a problem you don't understand out there in the terrible interconnection between culture and politics? […] And then we will find a way of studying that seriously. (1990: 13)

In this account, Hall identifies the direct challenge that I faced as I first stepped into graduate school in the mid-1970s. But from high school onward, I knew that learning for me was more than scholarly understanding or aesthetic appreciation, and certainly not a matter of acquiring cultural capital. For me, learning—as I had been given to understand from those diverse early influences—was an existential, intellectual, and spiritual way to know the world critically and thus a way to help change that world for the betterment of all its people and not the privileged few. Having left behind the study of medicine in my first year of college, I immersed myself in the undergraduate study of literature, history, and philosophy, as I looked for knowledge that would clarify what society was, how it worked, and how I and others could work to change it. Since I was studying at St. Mary's College in Minnesota, I learned these subjects with Christian Brothers and fellow students who were already affiliated not only with the progressive sensibility of the Second Vatican Council and existential philosophy, but also with the radical politics of the civil rights and anti-war movements (indeed, Brothers and students at St. Mary's took up leadership roles in the nonviolent anti-war actions of the Catholic Worker and the Catholic Left). And so, history, philosophy, and literary study on my campus were already in tune with the social and political world. In literature, especially, the interpretive frameworks of theological hermeneutics, existential philosophy, and the left populism of American studies gave me methods of social analysis that valued the aesthetic but did not stop at it.

However, in my master's work in the English Department at the University of Wisconsin-Milwaukee, the story was different. New Criticism reigned, and my MA studies did little to offer me the critical paradigm and method that I looked for (although it did give me a sensitivity and skill in formal analysis that has stood me well). Turning to my work as a community college teacher, from

1968 on, I searched for a critical problematic in my teaching. It was then that I was asked by my students to take my personal love of sf into the classroom; and by 1970, I was one of a very few teaching sf in a dedicated undergraduate course. Consequently, as one of the generation that broke open the English curriculum to allow for studies of popular culture, I began to find another way of working with literary texts. Then, as I returned to doctoral studies in the 1970s, Jack Zipes joined the faculty in Milwaukee; and, in his seminars (on Marxist criticism, the French Revolution, and the fairy tale genre) and in my work with the first editorial collective of *New German Critique* (NGC), I studied the critical theory of the Frankfurt School. With a combination of an orthodox Marxism (learned from the study groups of my activist life) and the Frankfurt problematic (learned in seminars and in the NGC collective), I began to develop a way to approach the literary landscape in ways that went beyond the isolated form of the text, but took that form seriously in a broader historical approach.

And then I encountered the work of Jameson on the politics of form in his early books, especially *Marxism and Form* (1971), and in his lectures at the July gatherings of the Marxist Literary Group (MLG). During my three summer sessions at the first meetings of the annual MLG Summer Institute of Culture and Society, I was able to work with Jameson and with others such as Stanley Aronowitz, Gayatri Spivak, Stuart Hall, and Terry Eagleton. Thus, what became a familiar matrix for many of us—German critical theory; French structuralism and poststructuralism; British cultural studies; American New Left, anti-racist, and feminist/gay cultural critique; and third-world liberation theory and criticism—gave me a more dynamic framework within which I could read literature in the context of the sociopolitical. With this framework, I was able in my Ph.D. work to find that "way," in Hall's sense, to work with sf, and then utopian fiction.

From this point, my sense of utopian aspiration began to find a more distinct method of producing and teaching critical, and transformative, knowledge. Central to this effort, as the Birmingham problematic encouraged, was my decision to let my object of study—the history and form of sf and utopian fiction—shape my interpretive strategies. In 1976, while teaching a graduate seminar at UW-Milwaukee's Center for Twentieth Century Studies, research fellow and sf writer, Samuel R. Delany, argued forcefully that academic scholarship had to stop imposing the critical apparatus used in the study of "high" realist and modernist literature and to adopt a method that worked with the specificity of the sf form. Sf, he urged, had to be taken on its own terms, and thus we needed to look to the way sf writers, editors, fans, and now fans-become-scholars considered the sf genre. As Angela McRobbie put it, in one of the great insights of Birmingham cultural studies, it was necessary to let the object of study shape the research, not the other way around (see McRobbie 1982).

Enriching this framework, the new writing by Darko Suvin on estrangement and cognition then became central to my evolving sense of form and method in sf studies (beginning with his "On the Poetics of the Science Fiction Genre" in 1972 and "Defining the Literary Genre of Utopia: Some Historical Semantics, Genology, a Proposal, and a Plea" in 1973), and Jameson added to this in his general theory and his work on sf and utopia. His review essay on Louis Marin's *Utopiques*, "Of Islands and Trenches" (1977) was a key text in the identification of utopia's fundamentally negative quality: as he argued that, rooted in the historical situation, utopia's trajectory moves from its formal negation of that moment into the figuration of another possibility, one not attainable in the world as it is but one that pulls humanity into that not yet existent reality. Hence, Jameson made the first of several iterations that have recurred throughout his work: namely, that the "deepest subject" of the utopian text is precisely its impossibility in the world as it is. Only a revolutionary transformation can produce the future reality that utopia, working as it does with the "raw material" of the material and ideological world, can only ever prefigure (2005: 13). In addition, the 1976 special issue of *the minnesota review* on "Marxism and Utopia," with Jameson's introduction ("To Reconsider the Relationship of Marxism to Utopia") and Suvin's essay ("'Utopian' and 'Scientific': Two Attributes for Socialism from Engels") reinforced my decision to focus on the new utopian strain of sf that had emerged in the oppositional movements and countercultures of the 1960s and 1970s.

Thus, I developed my work on the "critical utopia" in my first substantial effort to study the political function of the utopian imagination as it informed a method of knowing and intervening in the world. My 1981 dissertation (with the ungainly title of "Figures of Hope: The Critical Utopia of the 1970s. The Revival, Destruction, and Transformation of Utopian Writing in the United States. A Study of the Ideology, Structure, and Historical Context of Representative Texts," directed by Zipes) led eventually to *Demand the Impossible: Science Fiction and the Utopian Imagination* in 1986. Therein, I argued that the new utopian sf of the period—by the likes of Joanna Russ, Marge Piercy, Le Guin, and Delany—revived and refunctioned the traditional literary utopia. Influenced by postmodern attention to self-reflexive form, political engagement enriched by self-critical practice (e.g., feminist consciousness-raising, New Left criticism-self-criticism), and a creative encounter with both anti-utopian critique and the utopian shadow of dystopian writing, these works (especially in the period between 1968 and 1976) offered a fresh approach to utopianism that emphasized its value as a critical, negative phenomenon even as it explored—in the form of figurative, not prescriptive, thought experiments—versions of a post-revolutionary society as well as, and significantly so, the radical activism required for movement toward that transformation. As I put it then:

> A central concern in the critical utopia is the awareness of the limitations of the utopian tradition, so that these texts reject Utopia as blueprint while preserving it as dream. Furthermore, the novels dwell on the conflict between the originary world and the utopian society opposed to it so that the process of social change is more directly articulated. Finally, the novels focus on the continuing presence of difference and imperfection within utopian society itself and thus render more recognizable and dynamic alternatives. (Moylan 1986: 10–11)

As it happened, my recognition in these works of a self-critical utopian method, and indeed of the figuration of a more open-ended utopian society of permanent revolution that develops through struggles deploying just such a process, was noted and worked with in both sf and utopian studies. Less attended to, however, was my argument that the critical utopias foregrounded a sharper focus on the nature and degree of political agency required for such practical and utopian transformations. My point was that in these works of a politically intense period the familiar structure of the literary utopia was reversed. Whereas, in more traditional utopian novels, the society is featured (with the visitor traveling through it and registering its wonders and differences from her or his homeland), in the critical utopias, "the primacy of societal alternative over character and plot [or the *iconic* over *discrete* registers] is reversed, and the alternative society and indeed the original society fall back as settings for the foregrounded political quest of the protagonist," a protagonist who is "part of the human collective in a time of deep historical change" (Moylan 1986: 45).[1] Hence, the systemic alternative, while still formally and ideologically crucial, is approached by means of the political work required to produce that new society (and in realized utopias to revitalize it); thus, the ideological raw material and its figurative reworking center more on the dynamics of the utopian process itself and "the ensuing strategy and tactics taken by a human subject once again able to carry on anti-hegemonic tasks aimed at bringing down the prevailing system [be it original or compromised utopia] and moving toward a radically different way of being" (49). Thus, the critical utopia emerges as a "meditation on action rather than system" (Moylan 1986).

While in his more recent review and reconsideration of utopian theory, *Archaeologies of the Future*, Jameson rightly insists on separating the utopian project from any *immediate* connection with practical politics (most especially at times of focused revolutionary change), I argue throughout this book that such imaginative explorations of the political process are nevertheless central to the utopian vocation (2005: 15). As he puts it, "politics is always with us," and it is utopia's special contribution to be able to foreground the political when it appears most "suspended" in "transitional periods" or most fulfilled in "postrevolutionary" ones (Jameson 2004: 44, 43; 2005: 15–16). It is in such moments, in the "calm before [or after?] the storm," that utopia's thought experiments on political possibilities can be most eloquent. That is, both in "periods of great social ferment" (e.g., the 1880s–1910s, the 1960s, the 1990s, now?) that appear to be "rudderless, without any agency or direction" and in achieved, concrete utopias (e.g., the utopian societies imaginatively challenged by the critical utopian protagonists, or Ernst Bloch's actual dilemma with regard to the Soviet Union, as discussed below), the process of "utopian-creative free play" can feed and enliven the political imagination (2004: 45–6).

Looking at the larger historical periodization, it does seem to be the case that utopia's articulation of political challenges to, and transformations of, the hegemonic system became increasingly necessary, and evident, after the "victory" of capitalism in the late nineteenth century—as argued, for example, by Raymond Williams and Miguel Abensour as they traced the shift from systemic to heuristic utopias after the revolutions of 1848 (see Williams). Thus, from William Morris's chapters in *News from Nowhere* on "How the Change Came" through the (successful and defeated) struggles in the modern dystopias to the existential and systemic political meditations in the critical utopias, and to contemporary sf utopian and dystopian narratives, the calling of the *political* has been brought to the fore. To be sure, Jameson is right to note that an indulgence in matters of practical politics in their own right has little place in the anticipatory utopian project: for, in times of outright revolution, there is, for that moment, little room for utopian speculation; and in times of growing tension caught in a "reality paralysis," such reductions tend to produce reformist plans and containing maneuvers (2004: 44). However, at least since that historical/formal turn marked by Williams and Abensour, the utopian persuasion reveals, over and over, that *something* must indeed be done to begin to change a prevailing, apparently closed, system in order to assert that not only can an alternative exist but that a political capacity exists to achieve it.

Politics in these utopias of capitalism are indeed "vexed," as Jameson puts it, not because they are named and explored at the deeper, utopian, level of possibility and possibilities but because they have been—in so many instances by writers, theorists, artists, activists, and readers alike—taken up, reductively, as immediate, workable, practical steps (2005: 205). The "registering apparatus" of utopian texts is certainly not a social inventor's how-to manual or cookbook of revolution but rather is a meditative and subversive expression (as text or lived social experiment in an intentional community or political movement) on the reality, the necessity, of collective political (as opposed to personal, ethical) action (2005: 13). Utopia—again, especially from Morris up through sf by the likes of Margaret Atwood, Octavia Butler, Ken MacLeod, China Miéville, Kim Stanley Robinson, and beyond—offers a "poetic" rather than an instrumental exploration of the means of making radical change. Thus, in my focus on the political agency of the critical utopias (as enacted by individual characters, such as Le Guin's Shevek or Piercy's Connie in *Woman on the Edge of Time*, who both represent individual ethico-political choices as well as typify the collective political action of an entire movement), I identified the ways in which the utopias of those burgeoning, activist times of the Long Sixties zeroed in on precisely this imaginative operation, as they took the literary utopia's activist anticipation into a fuller consideration of directions and choices, and doing so in both pre- and post-revolutionary registers, thereby figuring not the *what* that is to be done but rather the *doing* that is, always, needed.[2]

Working

As I continued my studies of utopian method as well as the related processes of political pedagogy and consciousness-raising/organizing, a period of living in Ireland in the mid-1980s turned my attention to a non-literary discourse: namely, liberation theology. As it developed out of a European context (through the Catholic Action movement and progressive theologies, shaped by philosophical anthropology, hermeneutics, existentialism, and the Marxisms of French communism and the Frankfurt School/Ernst Bloch) and a Latin American context (with national liberation movements and writings by Bartolomé de las Casas, José Carlos Mariátegui, and Che Guevara), liberation theology took on a more politically engaged quality than its allied counterparts in Catholic "political theology" (see Johannes Metz) or Lutheran "theology of hope" (see Jürgen Moltmann). This situated and activist dynamic grew especially as the work of theologians and philosophers such as Gustavo Gutiérrez, Juan Luis Segundo, and Enrique Dussel was informed by, and in turn informed, the political alliances arising from the collaboration of indigenous and working peoples and Left cadre throughout the Southern continent.

Thus, as I considered it in a fresh postsecular light, liberation theology articulated an overt utopian project in both its theological and pastoral dimensions and in its resonance with secular revolutionary theory and politics. Unlike official Christian discourses since the Middle Ages, liberation theology does not attack utopia as a heretical turn away from the narrative trajectory of redemption and salvation. More in keeping with the apocalyptic theology advanced by the Franciscan Joachim of Fiore in the twelfth century, liberation theologians regard the collective political movement toward a just and emancipated future as a "graceful" sign of the larger promise of the Christian message and further recognize humanity's participation as central to what they openly called a "revolutionary process" of transformation, thus positing an activist view of the redemptive process (Gutiérrez 1973: 213). Theologically, liberation theology draws on an eschatological understanding of a transformed humanity in history, as it figures the horizon of a salvation that is both spiritual and material, a horizon that grows out of a critique of contemporary capitalism and anticipates a better world in its engaged re-interpretation of the "signs of the times," as the Gospel of Matthew put it. Pastorally, it locates the core of that process of transformation in the situated experiences and knowledges of the oppressed, thereby expressing a preferential option for the poor that could inform the leading edge of spiritual and political work in the world. Indeed, it was the pedagogical and political work of the grassroots Christian base communities in Brazil, Nicaragua, and elsewhere that most directly created what José Miguez-Bonino called the "new prophetic temper" of the mode of religious and political praxis.

Thus, in several essays, I wrote about the utopian methodology and pedagogy of liberation theology, and the substance of this work appears here in Chapter 4 "Bloch Against Bloch" and Chapter 5 "Denunciation/Annunciation" and informs my overall discussion of the processes of the utopian method and of becoming utopian. As a transformative method that aims to change and not simply know the world, liberation theology combines a negative hermeneutics of suspicion with a positive hermeneutics of recovery. Through this double move, named by some as a process of "denunciation" and "annunciation," liberation theologians provide a utopian mediation between spirituality and politics that challenges and transcends the limitations of the present in the name of the dispossessed.

In this context, I noted the resonance between liberation theology and its base community work and that of Marxist theory and left activism (a connection was already evident in the politics of the religious left). Following a similar hermeneutic trajectory, in an equally utopian mode, liberation theology enacts a "problem-posing" strategy that creates opportunities for the most oppressed of people to interpret their situation and to change it within the worldly perspective offered by a utopian horizon. As seen in the base communities, this transformative method operates in a pedagogical/political as well as an analytical/theological mode. As they carried out their adaptation of Paulo Freire's pedagogy of the oppressed, the base communities enabled their members to speak a "truth" appropriate to their needs and aspirations. Here, what Phillip E. Wegner calls utopia's "pedagogical and transformative dialectic" produces a radicalizing knowledge that allows its engaged practitioners to generate cognitive maps of reality that critique the existing society and prefigure new possibilities—again, realizing that such possibilities can only, like the figures of the Kingdom of Heaven or the Realm of Freedom, be pointed toward and not lived or known, until the "real work" of historical change occurs (1998: 53). Thus, the pedagogy of the base communities and the hermeneutics of liberation theology inform a praxis that accords with the utopian process, in that both produce the machinery of knowledge and action that the transformation of the present world system requires.

After working on the disruptive and creative utopian elements in liberation theology, I looked back to the influence of Bloch's utopian philosophy on the development of progressive theologies and on liberation theology in particular. While this allowed me to say more about liberation theology and its relationship with Marxist thought and practice, it also led me to focus on Bloch's own method. I therefore came back to considering the ways in which the critical method of utopia can often conflict with the prescriptive substance of utopia—or, how utopia as process works with and against utopia as ideology. I therefore revisited Bloch's extensive exploration of the trajectories of hope in the imaginative surplus of world history, as he discovered insistent strands of utopian anticipation in an amazing array of human expression and action. More pointedly, I examined the ways in which he deployed a critical utopian method within his own body of work. I reread *The Principle of Hope*, following Bloch's moves from meditations on the daydreams of everyday life to the ultimate transformation of the world and its history in the name of his most concrete utopia, the Soviet Union. In this process, I explored Bloch's Marxist contribution to Christian theologies and commented on the ways in which the dialogue between Christianity and

Marxism opened both progressive discourses to pressing historical needs, but I also examined how his utopian method interacted with his own, compromising, preference for the utopian ideology embedded in his reading of the work of Karl Marx and Soviet communism at the end of *Principle.* Drawing on Walter Benjamin's recommendation that historical materialism could become the victor in the battle against fascism if it enlisted the services of theology (see "Theses on the Philosophy of History"), I brought this productive suggestion up to the moment of the 1960s, when Bloch's Marxist utopianism helped to bring progressive theology down to earth (thereby enlisting it in the service of the revolutionary transformation of society and providing a refunctioned utopian framework for the emergent critical Marxism and activism of the contemporary Left). Thus, I argued that the debilitating authority of a closed, orthodox and teleological, Marxism could itself be challenged by a postsecular deployment of this new religious discourse as it contributed to that period's revival of the radical process of utopian anticipation and transformation.

However, a consistent use of this critical method was not an easy move for Bloch in his own work: while his intellectual and political commitment to a radical utopian hermeneutic carries through his entire body of work, his affiliation (in the face of the twin evils of Nazi and US power, of fascism and capitalism) with the counter-hegemony of the Soviet Union, and indeed later the German Democratic Republic, threatened to deflate the effectiveness of that very method. I therefore noted that Bloch's political commitment to the USSR not only trapped him in a historically static loyalty, but also revealed a twofold error in his method: on the one hand, his strategic belief in the power of the utopian *telos* led him to locate the USSR as the leading edge and telos of that trajectory and thus displaced all other radical possibilities; on the other hand, that ideological cathexis led him to set aside the critical and negative aspects of the utopian function that could have challenged his concrete utopia and consequently enlisted him in the forward movement so desperately needed by an internal communist critique in the emergent New Left.

Thus, as expressed more fully in the next chapter, I explored the conflict between Bloch's utopian politics and utopian method, and I developed my analysis in the spirit of what I had earlier written regarding the literary critical utopias of the 1960s. I examined this political and methodological dynamic through a reading of *Principle,* wherein I identified a dialogic tension between a historically frozen orthodox Marxism with its commitment to a linear progression toward the communist telos and an unorthodox understanding of the fragmentary, disruptive work of utopia throughout history. In some of his strongest utopian maneuvers, Bloch insists that utopia is not matter of finalized achievement but rather a phenomenon of motion toward a not yet existent reality, albeit a movement that necessarily has to work through, against, and beyond the actual tendencies and latencies of the given moment. Even as he evokes a "kingdom figure" that bespeaks a revolutionary telos, he resists equating that figure with an achieved reality: for these are anticipatory not established evocations, and thus "frontier concepts [...] that [move] toward the Absolute of human wanting" (1986: 1345, 1353). And in the closing pages, he speaks of "the process-world, the real world of hope itself" and reminds his readers that the "best still remains patchwork" (1374, 1375).

I therefore concluded this analysis by asserting that throughout *Principle* Bloch continually ruptures the ideological suturing of his own system, demonstrating his own method of reading against the ideological grain of the most compelling beliefs and affiliations. Even as he himself falls short of that very method, locking into his own Soviet solidarities, he offers the opportunity to turn the utopian impulse against his own position and to continue to learn from him even in his compromises and failures. As with the critical utopias that discovered the utopian germ in the hypostatization of actually existing "utopias" and sought for ways to move forward yet again, so too Bloch invites us to read beyond his last chapter in an open process of utopian anticipation.

This invitation to engage a utopian method of reading, and acting, beyond compromise, closure, or desperate affiliations recurred a few years later in the face of the revival of dystopian writing during the emergent period of neo-conservative/neo-liberal hegemony and left oppositional uncertainty and diffusion. Challenged by Lyman Tower Sargent's work, in *Scraps of the Untainted Sky: Science Fiction, Utopia, Dystopia* and *Dark Horizons: Science Fiction and the Dystopian Imagination* (introduced and edited with Raffaella Baccolini), Baccolini and I collaboratively wrote on the generic mode that Baccolini termed the "critical dystopia." In this new current of sf narrative, we found yet another manifestation of utopian anticipation: one that, like the earlier critical utopias, foregrounded the question of political agency; for here too, the renewed possibility of oppositional political movement rather than the formulation of a utopian system was of central concern. Thus, in literary and filmic works from the late 1980s to the late 1990s—by the likes of Piercy, Robinson, Margaret Atwood, Octavia E. Butler, Gary Ross, and the Wachowskis—critics such as Baccolini, Sargent, Peter Fitting, Jenny Woolmark, Ildney Cavalcanti, and I examined the refunctioning of the dystopian mode in this period when the radical anticipations of utopia were being denied, suppressed, and refused (when they were not simultaneously being co-opted into the global commodity culture).

Dystopian writing had certainly made its mark in the twentieth century. From Jack London's *The Iron Heel* and E. M. Forster's "The Machine Stops" to the classical dystopian "trilogy" of Yevgeny Zamyatin's *We*, Aldous Huxley's *Brave New World*, and George Orwell's *Nineteen Eighty-Four*, to works such as Katharine Burdekin's *Swastika Night*, Ray Bradbury's *Fahrenheit 451, and* John Brunner's *Stand on Zanzibar*, the genre provided an avowedly pessimistic form wherein the closure and terror of modern societies could nevertheless be registered and wherein, in some, warnings could be issued to readers to take heed, or else. As Baccolini and I noted, this dark shadow of the utopian genre had faded in the period of the critical utopias but had reappeared in the 1980s and 1990s. The new dystopias especially confronted "the devaluation of utopia by an official, neoliberal discourse that proclaimed the end of history and celebrated simultaneously the end of radical social dreaming and the achievement of an instantaneous 'utopia' of the Market" (2003b: "Introduction," 6–7). Yet these texts manage not only to rekindle the observant pessimism of their predecessors but (in works such as Atwood's *The Handmaid's Tale*, Robinson's *Gold Coast* and *Antarctica*, Butler's *Parable of the Sower*, Piercy's *He, She and It*, the Wachowskis' *Matrix*, and Ross's *Pleasantville*) they also explore, within their pages and images, new possibilities of political opposition "based in difference and multiplicity yet cannily reunited in an alliance politics that speaks back in a larger though diverse collective voice" (Baccolini and Moylan 2003b: "Introduction," 8). Consequently, they not only critique the present system but also posit new forms of oppositional politics that supersede both the Left micro-politics and social-democratic reformism of the time and build toward a new revolutionary vision and direction.[3]

As with the critical utopias, the political thought experiments of this new sf direction are best seen as poetic meditations on transformative possibilities. With their formal strategy of producing open texts by way of what Baccolini calls "genre blurring" and with their iconic generation of dystopian worlds that nevertheless include utopian enclaves of resistance (e.g., Earthseed in *Parable*, Tikva in *He, She and It*) and broad political alliances (e.g., the workers, scientists, feral Antarcticans, and government leaders in *Antarctica*; or the multiracial, sexual, class Resistance in *The Matrix*), the critical dystopias tap into the "necessary pessimism of the generic dystopia" but also express an "open, militant, utopian" political vision and trajectory that refuse "the anti-utopian temptation that lingers like a dormant virus in every dystopian account" and challenge the dominant system imaged in the text's alternative world (Baccolini and Moylan 2003: 7; Moylan 2000c: 195).[4]

This political charge, then, is not to be dismissed as a descent into unmediated practical politics, but rather is best seen as the outcome of imaginative work that maps, warns, and delivers an activist hope in times that are bereft of a strong political opposition. Thus, "generally, and stubbornly, utopian," the critical dystopias exemplify another moment in which the utopian method engages with an enclosed present. While their scenarios point toward a utopian horizon, their militantly pessimistic narratives "do not go easily toward that better world"; instead, they "linger in the terrors of the present even as they exemplify what is needed to transform it" (Moylan 2000c: 198–9). Again, the persistent utopian maneuver is one of breaking radically with the present in the name of a movement toward a transformed future, but at this moment not even daring systematically to image that future, opting instead for speculating on the next steps of a viable collective opposition—one that, as it happened, anticipated the anti-globalization and social forum movements of the last years of the twentieth century.

Keeping On

Looking back on all this work, I see a common thread that has been there from the beginning: namely, that of seeking and tracing evidence of the utopian function in the political imagination of the (ongoing) contemporary moment, carried throughout this sustained body of work that has led to this current re-assemblage with its focus on the personal and political process of becoming utopian, especially in these dark in apocalyptic times. Never regarding utopia as static or normative, I have consistently valued its quality as a critical, negative, and deeply political phenomenon, one that invites humanity to reach to horizons of possibility—even, and perhaps especially, in the most apparently achieved "utopian" situations. While utopia's alternative social realities are in and of themselves compelling figures of total social transformation (and doubly inspiring, as they both name actual possibilities and point to those we cannot yet know), no singular utopian solution can ever do the job of bringing humanity into that much-needed better world. The utopian *problematic*, therefore, must always enable further openings, further movement, so that its mobilization of desires and needs for a better world will always exceed any utopian formulations that arise from that very process, always look through any utopian answers, and always seek for more.[5] In doing this, the utopian vocation—as lived by activists, artists, scholars, and teachers, not to mention each of us in our everyday lives— must include an apprehension of its own internal and external limitations and challenges.

To be sure, in the long, and varied, trajectory of anti-utopian thought (from Aristophanes or Augustine to Edmund Burke, Karl Popper, Jacob Talmon, Francis Fukuyama, or Joseph Ratzinger), utopian aspiration has been rejected as, at its most benign, an undertaking that is boring and stifling or, at its most oppressive, one that is authoritarian and destructive; and, while utopian practitioners and theorists consistently oppose these judgments, they are often the first to recognize the dangers of closure and concentration of power that can develop in the progression from initial utopian impulses to an organized movement toward a better society or indeed the building of that society. Thus, the tendency of disciplined political practice or the systematic ordering of a better society to temper or repress the transformative energy that started it all has been soberly recognized in the utopian tradition, most especially in the self-reflexive critical utopian work coming out of the 1960s and 1970s.

And yet, no utopian worthy of the calling would embrace a transformative impulse alone. Winning the revolution, not simply making the revolution, is essential. The risk of closure and control is unavoidable if totalizing utopian transformation, rather than reformist or gestural politics, is to be seriously pursed. The threat of an effacement or cooptation of "utopian energy" (as the movement is disciplined, as subversive energy is tamed in favor of a post-revolutionary equilibrium, as the power of leading the movement or administering the new society settles into habitual hands, or as the prevailing hegemonic order taps into that utopian energy for its own ends) cannot be denied, but rather must be admitted and addressed at each step in the revolutionary process.[6] The sheer tendency toward compromise and suppression cannot justify the step backward from revolutionary change that is called for in anti-utopian resignation; nor does the apparent freedom of total negation justify the refusal of the hard work demanded by the process of building concrete utopia. Utopian transformation is a *dangerous* act, but it is no less worthy, or less necessary, for being so.

Thus, in these "bad new times" (as Bertolt Brecht might have called them), neither a politics based on maneuver solely within the current system nor a politics of sheer refusal is sufficient if one is still interested in being part of the historical movement toward a socioeconomically just, ecologically healthy, fully inclusive, and fully emancipatory world—if, that is, one is still to be with the diverse alliance that is the Party of Utopia. In these times, replete with their own "reality paralysis," it is more necessary than ever to "choose utopia" and to value the legitimation of the transformative work required by that choice (Sargent, "Choosing," 306–8). I want therefore to suggest that it is time to re-embrace, or more so to re-function, a bolder position: namely, to think of the power of the strong thought of utopia. By using this phrase, I am arguing against the characterization of the culture of postmodernity as it was symptomatically captured in Gianni Vattimo's concept of "weak thought": that is, the *pensiero debole*, the "positive nihilism," that he pitted against the earlier strong thought of foundational, Enlightenment master narratives. I suggest that it is time to move beyond this valorization of melancholy, exhaustion, and accommodation. It is time not simply to "allow" or "listen to" stances of difference and rehearsals of opposition, but rather to enable them, to empower them, or, at least, to create the utopian spaces within which they can flourish so that humanity's needs and desires might one day be met.

It is time, therefore, to increase the charge on critical and political thought, in this post-postmodern period. Here, then, I do not use strong thought as a return of the repressed, but rather as a way to dialectically reassert the fundamental quality of utopia: one that nevertheless needs to be taken, to be quaint, as "under erasure," as it envisions a total sociopolitical transformation while it adopts the negative hermeneutic, as seen, for example, in the critical utopianism of the 1970s or Bloch's own critical utopianism. Within this framework, then, utopia must be mobilized as a force that is equal to opposing the globalizing forces of global capital and US imperialism. Such strong utopian thought (as it grows out of the diverse micro-experiences of everyday lives) can opt for the macro-perspective and the global-scale alliance politics required to give it flesh (as does the comparable, related, *totalizing* analysis of ecology that must take everything into account to understand anything).

In this light, I want also to suggest another description by which we might better understand the nature of the utopian method, in an expression that bespeaks the strength of utopia as specifically rooted in an ever-insistent need to be critical, negative, and open. Thus, I think it could be helpful to borrow the terminology of nuclear physics and apply it to utopia: that is, to accept that any given instance of utopian aspiration has a certain *half-life*. In physics, half-life is the time span required for the quantity of a radioactive material to be reduced to one-half its original value—that is, the amount of time it takes for half of the atoms in a sample to decay (see "Radioactive Half-Life" online). Hence, as a metaphor for utopian dynamics, *half-life* captures the explosive energy of utopia yet recognizes that force will eventually diminish. By understanding the tendency of the utopian process to crack open the present, provincial moment but then, always, to diminish after its catalyzing work is done (by being deflected, defeated, or depleted), we are perhaps better able to understand utopia's potential and thus to work more adeptly with its recurring cycle of openness and ordering. Given this sense of utopia's effective duration, it is perhaps even more important to appreciate the primacy of its disruptive qualities. As Susan McManus argues, to stay its course, an authentic utopianism must be firmly based in its disruptive impulse even as it goes on to inform the building of movements, institutions, or societies. While both the disruptive and the institutional moments are "epistemologically and politically necessary, and dialectically related," the "second moment, of institutionalization must itself always be subject to the disruptive and imaginative moment" (McManus 2003: 3).

If, then, utopian justice and fulfillment are to be fully embraced, what is needed, perhaps now more than ever, is a courageous engagement with the utopian project, enacting not self-denying resignation but self-aware engagement. As this chapter and this book argue, however, the political work of utopian transformation requires the (theorized) knowledge of its dangers *and* its opportunities, its negative and positive tendencies. If, and when, a political movement again reaches forward or a better social order is successfully established, the subversive and creative utopian energy of the project at each and every moment must be reviewed and re-energized within the very problematic and practices that inform and drive it. To prevent closure and privilege—or at least to enable successful challenges to any such that develop—the conditions for a renewable utopian function must be made available.

Thus, along with this sense of utopia's strength and its temporary duration, another important element in the utopian method is *memory*, in particular, that form of memory that is productive rather than consoling or disempowering. While the maintenance of an open method that discourages exclusive power (be it in the form of overt force, wealth, information, or hierarchy) is essential, the ability to reach back and learn from the lessons of past victories and defeats is also required in that process of rekindling utopian opportunity. As Vincent Geoghegan argues, what is needed is that form of memory named by Bloch as *anagnorisis* (recognition); for with recognition, "memory traces are reactivated in the present" as "a repository of experience and value in an inauthentic, capitalist world" (1997: 22). In regard to the utopian process, the recognition of and reflection on, past struggles can inform the contemporary process so that it becomes imbued with an educated grasp of previous campaigns even as it proceeds with the work of negation, revision, transformation. Thus, forward-looking memory can catalyze the refunctioning of utopia and feed into what I call the temporal solidarity of the world's many utopian efforts.[7]

And so, in these apocalyptic times, the dangerous project of utopia must, will, continue. Emerging within the actual tendencies and latencies of the current conjuncture, new utopian manifestations (be they cultural or political) can help humanity to move beyond the current dark moment into yet another era of struggle and possible change. As each utopian effect breaks new progressive ground, and as each falters, the histories of previous utopian aspirations and achievements need to be remembered; and the stories, lessons, and inspirations of these past efforts need, ever again, to feed the emerging one. Utopia's work is never done.

Bloch Against Bloch: Liberating Utopia

I

In the 1930s, Walter Benjamin recommended that historical materialism could become the victor in the battle against fascism if it enlisted the services of theology (Benjamin 1969: 252). That critical encounter never occurred, but developments in postwar progressive theological and pastoral circles in Christian and Jewish communities helped to foster an interchange that resembled what Benjamin had recommended. This time, however, the pressing issue was not fascism as such but a constellation of problems that included the conflicts of the Cold War, the effects of decolonialization and neo-colonialization, and the impact of the totally administered bureaucratic consumer societies of late or postfordist capitalism. Furthermore, the initiative was taken by progressive theologians rather than by Marxists, and yet an important influence on this theoretical rejuvenation was the unorthodox Marxism of Benjamin's friend, Ernst Bloch. In this provocative conversation, what had become the enclosed discursive space of Western theology was broken open by the external, secular discourse of critical Marxism. In turn, the rigidity of the residual orthodox Marxism that runs through Bloch's own polyvocal text was also challenged.[1] As a result, the reception of Bloch by liberal and left theologians in the late twentieth century broke through the philosophical and ideological limitations of his work and refunctioned it for a post-Western appropriation of the utopian function in what Gustavo Gutiérrez calls the "entirely worldly world" (1973: 65).[2]

II

Having worked on it for decades, Bloch completed *Das Prinzip Hoffnung* in 1959, just a few years before leaving the German Democratic Republic and accepting a professorship at Tübingen University in the Federal Republic. The reception of Bloch's "esoteric Marxism" (Moltmann 1968), with its extensive and sympathetic analysis of religion and utopia, began at Tübingen in conversations between Bloch and theologians such the Lutheran Jürgen Moltmann and the Catholic Johannes Metz. From there, it spread rapidly, and his philosophy of radical hope became what one theologian in 1968 described as the "cultural pivot in historical theology as well as a contemporary point of contact between Christian theology and the world culture" (Heinitz 1968: 39). Wolfgang Pannenberg, one of the theologians influenced by Bloch at that time, noted that Bloch "taught us about the overwhelming power of the still-open future and of the hope that reaches out to it" (quoted in Gutiérrez 1973: 240). And, in the *Journal of Religion* in 1969, Ronald Green clearly appreciated that Bloch was concerned "not with the negation of religious belief, but with the attainment of a positive position by means of the criticism of religion" (Green 1969: 128). As Green saw it, Bloch's dialectical critique involved a "constructive and creative re-appropriation of the kernel of religious experience itself" (Green 1969). Over the course of the past fifty years, then, Bloch's work has had a major impact on political theology in Europe, on secular theology in the United States, and, perhaps most importantly, on liberation theology in Latin America and elsewhere in the developing world, as well as on progressive postsecular and utopian thought.

At the heart of Bloch's theory is his concept of the utopian function. For Bloch, as he puts it in his unique mix of philosophical and poetic language, the category of the Not-Yet-Conscious is the "psychological representation" of the materially "Not-Yet-Become in an age and its world" (Bloch 1986: 127). In the unfolding of the forward-looking wishes of humanity, the Not-Yet-Conscious becomes "*conscious* in its act, *known* in its content" (144) in order to be an effective force in society. In this process, hope, the "expectant emotion in the forward dream," emerges "in a *conscious-known way* as *utopian function*" (Bloch 1986). Consequently, the imaginative ideas and images generated by the utopian function "extend, in an anticipating way, existing material into the future possibilities of being different and better" (Bloch 1986). Always the historical materialist, however, Bloch stresses that this utopian capacity achieves concrete expression only when it is "set on its feet and connected to the Real-Possible" conditions in a particular historical situation (146). Thus, the utopian function is rooted in the world yet "is transcendent without transcendence" (Bloch 1986).

Bloch's exploration of the utopian function in the history of religious discourse dialectically superseded the mechanical materialism of Feuerbach and the positivist versions of Marxism that had relegated religion to the dustbin of history.[3] Bloch returned to Marx's own assessment of religion as not merely a disempowering opiate but also a powerful sigh of the oppressed or haven in a heartless world that must be accepted as a valid component of the long-term human efforts toward emancipation.[4] The central theoretical move in this deconstruction of religious discourse is a philosophical and historical critique that removes the hypostatized figure of God from the social space of religious discourse and practice and refunctions that "hollow space" for the utopian impulse (1294). In his study of the major world religions, Bloch traces the historical movement away from non-human astral gods of nature toward gods who are implicated in the human project and finally toward the elimination of God and occupation of the site of religious mystery by the human utopian function itself.[5]

In Judaism and Christianity, especially, Bloch finds historical individuals who founded their religions by reacting against traditional customs and natural religion. Moses first establishes a contract with a single God and "forces his god to go with him, makes him into the exodus-light of his people" (1986: 1191). The God of Moses is less a creator God and more a *Deus Spes*, a God of Hope who helps his people arrive at the promised land. By the time of Jesus, religious hope had been placed in the figure of a messiah who "appears as a scarcely concealable vote of no-confidence" in a God: Yahweh, who had become identified with the "opium-priests" (1235) of an institutionalized religion that had lost its prophetic exodus mission.[6] Instead of representing such an institutional God, Jesus "pervades the transcendent as a human tribune" and "utopianizes" the transcendent figure of God into the Kingdom of God (1191). Consequently, Jesus places the responsibility of building the new heaven and the earth in the hands of the community of believers.

The radical heart of the Christian message, then, is *Eritis sicut Deus*: you shall be like god. Thus, the novum of religion moves away from that which is above humanity to humanity itself: "the glory of God becomes that of the redeemed community and of its place" (1274). Yet, in Bloch's version of the humanization of religion there is a synchronic as well as a diachronic factor. For all along the way, he recognizes the importance of religious discourse as a privileged place of awe and mystery, as the site of the Utterly Different. It is only that the Utterly Different is now articulated within the realm of a human anticipation that is itself constantly open to that which has not yet been imagined or achieved.

Underlying this liberation of religious space is a "properly understood atheism" (1199): not the nihilistic atheism of the mechanical materialists that eliminates both God and religious (or better, spiritual) space but rather a creative atheism that negates the idolatrous god figure yet retains and transforms the space of religion so that "the kingdom, even in secularized form, and all the more so in its utopian-total form, *remains as a messianic Front-space even without any theism*" (1200). This liberating atheism is therefore the precondition for spiritual utopia, for "without atheism messianism has no place" (1200). Consequently, Bloch concludes that "religious imagination certainly cannot be dismissed in toto by the achieved demystification of the world-picture" (1202), for "in the midst of the ... nonsense about the mythical there lives and rises the undischarged question, which has been a burning question only in religion, about the unestablished-meaning of life" (1986).

Bloch argues that with historical materialism, the mythology of the divine and theology as "real science" is finished, and yet, contrary to Feuerbach and positivist Marxists, the "hope-content" that mythology and theology sought to express is not finished—nor will it ever be. Bloch, however, does not claim full credit for historical materialism or his own project. Rather, he sees this atheist strategy as a fundamental aspect of the Jewish and Christian traditions. He interprets Moses' replacement of the astral gods with a god under contract for the exodus as an implicitly atheist gesture, and he argues that "long before God as an existent object of being had been overthrown by the Enlightenment, Christianity put man and his claim, or precisely the *son of man* and his representative mystery, into the Lord of Heaven of former days" (1284).[7] In this religious elimination of what is basically idolatry, the critical atheist is not an anti-Christ but actually a prophetic voice first spoken by Moses and continuing into the present. Paradoxically, then, the utopian element in this religious tradition is "irreligious" because it is insistently "meta-religious" in that it "keeps the world open at the front and frontwards" (1293).

The result of this atheist religious tradition and Bloch's own secular analysis that continues in its spirit is the preservation and transformation of the "*hollow space* that the dispatching of the God-hypostasis leaves behind" (1294). What persists in that meta-religious zone is "the Novum into which human ranks of purpose continue to run in mediated form" (1296). In this space of mystery and undischarged questions, humanity has projected not only its nostalgic myths of perfection but also its expressions of tendencies toward a fulfillment not yet achieved. In this way, Bloch distinguishes between religious hypostasis and the field wherein religious hypostasis occurs, for that field is the most profound site of the utopian function. As Bloch puts it: "If there is no utopia of the kingdom without atheism, then there is implicitly also none without the utopian-real hollow space itself which atheism has both left behind and revealed" (1297), for

> here and nowhere else the entire history of religion has journeyed; but the kingdom needs space. So much space that all expressions and extensions so far are not enough for it, and again so little space, such intensively penetrated space, that only the narrow path of Christian mysticism indicates it ... For this and for this end the religious hollow space is and remains non-chimera, although all the gods in it were chimeras. (1298)

III

Bloch's transformation of religious space into a privileged site of the utopian function profoundly influenced liberal and left theology in the postwar decades. His critique enabled theologians to break out of inherited religious discourses and to pursue an agenda of hope without becoming trapped in the compensations promised by a supernatural deity or a technocratic society. In his introduction to a 1986 English-language edition of Bloch's essays, the US theologian Harvey Cox summarizes Bloch's dialogue in the 1950s with Paul Tillich and then explains Bloch's impact on the younger group of theologians of the 1960s. According to Cox, Bloch and Tillich agreed that the supernatural, personal God created through centuries of institutional Christianity no longer existed in any meaningful way and that humanity was no longer subject to that overwhelming and distant deity. They disagreed, however, on where the reality previously signified by that transcendental signifier was now to be located. Tillich looked, existentially, to "the depths" of existence for God as the source of being, while Bloch looked, politically, to the "forward edge" where humanity moves into the future (Cox 1968: 201).

The younger theologians influenced by Bloch included three basic groups: (1) the "death-of-God thinkers" such as Thomas Altizer, who saw Bloch as a "threat from the left" to their non-historical, "quasi-pantheistic mysticism"; (2) the "development" theologians such as Leslie Dewart, who sought to retrieve some acceptable concept of a personal God, but who became trapped in phenomenological notions of "presence" rather than the possibilities of an emancipating future; and (3) the "secular theologians" such as Cox, who welcomed Bloch's insight that the secular society is "bounded by a future toward which it hastens every day, a future it never attains but which continually prevents it from accepting itself as finished and final" (Cox 1968: 201–2). For secular theology, Bloch's principle of hope provided a way to be concerned with the everyday world "without sacrificing the transcendent," for Bloch helps to locate the space represented by the figure of God at the horizon of a future that challenges the secular society not to be content with the false promises of its apparently fulfilling present.

Bloch's contribution to the erasure of the traditional God of Christianity and his insistence on the power of future possibilities that humanity has yet to know and appreciate also had a major impact on two influential theologies developed at Tübingen in the 1960s. The "theology of hope" grew out of the work of the Lutheran theologian Jürgen Moltmann. His book *The Theology of Hope*, published in German in 1965 and English in 1967, restored eschatology, or the doctrine of the "last things," to a central place in Christian thought.[8] Although Moltmann was directly influenced by Bloch, a substantial difference between the two rests in their assessments of the role of human activity in the movement toward the eschaton. For Moltmann, the first cause of this forward movement is the non-historical Promise of salvation given by a God who resembles the Aristotelian prime mover. That is, the hoped-for salvation of humanity comes about not in the historical incarnation of hope represented in the activities of Jesus and a community of believers but rather in a transcendent future that makes the Promise available to a receptive humanity. Thus, although Bloch's influence on Moltmann furthers a theology that gives primary emphasis to the process of hope and the powerful pull of the future, the theology of hope itself remains locked in a set of non-historical categories.

A more dynamic Blochian influence is evident in the work of another colleague, Johannes Metz, a Catholic theologian who developed what he called "political theology." Metz, too, situates eschatology at the core of his work, but he goes further than Moltmann and links eschatology and hope with human political struggle. Celebrating the political maturity of the Enlightenment, Metz asserts that the proper concern of politics in the modern age is the question of freedom. Influenced as well by the analysis of the public sphere by Jürgen Habermas, Metz first identifies a public sphere for religion that negates the privileging of religion as an activity reserved for an entirely "private" sphere that ignores the political world. He then distinguishes between the public sphere of politics and the public sphere of religion in order to remove religious institutions from the temptations of direct political rule (a rule that in the history of the Roman Catholic Church was all too regularly associated with privilege and wealth rather than with the needs of the poor and exploited, but also all too regularly violated). He consequently stresses that while modern religion as a public entity must involve itself in questions of political agenda, it must remain aware that it works in a sphere separate from that of direct political rule. Given this distinction, Metz sees the appropriate involvement of religion in the political quest for human freedom as one of engagement through critique rather than control (Metz 1969: 110–14).

The shortcoming of Metz's theology, as interpreted by the more radical theologians developing "Third World" theologies of liberation (such as Gustavo Guttiérez), was that his analysis comes from a position of relative freedom in the "First World" (to use the terminology of the time). Consequently, Metz's understanding of religious engagement in politics does not take into account the more complex and acute situations in countries wherein exploitation and suffering are more pointed, and where the Church itself is often the only public institution capable of effective opposition. Thus, this critique of Metz's binary opposition of the public spheres of religion and the state explains how the privileges of the secular societies of the advanced industrial world prevent a non-mediated political theology from recognizing the difficulties of engagement required by people in areas of greater, or at least more overt, oppression. As Guttiérez, also influenced by Bloch, puts it, "in places like Latin America, things are different. The process here does not have the characteristics it exhibits in Europe. Faith, the Gospel, the Church, have … a complex public dimension which has played (and still plays) an important role in support of the established order" (1973: 225).

Bloch's critique of religious discourse and his analysis of the utopian function consequently had its deepest and most persistent influence in those religious circles that sought to confront situations of suffering and political struggle in Latin America and in other locations such as South Africa, South Korea, and the Philippines.[9] Guttiérez's *Theology of Liberation*, published in Spanish in 1971 and in English in 1973, is one of the key texts of Latin American liberation theology.[10] Bloch's influence can be seen throughout the book: for example, in Gutiérrez's dialectical argument for an "entirely worldly world," which refuses the traditional separation of reality into distinct supernatural and natural planes of existence and instead claims that "the world has gradually been acknowledged as existing in its own right" (66), or in his related argument that rejects the notion of separate sacred and profane histories and recognizes only "one human destiny, irreversibly assumed by Christ, the Lord of history" (153). Guttiérez, therefore, regards human history as the privileged complex of *both* material and spiritual liberation, which are themselves interconnected in the movement of humanity toward the Kingdom of God. This interconnection is explained by Guttiérez in his chapter on "Encountering God in History" as he discusses the dynamics of Christian conversion in the ongoing project of liberation:

> To be converted is to commit oneself to the process of the liberation of the poor and oppressed, to commit oneself lucidly, realistically, and concretely. It means to commit oneself not only generously, but also with an analysis of the situation and a strategy of action. To be converted is to know and experience the fact that, contrary to the laws of physics, we can stand straight, according to the Gospel, only when our center of gravity is outside ourselves. (205)

Here Christian theology and pastoral service connect with Marxist analysis and political action in the figure of Bloch's "upright gait" as it is inspired by that which is Utterly Different and beyond the limits of any given individual or people (see Bloch 1971b: 168–75).[11]

Guttiérez's debt to Bloch is most directly found in his chapter on "Eschatology and Politics." He says straight away that the "commitment to the creation of a just society and, ultimately, to a new man presupposes confidence in the future" (1973: 213). This future orientation calls for people to take control of their "own destiny" and to engage in a "revolutionary process" that leads to the "building up of a just society, qualitatively different from the one which exists today" (213–14). In this process, then, the premises of a revised eschatology enable the Church to become directly involved in history in a way that does not compromise its basic agenda of salvation. Guttiérez directly refers to Bloch's principle of hope as an activity that "subverts the existing order" (216). Referring to the utopian function that mobilizes human action in history, he argues that Bloch's important concept "brings us into the area of the possibilities of potential being" in a way that "allows us to plan history in revolutionary terms" (216). Indeed, while he respects and uses the theologies of both Moltmann and Metz, Guttiérez finds that Bloch's analyses are much more soundly connected to material history and human struggle than either of the European theologies (217–53).

Guttiérez proceeds by developing an interpretation of Jesus that dehypostatizes the founder of Christianity in much the same way that Bloch does. He breaks with the dominant Christian tradition that reduces the historical Jesus to the status of a theological icon "unrelated to the real forces at play" (226). Instead, with clear echoes of Bloch's critique of idolatry, he accepts Jesus as a complex, historical actor whose insights and agenda exceeded the goals of both the political zealots and the religious reformers of his own time even as he combined both tendencies in his call for humanity to enter the Kingdom of God. The subversive message of Jesus's story, then, is not only the end of the domination of God over man but also the end of the domination of man over man. Guttiérez, like Bloch, cautions that this anticipated Kingdom exceeds any given hope-content known to humanity, for "the announcement of the Kingdom ... leads it to discover unsuspected dimensions and unexplored paths" (231–2).

In the closing section of the chapter, Guttiérez links "faith, utopia and political action" in a dynamic relationship that constitutes the core structure of liberation theology. He first rescues the term "utopia" from its negative connotation of useless dreaming and identifies it as the necessary mediation of a progressive faith and politics. He then argues for its "quality of being subversive to and a driving force of history" by identifying three elements that characterize utopian longing as a material force: "its relationship to historical reality, its verification in praxis, and its rational nature" (232). He explains the three elements by means of the radical pedagogy of Paulo Freire. First, he recalls Freire's characterization of utopia's negative denunciatory power that repudiates the existing order of things and its positive annunciatory power that calls forth a new and just society. Then, he links both approaches to historical praxis, for "if utopia does not lead to action in the present, it is an evasion of reality" (234). Finally, drawing on Freire's understanding of the relationship between learning and political action, he situates the utopian function as a "mediation of the creative imagination" within the larger processes of a critical reason by which one can not only know the world but also change it (234). Thus, for Gutiérrez, the utopian function provides the unalienated connection between salvation and history that Moltmann's theology avoided, and it provides the material connection between the religious and the political public spheres that Metz's theology lacks.

The Blochian version of utopia, therefore, is the keystone of Gutiérrez's theology of liberation. It is the element that allows this radical theology to link, but also to challenge the limits of, Christian and Marxist thought and action. For within the single process of liberation, the complexity of levels that include the economic, the political, the social, and the spiritual is negotiated by means of the utopian function with its multiple dimensions of anticipation—some of which speak to the immediate moment and some of which go beyond all known images of the possible future society. In the interrelationships of faith, utopia, and politics, then, a complex intersection of discourses ensures that no provisional positions will hold back the larger revolutionary process. Political discourse keeps both faith and utopia focused on current struggles and future developments. Arising out of those struggles, the spiritual attitude of faith inspires both political action and utopian anticipation to resist their tendencies to be frozen in historically bound ideologies. And, utopian discourse—energized by the specificities of politics and the mysteries of faith—keeps faith and politics from becoming limited to present power structures, whether religious or secular. Guttiérez ends his chapter with an account of Christian hope as it has been transformed by Blochian theory:

> Christian hope keeps us from any confusion of the Kingdom with any one historical stage, from any idolatry toward unavoidably ambiguous human achievement, from any absolutizing of revolution. In this way, hope makes us radically free to commit ourselves to social praxis, motivated by a liberating utopia and with the means which the scientific analysis of reality provides for us. And our hope not only frees us for this commitment, it simultaneously demands and judges it. (238)

Thus, the theologian breaks open the hypostatizing ideological limits and idolatries at work in the Christian tradition and radicalizes that deconstructed Christianity with the infusion of the utopian function so that he can support and transform the secular revolutionary project in his own region of the world and beyond.

A more overt example of the dehypostatizing or deconstructive power of the discursive intersection of a Christianity and a Marxism that reciprocally subvert each other's traditional tendencies toward teleological closure can be found in the work of another Latin American liberation theologian, Franz Hinkelammert. Although his 1977 book contains only one direct reference to Bloch, Hinkelammert's *The Ideological Weapons of Death: A Theological Critique of Capitalism* (1986) is written in the spirit of Bloch's method of denunciation and anticipation and Gutiérrez's use of that method in liberation theology. However, Hinkelammert focuses more specifically on the immediate conditions of exploitation and suffering caused by capitalism and its allied national security states in Latin America in the 1970s. In a direct engagement with economic theory, Hinkelammert employs a combination of Marxist political economy and biblical exegesis to interrogate the theories of Milton Friedman and the Trilateral Commission as they have affected Central and South America. In addition, he challenges the conservative theologies that justify the institutional Church in its legitimation of those capitalist and imperialist theories and the practices that result from them. Following from this indictment of the dominant secular and sacral ideologies of power, Hinkelammert works from liberation theology's epistemological privileging of the poor to develop a "theology of life" that recognizes the rights and needs of the poor and that opposes the dominant "theology of death" that only offers patient suffering in this world and a transformed existence in a non-historical afterlife.

The central concept of the theology of life comes from Hinkelammert's reinterpretation of the resurrection of the body of Jesus as the fundamental sign of the material salvation of humanity. Hinkelammert argues that the promise of the resurrection provides the necessary link between present human existence and the utopian anticipation of the "new body" and "new earth" that challenges sacral and secular power. He notes, however, that such challenges must be continually "self-correcting" (1986: 225). For even as utopian praxis clashes with the limits of reality, it has to negotiate within those limits since it cannot in actual practice go beyond them. This does not deny the powerful, pre-conceptual activity of the utopian impulse, but it does acknowledge material reality's "invisible hand" in its call for a more critical utopian engagement. Against this sober recognition of the persistent drag of necessity, Hinkelammert's theology motivates a grounded human hope to push beyond the limitations of the present by offering it the assistance of a divine power.

The "God" of Hinkelammert's theology, however, is not the hypostatized deity of traditional Christianity. Nor is it the obsolete image that Marx deconstructed through his appropriation of Feuerbach's secularizing anthropology. In opposition to these hypostatized and alienated images of God, Hinkelammert offers a renewed image of the "Biblical God," for the deity that emerged in what Bloch called the atheist religious culture of the Bible is one that has progressively abdicated absolute power through the historical covenants with Moses and Jesus. In these two covenants, then, God is changed. With the first covenant, God "ceases to impose divine will on the human being in any way" (231) and works in partnership "within the human praxis of liberation" (230). With the second covenant, "the human being becomes sovereign" (231), and God's will and that of the liberation of the human community "coincide completely" so that "the imperatives of human liberation indicate what God's will is" (1986). As Hinkelammert suggests, the figure of the deity available for his Christian-Marxist discourse "derives from the liberated human being" (1986).

In this nearly postsecular rereading of Scripture, Hinkelammert's theology does not mechanically eliminate God, nor does it conflate humanity and God. Rather, as expressed in what Bloch would identify as the social space of religious discourse, God remains as the available signifier of an Otherness that empowers humanity to reach beyond its own utopian aspirations. Standing outside humanity, but in partnership with it, the "God of the Bible" provides a symbolic source of radical non-identity that ensures the openness of the liberation process. This signifier of the ability of humanity to transcend its limits therefore provides the nexus between Christian and Marxist concepts of transcendence and freedom that facilitates the move to a stronger form of oppositional praxis.

However, to make this connection viable, Hinkelammert must first surpass Marx's rejection of the image of God and the dilemma that resulted from that understandable and necessary theoretical move. The traditional Marxist concept of the deity is the medieval supreme being who is the surrogate of human reason, but this is a figure that can be dispensed within modernity. For with the prospect of the journey to the new earth by means of human labor and reason, Marx can replace the other-worldly supreme being with a humanity that makes its own history. Therefore, the compensatory deity of the medieval Church no longer has a use value in history. Yet Hinkelammert notes that in rightly dismissing that God, orthodox Marxism faces a new dilemma. The realm of freedom called forth by historical materialism is still a transcendent goal, yet the theory provides no mediating bridge to join the present struggle to that hoped-for emancipation that challenges humanity to exceed the limits of necessity. What is at stake is "the whole question of legitimating a human praxis of approaching the realm of freedom when one realizes that achieving it is a goal infinitely far off" (229). Without mediation, the gap becomes absolute, and any hope of crossing it is reduced to the status of myth. As Hinkelammert points out, this is a serious theoretical problem, but it is also a practical problem "found in socialist countries and socialist movements in the capitalist world." That is, "if utopian praxis is aimed at ends that cannot be achieved, why should there be such a praxis at all?" (1986).

The solution Hinkelammert proposes for this legitimation crisis in the Marxist social vision is "to insert Christian faith into it" (1986). This is not an act of opportunism but rather a seriously positive contribution to creating the conditions for orienting human life in its movement into a better future, for without such hope, humanity faces the possibility pointed out by Teilhard de Chardin that "humankind might go on strike and refuse to work for its own survival" (1986). Thus, in order to empower the steps of utopian praxis in its real forward movement, the God of liberation theology, the God that is now the externalized image of the liberated human being, can serve as the material signifier of Otherness that makes possible and mediates human movement across the apparently unbridgeable gap.

The human response to the God of the biblical covenants must therefore be understood in light of the radical reinterpretation of Scripture and Church doctrine undertaken by a liberation theology that is dialectically transformed by Marxist theory. For in following the covenant commandment of love of God through love of neighbor, the solidarity and mutual aid of the human community fulfil its side of the bargain, and in return, the signifier of divine power motivates human effort far beyond its perceived limits. Thus, Christian praxis—based in suffering and exploitation and informed by a partisan faith, hope, and love—challenges secular revolutionary praxis never to rest content, never to say enough, never to close off possibilities. In its turn, the Marxist critique of fetishism challenges liberation Christianity to remain based in concrete material reality and not to fall into the trap of absolutizing values or actions, not to fall into the trap of closing off or reducing reality to abstractions unrelated to the historical situations of suffering people.

In this manner, Hinkelammert correlates Marxism and Christianity in terms of the utopian function. However, in this correlation, Christianity is not reduced to the "truth" present in Marxism, nor is Marxist analysis based in a material praxis of social analysis reduced to the paradigm of a liberated theology. Rather, in provocative interaction, the two discourses dialectically transform and extend each other. As Hinkelammert argues, the fact that Christianity was unable to maintain its earlier message of liberation and—from the time of its fourth-century compromise with the Emperor Constantine—degenerated into a form of anti-utopian, institutional Christianity that was complicit with hegemonic secular power may be explained by its lack of a concept of human praxis. Yet, as Marxism developed its own concept of praxis, it drew on the very tradition of transcendence that had been largely lost in the mainstream Christian tradition but that had been continued in the minority and heretical movements led by the likes of Joachim of Fiore and Thomas Münzer.[12] Therefore, with the rediscovery of its own radical tradition of praxis, as carried forward in Marxism, Christianity can once more propose the liberation found in its origins, but it can also benefit from the progress of history and offer a methodological mediation that incorporates and legitimizes the Marxist goal of the realm of freedom.

IV

As can be seen in the above survey, progressive theologies have been transformed by their encounter with Bloch's utopian Marxism. In return, Bloch's own theory of the utopian function has benefitted from its reception by these radicalized

Christian discourses. As I described above, the European and North American theologies of the 1960s especially stimulated a discovery of Bloch's utopian method that extended beyond religious circles into the political imagination of sections of the New Left, especially in West Germany and to a lesser extent in the United States. In a more direct intervention into the political struggles of their region, Latin American liberation theologians preserved and transformed Bloch's understanding of the utopian function for an emerging postcolonial oppositional discourse that goes beyond the limitations of the Western sacred and secular traditions.

That revitalization and transformation, however, did not come easily. Because of Bloch's failure to challenge his own hypostatization of the "concrete utopia" of a Soviet Union deformed by Stalinism long after his methodology should have warned him of his error, the emancipatory value of Bloch's work has regularly been questioned. There is, of course, no doubt that Bloch's silence on the obscenity of Stalin's actions represents a betrayal of his own utopian vision and opens the way for serious questions about the validity of his approach.[13] Reflecting on the criticisms of Bloch's position that appeared in reviews of the 1986 publication of the English translation of *The Principle of Hope*, Jack Zipes observes that what is most disconcerting about Bloch's utopianism is that "it simply labels other philosophical positions as bourgeois and irrational when they do not comply with the direction his own thought takes" (1988: 4). Zipes sees this tendency toward "rigid uncertainty" stemming from Bloch's "firm belief in the messianic telos of his philosophy" and his insistence upon holding to what he considered to be the correct positions of Marxist analysis (4–5). Although he recognizes the creatively negative side of Bloch's utopianism that attacks orthodoxy and seeks for ways to work through it, Zipes persists in asking if Bloch's utopian Marxism itself "prevented him from seeing reality" (6). He questions the extent to which Bloch's interpretation of the October Revolution as a step along the "red line of history" was the result of a flaw in his theory of utopian discourse, a flaw that prevented him from confronting the problems inherent in Stalinism. In other words, what Zipes and other contributors to the special 1988 issue of *New German Critique* explore is whether Bloch's blindness to Stalinism was due to a problem inherent in his very philosophical method— or to what extent it was due to a personal/political accommodation with the apparently leading edge of the communist movement of his time (Zipes 1988; see also Negt and Zipes 1975). In actuality, it seems to have been a combination of both. Although, as can be seen in others since the 1960s, Bloch's utopian

Marxism ultimately surpasses his Stalinist accommodations—and does so most effectively in his analysis of the radically subversive function of religious discourse. Indeed, as an examination of the dialogic tensions in *The Principle of Hope* indicates, Bloch's utopian method includes the necessary elements for overriding the very hypostatization that led to his tactical accommodation with Stalinism and thereby inhibited the further development of a utopian communist strategy in his time.

Jan Robert Bloch, Bloch's son, writing in the same issue of *New German Critique*, addresses these painful and complex contradictions in ways that uncover the more personal side of Bloch's accommodation with Stalinism. While the younger Bloch recognizes the value of his father's privileging of the "upright gait as the basic ethical rule," he also observes that the revolutionary history of the upright gait "contains the negation of human dignity, contains crimes, above all, the crimes of the avowedly upright on the basis of their law" (1983: 10). In a clear example of the anxiety of influence, he asks how it was possible that his father's "revolutionary-utopian Humanum went along with inhuman despotism" (15). In unlocking this riddle, however, the son does not seek to kill the father by invalidating Bloch's entire method. Rather, in a dialectical effort to redeem Bloch's work from its own worst tendencies, he seeks "to liberate the philosophical gold from the debris of a moral system which clung abstractly and therefore relentlessly to the upright gait, though humans broke under its force" (15).

Jan Bloch begins his analysis by explaining that in the face of the overt evil of fascism, Bloch "transfigured the USSR into a revolutionary emblem" (16) that prevented further criticism of that concrete utopia as long as the twin evils of German and US oppression existed.[14] He argues that this short-sighted political commitment prevented Bloch from further investigation of the wrongdoings of the "utopian" society upon which he had placed all his bets. In the Soviet Union, for all of his warnings of the dangers of conflating ideology and utopia, Bloch described a utopia without darkness—or at least a utopia whose darkness was less vicious than that which raged beyond its borders in Germany and the United States.

Ernst Bloch's analytical skills failed him, then, at the point where because of his personal commitment he neglected the critical strength of his own method. His personal stubbornness combined with a privileging of his teleological principle of hope produced the ideological trap that led to his uncritical support for the Soviet Union. As his son put it, Bloch's

heart ... was so much with the new Jerusalem, with Lenin, that until our times
he shut his eyes to the victims of the "red tsars" of Soviet reality, whose existence
he himself had suspected early on. He never grasped the scope of the disaster
and was not able to: just as love makes one blind. (24)

Jan Bloch finds the flaw in his father's thinking in the gap between "his long
breath sweeping over eons" that expresses the utopian hope in the telos of
history and his myopic inability to see the real problems in his Soviet utopia.
Bloch was trapped not only by his loyalty but also by a twofold error within
his own method. On one hand, he adopted a tactical tolerance of Stalinism
that resulted from his strategic belief in the power of the utopian telos to pull
history forward, for he identified what he considered to be the concrete utopian
phenomena of Marxist science and the Soviet system as necessary steps along a
unilinear path that ended with the classless society. On the other hand, because
of this slippage into ideological hypostatization and because of his persistent
focus on what he believed to be the greater evils of the Nazi and American
powers, he neglected the critical and negative aspects of the utopian function
that could have challenged and subverted even the most apparently progressive
of concrete utopias.

Here, then, is the dilemma of Ernst Bloch's utopian politics and of his utopian
method. Although a long-range vision enables humanity to move beyond the
darkness of the lived moment, unless that vision includes an immediate and
ongoing critique of the ideological appropriation of the "utopian" achievements
along the way, that vision alone can betray the very processes that are meant to
lead toward it. If a given situation produces a fixation on the long-range goal by
either the arrogance of a triumphal Marxism or the fear of an impending defeat
by opposing powers—or, in Bloch's case, in a complex mixture of both—that
stunted application of the power of hope can readily destroy the utopian function.
In other words, unless both moments of the critical dialectic of the utopian
function are maintained—unless the negative, denunciatory moment and the
positive, annunciatory moment are both employed so that each challenges the
limitations of the other—the utopian method will fail through an acceptance of
the provisional "success" valorized by short-sighted ideology.

Jan Bloch's critique of his father's work, therefore, is partly a response by the
son to the stubbornness of the father, to the upright revolutionary patriarch who
refused to be swayed by the contradictions of political history as he remained
loyal to the October Revolution long after its agenda was betrayed. Yet it is also
a recognition of the limitation of the utopian method itself when that method

lapses into the very abstract hypostatization that it was meant to oppose. If the utopian goal and program are prized at the expense of the utopian impulse, the method fails. In this manner, at the very least during the years from 1934 to 1938, Bloch lost sight of his utopian dialectic and became a prisoner of his ideological allegiances (Zipes 1988: 7). That loss of perspective seems to have begun with Bloch's unwillingness to adhere to the critical heterodoxy of his early years. From there, the political position that resulted from the combination of his hatred of fascism and what he (rightly in my estimation) saw as its North American counterpart and his theoretical and political proclivity to trust in the Soviet Union as a necessary station along the yellow brick road of communist progress became a stance that he could not easily abandon. In a Faustian bargain with the Stalinist devil for the promise of the hoped-for future, Bloch discounted the price that he had to pay for his capitulation to the "official" version of the revolutionary process. In so doing, he sacrificed the philosophical gold of utopia for the fool's gold of Stalinist ideology. Hence, the times in which Bloch lived (and the way in which he was faithful to them) led him to refuse to engage in an effectively utopian critique of his own adopted concrete utopia, the Soviet Union.

At the end of his examination of his father's work, Jan Bloch argues that it "was almost inconceivable that Bloch would have renounced the Red October" because he "was too religious for that" (36). On the contrary, given Bloch's understanding of the persistent power of religious anticipation to pull humanity forward (especially after the meta-religious discourse has been liberated from its accumulated abstractions), the problem that Bloch faced was that, in his fatal attraction to the Soviet Union, he was not "religious" enough. Rather than holding to the dual strategy of negative dehypostatization and positive anticipation, he settled, at least until late 1955, for a tactically hypostatized vision. Even here, however, that tactical move paradoxically allowed him to carry on his own utopian strategy—for the benefit of many to come after him.[15]

V

There is, then, in Bloch's *Principle of Hope* a dialogic tension between a historically entrenched orthodox Marxism with its strong belief in the linear progression toward the communist telos of history and a heterodox understanding of the fragmentary and disruptive play of utopia throughout human existence.[16] The major methodological difficulty in Bloch's philosophy of hope lies in his uncritical cathexis to the traditional Western category of the telos, the apparently powerful omega point at the end of history that pulls human emancipation forward. To the extent that Bloch privileges this abstract telos as the locus of communism's triumph, he dilutes the subversive power of the concrete utopian function as it wends its way through the cracks of everyday life toward a liberated and fulfilled horizon. Furthermore, to the extent that he emphasizes the purely rational, scientific nature of his work as it grows out of Enlightenment thought, he also devalues his discoveries of the persistence of the utopian function in social and cultural spaces where the rational Marxist would no longer look: in the culture of fascism, for example, or in religion, or in the finality of death.

Bloch reveals his linear, teleological side throughout his work. In his discussion of religion, he often presents a version of utopia that draws on metaphors of *maturity* and *perfection* achieved at the end point of history. In his discussion of the contribution that religious founders make to the conscious movement "towards utopian reality," Bloch makes the following statement:

> And the growing self-commitment (of the founder, such as Moses or Jesus) is finally grounded in that specific venturing beyond with which every religious act begins. This specific venturing beyond, the *more mature religions become,* proves to be that of the most powerful hope of all, namely that of the Totum of a hope which puts the whole world into rapport with a *total perfection.* (1986: 1192, my emphasis)

Here, the careful interpretation and appropriation of religious space as a contested site for the utopian impulse collapse in a heavy-handed imposition of images of maturity and perfection that are part of the legacy of Bloch's inheritance of the Western Enlightenment, with its accompanying attitude of bourgeois arrogance and confidence.

One of the best indicators of Bloch's reduction of utopia's creative potential by means of his uncritical adherence to Soviet ideology and unmediated teleological thought occurs in his discussion of ideology and utopia in the first volume of *The Principle of Hope.*[17] Certainly, he grasps the power of the anticipatory consciousness as it informs and exceeds the ideologies in which it has been enlisted as a motivating force throughout Western history. Yet, once he addresses the role of the utopian function within the Soviet movement of his own time, he enters the dead end of his own historical hypostatization.

In his analysis of the symbiotic relationship between ideology and utopia, Bloch describes how ideology exploits utopian vision even as it restricts the potential of that vision to the requirements of a dominant class. He recalls Marx's comments in *The Holy Family* that the historically successful "interests" of a rising class produce a "cultural surplus" as their limited thoughts are phrased in terms of ideas that express the needs and aspirations of humanity in general, and he identifies that surplus vision as the "effect of the utopian function" (156). That surplus, he argues, can be revived for further movement forward. As he puts it, "these blossoms definitely can be removed from their first socio-historical soil, since they themselves ... are not bound to it" (155). He effectively understands the utopian function as a dynamic social force that both motivates ideologies and carries human aspirations beyond their encapsulation within ideologies, and he understands that such aspirations can be enlisted long after their particular historical moment in the further movement of human emancipation.

However, once Bloch turns to the discussion of the role of the utopian impulse within actually existing socialism, he reduces the power of the utopian function to the status of a programmatic tool in the hands of the correct and inevitable masters of history who operate without the limitations of ideological mystification. To be sure, he rejects "merely abstract utopianizing," which is not rooted in the objective considerations of the material possibilities at hand, and he privileges the "power of anticipation" carried out within "concrete utopia ... with its open space and its object which is to be realized and which realizes itself forwards" (157, my emphasis). Yet the difficulty arises when he identifies the role within socialism of this powerful "methodological organ for the New" as one that simply reorganizes the surplus of utopian visions that have survived beyond their own, ideological moments and have remained latent in the history of the Western consciousness (157). In its socialist or communist manifestations, the utopian function awakens the utopian surplus of the past from its ideological slumber only to send it along "the attempted path and content of known hope," which has become synonymous with existing socialism.

The tension between the critically utopian and the teleologically utopian in Bloch can be more extensively seen in the contrast between the closing section of *The Principle of Hope*, "Karl Marx and Humanity: Stuff of Hope," and the penultimate section, "The Last Wishful Content and the Highest Good." In "The Last Wishful Content," Bloch cautions against the trap of false utopias whose contents have become ideologically fixed in an overconfident sense of what is better at the given moment. Recalling the proverb that "the better is the enemy of the good," he warns against foolish wishes and ideal value-images that prevent movement toward a utopia that, in the best sense of Bloch's work, is never fully understood in terms of fixed content. He insists that the primary utopian drive rooted "in hunger, in need" can be found as "surplus" in most of the idealized formations of ideology (1321). In this light, he reads particular utopian figures such as the image of Jesus in the heretical sects of the Middle Ages or the revolutionary ideal of the bourgeois citizen as subversive signifiers that lead to versions of existence beyond what they signify in their own time. Even in this section, however, Bloch tends to explain the forward pull of these guiding images in terms of an "all-embracing purpose" of what is "humanly final" (1317). Yet, as long as he maintains a balancing caution against ideological fixation, his use of the categories of *totality* and *finality* remains at a level of provocative utopian tropes rather than categorical imperatives that order all that comes before them. In the temptation to "stay awhile," which carries with it the danger of becoming encased in a given ideological matrix, Bloch still identifies a moment when one is on the edge of a "good" that goes beyond what is offered (1179).

Bloch, therefore, understands the danger of hypostatizing the category of the "highest good"; utopian images, even of the highest order, provide not finished content but rather "relentless invariance of direction towards a content" so that the highest good is the sliding signifier of a "goal which is not yet formed" (1324). He recognizes that the key images of that highest good—the religious God, the atheist Kingdom of God, or the communist realm of freedom—are ideals that reveal abstract tendencies but not concrete constructs of what human existence must be. For the world is "a process" based in the materiality of existence, which may be subjected to human intention and goals but which always remains a separate category, with its own "allied potential" (1327). This process discourages human intentionality from exclusively determining the shape of things to come because "every formation of value is dependent on the tendency-latency in its material" (1333) so that a hypostatized version of attainment gone cannot fully account for the process. Therefore, "the hope of the highest value or of the highest good, this last conceivable border-ideal, contains both Self and World, in a manner that points to the utopian way" but that does not reduce that utopian movement to one system of perfection (1986). In the encounter of human aspiration and the materiality of the world, there is always a surplus; for "only the best still hungers" and resists whatever attempted "figures of perfection" are superimposed upon it. Consequently, "real-utopian ciphers" need to be understood by means of a "material theory of signs" wherein such ciphers are read as provisional encapsulations within "available meanings" but which also always already exceed those meanings (1334, 1345). Although Bloch argues that there is movement toward what is felt to be a "final figure" (1345), at its best Bloch's philosophy of hope never rests satisfied with that absolute sign.

Authentic utopian symbols are ones where "the thing signified is still disguised from itself," but they also are figures that have to be played through a concrete mediation with the possibilities of the given material world. They are not simply "attainable by a mechanical-levelling world picture" (1346). Utopian symbols, in other words, are "solely tension-forms, dialectical material process-figures" that "have around them, before them, the *uncompletedness* of latency" (1351). There may well be "utopian edges of meaning" around all signifiers, but they are not reducible to the content of those signifiers (1352). Bloch therefore cautions against "mythical hypostases" that reduce the images of the highest good to static accomplishments (1332). He states that the authentically highest good

> dawns thus in the entire potential of matter .... This, its kingdom-figure which does not yet exist, governs throughout great dangers, hindrances and orbitings, all the other figures of the good path, and in it the Authentic, according to the intention, is formed like joy. *These are frontier definitions of intention towards the highest good and the frontier concepts of every thought that moves toward the Absolute of human wanting.* (1353)

At this juncture, Bloch is at his critical best. He insists that the utopian function includes both the power to define fulfilment and the power to resist all efforts to contain its potentially unbounded hope in a hypostatized definition.

Unfortunately, in the next section, the narrative telos of his entire study, Bloch violates this methodological strategy. In "Karl Marx and Humanity: Stuff of Hope," he commits the very act of mythical hypostatization that he rails against throughout the three volumes. Driven by the contradictions of his times and his inherited Enlightenment and Marxist confidence, he puts the brakes on his utopian process by hypostatizing the Absolute Subject of Marx and the fixed communist project of a scientifically attained classless society. In this section, Marx becomes the "true architect" who *finally* empowers humanity to actively comprehend itself (1354). "Genuine Marxism," for Bloch, "in its impetus, its class struggle, and its goal-content is, can be, will be nothing but the promotion of humanity. And, in particular, all the cloudings and deviations along the way can only be really criticized, indeed removed, within Marxism" (1358). Going further in this hypostatization, Bloch makes theory and not people the active agent of progress as he asserts that "in those countries *where Marxism took power* ... quarters are arranged for the future" (1367). This, then, is the site of Bloch's methodological fault line and the source of his emotional and political blindness that found its expression in his uncritical support of Stalinism. This is the deep flaw in the philosophy of hope: namely, that it can settle for a teleological end point located in a militant hypostatization of those items that inspired its forward motion in the first place— reducing them, in this case, to the limits of Soviet Marxism and the Soviet State. At the point where Bloch's method should be opening up to whatever historical developments may yet occur in the unknown future, he clings tenaciously to the Soviet achievements of his era and thereby denies the future potential of the communist movement and his own method.

Nevertheless, contrary to the dire assessments of either his anti-communist or his revisionist critics, even at this darkest moment of his work Bloch still argues against the closure to which he himself had fallen prey. For even in this hypostatizing chapter, Bloch provides future students and practitioners of the utopian function with the wherewithal to deconstruct his own worst failures—to turn the utopian Bloch against the ideological Bloch. That countervailing strand of dialogic engagement begins with the epigram from Lessing that introduces the section: "It is not true that the shortest line is always the straightest" (1354). In this quotational gesture, he makes an opening cautionary gambit against the simplest way forward, whether that be in the act of making history or of reading the chapter at hand. Thus, even as he celebrates Marx and the communist goal, Bloch warns that "no dreaming may stand still," and he wisely observes that people have "always been expected to cut their coat according to their cloth" even as "their wishes and dreams did not comply" (1365). Even when he mentions the "legitimately expectable and attainable goal" of "socialist humanization," he cautions that such a goal can be approached only if it is "not obscured by the inadequate, is not bitterly led away down false roads"; for human emancipation, he asserts, can be decided only in "open history, the field of objective-real decision" (1372). He argues that "the unfinished world can be brought to its end, the process pending in it can be brought to a result, the incognito of the main matter which is really-cloaked in itself can be revealed" only if the tendency-latency of those hopes is constantly held open (1373). "Hasty hypostases" and "fixed definition" cannot serve utopian anticipation. Bloch clearly sees that there is "no pre-ordered" teleology at work "in the dialectical tendency-latency, open to the Novum, of material process" (1986).

To be sure, in defining such a pre-ordered discourse, Bloch refers to "old teleologies" and ones that "are mythically guided from above," and simply positing Marxism against those dated positions, he again moves away from the potential of his method (1986). At this point, Bloch's critical utopian logic demands that he reject the orthodoxy and the fixed telos of his Soviet comrades, for they too would lock the tendency-latency into a premature solution. His inability to do so, as I argue above, is the result of his teleological bent and his own tactical blindness, but Bloch's failure of nerve at this point does not bring down the entire structure of his utopian philosophy. Indeed, in his closing pages, he argues against that failure when he discusses the "ontic hypostasis" of pre-Marxist philosophies whose self-fulfilling method leads to a result that "becomes the palace which is already complete anyway at the end of the path" (1374). In contrast to such self-enclosed outlooks, he offers the concept of "the process-world, the real world of hope itself" wherein the "dialectically aimed, systematically open view into tendency-shaped matter" is the authentic form of utopian expectation (1986). At the end of his own work, then, Bloch gives his best advice to his readers—and ironically to himself had he heeded it. He cautions against absolute goals, and asserts that the "best still remains patchwork" (1375). He understands that "every end again and again becomes a means to serve the still utterly opaque, indeed in and for itself still unavailable goals, final goal" (1986). The "final goal" at the end of *The Principle of Hope*, therefore, is not an achieved or predicted end but rather a hope for that which is never fully attained. To settle for any goal "on the way" is therefore to pause fatally on the path to a homeland that still lies ahead; movement toward the horizon is essential. Thus, his powerful concluding words in *Principle*:

> True genesis is not at the beginning but at the end, and it starts to begin only when society and existence become radical, i.e. grasp their roots. But the route of history is the working creating human being who reshapes and overhauls the given facts. Once he [*sic*] has grasp himself and established what it says, without expropriation and alienation, in real democracy, there arises in the world something which shines into the childhood of all and which no one has yet been: homeland. (1375–6)

Thus, Bloch ends his massive study by playing out the dialogic tension that runs all through his work. In so doing, he reveals the nature of his dilemma. As he asserts in his discussion of ideology and utopia, the utopian function serves as a critical and forward-looking force up to the point of socialism. Yet, within existing socialism, the utopian challenge to the limits of any given definition of reality and its possibilities—especially as that reality is defined within the terms of a ruling ideology—is no longer required. Consequently, the utopian function under such conditions becomes a compromised method for appropriating the lost visions of the past for the apparently clear-headed work of what is taken to be the new society. In the privileging of the inheritance of Western culture that stems from his European bourgeois background and in his political loyalty to the Soviet Revolution that stems from a combination of his philosophical belief in the correctness of Marxism and of his existential interpretation of both the

United States and Nazi Germany as far greater evils, Bloch represses the most critical aspects of his utopian function precisely at the moment when they were most needed in his own time and place.

Throughout *The Principle of Hope*, therefore, Bloch pushes against his own best insights. He articulates the critical power of the utopian impulse, and in so doing, he teaches others to read against the grain of their time and to tease out the traces of human expectation. Yet, from the beginning to the end of his magnum opus, he regularly falls short of applying the power of that utopian critique to his own historical situation. Thus, Benjamin's advice returns. For what Bloch's principle of hope needed was an external challenge that would have exposed the dialogic contradictions of his work and set its best insights free. Or, as Laclau and Mouffe would put it, his work required the rupture of its sutured integrity by means of an encounter with another radical discursive system in order to free it from its own discursive blindness. As the progressive theologians realized, a demystified and open-ended critical theology—rooted in present suffering and struggle and suspicious of all provisional teleologies— appears to have been Bloch's methodological path beyond this dilemma. Filtering the utopian function through the medium of theological critique and vision provided the needed mediation between political praxis and the hoped-for realm of freedom.

Obviously the discursive and political power of such an external challenge did not fully develop until after *The Principle of Hope* was completed, but then— echoing Benjamin's original advice—the progressive theologians of the 1950s and 1960s carried out such an operation in their appropriation and in doing so made Bloch's radical utopianism more readily available for the secular New Left. Seeking ways to rewrite religious discourse so that it spoke to conditions of the modern world, European, North American, and Latin American theologians found a theoretical fellow traveler in this Marxist philosopher who both respected their own accumulated tradition and provided them with a method for dialectically transcending it. Unlike Bloch, however, the most progressive of them did not inhibit their thinking with an ideological hypostatization of their own theology. Instead, they turned Bloch's critical utopian Marxism against his limitations as well as their own and thereby generated a radical method that apprehends the signs of the times and constantly looks beyond them to newly emergent possibilities in human society.

In the work of the Latin American liberation theologians, especially, Bloch's articulation of the power of the utopian function resists closure by any ideological position—even one that occurs within the theoretical and pastoral structures of the liberation church itself. The liberation theologians have been able to "pluck the living flower" of Bloch's utopian function from the shortcomings and failures of his method and his own employment of that method. They have dialectically taken the utopian function to a new moment in the history of the human struggle for justice and fulfillment. Rather than simply exposing the failings of this unorthodox Marxist and cynically accepting the status quo of a world informed by anti-communism and dominated by transnational capitalism, they have dared to challenge that pervasive system in the name of a future that draws on the best of both Christian and Marxist praxis. Their critical strategy is not a backward, nostalgic opportunism, but rather an embracing of a revolutionary process that is still emerging from and beyond the limits of Western discourse.[18]

Denunciation/Annunciation: Utopian Method

I

As I note in the last chapter, in his "Theses on the Philosophy of History," Walter Benjamin, with not a little irony, recognized the ability of the hunchback of theology to win the game for the puppet of historical materialism.[1] While this might surprise those who cling to the stereotypical Marxist reduction of religion to a social opiate or sigh of the oppressed, Benjamin's sense of the disruptive power of religious discourse was better understood by those who were aware of the radical potential of contemporary political theologies, for, as I argue above, theology was given a fresh lease on life by historical materialism, and historical materialism's own horizons have been extended by politicized theologies. In those social contexts wherein historical materialism now participates in a game played out in the open by the more popularly accepted discourse of religion, theology is no mere puppet playing someone else's game. In these situations, the "messianic" interruption of the continuum of history is effectively carried out through a religious discourse imbricated with the larger, secular project of human emancipation. This development brings into theoretical action what Theodor Adorno called for in a letter to his friend in 1935: "A restoration of theology, or better, a radicalization of the dialectic into the very glowing core of theology, would at the same time have to mean an utmost intensification of the social-dialectical, indeed economic, motifs" (quoted in Lamb 1982: 132).

Although, at least since the 1950s, while progressive theologians have engaged with Marxism as an important methodological and political basis for their work, the reciprocal acceptance of the praxis of theology by those involved in secular revolutionary projects has not been as forthcoming. More attention must be paid, however, for the utopian praxis of religious discourse is not solely a mechanism of internal Church reform.[2] It has also been an important intervention against domination—by structures and practices based on class, gender, race, sexuality, and other lived differences; by the economic and military power of late capitalism and imperialism; and by the bureaucratic and ideological restrictions and deformations of postrevolutionary socialist states. Consequently, a further examination of the critical power of religious discourse—in particular, Latin American liberation theology—to challenge sacred and secular systems as well as to articulate oppositional moral-political insights can help to inform a clearer understanding of the synergy between progressive theology and historical materialism and the impact of that productive relationship on the developing theory and practice of the secular utopian method, indeed of the process of becoming utopian.

II

Liberation theology is not simply another step within the parameters of the modernization of religion. It is, instead, a self-conscious, revolutionary effort to develop a method and agenda for change that addresses the needs and aspirations of the majority of Latin American people on their own terms— replicating neither Western hegemonic nor counter-hegemonic views of what is to be done. Although influenced by Western culture, liberation theology is "not a mere reproduction, adaptation, or transcription of the 'academic theology' of the traditional centers" of religious thought (Míguez Bonino 1975: 62). Nor is it an uncritical continuation of Western political theory, Marxist or otherwise. Although liberation theologians draw substantially from Western Marxists and theologians, they claim their "right to 'mis-read' their teachers … to offer their own interpretation of the theological task" (Míguez Bonino 1975).[3] As the Jesuit theologian Matthew Lamb put it, these radical theologians transcend the limits of both the "sacralism" of the institutional Church and the "secularism" of the modern corporation and state bureaucracy (1982: 52–4).

The epistemological and political paradigm shift nurtured by Latin American liberation theology challenges the meaning of Christianity and the mission of the Church at the same time as it expands and deepens the process of social revolution.[4] In the late 1950s and 1960s, church activists—faced with the exploitation and poverty of the majority of Latin American people—asked what it meant to be a Christian in a world of suffering. Inspired by both the Cuban revolution and the Second Vatican Council, they worked to redirect the Church to the service of the most oppressed. The result was a "people's church" that begins from the daily experience of the "nonpersons of history," those who are "external" to the benefits of current social systems: workers, peasants, and the displaced populations in the squatter camps surrounding Latin America's cities from Tijuana to Santiago.

Although liberation theology had its roots in the context of oppression and resistance within Latin America, its origins and growth can be traced back to a wider set of historical developments, inside and outside the Church, after the Second World War. One major influence was the rejection of neocolonialism by national liberation struggles from Algeria to Cuba to Vietnam. As Míguez Bonino puts it, the "triumph of the Cuban revolution marks a new time in Latin America. It indicates that the capitalist and imperialist system can be overcome, even at a scant seventy miles from the USA" (1975: 33). No longer would "First World" economic and cultural models be accepted uncritically by the people seeking self-determination and social justice. Latin American clergy and religious studying in Europe in the 1950s—such as Gustavo Gutiérrez and Camilo Torres—benefited in their intellectual work from the perspective of national liberation opened up by these movements. As a result, revolutionary action informed by Marxist theory came to be accepted as a legitimate means toward a better life for people of the non-Western world. Since that time, the efforts of the grassroots and organized Left in Latin America—from movements led by Fidel Castro, Che Guevara, and Salvador Allende to the base community struggles in Brazil, Venezuela, and throughout the region—have continued to expand the secular political ground for the liberation church.

Within the Roman Catholic Church, Latin American theologians moved toward the liberation paradigm through their critique of the existential theology of postwar Europe and the pastoral practices of the New Christendom.[5] Existential theology—informed by the phenomenology of Heidegger, Sartre, Merleau-Ponty, and Gadamer—extended the trajectory that liberal theology had been following since the end of the nineteenth century as it moved from an otherworldly, God-centered perspective to a human-centered one. From the hope in the "new man" expressed by Teilhard de Chardin, to the "I-Thou" relational philosophy of Martin Buber, to the spiritual existentialism of Gabriel Marcel, to the Christian anthropology of Karl Rahner, existential theology focused on the meaningful existence of the human individual in the spirit of the insight of Dietrich Bonhoeffer that "being for others is the one and only experience of transcendence" (quoted in Fierro 1977: 11). As articulated by Karl Barth, Rudolph Bultmann, Paul Tillich, Karl Rahner, and others, this radical Christian version of liberal humanism allowed theologians to take seriously the realm of everyday life in the secular world and to abandon the traditional split between the supernatural and the natural. For existential theology, borrowing the words of Merleau-Ponty, "the transcendental descends into history" (quoted in Brenkman 1987: 19).

Freed from the tyranny of the supernatural by the existential problematic, the emerging liberation theologians gradually moved beyond Christian anthropology (and the Gadamerian hermeneutic that deeply informs its interpretive method). In particular, they saw that, despite its privileging of human existence in this world, existential theology did not speak directly to the people of the Third World, or anywhere else for that matter. As with John Brenkman's critique of Gadamer's hermeneutics, the new theologians found existential theology to be "unmarked by class, race, or gender, and unaffected by any concrete social interests or ideological commitments" (1987: 38). Thus, its anthropological consensus was exposed as too abstract: on the one hand speaking of generic humanity, on the other speaking of the isolated individual. The liberation theologians argued that without a material base in the historical, social, and economic specificities of communities of people in their own regions, theology was destined to remain a First World reflection upon the lone consuming individual, making his or her way through mass society or secular city, neither linking up with others nor radically breaking from the alienation of postwar consumer society. As the feminist theologian Sharon Welch noted in her critique of this overwhelmingly male and middle-class "academic" theology, the "specific historical concerns are bracketed" in the emphasis on the "ontological structure of existence" and "the experience of certain groups of people is excluded from contributing to or determining that analysis" (1985: 38).

In the pastoral arena, a new praxis linked to liberation theology's theoretical work grew out of the 1940s French worker-priest movement and the postwar Catholic Action movement based in the ruling ideology of New Christendom. From the turn of the century, Catholic social thought had posited a model of a New Christendom that represented the Church's efforts to project itself as an alternative to both capitalism and communism. Accepting the end of medieval Christian culture and the inevitability of modern secular society, the New Christendom model advocated specifically Christian institutions that would incarnate Christian policies and politics in a society dissociated from direct Church rule. While in the 1930s this approach favored a corporatist society (a view adopted by fascist regimes), in the postwar years the emphasis shifted to a liberal, yet anti-communist, agenda that marked a call to action for Christian Democratic parties, Catholic labor organizations, and social movements of young workers, students, and families. Organized on a cell basis, and stressing biblical study and social action, Catholic Action groups such as the Young Christian Students and the Young Christian Workers trained lay people for Christian political work much in the manner that Communist parties trained their own cadres. Theoretically propounded by Jacques Maritain, who did not go so far as to suggest a Catholic hegemony over society but who did envision a social order that was inspired by moral principles that stressed the dignity of the individual, Catholic Action was anti-communist but socially progressive. It developed leaders of the profane world who would organize social movements around a Christian "third way" between communism and secular liberalism. Drawing on the doctrine of the Mystical Body of Christ, in which each person is meant to fulfill her or his particular role in the social body with Christ as the head, Catholic Action combined a progressive side that spoke for the needs of the individual with a conservative side that tended to merge with fascism in its corporatist emphasis on hierarchical power and technical reform of the existing order.[6]

Influenced by participation in Catholic Action—especially as it shifted to the left through its immersion in South American revolutionary politics and North American anti-racist and anti-war struggles—liberation theologians and pastoral workers developed a militant attitude toward political practice while they rejected the anti-communist and conservative premises of the New Christendom ideology. In particular, they denied the validity of a social order directed by Christians, and they moved beyond New Christendom's narrow and immediate conflation of theology and social ethics to a more mediated understanding of the relationship between theology and radical social change. As a result, in a decidedly secular utopian move, they envisioned a broader public sphere in which Christians would constitute one group among many, and not the determining leadership. They abandoned the notion of a "third way" in favor of a specific allegiance to anti-capitalist, anti-Western movements. They saw their work taking place in an "entirely worldly world" (Gutiérrez 1973: 66) where neither the nostalgic retreat to a conservative Christian "paleodoxy" nor the technocratic reforms of a liberal Christianity willing to accommodate itself to the prevailing power structures of the West could serve as the basis for a Christian involvement in the process of addressing the anguish of contemporary society.

Liberation theology and praxis, then, represent a dialectical move through and beyond existential theology and Catholic Action. It represents an approach that attacks the "monster of contemporary alienation" (Lamb 1982: 128) and extends its own presuppositions by constantly basing its hermeneutic interventions upon the experience of real people in real, and terrible, contexts. In the early 1960s, the liberation project was greatly enhanced by the teachings of the Second Vatican Council and the leadership of Pope John XXIII. The vision of a worldly Catholicism advocated by the Council and the encyclicals of Pope John (*Mater et Magistra* and *Pacem in Terris*) and a few years later by Pope Paul VI (*Populorum Progressio*) extended the legitimacy of liberation theology. Vatican II's emphasis on the importance of transforming the existing world, on the need for participatory democracy in church and society, and on the importance of cultural forms in the formation of people reinforced the themes and strategies of liberation theology. Furthermore, the Council's recognition of the importance of the social sciences as tools for analyzing the "signs of the times" paved the way for liberation theology's appropriation of Marxism as a useful method of social analysis and vision.

Other directions in European theology developed in the 1960s that influenced the theology emerging in Latin America. In France, especially impacted by worker-priest pastoral action and the growing anti-Stalinist debates, the Christian-Marxist dialogues between and among theologians and party theoreticians, as well as pastoral workers and political organizers, helped to legitimate Marxism among progressive theologians (and opened secular theorists and activists to the possibilities of religious/theological discourse). In Britain, the articulation of a Catholic Left by Terry Eagleton and others around the journal *Slant* performed a similar function.[7] As seen in the last chapter, however, it was in the emergent West Germany that the most advanced theoretical work was launched. In a move beyond liberal theology and Christian Democracy, German "political theology" turned to critical, rather than orthodox, Marxism in order to find its way forward. The work of Jürgen Moltmann and Johannes Metz was influenced by the "warm" Marxism of Ernst Bloch and the cooler analyses of the Frankfurt School (especially Benjamin, Herbert Marcuse, and Jürgen Habermas). In the spirit of Bloch's philosophy of hope, they postulated that God is revealed in history through the promise of a "new heaven and a new earth" in a future that can only come about through the activity of humanity in transforming its own world. Drawing on Habermas, they described the role of the Church in actively involving itself in this process through a fresh assessment of its place in the secular public sphere. Again, while Latin American liberation theology clearly expressed its indebtedness to this European progressive theology that rejected the otherworldly, supernatural plane of reality so long privileged by traditional dogma and that recognized the role of human action in building the Kingdom of God in this world, it also distanced itself from it. Latin American theologians regard political theology as still too academic and abstract and are particularly critical of its Eurocentrism, its privileging of individual rights, and its tendency to favor social democracy.

Working beyond this complex heritage, liberation theology acknowledges its debt to the theology, philosophy, and politics of the West but also breaks away from those progressive, yet nevertheless hegemonic, discourses in order to find its voice within the process of the social transformation of Latin America. It therefore rejects the false promises of liberal modernity as a strategy that serves the interests of the First World governments and corporations and their collaborators among the national security states and the ruling elites in neo- and postcolonial regions. As Míguez Bonino stresses, it is important to realize the "gigantic fallacy of the whole modernizing attempt, because the efforts to prolong, consolidate, and carry through this project can only mean greater misery and tragedy for our continent" (1975: 15). Thus, liberation theology takes a strong position against capitalism because it enforces "a form of human existence characterized by artificiality, selfishness, the inhuman and de-humanizing pursuit of success measured in terms of prestige and money, and the resignation of responsibility for the world and for one's neighbor" (31).

In its criticism of the dominant Christian tradition and the modern industrial and postindustrial systems—Lamb's "sacralist" and "secularist" traditions—liberation theology calls for a "post-colonial and post-neocolonial understanding of the Christian gospel" within the "Latin American socialist project of liberation" (18, 39). Thus, this radical theology places a high priority on overcoming the chasm between the institutional Church and the poor and exploited. In this project, liberation theology adapts Marxism's critical and utopian method and vision to its analysis of the specific realities in Latin America. Although many commentators and theologians are reluctant to emphasize the importance of Marxist theory in liberation theology—whether for strategic or tactical reasons—it cannot be denied that the work of Marx and others such as Antonio Gramsci, Louis Althusser, Bloch, Marcuse, and Habermas plays a key role in this new religious discourse. As Juan Luis Segundo calmly admits in *The Liberation of Theology*:

> After Marx, our way of conceiving and posing the problems of society will never be the same again. Whether everything Marx said is accepted or not, and whatever way one may conceive his "essential" thinking, there can be no doubt that present-day social thought will be "Marxist" to some extent: that is, profoundly indebted to Marx. In that sense Latin American theology is certainly Marxist. (1973: 35)

Or, in Gustavo Gutiérrez's words, "it is to a large extent due to Marxism's influence that theological thought, searching for its own sources, has begun to reflect on the meaning of the transformation of this world and the action of man in history" (1973: 9).

Liberation theology won the regional Church's commitment to its central slogan (and underlying epistemology) of "a preferential option for the poor" at the conference of Latin American bishops at Medellin, Colombia, in 1968. In expressing its solidarity with the poor, the liberation church abandoned the "theology of death" identified with the forces of late capitalism. Instead, it chose the "theology of life" embodied in the community-based activism of the thousands of base Christian communities located throughout Latin America and in the secular revolutionary movements themselves. Inherent in the work of liberation theologians, then, is a recognition of the power of "diffused religiousness," as Frei Betto has described it, in the culture of 90 percent of the Latin American population (1987: 183). The religious narratives and rituals that shape people's daily lives are taken seriously, not as elements of a false consciousness or an opiate to be dismissed abruptly but as valid vehicles of memory and anticipation that can lead to the transformative empowerment of those who are denied life. As Betto says, in words that clearly reveal his understanding of the enduring force of cultural heritage and formation:

> If we were to ask a Latin American farmer, a worker, or a domestic servant what concept he had of the world, he would surely couch his reply in religious terms. The most elementary concept that the oppressed Latin American people have of the world is a religious one. I believe that one of the most serious mistakes of the Latin American left, particularly of the left within the Marxist-Leninist tradition, has been to preach atheism to the masses. It's not that they shouldn't say what they really think. It's not that at all. The thing is, they weren't being sensitive to the people's religious concepts, and, by acting in that way, they were, in fact, foreclosing the possibility of establishing a link between their political outlook and the masses. (239)

Accordingly, liberation theologians refuse to abandon religion and spirituality to either the dominant or the oppositional social and political forces. As Lamb puts it, those who choose the "religious option" within the oppositional spectrum must take care not to abandon Church structures in despair or bitterness, for total repudiation would only allow the dominant ecclesiastical authorities to continue in their biased flight from understanding and responding to those who suffer (1982: 12). Rather, they can work to transform and redirect those structures to the service of those who most need it. Conscious of Marx's Third Thesis on Feuerbach—that the revolutionary task includes both altering conditions and transforming consciousness—liberation activists seek new forms of what the North American theologian Edward Farley terms "ecclesia," or smaller communities based in "intersubjectively shaped redemptive consciousness" (quoted in Welch 1985: 93). Whether they are the base Christian communities of Latin America, the "communities of resistance" of North American peace or feminist groups, or local structures such as Afrocentric or Hispanic congregations, these "transformative communities" create a dialectical tension that shatters the "sociological dualism of institution versus charisma, of church versus sect" and that moves forward to a religious experience and discourse that is a critical and transcendent part of the revolutionary process (see Lamb 1982: 12). Drawing on the apparently residual discourse of religion, they further the emerging secular project of emancipation. They take what appears to be one step backward to move two steps beyond the paralyzing stasis of sacral and secular modernity.

The primary pastoral work validated by Latin American liberation theology, therefore, is not military counterviolence or service in postrevolutionary governments—although both are accepted as necessary tasks in given instances—but rather the base communities (*comunidades de base*).[8] These local communities of twenty to forty people provide spiritual and material sustenance and strength in the midst of poverty and terror through the process of *conscientización*. Initially inspired by Gadamerian hermeneutics but brought down to earth by Paulo Freire's "pedagogy of the oppressed" as it was worked out in the literacy campaigns in Brazil during the early 1960s, this consciousness-raising process is carried out by community leaders who serve as both spiritual ministers and political organizers. Through the steps of reflecting on experience, reinterpreting that experience in terms of a radical rereading of Scripture, and reflecting on the necessary changes in their social expectations and practices, the members of the base communities work toward an empowerment that allows them to re-enter history and challenge the dominant powers.[9] The development of the base communities is clearly the primary task for the popular liberation church, as well as the source of its original and continued theological development. Liberation theology at its best is never far from this decentralized pastoral work. Indeed, it is the theoretical expression of this pastoral politics.

III

Central to this "new prophetic temper" (Míguez Bonino 1975: 56) of liberation theology and its radical pedagogy is an overtly utopian method that combines a negative "hermeneutics of suspicion" with a positive "hermeneutics of recovery."[10] Through this double move—named by some theologians denunciation and annunciation—liberation theology provides a critical mediation between faith and politics that challenges and transcends the limitations of the present in the name of the dispossessed.[11] Its negative hermeneutic is not unlike that anticipated by Benjamin and developed by critical Marxists such as Adorno who insist on a "negative dialectic" that refuses the closure of an orthodox Marxism based in notions of representational identity, historical inevitability, and rigid totality (Adorno 1994). For only a method that recognizes the role of *difference* or *nonidentity* in its critical practice can provide the necessary negation and reappraisal of historical situations. Of course, for liberation theology, this negation challenges the canonical "truths" of religious as well as secular powers. It exposes dehumanizing practices and resists accommodation with any provisional achievement in the process of human emancipation, for as Welch insists, "the events of the twentieth century make it impossible to honestly assert with any assurance the likelihood of certain knowledge and final liberation" (1985: 14).

However, liberation theology moves beyond this negative moment to a positive recovery of emancipatory possibilities from "the perspective of the victims of history" (Lamb 1982: 17). It enlists the utopian impulse in order to articulate a utopian program for freedom not yet possible in the present situation. Indeed, this capacity for a nondogmatic utopian vision, based in the recognition of difference, constitutes one of liberation theology's most substantial contributions to transformative or revolutionary praxis. While fundamentally necessary, negation is not sufficient, for it does not itself articulate the powerful utopian element at work in any discourse, namely, one that taps the political unconscious of a people and allows them to break through the hegemonic ideological system in a concrete anticipation of a redeemed and just world for all. As Fredric Jameson has noted, "a Marxist negative hermeneutic, a Marxist practice of ideological analysis proper, must in the practical work of reading and interpretation be exercised *simultaneously* with a Marxist positive hermeneutic, or a decipherment of the Utopian impulses of these same still ideological texts" (1981: 296). As I discussed in *Demand the Impossible*, this *critical* utopian method self-reflexively works against bleak cynicism and naive escapism, either of which can all too easily be coopted as forms of artificial negativity that deflect and defeat engaged struggles.

The starting point for liberation theology's methodology is the *experience* of what Enrique Dussel terms "exteriority"—the "ambit whence other persons, as free and not conditioned by one's own system and not as a part of one's own world, reveal themselves" (1985: 40). Beyond the horizon of the rationality and order of dominant powers, the "reality of the other resists" (46) and reveals the possibilities of a radically different society. From this experience of exteriority, the process of liberation rejects that which is "established, fixed, normalized, crystallized, dead" (58–9) and proceeds to "the procreation of a new order, of its new structure, and at the same time of the functions and beings that compose it" (64). As Dussel puts it, liberation is a "goodness" (a "grace," in both theological and postsecular terms) that leads to "detotalizing the system or annihilating repressive frontiers" (66). Echoing Brecht, and anticipating Ruth Levitas' later work on utopia as method, he notes that "the liberating act ... can only be illegal, contrary to present laws, which, because they are those of an old just order that is now oppressive, are unjust. It is the inevitable position of liberation: subversive illegality" (66). From this base in subversive exteriority, liberation theology can chart the possible responses of a revolutionary Christian praxis.

As with the pastoral process of *conscientización*, liberation theology follows a "problem-posing" strategy that creates opportunities for people to interpret their situation and to change it. As in Freire's pedagogy, the method includes stages of decoding the dominant ideological construction of reality and a subsequent stage of renaming reality in order to speak a "truth" appropriate to the needs and aspirations of the community. Praxis, therefore, is central to the method. Passive learning or meditation is not sufficient. Rather, as Levitas would put it, the "graceful" transformation of reality is necessary. This process of interpretation and action does not reject the role of previous knowledge or theory, secular or sacred; however, such theories must be carefully and concretely adapted by the community rather than uncritically and abstractly adopted in their entirety. Thus, for liberation theology, "there is no knowledge except in action itself, in the process of transforming the world" (Míguez Bonino 1975: 88). As in the Gospel of John, the Word, the subversive truth, is "an incarnate word, a human flesh which has pitched its tent in history" (90). In this perspective, Christianity cannot step outside history, and cannot claim a neutral position outside of concrete political praxis.

One of the clearest accounts of the method used by the liberation theologians in their "critical reflection on Christian praxis in light of the Word" (Gutiérrez 1973: 13) is Segundo's essay "The Hermeneutic Circle." Working from a traditional, Western hermeneutic but moving beyond its theoretical and political limitations, Segundo defines the hermeneutic circle as "the continuing change in our interpretation of the Bible which is dictated by the continuing changes in our present-day reality, both individual and societal" (1973: 8). For the most effective use of this method, he posits two pre-conditions. One is that "the questions arising out of the present be rich enough, general enough, and basic enough to force us to change our customary conceptions of ... the world" (1973), for only this *activist* attitude will "force theology to come back down to reality and ask itself new and decisive questions" (9). The other is that the interpretation of Scripture, the central text of this "religion of the book," must change "along with the problems." If not, the problems of the present will "go unanswered, or worse, they will receive old, conservative, unserviceable answers" (1973).

The four decisive stages in the method are as follows:

> Firstly, there is our way of experiencing reality, which leads us to ideological suspicion. Secondly, there is the application of our ideological suspicion to the whole superstructure in general and to theology in general. Thirdly, there comes a new way of experiencing theological reality that leads us to exegetical suspicion, that is, to the suspicion that the prevailing interpretation of the Bible has not taken important pieces of data into account. Fourthly, we have our new hermeneutic, that is, our new way of interpreting the fountainhead of our faith (i.e., Scripture) with the new elements at our disposal. (9)

Thus, for liberation theology, each new reality requires a suspicious recognition of the conditions of the social situation, a subsequent reinterpretation of Scripture and official theology that responds critically to those conditions, and a renewed effort to change reality accordingly—and then, beginning the circle again, another reading of Scripture and theology in light of the actions undertaken. The process is ongoing—a permanent revolution of religious response to the needs and aspirations of the oppressed: one that begins in a process of Scriptural transformation but then leads outward to sociopolitical intervention and contestation.

Thus, Segundo rejects the traditional Marxist view of religion as an "affirmative" discourse fixed in the dominant ideological superstructure and inimical to the revolutionary project, but he also breaks from the universalizing hermeneutics of a liberal, existential theology that, for all its potentially critical intent, reproduces the Western status quo. Viewed through the lens of a hermeneutics of suspicion, religion can be a "weapon in the class struggle through a new and more faithful interpretation of the Scriptures" (1973: 16). Segundo observes that Marx himself stopped short of recognizing the full potential of this oppositional power of religious discourse, for Marx abandoned his own critical analysis and accepted the narrow Enlightenment view of religion as an irrational, mythic discourse belonging to "a purely spiritual plane." Going farther than Marx but in Marxist terms, Segundo regards religious discourse as "a concrete spiritualized form of ... protest against suffering in each age" (17).

However, this suspicious reflection cannot work on its own, for an effective use of the hermeneutic circle must include the positive step of articulating a way forward, a way beyond suspicion and negation. This requires, therefore, the creative work of recognizing and articulating the forward-looking utopian visions that arise within the daily lives of the suffering and oppressed as well as recovering the residual "dangerous memories" (Metz) of past moments of resistance and of extrapolating these "concrete utopias" into the motivating promises of the Kingdom of a new heaven *and* earth. Thus, as with the other forms of becoming utopian explored in this book, liberation theology incorporates the critical utopian impulse as the key mediating act in a praxis that does not settle for any enclosing equilibrium.

IV

Liberation theology has therefore generated a hermeneutic and activist method that helps to free the utopian impulse from the dominant structures and practices of the contemporary world. By restoring the "moral option" to the processes of political life, liberation theology offers one more way to reject what Stanley Aronowitz calls the "normative structures of modernity, which view spirituality, intuition, and experience as forms of ideology to be overcome by scientific rationality" (1981: 119–20). In what are now outdated terms, Aronowitz rightly saw the "contemporary spiritualism" of liberation theology as a "postmodern" discourse that challenged the hegemonic assertion of identity between reason and reality. Such a discourse goes far beyond the obligatory nod to plurality and pragmatic action offered by contemporary liberal theory, in any of its sacred or secular versions. Indeed, liberation theology is a dangerous discourse that is outraged and outrageous in its demands for justice and freedom. It is clearly suspicious; for, as Welch insists, without a "skeptical edge," liberatory affirmations of emancipation and justice "lose their reference to concrete situations" (1985: 14) and fall prey to cooptation by any power/knowledge system with an interest in keeping things as they are, or as they have become. It is also radically *utopian*, for in its articulation of dangerous memories and subversive horizons, the preconceptual activity of the spiritual imagination resists the rational, linear restrictions of modern life, whether those restrictions come with reaction or revolution.

Thus, liberation theology identifies the power of anticipatory fantasy or social dreaming to disrupt history's mythic spell. The organized Left has taken a long time to learn this—even with the help of writers such as Benjamin and Bloch. However, current postcolonial and decolonial movements—formed, on one hand, by the theories of critical Marxism, feminism, and ecology, as well as by the linguistic turn in philosophy, and, on the other hand, by the adamant practices of those who live at the peripheries of Western power to determine their own lives, their own forms of resistance and revolution—have proven to be more open to the political dimensions of spirituality, as well as to the spiritual dimensions of politics. These movements have recognized the importance of an anticipatory discourse in the process of moving from the bad old society to the good new one.

In a similar vein, Michael Taussig discusses the ways in which the discursive strategy of magical realism (*lo real maravilloso*) works not only in Latin American high culture but also in the popular culture of indigenous groups such as the Putumayo Indians of the Upper Amazon to subvert the sacred and secular colonial myths of conquest and redemption by reworking them into expressions of resistance and revolution. Taussig explains this discursive strategy in terms of Bloch's concept of "nonsynchronous development" in which images of the past are refunctioned to serve the hope of a better future (165–6) in a social expression of the subversive spiritual dimension in human experience.[12] In the Upper Amazon Indian cultures in which he lived and worked, Taussig encountered such counterhegemonic practices rooted in everyday existence that refunctioned the very myths imposed by the invading secular and ecclesiastical powers into powerful fictions of resistance. Thus, the image of the devil imposed on the Indio cultures by a colonizing Christianity is adopted as a signifier of resistance against those who try to dominate them; thus, the figure of the Virgin mobilized to bring new converts to their knees becomes a source of distributive magic that can punish envy and restore justice; thus, in the liberation Church, the image of Christ merges with the image of Che, and the Magnificat, that prayer of the Virgin Mary so often taught by the hegemonic Church as a prayer of submission, becomes a manifesto of resistance and justice: "He has put down the mighty from their thrones, and exalted those of low degree; he has filled the hungry with good things, and the rich he has sent empty away." To borrow Taussig's term, there is in the praxis of liberation—tempered by the materialist theology that reflects upon it and the social practices that give it concrete existence—a "wildness" that challenges the unity of the established order and gives voice to new possibilities. It is a wildness in the spirit of Benjamin's notion of messianic disruption—one that "creates slippage and a grinding articulation between signifier and signified" (Taussig 1987: 219). The questioning and transforming hermeneutic of liberation keeps this wildness alive so that it can "speak truth to power" in the utopian name of the integrity of nature and the human community. Here, then, the recognition by Benjamin and Bloch of the critical, utopian potential of religious discourse is perhaps more pertinent today than in their time—if only because of the provisional successes of liberation theology, of feminist, black, other national/ethnic theologies, as well as ecological and queer theology, in challenging the discursive, political, and economic monopoly of the global powers.

4

Look into the Dark: Dystopia and the Novum

I

Looking backward from this current moment, the political and intellectual milieu of the 1970s stands almost as an alternative reality, a moment in sharp contrast to our dark times.[1] I don't evoke this difference to dwell in nostalgia—for there were problems and contradictions, arrogant shortcomings and enthusiastic errors, internal failure and external repression then as now. Nevertheless, at least from my own perspective (at that time, within US culture), the spaces, and practices, of radical democratic socialist/communist opposition to the system of postwar capitalism and contending superpower bureaucracies were relatively more substantial and occupied greater "liberated zones" of praxis, before the ravages of the neoconservative and neoliberal counter-revolutions.

Within this larger Movement, an array of intellectual and cultural activity took place across the sociopolitical grid: from neighborhood and organizational study groups; to local theater companies, poetry groups, visual and performance art projects, film societies, poster collectives, fan formations, festivals, and rock bands; and on to new initiatives in the academy, critical and creative production flourished. In the universities, the new theoretical praxis (linked with political formations and campaigns) was broad, overlapping, and challenging to the official academic structure and the normative social system. In an historic move, inter-, cross- and trans-disciplinary work in African American, gay and lesbian, Third World, women's, ecological, and other "Studies" programs emerged as the intellectual and pedagogical dimension of the political struggles for self-determination and justice. Also, the elaboration and expansion of the Left's ongoing critique of the status quo, and the struggle through and beyond it, took several directions. To name two specific examples in the United States: in Milwaukee, Madison, and New York, attention was given to the critical theory of the Frankfurt School in the editorial collectives of the new journal *New German Critique*; and, from San Diego and New York, what came to be called "literary theory" led to the formation of the Marxist Literary Group, its annual Summer Institute in Culture and Society, and later the journals *Social Text* and *Mediations*. In addition, critical work in specific areas of cultural production took more solidly oppositional shape: this can be seen, for example, in the studies of film and popular music, and in science and utopian fiction.

In this richly layered spatiotemporal moment, therefore, intellectual and cultural practice moved between the academy and other social formations without the barriers, silos, and cages that have now become all too common. The result was the revitalization, after years of repression and marginalization, of the discourse of a broadly considered Left that included a refunctioned critical Marxism, a new wave of Marxist/socialist-feminism, African American and other racial and national liberation studies, gay-lesbian-queer studies, ecological studies, and anti-, non- and post-Western scholarship. This was a time when the personal, political, and professional dimensions of life were more, though not always easily, interrelated as facets of the self-conscious and self-critical practice of the Movement. This was a time just before the hegemonic rise of the New Right, a time just before the alienation, reification, and absorption of critical or theoretical practice into the market mechanisms of a newly rationalized knowledge industry (in publishing and in academia itself).

In this moment, in the December 1972 issue of *College English*, Darko Suvin's "On the Poetics of the Science Fiction Genre" made a significant contribution to this oppositional public sphere. For many engaged cultural scholars, trying to develop critical methods needed to analyze and change the existing order of things, as well as with finding effective ways to come to terms with the social meaning of forms such as science fiction, "Poetics" especially marked the beginning of a fresh approach to sf that dealt equally with its sociological and formal properties and led to the expansion of sf and utopian studies in ways that connected with the lived oppositional movement. Suvin's analysis of sf on its own terms, his identification of "the interaction of estrangement and cognition" and "an imaginative framework alternative to the author's empirical environment," shifted sf criticism beyond the limiting high culture approaches of the day: including those that followed New Criticism and canonical literary studies in a too-readily elitist elevation of some sf to the status of "serious literature," usually working with criteria appropriate for the realist or modernist novel, and those that deployed an unreflexive populist reading of sf as "paraliterature," but that did not make the distinctions required to comprehend sf's social production and consumption (375).[2] In "Poetics," sf was instead considered as a didactic literary form with its own history (however debated that would come to be) and its own formal operations. The object at last had shaped the critical response.

The paradigmatic shift marked by "Poetics" was followed by another key contribution in 1973 with Suvin's "Defining the Literary Genre of Utopia: Some Historical Semantics, Some Genology, a Proposal, and a Plea." Again, by way of historical analysis and careful definitions and distinctions, Suvin's essay sharpened the study of the literary utopia in a move that complemented what "Poetics" did for sf. It also significantly added to his examination of the kinship of the two genres as he elaborated on his historically disruptive argument that utopian fiction was *both* one of the roots of sf and one of its types: here, it's important to recall that he traced "science fiction" from ancient and medieval marvelous voyages and earthly paradises and argued that utopian fiction and the modern instances of sf shared in this heritage as kindred forms of "estranged" writing.[3]

These crucial contributions were soon joined by a paper Suvin delivered in 1977 at the University of Wisconsin-Milwaukee's Center for Twentieth Century Studies ("Science Fiction and the Novum") that was published in 1979 as Chapter 4 of his groundbreaking *Metamorphoses of Science Fiction*.[4] In "SF and the Novum," Suvin brought to his categories of "cognitive estrangement" and "alternative framework" the more developed argument that "sf [and utopia] is distinguished by the narrative dominance or hegemony of a fictional 'novum' (novelty, innovation) validated by cognitive logic" (1979c: 63). Here, however, this story of growing influence falters, for (as Suvin himself observed in his keynote address at the 1996 conference on "Envisioning Alternatives" at the University of Luton) the "SF and the Novum" chapter did not receive the attention given to the earlier publications.[5] In the published version of this address, Suvin surmised that the lack of response indicated a passive acceptance of his argument, indeed implied a "critical consensus" by "socialists and liberals" (1997b: 37). My own interpretation of this critical silence is, I fear, less optimistic. I would argue that it was not consensus but in fact deep discomfort with Suvin's argument that accounted for the neglect of the novum as a critical category. Indeed, in an exchange in *Science Fiction Studies* as recent as 1994–1995, a version of this discomfort emerges when Suvin and Carol McGuirk disagree over the function of the novum, with McGuirk, in postmodern fashion, distancing herself from Suvin's claim that a textual novum needs to be validated by cognitive logic (this, even after checking Suvin's clarification in his 1988 volume *Positions and Presuppositions in Science Fiction* that cognition includes the imagination as well as analytical discourse, a point which he had already made in "Poetics").[6]

Lurking in this friendly disagreement, therefore, is a hint of what might have been more aggressively at stake in this decades-long silence. Recalling the rising hegemony of the Right around 1980, I suggest that this critical dismissal is itself an early symptom of the systemic reaction against the thriving Left intellectual and cultural sphere—one that has continued, and indeed grown, in academic institutions and formations ever since. To be sure, needed, useful, and proper critiques, by what has often been inaccurately subsumed under the term "poststructuralism," challenged the orthodox Marxist tradition that uncritically employed categories such as scientific analysis, totality, or class struggle within the unyielding, authoritarian, stricture of a fixed teleological analysis that was itself closed to the specificities of history. Especially in critical Marxist, feminist, and postcolonial theory, these critiques aided the Left's political and intellectual project, as they stimulated the re-examination and refunctioning of such assumptions, premises, frameworks, and methods. However, by the 1980s (and drawing on the conservative reaction against the political and cultural impact of the Event of May 68), this substantial "poststructuralist" critique was all too readily conflated with a response that was neither critical nor dialectical but outright condemnatory of *all* left discourse, analysis, praxis. That is, the critical project was often appropriated for attacks based in old-fashioned anti-communism, albeit given renewed "professional" shape by the post-1968 reaction and the emergent New Right discourse. In this repressive atmosphere, however carefully nuanced at the time, Suvin's claims for the formal operation of a totalizing novum validated by critical cognition were too easily labelled as prescriptive and narrowly rational and consequently ignored and bypassed in the retreat to the safer professional zones of textuality, micro-politics, or yuppie postmodernity.

This tendency to coat the bitter pill of dismissal with the gel cap of critique was countered as early as 1983 in the paper (published in 1988 as "Cognitive Mapping") given by Fredric Jameson at the Summer Institute on Culture and Society, co-sponsored by the Marxist Literary Group and the Unit for Criticism at the University of Illinois. Jameson begins with a recognition of the "pedagogical function of a work of art" (1988: 347) that leads him to affirm the "historical merit of the work of Darko Suvin to repeatedly insist on a more contemporary formulation of this aesthetic value [of the didactic], in the suggestive slogan of the *cognitive*" (343). Later, as he concludes his argument for the use value of a (provisional, critical) "cognitive mapping," he notes how he has "infringed so many of the taboos and shibboleths of a faddish post-Marxism" that dismiss the categories of class, class consciousness, class struggle, and the mode of production and that stigmatize "the concept of totality and of the project of totalizing thought" (353–4). Pointedly, he observes that the post-68 French *nouveaux philosophes* said it most succinctly, without realizing that they were reproducing or reinventing the hoariest American ideological slogans of the Cold War: "totalizing thought is totalitarian thought; a direct line runs from Hegel's Absolute Spirit to Stalin's Gulag" (354). In 1994, Jameson updated this counterattack in *The Seeds of Time* as he again dismantled the postmodern equation of *totality* as an aesthetic or analytic category ("a combination or permutation scheme") with *totalitarian* practice (1994: xv). In what amounts to an auto-critique of aspects of his own postmodernism studies, he continues his review of the "paralysis of postmodern thinking" and argues in favor of "the philosophically correct use of the concept of totality, as something that by definition we cannot know rather than as some privileged form of epistemological authority some people are trying to keep for themselves, with a view toward enslaving others" (69). In other words, given the "totalizing force" of capitalism, in any of its historic transformations, it is only by means of representations and figurations of the social totality (and not by the enforcement of hierarchical/undemocratic strategy and tactics) that the mode of production can be adequately grasped, critiqued, indeed challenged. Such a process is not authoritarian, closed, or absolute, but rather a matter of "a preliminary working hypothesis" or "an indirect way of solving something that cannot be mastered head-on" (68–9). As Jameson puts it: "Totalization" is thereby "a project rather than the word for an already existent institution" (65).

A different version of this opposition to theoretical reaction is put forth by Paul Smith in his 1997 analysis of the "global" moment of capitalism. In *Millennial Dreams: Contemporary Culture and Capital in the North,* Smith claims, as part of his basic approach, the "logic of totality" that, quoting from Engels, he describes as a method depending on "a historical process and its explanatory reflection in thought, the logical pursuance of its inner connections" (2). Asserting that the "different descriptions of the world that [critical Marxism] can offer are still crucial," despite (or perhaps because of) the historic events of 1989 and the "thrall of the millennial dream" of a restructured capital, he argues that the "discovery and exposure of effective orders of determination in culture and society are still the tasks at hand and [are ones] in which a pragmatic politics might still claim a theoretical and analytical dimension directed at *structural* transformation" (56). That is, in the face of capital's totalizing practice, only an "alternative analysis of the totality" (57) can mount an effective oppositional response. Thus, Smith, like Jameson, challenges anyone who "parrots the shibboleth of the collapse of grand-narratives," who recites the standard refrain against Marxism's "totalizing" urge"

(59), or who "forgets" how much left critical praxis has rigorously challenged any and all authoritarian tendencies. As with Jameson and Suvin, by way of Raymond Williams, he reasserts the importance of "the explanatory power, and the power to change, that came from recognizing the existence of a completely structured totality" (60), and of being able not only to critique the social order but also to change it.[7]

In light of this reactionary riposte, I suggest that Suvin's argument for the novum fell victim to the theoretical and political dark ages of the 1980s. As the political culture of the 1970s was beaten back, and as its critical wing slid into shadows of suspicion, the 1979 essay was seldom explored, except by Jameson and others who were generally working within the ambit of the journal *Science-Fiction Studies*. Indeed, to return to my discussion of Suvin's 1996 keynote, I would note that, even though he expresses doubts about the "beneficence" of the novum, his concerns are not a rejection of its underlying logic but rather a caution about a too facile embrace of the capacity of a radical novum to survive the pressures of the current conjuncture (see Suvin 1997b: 37). Thus, he asserts that "we live in an ever faster circulation of what Walter Benjamin called *das Immerwiedergleiche*, the ever again recurring whirligig of fads that do not better human relationships," and he quotes David Noble who warns of the "perpetual rush to novelty that characterizes the modern marketplace, with its escalating promise of technological transcendence" in a "remarkably dynamic society that goes nowhere" (37). Suvin's 1990s suspicions, in other words, are not those of the earlier period of reaction and rejection but rather a needed correction of the effective apprehension of the viability of the novum in these times. Because of its cautionary tone, I would argue that Suvin's keynote commentary helps to revive his already nuanced argument in the light of the subsequent poststructuralist sensibility and in the shadow of the now more pervasive power of capital. Indeed, Suvin does not argue that the novum should be made redundant in an end-of-history implosion but rather that extreme care must be taken to distinguish between the novum of opposition and the "pseudo-novum" of commodification that have come to dominate the terrain of the "new." He consequently offers a sober reminder that utopian hope for what is Not Yet can be negated by the false utopia that the new market order offers as the prime site for individual experiences of hustle, success, and pleasure, and he further cautions that the novum of opposition itself must be interrogated (as in the critical utopias of the 1960s and 1970s and the critical dystopias of the 1990s) so that it is recognized as a novum when it generates a "formulation of a problem" but not when it offers the consoling "explanations" of a pseudo-novum (39).

With this historical perspective in mind, I want to examine more carefully Suvin's category of the novum. However, beyond explication, I will take the discussion into the present economic-cultural context and consider how the category of the novum—despite or indeed because of Suvin's own caveats— can contribute to an understanding of the literary mode that turned out to be particularly suited to the nasty 1990s (and indeed our own apocalyptic moment): namely, dystopian fiction. Whereas utopian—critical, heterotopian, or ambiguous—writing was at the leading edge of cultural expression in the 1970s, it was the *dystopia* that came to prevail in the 1990s and thereafter (and I say this even while recognizing, to cite but one example that I develop in later chapters, the exception to this tendency that manifested itself in the utopian and anti-anti-utopian novels of Kim Stanley Robinson).

II

With his argument that the common denominator of the sf, and utopian, text was to be found in the "estranged techniques of presenting a cognitive novum," Suvin sharpened the sociopolitical valence of his earlier definitions by clarifying how "history and society are not simply the contexts of fiction but its inly interfused factors" (1988c: x–xi). Thus, while novelty might be present in the *content* of any literary genre, in sf the novum is the *formal* element that generates and validates all elements of the text, from the alternative world to plot, characters, and style. Yet, the novum is meaningful only to the extent that it effectively intervenes in the author's historical context. Suvin makes this point eloquently:

> Born in history and judged in history, the novum has an ineluctably historical character. So has the correlative fictional reality or possible world which, for all its displacements and disguises, always corresponds to the wish-dreams and nightmares of a specific sociocultural class of implied addressees.
>
> (1988f: 76)

As he reveals in *Metamorphoses*, Suvin's immediate source for this category is Ernst Bloch's work, but he does not simply borrow from Bloch. Rather, working in a different historical and political juncture, he dialectically critiques and supersedes Bloch's more orthodox formulation of a societal novum. He consequently develops a radically democratic and diverse sense of the novum that enriches the deeper, political implications of his argument.

Bloch's introduction in *The Principle of Hope* usefully begins with his identification of the realism and pessimism needed to expose the "horrifying possibilities which have been concealed and will continue to be concealed precisely in capitalist progress": for only from such a "critical coldness" can a "militant optimism" proceed clearly with concrete utopian struggle (Bloch 1986: 199). Having taken this stand, however, Bloch then falls back into an orthodox framing of his version of the novum in company with the interrelated categories of Front and Ultimum, and here Suvin's critical refunctioning takes hold (see 198–205). First of all, Bloch's category of the Front, where the novum is to be found, is limited by its Leninist connotation of direct military engagement. Such a singular site of his movement betrays what the actually existing Left has come to know: namely, that the sociopolitical spaces and moments of contestation are multiple and shifting. In Suvin's refunctioned sense—informed by Antonio Gramsci and Raymond Williams—the metaphor of the Front gives way to a meaning closer to Williams' notion of a "structure of feeling," which allows for the identification of a variety of historically specific sites and instances (often contradictory but nevertheless oppositional) in which radical nova are to be found. To be sure, in his unorthodox moments Bloch himself catches this sense of a complex array of emergent possibilities, for he speaks of those spaces wherein the "world process" is most in motion, wherein one can locate the "little thought-out, foremost segment of Being of animated, utopianly open matter" (200). Thus, Suvin's novum is not the reified "novelty" produced by capitalism, or indeed the vanguard privileged by orthodox Marxism. Instead, it is the dialectical force that mediates material, historical possibilities and the subjective awareness and action engaged with those possibilities.

On the other side of the frame from the Front, Bloch's novum assumes full import only when grasped in terms of the Ultimum into which it will transmute, and for the Marxist philosopher, the Ultimum represents "the highest newness, the repetition (the unremitting representedness of the tendency-goal in all progressively New) [that] intensifies to the last, highest, most fundamental repetition: of identity" (203). The shift from novum to Ultimum registers the point of a "total leap out of everything that previously existed" (Bloch 1986), and so it is the pull toward the unrepresentable Ultimum that keeps the novum resistant to enclosure by the forces (whether hegemonic system or orthodox opposition) of the present moment. While the sense of a "total leap" keeps the Ultimum radically open, the connotation of finality compromises it with the sort of ahistorical fixation that predominates in both theological and Stalinist discourse. For Suvin, therefore, the Ultimum, with its anti-historical claim of fulfillment, must necessarily give way to the alternative of the always-unfolding horizon of a radical break from, or leap beyond, the present, one that refuses the legitimating claim of teleological arrival. In Suvin's formulation, the novum has revolutionary effect *only* if it functions in relationship to the changing, historically specific structures of feeling out of which it develops and the not yet nameable *horizon* of an ongoing history toward which it tends. Again, as I argue above, Bloch, working from his unorthodox standpoint, which always contends with his orthodox discipline, puts it this way: "the dialectic which has its motor in unrest and its goal-content, which in no way exists ante rem, in unappeared essence does away with the dogged cycle [of an Alpha to Omega movement around the new which endlessly repeats]" (204). Instead, in keeping with the "real-ciphers in the world," history itself can move in an open-ended, not determined or predictable, manner.

Working from this dialectically enriched philosophico-political framework, Suvin frees up the political valence of the novum as the mediation of form and history. As he puts it in "SF and the Novum": "An aesthetic novum is either a translation of historical cognition and ethic *into* form or (in our age perhaps more often) a creation of historical cognition and ethics *as* form" (1979c: 80). With the relationship established, he goes on to refine the treatment of readerly estrangement begun in "Poetics," and describes it as a "feedback oscillation" that

> moves now from the authors and implied reader's norm of reality to the narratively actualized novum in order to understand the plot-events, arid now back from those novelties to the author's reality, in order to see afresh from the new perspective gained.
>
> (71)

This process also provides Suvin with the basis for the critical evaluation of sf texts, for he notes that sf is a symbolic system that can be "cognitively validated within the narrative reality of the tale and its interaction with readerly expectations" (80).

The criteria Suvin employs to evaluate the meaningfulness or significance of a sf text vary slightly from essay to essay, but they are summed up most succinctly in "Science Fiction and Utopian Fiction: Degrees of Kinship" (published as "The River-side Trees" in 1974, reprinted in *Positions*). He lists three criteria for the evaluation of the novum and its correlate elements: "magnitude," "cognitive validation," and "relevance" (1988e: 34). Thus, the measure of magnitude (gauged from a "single event or gadget to a cosmic-cum-societal totality") primarily concerns textual content (38); for this is largely a matter of assessing a text in terms of "how much new insight into imaginary but coherent and this-worldly, that is, *historical,* relationships it affords and can afford" (1979c: 81). In his 1982

"Narrative Logic" essay (also in *Positions*), Suvin elaborates on the criterion of magnitude in terms of the related criterion of consistency, which, he explains, is a measure of whether the novelties are "sufficiently numerous and sufficiently compatible to induce a coherent 'absent paradigm'" (1988b: 67).[8]

The question of cognitive validation moves the readerly, critical process outside the text. Certainly, within the text, cognition requires "the necessity and possibility of explicit, coherent, and immanent or nonsupernatural explanation of realities" (1979c: 67). However, in "Not Only But Also: On Cognition and Ideology in SF and SF Criticism" (written with Marc Angenot in 1979, reprinted in *Positions*), the authors note that the validation of these realities must occur by way of a full "*interaction between the text and the history in which it is being written and is being read,* so that the contradictions and mediations of a history-as-process are [not] passed over in silence" (1988g: 48). That is, to avoid a response not caught in the present moment (therefore "ideological and mystifying"), cognitive validation must grasp the current conjuncture in its contradictions (48). To do so, however, it must draw not only on analytical discourse but "equally (and in all probability necessarily) … on imagination" in order to resist the reductions and closure of an all too easily instrumentalized rationality (1988d: 189). Indeed, a "truly critical attitude," Suvin and Angenot go on to say, works at the "horizon of a modern, epistemologically self-conscious and self-critical *science or cognition*" (1988g: 49). This cognitive horizon necessarily incorporates the viewer, reader, or critic into "the structure of what is being beheld" and therefore "permits the provisional method situated within it to be integrated into social practice and to become self-corrective on the basis of social practice, and which has a chance—if used intelligently—to show realistically the relationships of people in the material world" (49–50). Thus, cognitive validation stays open to its own presuppositions, historical specificities, and changing positions in the context of an ongoing social practice.

Finally, the criterion of relevance ("fake *vs.* superficial *vs,* deep and/or lasting") takes the evaluation to the "point where aesthetical and socio-political qualities meet," where the "transposition and condensation of history into an analogical historicity" make an epistemological impact on the reader's own situation (1988e: 38). This is the most didactic moment in the production and reception of this didactic literary form. It is the moment when the cognitive quality of the novum, which is manifest in reading protocols, reorganizes the "logical space of our conceptual frameworks" and increases "understanding of the 'dynamic processes of reality'" (Umberto Eco, quoted in Suvin 1988d: 190).

Underlying these evaluative discussions is Suvin's driving desire to differentiate between novum and pseudo-novum, between the open, political organ of the New and the economically or politically reified product. Indeed, by way of Benjamin, Suvin develops an extensive analysis of the "false" novum in his 1980 essay, "For a 'Social' Theory of Literature and Paraliterature: Some Programmatic Reflections," but he argues as well in "Narrative Logic" that "the distinction between the consistent and inconsistent novum as a special case of the distinction between true and fake novum) is ... not only a key to aesthetic quality in sf but also to its ethico-political liberating potentiality" (1988b: 70). Thus, simple, "capricious," market contingencies, passing fashions, do not a radical novum make, nor does the location of a universal meaning outside of history or the cycle of a static narrative masquerading as history. The novum, in short, must literally make a difference, and the determination of its quality is both an aesthetic and an ethico-political judgement that addresses the fundamental question of "power relationships" as they play out in the author's time-space (1979c: 82; 1988g: 55).

III

Throughout his work, Suvin asserts this ethico-political potential of sf and utopian fiction. In "SF and the Novum," in *Metamorphoses*, he argues that the "praxis" and "epistemé" of sf have the capability to lead into a "third dialectical term" that supersedes both "fatalistic collectivism and humanistic individualism" (1979c: 74). He demonstrates this claim in theoretical arguments and textual analyses, and he persistently demonstrates how the fictional novum undergirds and informs the readerly, or critical, feedback loop which, at its best, comes to terms with the absent paradigm of the social-historical situation, cracks through its ideological formations, and makes possible new ways of knowing the world. This powerful critical effort, however, has seldom dealt directly with the *dystopian* text.[9]

To be sure, early on in "Defining the Literary Genre of Utopia," Suvin steps into the field of dystopian writing when he notes that utopia, as the "logical obverse" of satire, "explicates what satire implicates, and vice versa," and he further suggests that a utopian text could be "gauged by the degree of integration between its constructive-utopian and satiric aspects," for the isolated extremes of "the deadly earnest blueprint and the totally closed horizons or 'new maps or hell' both lack aesthetic wisdom" (1979a: 54–5). Later, in "Science Fiction and Utopian Fiction," he describes "anti-utopias" as utopian variants that emerge from a novum generated by a "less perfect principle" of social organization, observing as well that a text that makes "a community claim to have reached perfection is in the industrial and post-industrial dynamics of society the surefire way to present us a radically less perfect state" (1988e: 36). Further on, he mentions the "intimate connection of utopian fiction with other types of sf (extraordinary voyage, technological anticipation, anti-utopia, and dystopia, etc.)" (38).[10] However, rather than address the specificities of the dystopia, he chooses to see it as satire one time, as anti-utopia another, and in yet another as a correlate form of sf.

In the interests of clarifying the form and function of dystopian fiction—and doing so in light of Suvin's concept of the novum—I want to turn to Jameson's comments in *The Seeds of Time*. In his discussion of the antinomies of utopia and anti-utopia, Jameson makes the familiar point that even the most anti-utopian expressions are "in reality Utopian ones," working as manifestations of a political unconscious acting on its "longing for transfigured collective relationships," despite the denial or suppression of the name utopia in doing so (1994: 54–5). However, as he reasserts the ubiquity of utopia, he cautions against "the facile deployment of the opposition between utopia and dystopia" (55). In an important move, he suggests that the pair be disjoined, and that the spectrum of utopia and anti-utopia be separated from the object of dystopian narrative. Indeed, it is the narrative quality of dystopia (with its attention to what "happens to a specific subject or character") that differentiates it from the non-narrative utopian text, which instead of plotting the trajectory of a subject "describes a mechanism or even a kind of machine" (56).[11] Thus, he posits dystopian stories of social disaster (as seen in near-future sf) as a counterpoint to utopian accounts of the imaginary construction of better social systems in the name of freedom, even as such accounts are exercises that name that which cannot be named.[12]

While Jameson's tendency not to consider the role of narrative in utopian texts is a matter for further consideration, his point about dystopias is provocative and useful. To be sure, it is immediately necessary to detach "dystopia" from "anti-utopia" and thus to agree that the proper philosophical opposition is that of utopia and anti-utopia. Indeed, Lyman Tower Sargent made this distinction in 1975 when, in "Utopia—The Problem of Definition," he reserved the term "anti-utopia" for "works, both fictional and expository, which are *against* utopia and utopian thought" (138, my emphasis). Working from the original pun, Sargent stipulates "ou-topia" as the generic name for the "no place" of alternative worlds of whatever valence, while "eu-topia" names the rendering of a "good place" and "dys-topia" becomes the term for accounts of a "bad place" (137–8). These distinctions support what Jameson later suggests, for within the socio-philosophical spectrum of utopia and anti-utopia, the textual forms of "eutopia" (now commonly "utopia"), "dystopia," and "anti-utopia" play out as related but different fictional sub-genres. Indeed, in "Science Fiction and Utopian Fiction," Suvin offered a less nuanced but apt version of this distinction in his comment that "sf can finally be written only between the utopian and the anti-utopian horizons" (1988e: 42).

Jameson's divorce of dystopia from utopia is, then, a crucial distinction for the generation of a dystopian poetics, for it separates the textual category from the philosophical relationship. However, instead of removing dystopias from the discussion, this separation opens the way for an examination of the dystopian text, which therefore is not to be read as an inversion of a utopia nor to be conflated with anti-utopia.[13] Rather, it is an object to be analyzed on its own terms. Returning to Suvin's framework, the dystopia emerges as another type of estranged writing, one whose fictional novum also negotiates the socio-political spectrum of utopia and anti-utopia.

Considering dystopia in terms of its own properties, Raffaella Baccolini therefore argues that the dystopian text works from the dialogic interaction of a narrative of the hegemonic order and a counter-narrative of resistance (see Baccolini 1995a). Given this structure, dystopian novels tend to begin right within the nightmarish society, with dystopian citizen immersed within it (see 1995b). Yet, despite the absence of the "utopian" process of dislocation, education, and return of a visitor, the "dystopia" generates its own didactic project in the critical encounter that ensues as the citizen, a rebel or misfit of some sort, confronts, or is confronted by, the society that is present on the very first page.

How that encounter develops, and especially how it ends, offers a starting point for investigating both the meaningfulness of the textual novum and the sociopolitical effect of given dystopian texts. Here, Suvin's criteria come back into play, but before returning to his critical matrix I want to recall Søren Baggesen's helpful analysis of dystopian tendencies. Working from Bloch's categories of "militant" and "resigned" pessimism, Baggesen distinguishes between dystopias that exhibit a "utopian pessimism," in which the social conditions are explained in terms of the material processes of history, and those that hold to a "dystopian pessimism," in which the destructive elements are based in ontological conditions that lead to "resignation" rather than "militance" (35–6). Although I prefer calling this second category "anti-utopian pessimism" and will go on to identify its typical form as "pseudo-dystopia," I agree that this analysis allows for a sharper understanding of how dystopian narrative plays out on the utopia and anti-utopia spectrum.

Taken in the light of Baccolini's and Baggesen's analyses of the structure of dystopian narrative, Suvin's criteria offer a useful entry to the critical re-assessment of dystopia. As outlined above, a text can be read in terms of the categories of magnitude, cognitive validation, and relevance. However, in addition to this tripartite matrix, Suvin offers a related approach, based on the difference between epic and myth, that is well suited for the specific operations of dystopian texts. In "The SF Novel as Epic Narration" (published in 1982 and in *Positions* in 1988), he identifies two complementary elements of the sf novel that serve as sites for formal and sociological evaluation: the novum as plot generator and as ending, as both are considered along the line from epic to myth (see 1988f).

Suvin begins his analysis of the novum as plot generator by noting that sf is "in proportion to its meaningfulness—under the hegemony of the epic" (1988f: 77), and he grounds this conclusion in the claim that sf texts share the common denominator, in one variant or another, of the "epic adventure or voyage-of-discovery plot," even if a narration is concerned with the discovery of an idea or the process of changed consciousness. The validity of such narratives, again, rests on the force of the novum: for a significant sf text must be based on "new configurations of reality in both inner and outer space, rather than an a priori dogma pretending to mythological status or a private impression" (77). The chronicle in the alternative setting pivots on the novum, as the epically new, not on "the mythic reconfirmation of cyclic processuality" (77). Consequently, a meaningful text will "represent spatial and historical configurations as partly but irreconcilably different from the norm dominant in the author's age" and will "refuse the mythological homeomorphy where all cycles and all agents are, centrally, such transformations of each other which can bring forth neither truly new values nor a hesitation as to the empirical success of existing values" (77–8).

Moving from plot to ending, Suvin argues that "epic events can be present as historically contingent and unforeseeable (and thus as a rule historically reversible)"; whereas, in a compromised, commodified, ending, the "events are cyclical and predetermined, foreseeable descents from the timeless into the temporal realm," hence mythological (80). In an epical text, "choice" shapes the agential relations and ending in "new and better" ways, ones not readily foreseen.[14] This, he asserts, is "the precondition for a narrative rendering of freedom" (80), whereas in a mythological text there is no clear sequence of narrative choices pulling forward as a novum. He concludes, "in sf novels, again more explicitly and testably than in most other genres, the ending is the moment of truth for the novum's cognitive validation and the narrative's believability—for the coherence, richness, and relevance of the text as significant sf" (81).[15]

In the dystopian mode, therefore, several critical moves can make possible an effective understanding of the operation of this textual form and its value. Considered as a separate subgenre of estranged fiction, the dystopia can be examined, on one hand, according to the manner in which its novum generates internal innovation and, on the other, according to its analytical and imaginative contestation with the author's historical situation.[16] However, given the above distinctions of utopia, anti-utopia, and dystopia, a further distinction can now be made between "dystopia" and "pseudo-dystopia": that is, between a text in the dystopian tradition and one that appears to be dystopian but fails (or chooses not) to challenge the ideological and epistemological limits of the actually existing society (see table). In this context, several questions arise. Where does a given text fall on the continuum of *militant utopian pessimism* versus *resigned anti-utopian pessimism*? How does it play out in the difference between epical and mythic form and substance? How is it informed by a novum or pseudo-novum? And, how does it situate itself in the contest between history and the "end -of-history," between utopia and anti-utopia?

		Philosophical Horizons	
		Utopia	*Anti-Utopia*
		Historical Novum	Universal Pseudo-novum
Estranged (sub)genres		u-topia/eu-topia (radical hope) dys-topia (militant pessimism)	anti-utopia (cynicism/despair) pseudo-dystopia (resigned pessimism)
		(epic, open)	(myth, closed)

The potential of a dystopian text thereby rests in the capacity of its novum to "reconcile the principle of hope and the principle of reality" by resisting mythological or ideological closure and opening toward a "more mature polyphony envisaging different possibilities for different agents and circumstances, and thus leaving formal closure cognitively open-ended, regardless of whether at the end of the novel the positive values be victorious or defeated" (1988f: 83).

IV

From Jack London's *The Iron Heel*, E. M. Forster's "The Machine Stops," and Yevgeny Zamyatin's *We* to Kim Stanley Robinson's *Gold Coast*, Octavia Butler's *The Parable of the Sower*, and Marge Piercy's *He, She, and It*, the web of dystopian writing offers specific cultural artifacts that negotiate the processes of history, perception, and social change.[17] While some dystopias explore the terrors and contradictions of fascist or bureaucratically deformed socialist states, others delve into the cruel chaos of capitalist systems. While some adopt an anti-utopian persuasion with no allowance for opposition, others stubbornly locate utopian enclaves of resistance or pockets of misfits at their margins. While some take the "classic" form of a conflict within an authoritarian society, others (often as sf set "twenty minutes into the future") provide "new maps of hell" that trace the complexities of a restructuring world system that, so far, offers few instances of appropriate resistance and utopian hope. Yet, each text leads to an aesthetic or epistemological encounter with its historical conjuncture: whether that encounter recasts the present in mythic traps of consolation or takes the reader radically beyond the order of things is a question whose answer begins with the textual novum as it plays out in history.

More specific studies of the dystopian mode were to follow, but for now I want to close this chapter with another "dystopian" text, another by Suvin.[18] This is not a critical essay or fiction, but a poem, "Growing Old Without Yugoslavia," partially published in 1994 in *Science-Fiction Studies*.[19] To frame my comments, I begin with a separate *utopian* fragment published some years earlier, in 1988: namely, Suvin's dedication in *Positions*: "To Ivan V. Lalic and the memory of Vojo Kuzmanovic—friends and sf swappers from the archaic torso of Zagreb in the 1950s, our socialist youth." Here is a utopian riff that comes from memories in which the personal and political, everyday life and revolutionary immersion, entwine in the concrete utopian moment of youth in Yugoslavia in its youth. This remembrance, however, is not a "recollection" or backward-looking exercise in nostalgia, but rather (and rightly, as the first words in a text devoted to history, cognition, imagination, and praxis) an act of "recognition" of the continuing power of past victories in the present, perhaps in the future.[20] It is a gesture against the cult of the New in a world-without-history, a terse challenge to the cooptations of commodified society. Unfortunately, since *Positions'* publication, this moment has passed more fundamentally than the dedication implied. The grinding motion of history, this time in neocapitalist triumph, has taken its awful toll. Nevertheless, the dedication is a figure of hope that stakes its claim on us, from out of history. As we read it, we are, momentarily, *in* history.

The dedication puts the tragedy and pain of the poem in sharper perspective, as if it needed it. Written in 1991 during the counter-revolutionary destruction of what once was Yugoslavia (the concrete utopia of the dedication), the poem verges on despair as it describes a world in which even "those who cannot die/ Also are dying." Indeed, on first reading, it struck me as a step into the hell of anti-utopia. As I reread it, however, the critical dystopian quality of the lines echoed through their insistent refusal to go gently. For in this poetic journey from hope, into terror, and beyond, a radical novum holds out against the darkness of reaction. This is the full poem:

Growing Old Without Yugoslavia

1.

By now i think with vague benevolence
Of events going on after me
Chocolate cake being tasted, palate-smacking,
Long-limbed women being ogled, white-skinned,
Chocolate-skinned,
Brown-skinned,
Ogling back,
Intricate theories being mantled & dismantled,
Other poetic delights & sweet sorrows.
Yet the Enlightened is right
Hunger torturing profit percentages 9–to–5 jobs
Not to mention intestines sickness aging
This dog-turd universe offends basic decency
I could do better as an all-powerful Creator
He must be an autistic child
Playing ricochet along the shore with meta-galaxies
Counting the bounces before they sink into the quark brew

A sight rather comic in that feeble way
If we weren't trapped inside
Ah what good is mental strife without Tito's
Fraternal Fudô-sword? Still, i shall not cease:
The soft mercilessness of reason hath me in thrall.

2.

Dein leben wird dir entrissen
Deine leistung wird dir gestrichen
Du stirbst für dich.
Badener Lehrstück
I would like to consent to my non-being
Usually called death
To make my peace i need a lot of good being
In the nature of Buck's anti-gravity belt
Around me or maybe a space-shuttle runway:
Well-kept, durable, solid
Making possible a glad & safe ascent
Into the giddy lightness of non-being.
Alas! the being around me is ill-kept
The keepers are corrupt & absolutely shameless
Their only integrity is the muddy massyness of hate
Spewing out black lava,
burning up gnarled olive-trees small kakadu
Yugoslavia disintegrates into dwarf malignancies
Gun-sighting each other with simulacra mantic
Slaughters romantic relics of saints
Byzantine & Holy Roman antics.
How can i consent to easeful non-being
When being for all i hold beloved
Becomes heavier & heavier? who unclutches
When assassins stick a bayonet into her entrails?
Ascensions drop bombs rip up lungs & eyes
Even if we find anti-gravity it will be for blowing up babies
Even if i die old in my bed, this system
Makes it impossible to die gladly.
With no Tito, bombers & warring angels
Recolonize the blissful anti-gravity skies.
Where nobody can consent to dying
The economics of life are all wrong.
Those who cannot die

Also are dying:
O Apollo, help us to change, to make a head
On the torso of our bank-ridden life!

Because of the "corrupt" and "shameless" keepers who have wrought the
destruction of individual lifetimes, of a society, of a social dream, "good being"
is banished. The actually existing locus of hope is disintegrating at the hands of
a system that "makes it impossible to die gladly." And, lest we Western readers
think it's only the "Eastern" bureaucracy to blame, we find by the closing lines
that the "system" has produced a world in which "The economics of life are all
wrong," in which we all face a "bank-ridden life." Under the gravitational force of
reaction, with its "dwarf malignancies," the desire for fullness of being is crushed.
The hope for a just and free world in which, as Bloch boldly argued, even death
would lose its sting, drowns in the lava flow of blood and hate.

Yet, faced with this brutal loss of the historically achieved materiality of a
socialist dream, a novum of hope persists. This can be traced, as Suvin's own
criteria suggest, in the poem's ending, but also in the creation of the poem
itself. Contrary to the sense of the Brecht quotation that recounts the terror
of being reduced to an isolated self, the narrator is a connected member of
a community, not a free-floating individual. This stubborn self journeys
internally from denunciation to annunciation, from the cold stream of critical
apprehension of the shameful order into the warm current of hope, and moves
toward an ending that culminates in an outrageous secular prayer to Apollo,
god of light and truth, protector against darkness, ultimate mediator between
humans and what lies beyond. The postsecular prayer, however, is not a cry for
salvation, or deliverance. Rather, as one would send to a skilled organizer, it is
an emergency message for help in mobilizing *change*. And, change begins with
work, with the re-creation of a head, that site of radical cognition, to enliven
the alienated torso of flesh and desire, and so to stand upright against the life-
denying system.

The novum, however, flickers not only in the ending but also in the
imagination that produces the poem. Even before the critical act of reading,
or organizing, the structure of feeling of anger, fear, and yearning moves the
poet, who will not surrender at the margins of dystopia, to write.[21] "Growing
Old Without Yugoslavia" thus resounds in militant, epical, utopian pessimism,
and stands as the "ultimate" moment in this meditation on the novum and
dystopia.

On the Vocation of Utopian Science Fiction

I

In Ken MacLeod's *Learning the World*, fourteen-year-old Atomic Discourse Gale begins her shipboard biolog with an account of her quest to learn the age of her world, which turns out to be an interstellar Ship in the midst of its multi-generational mission of discovery and colonization. Encouraging her to learn for herself, her care-mother sends her to the topmost sections of the "world" in which she has grown up, to the place where "the sunline enters the wall," where in fact the keel of the Ship and the base of the engine are located (MacLeod 2005: 2). Joined in the upper levels by Constantine, one of the Ship generation's leaders, she encounters the crew who live in the reduced gravity of the upper climes—those "strange people [...] long of limb and lithe of muscle and wild of hair"—and at the apex of her climb, she and Constantine locate the plaque that dates the Ship and names it: "Sunliner, But the Sky, My Lady! The Sky! Forged this day 6 February 10 358 AG" (6–7). At this point, Atomic goes through her first paradigm shift as her world becomes a ship and expands in its complexity and opportunity.

Thus begins MacLeod's science fiction tale with its familiar sf themes of exploration and first contact; of future history and inter-species conflict; and of learning, communication, and change. Most of all, it begins his account of characters who re-discover their own world in the process of exploring others. Atomic becomes an engaged learner and citizen on her Ship even as she takes in the new information about the planet revolving around the Destiny Star at which they finally arrive. With this knowledge comes a gestalt shift in her understanding of the universe and humanity's place in it. Viewing the planet for the first time, Atomic and her shipmates look at "a rocky terrestrial with a multicellular biosphere, the first in fourteen thousand years," essentially "another

Earth" (70). Not only is this discovery a step toward creating a new map of the universe, it is also a re-opening of species memory for the Shipboard humans; for this planet brings them a retrospective spatiotemporal view of world they never knew, the ruined world of Earth. Eventually, they encounter the planet's bat-like people who are the first intelligent life encountered in humanity's explorations. As a result, Atomic and her colleagues come to grips with the unforeseen, with the reality of a very different universe than the one they thought they knew. They must, as she says, "start learning the world all over again" (96).

Reciprocally, MacLeod describes the learning curve of the bat-like inhabitants of the planet Ground, especially through the viewpoint of two members of its University Faculty of Impractical Sciences, the astronomer Darvin and the physicist Orro, as they track the Ship's arrival in their solar system and then lead the way to contact between the two species. Especially for Darvin and Orro, the discovery of the Ship—with its implications for the nature of the universe and its challenges to the values and lives of their own people—becomes a "marvellous opportunity" for the production of new knowledge. For them, as they respond in this estranged version of our own cultural history, the frowned-upon speculations on aliens and space ships in their culture's popular science and "cheap-paper magazines" of "engineering tales" have turned into the experience of comprehending and dealing with their actual existence—in an echo of Rebecca Evans' argument that the cognitive estrangement capacity enabled in readers by science fictionality can be turned back on their own society so as to break through the presumptions of its ruling narrative (24; and see Evans 2018). In their subsequent actions, as they become involved in the hegemonic efforts to confront this new arrival, the scientists, along with all the people of Ground, make a historical leap as their society is reflected back to them through the perspective of the new arrivals. As they themselves are cognitively estranged, their world changes utterly: with slavery ending, war culture fading, and a new period of discovery and development looming.[1]

As is usually the case in this epistemological process, for each of the key characters the quantitative intake of information builds into a qualitative shift in consciousness that radically alters their standpoint and existence. The mission of Atomic and her colleagues is transformed, as is the perspective, social organization, and value system of the inhabitants of Ground. The outcome for both is a "break" that moves beyond agendas of exploitation and war and toward a new stage of cooperation between humans and this non-human sentient species. Of course, it is not just MacLeod's characters who confront the unforeseeable, who learn old worlds and new, and who change their perspective and behavior. For readers join in the same process of pleasure and pedagogy. More than many sf works, MacLeod's book enacts and teaches the sf protocol of worldbuilding, cognitive estrangement, consciousness-raising, and paradigm shifting. As Atomic's friend Grant tells her, "the way to learn the world is to look at the world" (2005: 138). But this is a disruptive process, as Orro well knows, for "by investigating the unknown," they have "diminished the known" and thus destroyed their present paradigm and produced the necessity for new perspectives and new ways of learning, and being (47).

II

Learning the World reaffirms the pedagogical potential of science fictionality, a potential that especially in its utopian mode enables authors and readers to revision their own world and to explore collective responses and possible solutions to the problems facing humanity and all of nature. Yet, as Fredric Jameson, in accord with Darko Suvin, consistently argues, the paradigmatic "method" of the literary utopian form must be understood as one that works not by direct representation but by figuration that can "defamiliarize and restructure" our experience of the "habituated," "intolerable," "occluded" present (Jameson 2005: 286–8). Herein, the "future" as such is "irrelevant or unthinkable," becoming instead the mechanism for "transforming our own present into the determinate past of something yet to come"; thus, at its core, utopian sf is a "vehicle" for a "meditation" on "our own absolute limits" (288–9).

In this chapter, however, I want to shift to another register of the utopian problematic, as I move from this core of negation to its positive penumbra. Certainly, the deepest theoretical aim of the negative hermeneutic is the disruption of the present by keeping utopia at the horizon. Especially in the face of the enclosure of neoliberal capitalism and its ideological repression of systemic alternatives, the mobilization of the negative in the utopian imaginary has been crucial in neutralizing the self-declared inevitability of the present world reality. And yet, when considering the reading effect and especially the pedagogical potential of utopian sf—and keeping to the spirit of Jameson's call that the "Marxist negative hermeneutic" should "be exercised *simultaneously* with a Marxist positive hermeneutic"—I think critical attention also needs to focus on the ways in which utopian writing not only negates the present but also generates the opportunity for a cognitive encounter with what might be and with what might be done to get there: for the present is not just made impossible by the invocation of utopia's horizon but also by the steps taken on the way (*unterwegs*) to it (1981: 296).

Indeed, it was sf's formal capacity for worldbuilding, with its cognitively estranged relationship to the present, that, at least in the Anglo-American tradition, stood available for the post–Second World War re-vitalization of the utopian imagination, as the literary utopia found another home in this genre of modernity and postmodernity. Whether one agrees with Suvin that utopian writing is the "socio-political subgenre" of sf (1988: 38) or with China Miéville's argument that it works within the mode of the fantastic, be it as sf *or* fantasy (2002b: 47–8), utopian expression has always historically morphed in the intertextual sweep of forms (developing in, among others, satire, travel writing, model constitutions, the romance, sf) and indeed elsewhere, especially as one looks beyond the Anglo-American lineage. And over the last few decades, especially from the 1990s, utopian writing has gone through further shifts, as in the critical dystopias, new iterations of the critical utopia, and fantasy with writers like Miéville and Phillip Pullman.[2]

And so, in this chapter, I want to open a line of thought about utopian sf and fantasy that addresses the power of utopia's strong thought. That is—given the formal disruption of the prevailing *Denkverbot* (as the editors of the *Lenin Reloaded* volume call the current prohibition on alternative thinking)—what can we then say about the positive hermeneutic that ensues? I will begin with two preliminary points.[3] The first is to note the inevitable importance of *content* in the literary utopia, wherein the textual details of alternative social values and political practices that are rendered invisible by the prevailing common sense are foregrounded with the intention of being taken seriously by readers, before, they deliquesce back into the very form by which they were given imaginative life. However much this content comes to us by way of estranged figuration, the subject matter has always mattered. From Thomas More and Margaret Cavendish to H. G. Wells and Charlotte Perkins Gilman to Ursula K. Le Guin and Kim Stanley Robinson and beyond, utopian writing has always refused the limits of its present time even as it draws on its possibilities in order to produce an alternative version/vision of reality that works as both an indictment of the present and a projection of forward movement (a projection whose power lies not in its ideologically bound representation of "real" political solutions but rather in its pedagogical provocation of new thinking and new action).

Following from this, my second point is to note the historically situated nature of Jameson's caveat: namely, that it especially speaks to the status of the utopian imagination *in late modernity*; and to this end, I want to recall his phrasing two paragraphs above his key point in "Progress Versus Utopia" as he writes of the "atrophy in our time of what Marcuse has called the *utopian imagination*" (1982: 153). In short, Jameson's most troubling observation is one that speaks most effectively *within* the context of what he has called the "windless closure of late capitalism" (1988: 21). While I'm not suggesting that we have seen a qualitative change in the present world system, I do want to say that it can be useful, in light of political movement around the globe, to look again at the pedagogical potential of utopian sf, to look at its capacity to meditate not just on the break but also on possible, even if still absent, "steps of renewed praxis" (Jameson 1994: 71).

Let me therefore pose two questions: what do we gain by not only working with the negative register of the utopian problematic but also with the positive? Consequently, what do we gain by taking another look at the *content* of utopian sf and fantasy? To be sure, Jameson himself is not closed to either question. Yet, he consistently keeps his distance from both. Of course, he is working out of Marx and Engels' caveats about utopia (as well as Ernst Bloch's later warnings about abstract utopia). As in his interview with Ian Buchanan, he often reiterates our incapacity to imagine a radically new future or to even to move toward transformative solutions from within the ideological limits of the situation in which we currently exist, and he keeps a good distance even from initially utopian content that settles into the ameliorations and co-optations of reformism (see Buchanan 2006). He is right to say that, from where we now stand, we have great difficulty "imagining the end of capitalism and its replacement by something else" (Jameson, quoted in Buchanan 2006: 131). And so, in the interview, Jameson concludes that his own approach to utopia has "generally has been a negative one," preferring to examine the "blockages on the future and on the utopian impulse" rather than proposing "positive new utopian visions," which he admits flourished "so brilliantly, from Fourier to Morris" (Buchanan 2006).[4]

However, even if it is not his preferred stance, Jameson recognizes the positive hermeneutic and its potential to enable readers to explore and make judgments about transformative models, values, and agency. He expresses its importance in his distinction between the moment of Jean Paul Sartre and that of Theodor Adorno: "If political practice is still possible, you have the Sartrean model and if there's a block or a stalemate, then in a way you have a very powerful countermodel in the German idea of keeping negative and critical thought alive" (quoted in Buchanan 2006: 122). As well, in taking a Marxist approach to social reality (in keeping with utopia's own totalizing method), he notes that, in this moment of globalization, we might be entering what Lefebvre calls a "new kind of spatial dialectic" that can occasion a "new conception of a Marxist politics" (quoted in Buchanan 2006: 128). He goes on to speak about the possible work of a Marxist myth criticism (one that accords with Bloch's reading of the utopian surplus in the cultural heritage) that could enable a "way of understanding what we've lost historically and as a charge of utopian energy on which we can draw," and he sees the utopian potential of the dialectical interventions on work practice and new technologies by the likes of Paul Virilio (quoted in Buchanan 2006: 130). And in *Archaeologies of the Future*, he has noted the disruption of the present system that would arise from such programmatic elements as the minimal utopian demand for universal employment and by the new possibilities for federalism, and almost everywhere he invokes the image of *collective action* as a utopian novum.[5] Nevertheless, for Jameson, the work of negation and the politics of form take strategic precedence.

However, in the interest of expanding the deployment of the utopian problematic and in further exploring the pedagogical function of the utopian genre, I want to ask: how readers in general and utopians in particular can usefully regard the effect of the provocative words, images, concepts expressed in its pages? How does the utopian imagination operate as a *method* that enables an analysis and judgment of the efficacy of concrete utopian scenarios to be found emerging *from*, as opposed to *beyond*, capitalism's own mechanisms and moving toward the "break"? How does utopian writing not only reflect upon but also *elicit* a transformative mode of agency? I will begin with a counterpoint to Jameson's invocation of Marx and modernism that calls up Bloch and Lenin and goes on to remember the epistemological value of popular science.

Let me take one step back from the negative base of Jameson's utopian paradigm and open a way toward a two-fold move of considering the political value of utopian content not only as negation or neutralization but as an estranged, positive anticipation of both movement and horizon. In doing this, I am not indulging a fascination with crank ideas or liberal reforms, nor locking on to a pre-determined revolutionary eschatology or to an unhistorical, abstract utopianism. I am, however, looking to the interpretive work of teasing out the didactic value of utopian writing that thinks about what Bloch calls the material tendencies and latencies of the current system and discovers immanent "traces" (*spuren*) of forward movement toward a more utopian horizon. And, I am further suggesting that we attend to Lenin's emphasis on revolutionary process as we adduce what Jameson describes as the "collective awareness of the way in which revolution is being played out symbolically and actually in each of its existential episodes," along with the correlative work of "underscoring the difference between systemic and piecemeal goals" (Jameson 2007b: 68, 70).

Keeping Bloch's anticipatory materialism and Lenin's revolutionary process in mind, I suggest that in our time there are new energies provoking utopia's radical vision, that the knots of sheer atrophy have been slightly loosened by emergent conditions in this dangerously destructive moment—as seen, for example, in the revived socialist movement; the radical environmental movement; the movements for diversity and against racism, sexism, homophobia, transphobia, and all forms of xenophobic hatred and violence; the alternative spaces being carved out by interventions such as the Mondragon Cooperative, the Zapatista Army of National Liberation, or other local creations of "real utopian" practices; and the rising movement of the multitude (including migrants, refugees, asylum seekers, and indeed all precarious workers and citizens).[6] And, in the work of some writers at least, I think we can discover a more nuanced utopian expression that has accordingly developed in these times of world crises and titrating politics. And so, with an eye toward breaking ideological chains and changing consciousness, it can be useful to look at what is going on in the work of writers such as Kim Stanley Robinson and China Miéville.

In reflecting on the use value of such content (in the spirit of Bloch's technique of reading utopian traces rather than heeding the siren call of reductive surface readings), I think readers might also re-consider its place not only in the lineage of the literary utopia but also in the origins of a deeply popular stream of sf: namely, the Gernsbachian "scientifiction" stories (as in Darvin's and Orro's "engineering tales") that were not simply the products of a new mass culture broadly considered but specifically of popular science magazines with their hope-infused tradition of amateur investigation and problem-solving.[7] Certainly, Jameson acknowledges sf's "capacity to provide something like an experimental variation on our own empirical universe"; but his argument tends to focus on the *formal* significance of the shift of the critical function from high art to mass art such as sf (1975: 223). He furthers his privileging of the *form* of sf in "Progress versus Utopia" when he writes of sf's "own dynamic, which is not that of high culture" even as he goes on to explore its "complementary and dialectical relationship to high culture or modernism" (1982: 283).[8] Important as this argument is, it elides the added value that comes from sf's cognitive roots in popular science. For the realm of popular science is a valuable and effective tradition of learning the world, of inventing and speculating on alternatives that might speak to its problems; and herein, we can look not only to the work of amateur scientific societies, workers' schools, and reading groups but also to that of popular campaigns such as those undertaken by the women of the Love Canal housing estate, who sought to protect their families from the aftermath of toxic dumping, and by other citizen groups (such as those challenging the economic and environmental racism of toxic waste dumps) who have rejected official scientific consensus with their alternative research and activism. To be sure, activist citizens always need to address the ideological function of the more reformist elements of these struggles as they can provide what Jameson terms an "elaborate shock-absorbing mechanism" that accustoms their practitioners and readers to capitalism's rapid innovation and adaptation, and we need not privilege one-dimensional tinkering or obsession even as the more radical movements break through into robust opposition (1982: 151). More generally, however, I do think it is possible to benefit from a Blochian recognition of the critical, utopian, heritage of amateur scientific discourse of learning, invention, and critique out of which this line of sf grew and from which it draws. It is, therefore, the estranged yet hopeful *problem-solving* quality found in the thought experiments of popular science that I want to bring back to the table alongside the effectivity of sf's form, and I suggest that this addition can provide a larger scope for understanding and working with utopian sf that pushes at the edges of what is known and leads outward to what is unforeseeable, or perhaps just looming into sight.

I am, therefore, opening a broader critical terrain that energizes the disruptive *and* constructive pedagogy of utopian sf. For if one lingers at the negative and focuses *only* on the break, one could well be trapped in some contemporary version of Zeno's paradox and thereby neglect expressions that register the tremors of emergent political movement. Caught in the headlights of the negative, might the opportunity for open spaces of political exploration and debate be missed? Is it not necessary to pay attention, as Miéville puts it, to what is "embedded in everyday life" in the spacetime between now and the horizon (2002b: 45).

In turning to content, however, I am refusing the temptation of what Jameson calls a "demotic Marxism or mass-cultural communism" or what Meagan Morris and others have seen as a banal romanticism that seizes on what are taken to be accounts of "real" political moves (Jameson 2007a: xviii).[9] In recognizing the pedagogical power of science fictional content to move through the ideological limits of its own representational imagery as it delivers an estranged (re)consideration of what might be done, I am still working within the realm of ideology and formal production. I want to hold on to the productive relationship of form and content, but in doing so to shift perspective in order to stress that utopian content as well as form can work against the grain of economic (and aesthetic) reification, ideological absorption, and the temptation of reformism. Here, I am looking at the Utopia-Ideology imbrication with less of an eye on the way in which dominant ideology taps and saps the power of the utopian imagination and more on the way in which the utopian surplus produces an oppositional pedagogy that can excavate materially resonant alternatives that are open to radical policies and activism, whatever their useful half-life may be in the dynamics of ongoing history.

I suggest that this identification of a prophetic or pedagogical vocation reasserts utopia as a form of what I have termed *strong thought* that moves beyond the melancholy and exhaustion of postmodern resignation and engages and enables processes of bold utopian opposition. Thus, utopia's strong thought can be mobilized against all accommodation with the present system: against the dominant ideologies that deny, fear, and absorb utopia and against limited reforms or ameliorations that end up preserving not radically altering the state of things. I would also add that it is also time not simply to privilege the negative vocation of utopia: that is, the Adorno moment.

While I am not proposing a competing paradigm to Jameson's, I do want to acknowledge a line, or more of a matrix, of thought that tends to put more stress on the positive alternatives and trajectories made available to readers by utopian writing. Here, I am perhaps closer to a contemporary Italian approach to the political imagination that works in a zone between Sartre and Adorno: as encapsulated in Paolo Virno's statement that in examining the present conjuncture we need to understand "the *ambivalence*" of its "modes of being and feeling to discern in them a 'degree zero' or neutral kernel from which may arise both cheerful resignation, inexhaustible renunciation, and social assimilation on the one hand and new demands for the radical transformation of the status quo on the other" (1996: 13). Or as Michael Hardt puts it: the theoretical work to be done is not only the analysis of forms of domination and exploitation, but also the identification, affirmation, and furtherance of the "existing instances of social power that allude to a new alternative society, a coming community," for, as he continues, the "potential revolution is always already *immanent* in the contemporary social field" (1996: 7).

Within a positive utopian hermeneutic, the focus on content usually revolves around two concerns: the systemic alternative and the political agency required to achieve it. While the formal/conceptual work of neutralizing the present must be done, the pedagogical (and organizing) work of utopia must also attend to this forward-bearing content. For many readers, it is the estranged figuration of the iconic alternative worlds and the motivations of the discrete narrative action in a utopian text that deliver the cognitive mapping, structures of feeling, and thought experiments that can challenge them with, admittedly temporary but nevertheless substantive, explorations of ways through and beyond the present world system. While the representations of such possibilities will always be trapped within the limits of the present (dependent as they are on the ideological matrix of the time in which they are imagined), their utopian surplus (with its models or scenarios) can nevertheless deliver a pedagogical effect that stimulates debate, subverts capitulation, and provokes steps toward a transformative praxis.

Certainly, Suvin has long taken this approach to the dual registers of the utopian method, albeit with greater focus on the production and potential of utopian knowledge. While his work on cognitive estrangement is perhaps best known, his contribution to the 1976 special issue of *the minnesota review* on "Marxism and Utopia" speaks to his appreciation of the historical materialist quality of utopian cognition. In this re-reading of Marx and Engels' "Socialism: Utopian and Scientific," Suvin contextualizes the authors' position and traces the historical shifts that have rendered their initial science-utopia binary "misleading and even counter-productive" in the present moment (1976: 59). In his concluding section, he argues for a contemporary synthesis "of the bold, vertical *utopian will to revolution* and the scientific, horizontal *knowledge of preconditions for revolution*" (67). To this, as discussed in the previous chapter, I will add his familiar stress on the ability of sf to explore its alternative realities as a "novum," an "'as if,' an imaginative experiment, a methodological organ for the New in the history of human relationships toward society and nature, a cognitive model" (Suvin 1988e: 42). And finally, in an essay in which he re-appraises Ursula Le Guin's *The Dispossessed*, he restates his point that "fictional narrative (as any thinking) can be understood as based on *thought experiments and models*" that subvert received norms and produce what he calls "*a cognitive increment* (that can range … from zero through very partial to very large)" (Suvin 2010: 509–10). He argues that this "better understanding permits what Brecht called intervenient, effective or engaged thinking … It allows the reader to pleasurably verify old and dream up new, alternative relationships: to *re-articulate* (in both senses of the word) human relationships to the world of people and things" (510).

More than Suvin, Lyman Tower Sargent directly stresses the necessity for attention to utopian subject matter in effecting a non-determinist process of utopian change. In "The Three Faces of Utopianism Revisited," he argues that utopia's "social dreaming" motivates deep transformation, and—in a maneuver that implicitly collapses the idealist-materialist binary—he cites Fredrick Polak's point that human society and culture are "magnetically pulled towards a future fulfilment of their own preceding and prevailing, idealistic images of the future, as well as … pushed from behind by their own realistic past" (quoted in Sargent 1994: 25). In "Choosing Utopia: Utopianism as an Essential Element in Political Thought and Action," he argues passionately for the necessity of utopianism in human history. In this essay, he is clear in his claim that "utopias generally contend that radical change is needed, not just piecemeal reform" (Sargent 2007: 305). Indeed, he adds that reform itself can only be "useful if we know where we want to go, as steps toward a larger transformation that will radically improve the human condition"; thus, he asserts that we "must choose Utopia … must choose the belief that the world can be radically improved … must dream socially; and … must allow our social dreams to affect our lives" (306).

Also aware of utopia's positive figuration, Raymond Williams, in his "Utopia and Science Fiction" essay, focuses as well on the utopian mandate for choice, and attends especially to the steps to be taken from the now to the Not Yet. Emphasizing utopias that privilege "willed transformation," he examines the way in which utopian thought has been refunctioned in sf as a "crucial vector of desire" (1978: 204, 206); and in his commentary on Miguel Abensour's periodization of the shift in utopian thought from the systemic to the heuristic, he argues that utopia's "education of desire" can encourage a radical response to "constrained reformism" as it offers a "strength of conviction that the world can really be different" (208). Not inclined to the idealism of fully fledged plans for the future, he privileges William Morris's emphasis on the "transition to utopia, which is not discovered, come across, or projected … but fought for," and he reads Le Guin's *The Dispossessed*—especially in its account of Shevek's experience—as marking a shift beyond Thompson as it explores the more active process of the "*learning*" of desire and renews the utopian impulse in doing so (209, 213).

This emphasis on the formation of a consciousness of political agency is also found in Peter Fitting's effort to deal with the "double-bind" of trying to work between Jameson's argument about the "true vocation" of utopia and his own reluctance to give up on the utopian text's ability to "portray an alternative" that can motivate a collective imagination and behavior (1998: 14). In his contribution to a *Utopian Studies* special issue on Jameson, Fitting recalls the long tradition of utopian texts written by authors who intended their radical content to be taken seriously and adopted as actual alternatives within political or social movements, and he recaptures the history of activists who first came to utopian literature because of the politically instructive, challenging, and empowering content they encountered on its pages. He grants that Jameson's focus on the text's critical function "helps us to understand the 'conditions of possibility' of a specific utopian work, and the buried contradictions it is attempting to resolve," but he also argues that "it does not satisfactorily acknowledge the positive aspects which brought us to utopias in the first place. For many of us became interested in literary utopias precisely insofar as they were visions of alternatives" (1998). In attempting to resolve his dilemma, he argues not so much against Jameson but through him, in a dialectical twist that retains Jameson's sense of figuration but incorporates the pedagogical impact of utopian content. In catalyzing radical change, he argues, the work of the utopian text lies not only in reminding us of the "insufficiency of our own lives" or in negating ideological contradictions but also in providing an exploration of "the look and feel and shape and experiences of what an alternative might and could actually be, a thought experiment … which gave us a sense of how our lives could be different and better, not only in our immediate material conditions, but in the sense of an entire world or social system" (1998: 14–15).

In a much more thorough fashion, Ruth Levitas has elaborated her account of the methodology of a positive, transformative utopianism. She argues that utopia's method can be understood as the "imaginary reconstitution of society" (or IROS). As with the others, she emphasizes the process wherein a reader encounters the material of the utopian text and responds actively to it. Building on Bloch's concept of "educated hope" and Abensour's utopian heuristic, she values the activist nature of this utopian method and describes IROS as "a device firstly to defamiliarize the familiar, and secondly to create a space in which the reader is brought to experience an alternative and called to judgement on it" (Levitas 2007: 56).

Levitas's articulation of IROS grows out of her interventions in two contexts: the discipline of sociology and the transdisciplinary project of utopian studies. In her reappraisal of sociology, she advocates a more engaged role for the scholarly field by directly linking its method to IROS. She notes that this form of modeling is central to both sociological and utopian interpretation, with the difference traditionally being that sociology has foregrounded "the elements that utopia backgrounds" (i.e., the descriptive, explanatory analysis of how existing societies work as systems) and backgrounded "to the point of repression—the elements that utopia foregrounds" (i.e., the critical judgment of that present system from the standpoint of the Not Yet and the anticipatory, at times even prescriptive, proposal for the elaboration of a radically other future) (Levitas 2007: 60).

In restoring the speculative quality of a *utopian* reconstitution of society to the purview of sociology, she draws on H. G. Wells's assertion in his 1914 essay, "The So-called Science of Sociology," that the "creation of Utopias—and their exhaustive criticism—is the proper and distinctive method of sociology" and argues that the discipline could become more productively, and politically, attuned to studies of the impact of "a society imagined otherwise, rather than merely society imagined" (quoted in Levitas 2007: 60).

While her discussion of utopianism and sociology stresses the importance of a holistic, and anticipatory, social analysis and evaluation, Levitas's response to work in utopian studies interrogates the relationship between that systemic interpretation and the political education and action required for radical change. Updating her argument in *The Concept of Utopia*, she acknowledges the tendency in utopian studies since the 1970s to privilege a "greater openness" in the delineation of the nature of utopian expression and in the shift in focus from content to process. She specifically cites Jameson's point that what is of utmost importance for utopianism is "not *what* we imagine, but *that* we imagine" (Levitas 2007: 57). While agreeing with the need for this theoretical move, she then goes on to express her deep concerns:

> All this openness is a bit much for me. We could do with a bit of closure. Abensour's commentary on [the heuristic value of] Morris suggests that it does not matter whether you agree or disagree with the institutional arrangements. What matters is that the utopian experiment disrupts the taken-for-granted nature of the present and proffers an alternative set of values. (Levitas 2007)

What concerns Levitas is the risk of "political evasion" that can occur in a concentration on an abstract process without a body of concrete ideas and options that are available to be considered, debated, and deployed. Thus, she argues that the education of desire that is so empowering for an oppositional political consciousness requires the subject matter of utopia's IROS, precisely insofar as "it deals with the concrete instantiation of values, enabling a level of real exploration and judgment," for "without a certain element of closure, specificity, commitment, and literalism about what would actually be entailed in practice, serious criticism is impossible" (Levitas 2007). Levitas supports her position by referring to Bloch's recognition that *existing* tendencies and latencies must be imaginatively worked with to reach toward any future-bearing alternative: as she puts it, utopian longing "cannot be articulated other than through imagining the means of its fulfillment. You cannot identify what it is that is lacking without projecting what would meet that lack, without describing what is missing" (2007: 57).

This method of IROS therefore offers two diagnostic modes for critique and change (one is analytical, the other is constructive), and it is one that resonates with the denunciation/annunciation hermeneutics of liberation theology that I outlined above. As *archaeology*, the analytical mode of IROS "involves excavating and uncovering the *implicit* utopia or utopias buried" in the political programs, social contexts, or texts in question (Levitas 2007: 57). Closer to Bloch's, and Jameson's, hermeneutic project of reading elements of the world cultural heritage so as to decipher their utopian traces of hope, the archaeological diagnostic lends itself to critical analysis of utopian implications in contemporary or historical contexts. As such, it speaks to the method of critical hermeneutics and cultural studies, as well as to Levitas's sense of a refunctioned discipline of sociology. The second, constructive, approach considers IROS as *architecture*, insofar as it asks *explicitly* what a utopian alternative to the inadequate, incomplete present would "look like, and how it could be attained" (Levitas 2007: 57). This approach can be found in the work of creating or analyzing overt utopian social policy, lived experience, or literary expression; and indeed, Morris's *News from Nowhere* stands as Levitas's textual exemplar for such creative work. As a methodological approach for the critical study of utopian writing, it constitutes a recognition of and engagement with the utopian method on two registers: at the level of the utopian project presented in the given text, and at the level of the reader's/critic's interpretive work of linking that utopian expression to what the text offers by way of an understanding of the steps available for reaching toward the utopian alternative. As ever for Levitas, the work of IROS in either of its diagnostic modes enables us to explore two questions that inform the underlying *ontological* quality of her method: "How, then, should we live?" and "How can that be?" (2007: 57).

I will end this sequence with two other, brief, references. The first is Lucy Sargisson's assertion that utopia "lies at the heart of politics" (2007: 42). In her research as a political theorist and ethnographer (whose objects of study have ranged from utopian theory, to literary utopias, feminist and green political thought, intentional communities, and a range of phenomena of everyday life), she reaffirms the way that utopian expression, be it textual or lived, offers "a route into the debates of [its] time ... [as it addresses] political themes critically and creatively, telling us what is wrong with the now and how it might be improved" (32); as with the others, she argues that the double move invited by utopia "can help us to think about the world" as it breaks "old patterns and paradigms" and showcases "new ways of being," and thus inspires and catalyzes the very agency required for change (39).[10] The second is Phillip E. Wegner's emphasis on the activist, pedagogical function of utopian content and form as he reminds us that utopia unleashes a process that "re-educates the desires of its audience, enabling them to grow the 'new organs' necessary also to 'live' and later 'perceive' a newly emerging social and cultural reality" (1998: 68).

III

What this adds up to for me is an appreciation for a critical apparatus for utopian expression that does not just focus on the "problem of content" but also on the *opportunity* of content (Jameson 2007a: xix). While the "gap" between the ideological limits of the present moment and the articulation of the not-yet-possible remains, those working models of concrete spaces and steps on the way to utopia still require acknowledgment and consideration. I'm suggesting therefore that critical work on the reading effect of utopian writing needs to ask readers to look at how a utopian literary text *thinks*, and *teaches*, with its form *and* its content, how it develops the capacity to think and act Otherwise, how it evokes the warm stream of hope as well as the cold stream of critique.

Turning laterally to political thought, we see one line of this tendency exhibited in recent studies revisiting Karl Mannheim—such as those by Sargent or Vincent Geoghegan—and we see another in the writing of political theorists such as Susan McManus who confronts normative liberal theory and its legitimation of pragmatic reformism by mobilizing a "deconstructive and utopian political imagination."[11] Closer to practical politics, in the work of David Harvey and Roberto Unger, one can find an activist utopian stream that challenges what Unger calls the "dictatorship of no alternatives" and engages with possibilities in *existing* formations of the city and the nation-state (Unger 2005: 1). For his part, Harvey proposes a "dialectical utopianism" that acknowledges the need for a non-authoritarian utopian process; but, like Levitas, he goes on to argue that any useful utopian project has "to crystallize into a spatially-ordered and institutionalized material world somewhere and somehow" (Harvey 2000: 185). And Unger's small volume from 2005, *What Should the Left Propose?*, stands as a manifesto for his proposals for intervention and change *within* the neoliberal moment. Harvey notes how the Brazilian theorist seeks radical alternatives to neoliberalism that can "emerge out of critical and practical engagements with the institutions, personal behaviors, and practices that now exist" (Unger 2005: 186). While Harvey and Unger propose immediate programs and steps to be taken within the nation-state that move toward a transformation that can occur without a *singular* revolutionary rupture or Event (as Alain Badiou would term it), Michael Hardt and Antonio Negri follow a more radical line within this new utopian tendency. Less focused on next steps and more on the horizon—and thus freer of the dangers of compromise, while also more prone to the dangers of abstraction—their developing argument in *Empire, Multitude, and Commonwealth* nevertheless resonated with and challenged the politics of the World Social Forum and other alter-globalization formations. Over the course of their trilogy, Hardt and Negri argue for a global, post-nation state, politics wherein the "extraordinary accumulations of grievances and reform proposals" will at some point reach a punctal moment and be "transformed by a strong event, a radical insurrectional demand" (2004: 358). In analyzing global capitalism with its achievement of the "full spectrum dominance" of biopolitical power, they not only identify the enclosure of the present system but also the engine of opposition to it in the new commons that can emerge from it, and they see in the coming-to-consciousness and resistance of the global "multitude" an agent of history that can break toward the "living future" of a new society (2004: 53, 358). Clearly, this agential tendency is far from a unified project. Deep differences and debates abound, and we see a plurality of utopian projects at work. Overall, however, the new utopianism breaks from present-bound institutional and ideological limitations and prohibitions, refuses the reduction to reformism, and nominates and explores new forward steps.

And so, to reprise my opening, I argue that it is this very invitation to discuss and debate alternative values and actions that lies at the heart of the pedagogical function of utopia's strong thought. In this regard, the estranged reading experience of utopian narrative has an affinity with other creative or critical projects that carry a utopian charge: as seen, variously, in the socialist-feminist pedagogy called for by Shelia Rowbotham, with its prefigurative possibilities that "consolidate existing practice and release the imagination to what could be"; in the "clarifying models" that Nathaniel Coleman sees at work in utopian architecture; in the "scenario building" technique employed by environmental biologists who work with grassroots communities by way of storytelling to assess their own ecology and what can be done to save it; or in the *conscientización* process practiced in base Christian communities (see Rowbotham 1979: 147; Coleman 2005: 24; Moylan 2004). And, while resisting a romanticization of fandom, and recognizing the more random individuality of sf and fantasy reception, I suggest that readers of these genres can engage in a pedagogy of change as they encounter the sf process of worldbuilding, with its call to "start learning the world all over again." To be sure, prevailing common sense usually regards this reading experience as escapist entertainment, and yet that readerly escape from the "reality" of the mundane present has a transformative potential as and when it exceeds the limits of the genre as commodity or ideological shock-absorber.

IV

Finally, let me turn to the exemplary work of Robinson and Miéville. While the two writers couldn't be more different in their creative output (with one working in a utopian sf mode and living in the United States and the other writing what Jameson has called "materialist fantasy" in Britain), both explore spaces for transformative change that can emerge between the present global order and the onset of a new society (Jameson 2002: 280). Working beyond the prevailing dystopian imaginary, both have adapted utopian sf in a way that concretizes it even more than the critical utopias, as they embed their utopian scenarios, with distinct creative strategies, so that their explorations grow out of the material conditions and contradictions of their alternative worlds and are not delivered as abstract agendas or answers. Both create the formal machinery that renders utopia impossible in the present world system even as they develop thought experiments that consider possible steps to be taken within that very conjuncture toward a utopian novum. While Robinson marshals a systemic perspective that looks to models of transformation developing in a mode of dual power operating within existing state structures as well as autonomous formations and Miéville works from a focus on embedded political process that emphasizes grassroots initiatives, movements, and parties working against state or global systems *before* the moment of a revolutionary event, each in his own way taps into immanent possibilities and generates imaginative raw material that resonates with current oppositional tendencies while it also reaches toward the utopian horizon.[12]

Of the two, Robinson has consistently written in a recognizably utopian mode. Even as he is always finding new approaches within the variety of sf sub-genres and developing a more nuanced sense of the utopian imagination as he does so, in each new work he negotiates a path between totalizing transformations and pragmatic maneuvers: or, in sf terms, between analogic portrayals of a utopian society and extrapolative accounts of responses to ecological, economic, and political issues that require attention now in order to make any significant move toward the Not Yet. To use Kathleen Spencer's phrase, the "irrealistic reality" of his narratives invites readers to engage directly with his subject matter and so to take seriously his anticipatory narratives both for their immediate interventions and for the horizon to which they point (1983: 38).

Robinson's utopias have ranged from the local to the planetary to the cosmic, and in the realm of alternative history, and they have consistently worked within an ecological problematic. In *Pacific Edge* (1990), he wrote a case study of an achieved utopia in one town that details its social system and the everyday life of its citizens as it especially focused on the debate between growth and a steady-state system. In *The Mars Trilogy* (1992–1996), he shifted to a broader canvas as he tracked the long history of a Martian colony, delineating the multiple utopias and political stages that developed on that world. Across these volumes, he generated a version of Levitas's architectural reconstitution of society that comparatively tests the aims and consequences of various political paths as it follows three revolutionary periods in its future history. In closely examining the incremental politics of change, he again addresses the ecological question of a sustainable relationship between human society and the rest of nature, doing so in a reflection on the constructedness of both as he recounts the debate over terraforming the planet, even as he also models, with traditional utopian detail, a variety of political-economic systems (socialist, anarchist, green, liberal corporate) as well as autonomous social arrangements based in the needs and desires of situated groups. In his alternative history, *The Years of Rice and Salt* (2002), he explores a variety of utopian systems and practices as they develop on a hypothetical Earth wherein Western modernity did not happen. Back in this timeline, present and future, he has moved to the very near future on this planet in *Antarctica* (1997a) and the *Science in the Capital Trilogy* (2004–2007), out again to the Solar System and beyond in *2312* (2012) and *Aurora* (2015), and back to Earth (and the Moon) in *New York 2140* (2017) and *Red Moon* (2018). Thus he develops an overarching meta-narrative that embodies his critique of the current sociopolitical and ecological deprivation and devastation produced by the present order of things even as he explores the utopian impulse and programs of pre-and post-revolutionary agency and society.

Throughout this ongoing body of work, Robinson reaffirms the negative charge of utopia even as he generates positive scenarios of steps beyond the present. As seen in the swing from the near future *Pacific Edge* to the epical *Mars* books to the alternative history of *The Years of Rice and Salt*, his invention takes many forms. Of course, he works with the narrative structure of sf and the literary utopia, but he also deploys other fictive devices that provide more overtly didactic opportunities to enrich his provocative challenge to the status quo. Certainly, his exercise in alternative historiography is an example, as is his work with the literary forms of the writer's journal and poetry (as in *Pacific Edge*, *The Mars Trilogy*, and *Antarctica*). He also extensively works with the discourses of parliamentary debate and public policy (as in his accounts of the council meetings in *Pacific Edge* on the question of land preservation and of the debates in the *Mars* books on the question of terraforming), and he takes up the utopian form of the imagined constitution in *The Mars Trilogy* and the political treaty in *Antarctica*. For example, in *Green Mars*, he recounts the meetings and debates that produced the Dorsa Brevia Declaration and established the framework for an independent Mars; and in the miscellany sequel to the *Trilogy*, *The Martians*, he continues this non-narrative modelling with the text of the Mars Constitution (1999: 225–41). In the same mode, in *Antarctica*, he offers the summary protocol of the Antarctic Treaty wherein the principle of a sustainable permaculture is upheld, with the additional requirement that "special attention should be given to cooperative, nonexploitative economic models" (1997a: 491). In an echo of Hardt and Negri, the continent is declared to be a "land without ownership, [a] *terra communis* ... not property but commons"; and, lest we think Robinson is proffering a utopia in one continent, item eight of the protocol concludes that "what is true in Antarctica is true everywhere else" (489) as the principles governing the utopian zone of the "science continent" are identified as a clarifying model for our own planetary society (491). I will discuss Robinson's texts more fully in the next chapter, after I have set up my analysis of his ecological framework. For now, I'll simply state that he generally presents readers with the terms and conditions of a longer game, in which the slow assault on the environment and society continues even as the struggles of humanity as a partner in nature continue to resist that end by aiming for a better society and a healthier planet.[13]

Unlike the reception of Robinson's work, Miéville has not always been seen to be working in a utopian mode. For one thing, he generally writes fantasy that pulls the utopian impulse through its narrative operations, and this has proven to be a distraction for some. Importantly for such readers, in the *Historical Materialism* "Symposium on Marxism and Fantasy," Miéville breaks from the familiar dismissal of fantasy as an art of mystification—most directly by questioning Suvin's version of that argument, albeit one he subsequently revised (see Miéville 2002b).[14] He opts instead for placing *both* sf and fantasy within the category of the "fantastic (the impossible-but-true)," and he connects the reading effect of the fantastic mode to Marx's argument that human productive activity is "predicated on a consciousness of the not-real" (2002b: 43–4). Thus, both the "not-yet-possible" of sf and the "never-possible" of fantasy can create mental spaces for comprehending the "impossible" as it is denied by the dominant system. In the spirit of Bloch, he argues that both privilege the not-real and disrupt the provincial present in ways that allow "one to think differently about the real, its potentialities and actualities" (45–6). Only then does he locate the utopian imagination as a development *within* the work of the fantastic, therein regarding it as an "an articulation of the fantastic marshalled to socially polemical, potentially transformative ends" (47–8).

While some might see this as a dismissal or diminution of the utopian project, I think Miéville's aim is more a matter of negating the *abstract* utopianism refused by Marx, Engels, Bloch, and Jameson. In his negation of that negation, he locates the utopian polemic in a more productive position *within* the reading protocol of the fantastic. As a *second* step in the subversion generated by the cognitive work of worldbuilding, the specifically *utopian* possibility becomes a political development within the world as it is concretely imagined (46). In this formulation, he opts for a materialist utopian expression rather than the castles in the sky that can be such dangerous distractions from the actually existing, utopian, project of revolution.

With this understanding of the relationship between the fantastic and the utopian, and of the strong *pedagogical* potential of that relationship, it is not surprising that Miéville's worlds are not recognizably utopian. Instead, to draw on a specific set of texts, the society in his Bas Lag Trilogy—*Perdido Street Station* (2000), *The Scar* (2002a), and *The Iron Council* (2004)—is exploitive and violent, even as it is diverse and dynamic. A utopian reading of the trilogy therefore requires an "archaeological" approach that follows the trajectories of activism emerging from the realities of the world as they are figured in his two spatial creations: the city-state of New Crobuzon and outlying countryside in *Perdido Street Station* and the floating-city of Armada in *The Scar*. Given Miéville's strategy of embedding, it is only after inhabiting the societies of the first two volumes that the reader properly arrives at the "architectural" revolutionary narrative in *The Iron Council*. When the Event does occur (in an echo of the "When It Changed" section of William Morris's *News from Nowhere* and the arrival of Lenin's train at the Finland Station), it develops on two fronts: one rising out of the labor struggle on the trans-continental railroad and one out of the uprising of the immiserated and angry citizens of New Crobuzon as they suffer under endless war and unremitting oppression. Both trajectories are brought to the reader by the storylines of individual protagonists (both gay men, one a young worker, one a shop owner) who are representative militants in each struggle.

On the railroad, the free workers, enslaved Remade, and prostitutes who follow in the train camp walk out in three independent strikes; but in the face of their common oppression by the managers and their police, and inspired by the agitation of the revolutionary newspaper, *Runagate Rampant*, they move beyond mistrust and antipathy and become a new collective agent of history. Resonant with the arguments of Hardt and Negri, this multi-species *multitude*—as workers (slave and free), camp followers, refugees, and bandits— forges a new "commonality" from their biopower and seizes the means of production, the Train. Out of this new historic bloc, the Iron Council is formed. Within its leadership, Ann-Hari and Uzman constitute complementary wings of the movement: with Ann-Hari, the charismatic leader of the prostitute strike, who values the novum of the liberated Train and speaks of moving forward into an unforeseeable future in direct utopian terms; and Uzman, the Remade worker and political organizer, who looks to an eventual re-linking with the movement back in New Crobuzon in more politically pragmatic terms. Initially, Ann-Hari's position prevails, and the people of the Train move off the known map to build a utopian enclave.

While the Train-Commune and its Iron Council settle into its "hinterland of democracy" for two decades, the citizens of New Crobuzon bear up under exploitation, repression, and war (Miéville 2004: 375–7). Eventually, the "unorganised complaints," strikes, and contestations with the militia reach a critical mass (80); and—again urged to a "unity in action" by *Runagate Rampant* (86)—the guilds, neighborhoods, war veterans, students, artists, proscribed dissidents, and political organizations rise up after yet another "Special Offensive" by the militia (336). Riots and strikes increase, and sections of the city are occupied. Civil war ensues, only to be interrupted by negotiations with the government. When the Collective's demands are rejected, the run-up to a final battle begins. At this point, the Collective sends word to the now-legendary Iron Council, imploring them to arrive at Perdido Street Station and spark the next stage of the revolution.

The Iron Council agrees in solidarity and sets out to join the Collective in a grand alliance (in the spirit of Bloch's concept of the Front, or indeed the Communist Party's Popular Front of the 1930s). As they approach the city, however, they receive reports that liberated neighborhoods are falling. Hearing of the "savage last days" of the "alternative city-state" (505), the debate begins in the Council as to whether they should join the battle, and surely go down in an act of "millennial absurdity," or hold back and stay free to fight another day (511). At this point, the narrative winds toward its close in an ambiguous utopian moment. Standing against the decision to bring the Train into the city, the intellectual and golem-maker artist, Judah, breaks ranks and creates a golem that takes the Train out of time, where—in a fantastic reprise of Bloch's cultural heritage transported to the future—it can wait until "things are ready" (560, 592). Judah's action denies the intention of the Council to join in the last battle, yet in the tension between them a utopian horizon remains. An edition of *Runagate Rampant* declares that the government has won and "order reigns" but asserts that "the Iron Council will move on again" (611), and the Trilogy ends with a declaration: "Women and men cut a line across the dirtland and dragged history out and back across the world. They are still with shouts setting their mouths and we usher them in. They are coming out of the trenches of rock toward the brick shadows. They are always coming" (614).

Reading this narrative, one can't help but think of Miéville's intellectual and political affiliation with Morris and his narrative of "How the Change Came." While in *The Iron Council*, the utopian time of rest and creativity never arrives, the steps toward it are delineated in a narrative of utopian process. At its end, readers are left in a moment of Brechtian problem-solving to ponder the relative merits of the two outcomes: considering whether the appropriate utopian direction lies in the spatial solidarity of apocalyptic engagement or in the temporal solidarity of surviving as a locus of hope. Bridging both, the Train and Iron Council constitute a spatiotemporal utopian surplus that denies and challenges the status quo. Like *News from Nowhere* in its time, *Iron Council* is an *imaginative* meditation on revolutionary politics, in its personal and collective, creative and organizational dimensions.

If Robinson gives us the bones of a utopian future history in his large-scale narratives of systemic and agential transformation, Miéville puts flesh on those bones in his story of individuals and groups who coalesce into a multitude and build a revolution. Robinson's sf vision offers utopian strategies that are put into motion at the levels of state power and everyday life, and Miéville's utopian scenarios of political movement follow the development of committed action from its basis in individual lives through to a collective agency capable of reaching toward transformation. For both writers, utopia can be approached only by working from and with the complex of possibilities of the world as it exists. Both provide examples of the way in which utopian sf not only negates the world readers know—rendering it insufficient, incomplete, and incapable of fulfilling utopian needs—but also figures modes of agency that move toward the unforeseeable utopian horizon.[15]

V

My aim in this chapter has been to focus on the positive hermeneutic in the utopian problematic, and to consider the ways readers might open textual figuration to a productive speculation on how its content as well as its form disrupts the present and explores what might be done to change it—not to find immediate, practical answers but to enlighten and expand the articulation of an alternative agenda and agency. As I was working on this question of the pedagogical vocation of utopian writing, I received an e-mail from a colleague who had long been away from the study of utopian writing. She wrote that, given the times we live in, she was returning to it, especially in her teaching. As she put it:

> I decided to return to the topic of utopian thought and teach an undergraduate seminar on "Good Worlds, Bad Worlds: Utopian and Dystopian Visions." It was triggered by remarks my current undergrads have made about things such as the Universal Declaration of Human Rights, that they considered "completely utopian," meaning "nice idea, but forget it … it's totally unrealistic." It made me realize that I wanted to return to my previous reflections and reconsider their relevance for these times.[16]

Like many of us, my colleague is concerned with the impact of managerial instrumental realism and what Unger calls the "dictatorship of no alternatives" on our students, and I was encouraged to hear her write of returning to utopian thought and writing as a way to motivate them to think differently, critically. In this regard, the pedagogical opportunity of utopian sf works like the "subtle knife" in Philip Pullman's *Dark Materials Trilogy*: as a device that enables us, as it did for Will and Lyra, to cut through the boundaries of provincial reality and open a "a gap in mid-air through which they could see another world" and, hopefully, learn that life in *this* world can be radically better (Pullman 1998: 194).

I will close with a utopian riff from another mode of fantastic writing, one of Subcomandante Marcos's "Old Antonio" fables, that also catches the nature of utopian possibility as it emerges from material conditions in the world and makes the present impossible in an evocation of the horizon of transformation and the steps to be taken toward it:

> You thought the road was already there somewhere and your gadgets were going to tell us where it was. But no. And then you thought I knew where the road was and you followed me. But no. I didn't know where the road was. We had to make the road together. And that is what we did. That's how we got where we wanted to be. We made the road. It wasn't there. (Marcos 2001)

N-H-N': Robinson's Dialectics of Ecology

I

There is no question that we live in conjuncturally dystopian times, negotiating a dark matrix of catastrophic ecological destruction, increasing economic exploitation, constant war, intensifying impoverishment and displacement of peoples, and pervasive racism and xenophobia. In regard to the state of the planet, James Hansen, former director of NASA's Goddard Institute of Space Studies, years ago argued that we are at the edge of "tipping points ... fed by amplifying feedbacks," the most significant of which are the drop in carbon absorption and growth of greenhouse gas; the rapid melt of polar sea ice and consequent rise in sea levels; the increasing toxicity of air, water, and land; and the resulting decimation of humanity and our nonhuman cousins (Hansen 2009: ix).[1] While still a provisional *stratigraphic* category, social and cultural discourse confronting this imbricated matrix of catastrophe has recognized that the "Anthropocene" (as that period of deep time characterized by the impact of humanity, whenever one begins it, be it the Neolithic, the industrial, or the late capitalist turns) is winding down, or, according to many, coming to a cataclysmic end.

As early as *The Ecology of Fear*, Mike Davis proffered this cautionary analysis as he argued that the causes and consequences of this ecological, economic, and sociocultural disaster are not to be found in the processes of nature but in human behavior. We know that the alienation, exploitation, and destruction of nature can be traced back to deep causes, but we also know that in modernity it is especially the dominance of the world capitalist system that has intensified the ruination of life on Earth. With the global incursion of neoliberal capitalism, the crises are increasing exponentially in scale and proving incapable of amelioration within the terms of the existing world system. Indeed, Joel Kovel reminds us that "the crisis is not about an 'environment' outside us, but the evolution, accelerating with sickening velocity, of an ancient lesion in humanity's *relation* to nature" (2007: 14).[2] For Kovel—and others such as Ted Benton and John Bellamy Foster—capitalism (racial, patriarchal capitalism) must be named the primary cause of this entropic relation (see 81; 23–5). In his words, "capital cannot recuperate the ecological crisis because its essential being, manifest in the 'grow or die' syndrome, is to produce such a crisis, and the only thing it really knows how to do, which is to produce according to exchange-value, is exactly the source of the crisis" (89). In this regard, I hold with Jason Moore's historical materialist argument that the more accurate term to describe the period that is cataclysmically engulfing the world is not the Anthropocene but the *Capitalocene*, which he defines as the "historical era shaped by relations privileging the endless accumulation of capital" (Moore 2015: 173).

Given the mechanisms of this totalizing system, I argue that the only option for survival is an equally encompassing eu-topian *transformation* of the way that humanity exists within that nature of which we are an integral part. Writing in *Utopian Studies* in 2016, Kim Stanley Robinson observed: "Climate change is inevitable—we're already in it—and because we're caught in technological and cultural path dependency, we can't easily get back out of it … It has become a case of utopia or catastrophe, and utopia has gone from being a somewhat minor literary problem to a necessary survival strategy" (Robinson 2016: 9). In her 2018 monograph, *Green Utopias: Environmental Hope before and after Nature*, Lisa Garforth supports Robinson's conclusion as she argues that the dominant challenge facing us is to develop a new, "green utopian," way of living "in a fundamentally different and unpredictable era," but she goes on to assert that this new way of living requires a radically new way of being, a utopian way of being: "once we start to think about the mixed-up, hybrid worlds that we have made and that we must live in and with, and about the complex ways in which we ourselves are simultaneously matter and culture, we need new ontologies, new ethics and new ways of thinking about better greener worlds" (4–5).

Here, however, it is important to be wary of the way the current world system generates its own "artificial negativity" to produce an ameliorating practice of, at best, reformist behavior (as in the "greening" of households, to use Andrew Dobson's phrase) that is all too readily contained and exploited (Dobson 2007: 202).[3] In an interview with Liz Else, Slavoj Žižek has named such ecological gestures the "new opiate of the masses," for while he acknowledges the ecological struggle as one of the key elements in the counter-attack on world capitalism (the other being the grassroots, emancipatory democracy of the multitude), he calls for radical engagement beyond the "privatization of ecology" that is produced by the green market and its green lifestyles (Else and Žižek 2010: 28).

Therefore, if humanity seriously chooses to develop these nova of thinking and acting in order to transform the way the world system currently works, there must be a radical *break* with the present: this requires a systemic rupture that opens the way to another world, and for this, as Garforth argues, it means thinking, and acting, outside the terms and conditions of the current order. And yet to focus only on the break, or even on the abstraction of an uprising of the global multitude, is not enough. In the quest for what is to be done, humanity needs to explore how to move from here to there. Together, we need to discern the "next step of renewed praxis" (Jameson 1994: 71). In this context, we need a strategic move away from what Dobson calls the "light-green politics" of environmentalism and into the "dark-green politics" of ecologism (2007: 194). Certainly, on a personal level, each of us needs to act responsibly in the moment—doing our share of good practice, however much it is encased within the prevailing economy and ideology. But collectively, and diversely, we need to develop a radical ecological consciousness and behavior: in a series of initiatives that could stretch from the actions of campus or neighborhood environmental committees, to local organizers developing "green schools," to residents fighting against toxic waste dumps, to environmental groups campaigning by a variety of means (from direct action and street campaigns to legal challenges and educational outreach), to the campaigns of the anti-capitalist and alter-globalization movements, to the growing militant activism of school children and their affiliated adults, and to the generation of radical ecosocialist policy within existing political parties and at the horizon of the subsequent long march through legal and legislative systems at national, regional, and planetary levels. Yet while this continuum maps a terrain of actually existing politics, there still needs to be an epistemological and political break between light and dark green (informed by a "red," materialist and anti-capitalist, movement) if significant change in the world system and in humanity's relationship to nature is to occur. While he puts it cautiously, this is the position Dobson favors when he identifies the limits of *environmentalism* and stresses the importance of radical *ecology*: "reformism is necessary in that it provides us with a green platform, a new consensus in our relationship with our environment, from which we can make the leap to more radically green practices" (201). The steps forward are important, but the break and the move beyond are also necessary. And it will only come out of the titration of the collective work of the moment into an "eventual" break, in Alain Badiou's sense (Badiou: 28). To paraphrase Shevek in *The Dispossessed*, we need "to be difficult and choose both" (Le Guin 1974: 197).

What is therefore called for is not business as usual, neither restricted reform nor scarcity guilt-tripping, but rather a far-reaching critique and vision of how this world works and a bold pursuit of radical alternatives that can gain traction, from the largest systemic levels through to the practices of our everyday lives. Humpty Dumpty cannot be put back together. Instead, the wall must be torn down, and in its place a new subject of nature and history can emerge. To make this move, we need the means to cast light on the darkness before us and to envision and revision what is to be done and what is not yet. As Garforth argues, we must directly face this dire situation and simultaneously admit the difficulty of thinking beyond this crisis and generating a radical utopian alternative: what we need therefore is a *utopian method* informed by a "green hope" that disrupts capitalist hegemony and enables humanity to live creatively within with multiple ecologies. Robinson reaffirms this two-stage response (in an interview appropriately titled "Still, I'm Reluctant to Call This Pessimism") as he explores his own efforts narratively not only to track the necessary break with the present order but also to draw on what we have already achieved to produce a new reality in which all of nature can survive (Canavan and Robinson 2014). On the second page of the interview, Robinson offers a simple one-sentence micro-fiction that speaks to us all: "This coming century looks like the moment in human history when we will either invent a civilization that nurtures the biosphere while it supports us, or else we will damage it quite badly, perhaps even to the point of causing a mass extinction event and endangering ourselves" (244). For those who still hold to this deep impulse of utopian hope, who have not capitulated, the imperative is to find ways to move forward. Throughout this transformative process, we ourselves will have to change as we develop a new mindset and a new sensibility (as in Kate Soper's "alternative hedonism") that refuse and transcend the terms and conditions of the global capitalist system. As we do so, we can construct what Badiou describes as "the space of thought" that can enable humanity to create and inhabit the next steps that enable the breakthrough to the new reality at the horizon (Badiou 2001: 28).

II

To help produce this radical reorientation, not only intellectuals and activists, scientists and policymakers, but also artists and shamans are needed: visionaries grounded in this world but able to generate social maquettes that offer immediate strategies, as well as figurations of another possible world.[4] We need to open ourselves imaginatively and cognitively so we can create this new space beyond the limits of the present. For me, at least, the science fictional imaginary has long been one of the most powerful sources of this re-visioning.

Throughout its history, sf has paid close attention to the state of nature, looking at its processes and potential as well as its plight in the hands of humans. In his study of ecocriticism and sf's place in it, literary critic Patrick Murphy notes that this generic strategy "shares with both nature writing and other forms of nature-oriented literature detailed attention to the natural world found in the present, as well as the scientific disciplines that facilitate such ... attention" (Murphy 2000: 90). And political theorist Ernest Yanarella identifies the "post-millennial politics appropriate to the ecological imagination limned in daily practices of the ecological, feminist, and peace and social justice movements and anticipated ... in contemporary science fiction" (2001: 289). He concludes his study of sf and the ecological imagination by asserting that sf will "continue to be [a] ... sophisticated intellectual guide for addressing portentous political and cultural issues of today and tomorrow as if the fate of the Earth and all its creatures—including humanity—mattered" (304). I am sure each of us can write our own list of sf works that address nature and its crises. My own choices, made as I was writing this piece, would move from the early exploration of the human-nature interface by Mary Shelley; to the evolutionary, deep time narratives of H.G. Wells and Olaf Stapledon; to the exploration of non-human agency in work by Clifford Simak, Cordwainer Smith, Samuel R. Delany, Octavia Butler, or Nnedi Okorafor. It would then focus on dystopian narratives such as George R. Stewart's *The Earth Abides* (1949), Neville Shute's *On the Beach* (1957), John Brunner's *The Sheep Look Up* (1972), or Starhawk's *The Fifth Sacred Thing* (1993), and move to eutopian writing such as Ernest Callenbach's *Ecotopia* (1975), the work of Ursula K. Le Guin—especially *The Word for World Is Forest* (1972), *The Dispossessed* (1975), and *Always Coming Home* (2000)—and Gwyneth Jones' more ambiguous treatment of green utopia in her *Bold As Love* cycle (2001–2006). And then, there is the contemporary sf that comes under neologism of "cli-fi," such as Jeanette Winterson's *The Stone Gods* (2007), Ian McEwan's *Solar* (2010), Omar El Akkad's *American War: A Novel* (2017), Margaret Atwood's *Maddadam Trilogy* (2003–2013) and *The Testaments* (2019), or N. K. Jemisin's *Broken Earth Trilogy* (2015–2017). And, to be sure, there is the work of Kim Stanley Robinson.

It's not surprising that sf writers who think and speculate about this world should pay attention to nature. However, it's not just a matter of addressing ecological matters in the *content* of their writing; for the *form* of this genre of alternative worlds *privileges* large-scale attention to the fate of the Earth. It therefore bears paraphrasing Delany's formulation that the background or setting that one encounters in mundane fiction is in sf the foreground, and driving force, of the entire narrative (Delany 1991). In this iconic register of spatial creation, an alternative world, with its estranged reflection on the author's own time, is presented in thoughtful and totalizing detail; and it is within this elsewhere and elsewhen that the plot and characters can play out in the discrete register of the narrative. As I argued in Chapters 4 and 5, it is in this *formal* quality of worldbuilding that readers can especially discover the science fictional capacity for exploring the complex of ways in which nature operates and the ways humans use and abuse this ground of existence. Within this ecocritical sphere, writers can move from extrapolating on near-future consequences of immediate dangers and opportunities to imagining radically other worlds that may well begin in a reflective sense of the present world but go on to pull readers into figurations of an entirely different way of being.

However, while *form* is crucial in appreciating the transformative contribution of which sf is capable, it is important to recognize the power of its very *method*: rooted in sf's capacity for generating a "cognitive estrangement" (Suvin) that enables readers to develop critical perspectives on their own world situation by way of its alternative representation and figuration in the imagined world of the text. As Rebecca Evans has argued, this cognitively estranging quality at the core of the sf method can enable readers not only to work from the estranged account of the textual world back into the known world but, more dynamically, to carry this readerly method into everyday experience by regarding the provincial reality of the given world as itself a dangerous fabulation and consequently forging a new way of being out of the shell of that fabrication (Evans 2018).[5] As Robinson puts it, "we are now living in a science fiction novel that we are all writing together" as we try to grasp "the real situation more imaginatively, while imagining what we want more realistically" (Canavan and Robinson 2014: 255). Working with this estranging method (especially when driven by a utopian impulse), we, as readers and as citizens, can approach this moment at the end of the Anthropocene (or Capitalocene) as itself a narrative that can be dislodged from its status of certainty by a cognitively estranged response that is both temporally and politically reorienting so that we can not only imagine new, utopian, alternatives but work together in realizing them.

In this context, I want to look more closely at Robinson's sf in terms of his ecological imagination and engagement; for, as a leading writer and intellectual, in the tradition of Ursula K. Le Guin, he demonstrates in all his work how science fictionality can contribute to the pressing transformative project. Although he is adept at working in a dystopian imaginary—the best example is *The Gold Coast* (1988), the second volume in his Three Californias Trilogy—Robinson favors the eutopian mode. As he recently put it in *Science Fiction Studies*:

> The need is clear, the solution is obvious: we have to invent a just and sustainable civilization … Putting any such new system into practice against the intense resistance of currently existing privilege, greed, stupidity, and fear will be very difficult. We will blunder and fight our way to any better state. Those are good stories to tell, that's the science fiction we need now. (2018: 427)

Yet, this preference does not produce a one-dimensional wish-dream of a better world (which Bloch would characterize an "abstract utopian" gesture).[6] Rather, Robinson works with an approach that is simultaneously pragmatic and utopian—not unlike David Harvey's "dialectical utopianism" that braids together the realization of a given production and a visionary process (Harvey 2000: 182–99). Robinson argues that the cognitively estranging thought experiments generated through the process of science fictionality can generate

> historical simulations, which start in the present and then state *if we do this we will reach here*, or *if we do that we will reach there* [and thus sf is] a mode of thought that is utopian in its very operating principle, for it assumes that differences in our actions now will lead to real … consequences later on—which means that what we do now matters. (1997b: 9)

Sf provides what he describes as "an enjambment of facts and values in a way that our culture desperately needs right now" (Foote 2009: 279).

Robinson therefore prepares our minds for a leap beyond the current ideological mindset. Picking up on the author's science fictional method, Eric Otto has described how Robinson's "multi-positional narrative attests to his desire to move closer to utopia by encouraging readers to synthesize continually a complex array of political positions" (2009: 254). In doing so, Robinson transcends the antinomies that blind and stifle us: be they nature and humanity, organic and scientific, sacred and secular, personal and political, or red and green politics. In *Green Mars*, for example, he describes the struggle of the liberated colonists "to yoke together impossible opposites," and he himself does this throughout his work as he recasts the stasis of such binaries in his narrative *combinatoire*, turning them in a double helix of possibilities that ultimately imagines a novum for a world that has been changed utterly (Robinson 1993: 229). In doing so, he creates a structure of feeling that enables a dialogue between present conditions and future possibilities that reconfigures the range of positions mobilized in the quest for social and ecological justice.

III

One way we can fruitfully consider Robinson's eco-politics and eco-ontology is by taking account of the conceptual and formal registers that resonate with his pragmatic/responsive and utopian/transformative perspective. Beginning with the conceptual, I will draw on Jameson's distinction between utopian program and utopian impulse. On one hand, utopian program is the systemic alternative committed to realization within a given totality, be it "the Utopian city, the Utopian revolution, the Utopian commune or village, and of course the Utopian text itself" (Jameson 2005: 5). A utopian program informs those efforts that generate a revolutionary praxis arising out of struggles within a given situation; yet while such a program is presented in a "realistic" mode in its extrapolation of what is to be done, the activist or reader needs to recall the necessity for an ontological, epistemological, and political break from that present so as to continue the movement toward the totalizing transformation implied in the program. The utopian impulse, on the other hand, is the more elusive (indeed poetic) mode of learning the world, one that finds "its way to the surface in a variety of covert expressions and practices" (3). While a utopian program is produced by a "deliberate and fully self-conscious" articulation of a transformative agenda, the utopian impulse, as an initial or a continuing force, drives a method of interpretation and intervention wherein practices or images can be read as allegorical figures whose radical invocation of a better world exceeds their immediate meaning—within the existing world system, in the revolutionary program, or in the new society (Jameson 2005).

Formally, as I discussed in the last chapter, the expression of program and impulse can be tracked in terms of the modes of representation and figuration. On the surface of the sf text, the worlds generated are generally presented through a fictive verisimilitude that allows for a consistent presentation of a knowable world. It is in this *representational* tendency that sf's anticipations offer up the details of a utopian program. In Harvey's architectural terms, this "materialization" of a possible alternative system or practice can be "a particular set of institutional arrangements and a particular spatial form" (2000: 188). In and of themselves, these provisional pathways, especially when closely resonant with the author's and contemporary readers' present time, can produce immediate political inspiration: hence, the Nationalist Clubs that arose from the reception of Edward Bellamy's *Looking Backward* (1888) or the reconceptualization of the political geography of the Pacific Northwest in light of Callenbach's *Ecotopia*. This pedagogical quality of sketching realizable alternatives is captured by Peter Fitting when he describes his own appreciation of utopian texts as they explore "the look and feel and shape and experiences of what an alternative might and could actually be," seeing them as thought experiments "which gave us a sense of how our lives could be different and better, not only in our immediate material conditions but in the sense of an entire world or social system" (1998: 14–15).

And yet the science fictional imaginary does not adhere to the strictures of bourgeois or instrumentalist realism and is not to be reduced to the closure implied in a representational mode. As I've argued, as an estranged genre that produces alternative worlds that grow out of and beyond the worlds of its authors, the genre's "irrealistic realism" leads into *figuration*. As Philip E. Wegner (drawing on Louis Marin) puts it, figuration offers "a process of allegorical representation for which there is not yet a referent, a giving of representational form to that which has not been named" (2009: 201). In this pre-conceptual mode, sf's thought experiments articulate not what is immediately to be done but rather a radically new world (Ernst Bloch's Not Yet) that can only appear beyond the present enclosed reality. Wegner argues that such figuration can work as a form of what Badiou names a Truth Event, a supplement to or "going beyond" the current situation, the "what there is," which thereby "compels us to decide a *new* way of being" (quoted in Wegner 2009: 201).

For his part, Jameson privileges *figuration* as the mode that negates the ideological and systemic closure of the present, hence his Zen-like conclusion that the "deepest subject" of the utopian text, and its most "vibrantly political" intervention, is "precisely our inability to conceive it, our incapacity to produce it as a vision" (1977: 21). Working from the other direction, Harvey (aligning himself with the political analysis of Roberto Unger) argues that utopia's visionary power may well point toward a radical reconstruction of the world, but in its most effective form it needs to "emerge out of critical and practical engagements with the institutions, personal behaviors, and practices that now exist" (Harvey 2000: 186). While I agree with Jameson's position, I argue, as I did in the previous chapter, that while utopia's negative maneuver properly stresses the break and evokes the future realm of freedom, its positive approach (in politics and in this case in its expression in sf) usefully concerns itself with the next steps, and therefore with radical articulations of possible action. For me, therefore, figuration does not simply negate the mode of representation; rather, it liberates it from the ideological drag of present realities, thus ensuring that its radical content can be considered seriously on its own terms even as it can further be read as an allegory that evokes a very different future. Again, I argue that we need to choose *both* (the vision of program and impulse, the material of representation and figuration) so that we can approach these political and formal modes in a dialectical fashion, thereby seeing how each opens up and transforms the other. Working from the negative hermeneutic, we can see how the utopian impulse can pull a program beyond the exhausting limits and compromises of the present system and how it can figure the horizon of an alternative that exceeds the stated content of any given thought experiment. Whereas, by engaging with proffered alternatives through the second stage of a positive hermeneutic, a utopian/represented program can negate the reductive *abstraction* of a utopian allegory by situating it *concretely* in the tendencies and latencies of the present.

IV

Robinson's utopian sf can be read in terms of these double moves of program and impulse, representation and figuration, as he develops his holistic critique of the present world and forges radical visions for a transformed natural reality in which humans are important agents but not dominant. From early on in his writing, he has focused on the ways in which humanity can further the unfolding of nature, as opposed to the anthropocentric domination of it that has persisted so far. In so doing, he has created a series of narratives that express ecologically informed utopian programs for a better recognition and treatment of nature and society, but it is important to always recognize that it is his overall utopian impulse that figures the critical negation of the world as we know it and then opens up into his representation of these programmatic narratives. Most often working closely in the present, driven by a deep utopian impulse, his narratives address the most pressing of immediate concerns (capitalist exploitation, corrupt power, abrupt climate change, the violation of Earth's carrying capacity) as they explore possible political responses. Yet, as he conveys readers across the utopian trench and into the locus of these alternatives, the utopian impulse continues its work by layering on a figurative register over the representation of these programs that then transforms them in a second order of meaning into allegorical evocations of a new utopian horizon that we cannot yet know or experience.

Central to what Robinson calls the "consensus vision of what might be" is therefore his sense of nature and humanity's place in it (1997b: 10). He stated this position early on in his work in his introduction to the *Future Primitive* anthology:

> The biosphere is our extended body, and we can no more live without it than we could live without our kidneys or our bones. The old paradigm of the world as a machine is being replaced, in modern science and in the culture at large, by a more accurate and sophisticated paradigm of the world as a vast organism, complexly interpenetrative in ways not previously imagined. The world is not a machine we can use and then replace: it is our extended body. If we try to cut it away we will die. (1997b)

In a later interview, he reiterates this view by refusing the binary between human and non-human in a more personal key: "The more I think of us as animals, the easier it becomes for me to understand things that I didn't understand before" (Foote 2009: 286). Crucially, for Robinson, humans are *part* of nature. They are not masters of some material universe or stewards of lives external to themselves; rather, they are, so far, the most self-aware species within the natural realm.[7] Shaun Huston has suggested that Robinson's view of nature resembles Murray Bookchin's concept of "third or free nature" (Huston 2009: 231). As Bookchin conceives it, "first or bio-physical nature" produces "human or social nature," but rather than holding to this binary division the potential exists for a conscious *synthesis*, "wherein the human species actively participates in the differentiation and evolution of life" (quoted in Huston 232). Third nature can produce "an ethical humanly scaled community that establishes a creative interaction with its natural environment" (Bookchin 1996: xvii). Huston, however, pauses on Bookchin's continuing emphasis on *human* community; he cites Robyn Eckersley's argument that the concept of third nature does not go beyond an anthropocentric vision of stewardship: in his reading, therefore, third nature still posits humanity and nature as separate, wherein humans act, however wisely, *with* nature and not *in* nature. He therefore concludes that Robinson does not reproduce Bookchin's position but rather interrogates it throughout his fiction (see Huston 2009: 232–3; Eckersley 1992).

My own reading of Robinson goes further than Huston's. I suggest that his approach breaks through the binary that entraps Bookchin. Throughout his critical analyses, working from his own situated position, Robinson explores, as Huston aptly puts it, "what human *participation* in the evolution of nature might be like" (Huston 2009: 233). Given this focus, he doesn't write narratives about the long-term transformation of sentient life and agency, as found in his admired Stapleton; nor, to acknowledge the questioning of Robinson's humancentrism by Sherryl Vint and Mark Bould, does he focus on non-human life and agency, though, as Vint and Bould observe, his treatment of animals liberated from the Washington DC Zoo in *Fifty Degrees Below* is a step in that direction, and certainly the planetary minds of Jupiter and Europa that we find in *Galileo's Dream* constitute a significant evocation of intelligent non-human life (see Vint and Bould 2009). Thus, as he consistently works beyond an abstract politics of *alterity*, he does not posit nature as an Other with which humans should ally; rather, he declares the comradely unity and solidarity deriving from what Badiou terms the "constitutively situated dimension of all being" as an integral part of nature (Badiou 2001: xxv). His creative project therefore begins with where we humans find ourselves, and yet as he develops his narratives he points to a larger nature of which we are a part. In this context, his human standpoint is not reducible to a hegemonic anthropocentrism but rather evinces a critical examination of what we humans have done and generates a transformative vision of what we could go on to do as one species in the biosphere.

Rather than Bookchin's, I suggest that Robinson's concept of nature is closer to that proffered by Bloch. While Bloch, like Robinson, is politically concerned with human agency and potentiality in history, it is important to recall the utopian philosopher's debt to dialectical materialism and see that his meditations on the human utopian impulse take place within the larger realm of an evolving material nature (as opposed to the idealist anthropomorphic domination of nature). As John Bellamy Foster argues, the "immanent materialist dialectic" developed by Marx and Engels (which we can no longer reduce to its received attribution as a form of positivist, mechanistic determinism) articulates the emergence of an all-encompassing material reality in which nature, including the human species, develops by contingency and co-evolution (2000: 233, 230, 254). Within this framework, as Vince Geoghegan notes, Bloch's "radical materialism expresses an imbricated belief in the natural element in human dynamics and the dynamic element in nature" (Geoghegan 1996: 153). Herein, nature demonstrates its own unfolding process, its own story, part of which involves humanity, part of which will go on long after humanity has passed on. Again Geoghegan:

> For Bloch the great material drama, of which humanity is a part, is far from over; the processes which gave rise to human consciousness within nature have not exhausted their creativity. The utopian tendencies within the human world need to be related to an even larger and more awesome process—the onward development of the material universe itself. (Geoghegan 1996)

In Bloch's view, nature is not an external force to be dominated or exploited. Rather, in a move that goes beyond Bookchin's binary two-step, it is nature's own "creativity and productivity" that have led to humanity becoming one of its conscious elements (1986: 670). Furthermore, as I explore in Chapter 2, the unorthodox Bloch refuses a unilinear teleology that begins with passive nature and ends with human history: instead his vision revolves around "continuing temporal modalities" (Geoghegan 1996: 157). He therefore argues that nature follows a "noteworthy future mode of its own" (Bloch 1986: 76). Thus, Bloch identifies a "natural subject," one that lies in the future, one that will emerge from the co-productivity of nature and humanity. Quite beyond Bookchin's teleology, "Bloch's speculations on nature," as Geoghegan puts it,

> reflect his belief that genesis is at the end, and not in the beginning. His system [growing out of Marx and Engels but going back to Democritus] starts with matter and its potentialities, and arrives at a utopian vision of a *supernature* where humanity, itself a natural product, co-produces with a still dynamic nature. (1996: 159)

Within this perspective, as Geoghegan aptly concludes, humanity "is thus exalted *and* humbled" (1996).

Bloch's sense of a supernature can be understood as what I would term *Nature Prime* (N')—or the dialectical sublation of primary nature (N) and humanity (H). This is a more dynamic outcome than that allowed for in Bookchin's synthesized third nature. Here, nature itself is the transformed and transforming reality; and this, I argue, is a position that accords with Robinson's. Given the emphasis he places on social problems and struggles in the discrete register of his narratives, it is not surprising that some readers underestimate the degree of Robinson's epistemological and ontological immersion within the realm of Nature Prime. However, in his iconic worldbuilding and in the resulting content of his narratives in which humans come to terms with their environment, the nature expressed in each work and in the overall intertext of Robinson's alternative realities is not that of a passive *landscape* for human plots and counterplots (as Vint and Bould suggest). Rather, Robinson's biosphere is, like Bloch's supernature, Nature Prime itself, the substrate and subject of all existence and subsequent action.

V

In the last chapter, I offered a summary discussion of the way Robinson's political engagements and projections work with his mobilization of sf form and offered that in a critical reading of both his work and one novel by China Miéville. Now that I've more fully examined Robinson's understanding of the relationship of humanity and nature, especially taking account of his figuration of Nature Prime, I'll move on from that initial overview and proceed with a closer account of his individual texts. As I've noted, Robinson has moved from portrayals of ecological politics in one town in *Pacific Edge* (1990), to a city in the *Science in the Capital Trilogy* (2004–2007), a continent in *Antarctica* (1997a), an entire planet (and Solar System) in the *Mars Trilogy* (1992–1996), and in the alternative histories of *The Years of Rice and Salt* (2002) and *Galileo's Dream* (2009).[8] In *2312* (2012) and *Aurora* (2015), he again reached out to the Solar System and beyond, only to return to our own near future on Earth in *New York 2140* (2017) and *Red Moon* (2018). And, as I will argue, in the prehistoric sf of *Shaman* (2013), he created a compelling meta-commentary on the overarching "geohistorical imaginary" by which he creates this entire panoply of critical and visionary creations.

Pacific Edge set a pattern for the later works, as the dignity and integrity of the land stand at the core of the sociopolitical crisis of the narrative. As remembered by Tom Barnard (retired activist, now writing about the potential of the utopian imagination), a global revolution has succeeded in overthrowing the capitalist system and has produced a new society (albeit in a biosphere ravaged by that previous system) that operates on the basis of radical democracy, socialist economics (with a mixed use of market technologies), cultural diversity and freedom, and a relationship with nature based on the principles of permaculture. Set in the post-revolutionary desert town of El Modena, California, the main plot recounts a local political battle (led by Tom's nephew, Kevin Claiborne) against resurgent greed, personal power, and a renewed violation of the integrity of the land. True to the form of the critical utopia, reactionary darkness falls when it becomes evident that some citizens, including Alfredo the leader of the town council, are more interested in development and wealth than in the new eco-utopian way of life. A bitter council fight erupts over the question of whether Alfredo and his company will be allowed to build a commercial center on Rattlesnake Hill, the last open land in the area. The crucial battle to stop the venture and save the Hill is lost when the council votes in favor of the development. However, when Tom, who lived near the Hill, dies, Kevin arranges a memorial service to mark his passing. In the eulogy, in an act of radical spirituality, the town minister links the integrity and sacredness of the Hill with Tom's revolutionary contributions, and the subsequent commitment of the townspeople to declaring the Hill an "inviolate" shrine guarantees that it will not fall prey to Alfredo's scheme.[9] What was lost in the civic sphere of the council is subsequently won on the cultural front by way of the memorial ritual. As a result, the utopian impulse of the long revolution is preserved; and Rattlesnake Hill stands as both motivation and beneficiary of the utopian program, while on the utopian horizon it also figures the transformed status of nature and humanity's relationship to it.

In the *Mars Trilogy*, the revolutionary process (helped by a longevity treatment that extends the lives of the original colonists) forges an independent Martian society that has broken away from the greed and toxicity of Earth. The new society is organized around principles and practices very like the utopian program detailed in *Pacific Edge*, even as they are developed in the greater polyphony of what Jameson describes as "a re-flowering of elaborate and varied left traditions and alternatives" (Jameson 2000: 230). Furthermore, and working at the utopian intersection of science and politics that Robinson celebrates throughout his writing, the debate on *terraforming* opens the productive connection between program and utopian impulse.[10] Ranging from charges of arrogant anthropocentrism linked to an emphasis on the tendency for industrial terraforming to positive responses to the liberatory potential of an ecopoesis that works with and not just on the land, the many published debates and discussions on terraforming have proven the value of Robinson's provocative thought experiment.

Much more could be said about the politics and science of the Trilogy (especially in regard to the principles and protocols of the new society—including the designation of inalienable rights for nature itself—that emerge in Robinson's revival of the eighteenth-century form of the utopian constitution, as in the previously mentioned Dorsa Brevia Document and the Martian Constitution). For now, I want to focus less on matters of revolution and terraforming and more on the convergent outcome of both in regard to the dialectics of humanity and nature as Robinson understands them—see his further reflections in *The Martians*, the volume of out-takes from the Trilogy (1999). After the multi-generational unfolding of the utopian program, what emerges at the end of the Trilogy is a new, dual, subject of history, as humanity enters into a qualitatively new "state of free nature with Mars" (Huston 2009: 239), which, in the biologist Ann's words, has become "something entirely new" (Robinson 1996: 730). First, the post-revolutionary human, figured as the *martian*, representative of what Huston terms a "biotic citizenry," appears in the renewed personalities of First Hundred survivors such as Sax and Ann (who is described at the end of *Blue Mars* as a "fully Martian Ann at last") and in the indigenous generations represented by Nirgal, Jackie, and Zo, with their tall, birdlike bodies (Huston 2009: 248; Robinson 1996: 754). Unlike the historical Earth-bound human, the new *martian* subject has cast off its biological and historical chains and is consequently opened to the potential of a radically responsible and free life.

Second, Nature Prime is directly figured in the utopian transformation of bodily death, which in Bloch's writing can be read as the elimination of the Faustian "sting" of premature death (indeed, such a victory over death is reprised even more powerfully in the reincarnation revolution in Robinson's alternative history, *The Years of Rice and Salt*).[11] However, the emergent subject of Nature Prime is also, and most fully, realized in the ongoing evolution of Mars itself. To be sure, the planet has been transformed by humans; but in return, it has transformed them. While its material integrity has eventually been legally and scientifically secured, Mars itself has further enfolded the entire project of human settlement within its larger, natural scale.[12] The emergent subject position of Mars is perhaps best summed up by Sax when he concludes that what is important is "not nature, not culture: just Mars" (1996: 679). Or, as Robert Markley puts it (in an echo of Kingsley Amis's recognition of the "idea as hero" in postwar sf), the ultimate "hero" of Robinson's trilogy "remains Mars itself" (2009: 131; Amis 1969). But if there is a third figure that encapsulates the radical convergence of humanity and nature, it is that of Hiroko who, by the end of the Trilogy (in anticipation of the mega-narrative scale we find in *The Years of Rice and Salt* and in *Galileo's Dream*), is a matriarchal specter hovering somewhere in a postdeath realm between life and death, and whose principle of the life force of "viriditas" has ultimately conjoined her green vitality with Ann's red "viriditas of rock" (Robinson 1996: 558). As a consummate figure of Robinson's dialectical resolution of the antinomies of nature and culture, life and death, red and green, Hiroko emerges as the most developed expression of humanity's contribution to the ongoing evolution of Nature Prime.

In the wake of the Trilogy, which Jameson describes as "the great political novel of the 1990s," the very near future sf of *Antarctica* and the *Science in the Capital Trilogy* pulls readers two steps backward into pre-revolutionary narratives that explore political steps closer to our present situation (Jameson 1994: 65). In both, Robinson's utopian program and impulse are shaped by the more pragmatic valence of his vision and invite readings that are immediately political—and as such arouse suspicion by some critics that he has been compromised by the parameters of the current conjuncture.[13] Yet, in each of these works, Robinson's program reaches toward, even if it does not yet arrive at, his transformative horizon of radical democracy, socialist/mixed economics, liberated culture, and permaculture. Intertextually, the radical figuration of the earlier *Mars Trilogy* can linger in a reader's mind and stand as the fictive future of the fictive present of these later works; and from this point of view, we can return to the longer perspective of the *Mars Trilogy* and consider these proto-utopian realizations in light of that horizon.

In *Antarctica*, budgetary cuts delivered by a right-wing president and the need to negotiate a new Antarctic treaty produce a critical moment in which a progressive power shift unfolds. The radical reform of the power structure that governs the "science continent" is won by an oppositional alliance that includes on-site scientists, technicians, artists, tourist guides, labor leaders, and feral "transantarctic" citizens, as well as eco-saboteurs, lawyers, scientists, and politicians from the higher echelons of the US world superpower (1997a: 2). Through the complex campaign of this exemplary united front, Antarctica is transformed into an autonomous zone—as its scientific base is protected, its workplace turned into a cooperative, and its resources tightly regulated. It is therefore declared as "its own place" in the revised Treaty, but this liberated Antarctica also stands metonymically as a utopian alternative for the entire planet, with the final protocol of the Treaty declaring that "what is true in Antarctica is true everywhere else" (491). In terms of the figuration of new subjects of history, the unfolding of the narrative focuses on X and Wade as radicalized political activists, Carlos as the enlightened representative of local South American interests, and especially Val and Mai-lis who reach to the horizon as the "future primitive" feral citizens. In terms of nature itself, the liberated continent (reinforced by the utopian clauses of Treaty) is established as a liberated evolutionary zone—and not an imperialist or capitalist enclave. In the renewed Antarctica (described in the Treaty as both a "world site of special scientific interest" and a "sacred ritual space," phrases that echo Robinson's ontological treatment of the land in the *Mars Trilogy* and *Pacific Edge*), the figurative convergence that points toward Nature Prime is summed up by Mai-lis who (as an iteration of Hiroko) describes the feral inhabitation as "the land's human expression and part of its consciousness, along with the rest of its animal and plant consciousness" (488, 444).

In the *Science in the Capital Trilogy*, Robinson brings readers closer to the present moment as the disasters brought on by abrupt climate change (coming like biblical, but all too real, plagues in the form of flooding and freezing) are, at least temporarily, dealt with by a similar united front led by an alliance of government officials and scientists.[14] In this series, Robinson evinces a more immediate utopian politics (closer to the work of Harvey or Unger than to Hardt and Negri) in a nearly realist narrative of a combined scientific and political intervention to, explicitly, save the Earth and, implicitly, move toward a utopian order. Indeed, the Trilogy is barely recognizable as utopian, although he calls it that in his essay on the series; for the utopian trajectory grows out of the crises produced by abrupt climate change and the efforts of the protagonists to save the Earth (Robinson 2016). Thus, *Green Earth* (*Forty Signs of Rain, Fifty Degrees Below,* and *Sixty Days and Counting*) can be seen as a strong example of Levitas's utopian reconstitution of society within which utopian lessons of sociopolitical transformation can be discovered (Robinson 2015b, 2004, 2005, 2007a). Robinson's account of the extreme flooding and freezing produced by global warming and the consequent destruction of the Gulf Stream evokes the Old Testament jeremiads, but the form and substance of the volumes are a more complex combination of hard sf, science writing, and political discourse, all given a utopian valence by the account of the collective agency (including the US president and a community of Buddhists from a Pacific island state that was flooded out of existence) that realigns the world infrastructure on a scale that Robinson compares to Franklin D. Roosevelt's American New Deal and Hugo Chavez's Bolivarian Revolution. The result not only saves the planet but also produces the preconditions for a transformed society based on Robinson's familiar principles of permaculture, justice, and democracy.

What is most striking about the utopian program of this Trilogy is its synthesis of the macro-politics of state power and the micro-politics of everyday life (inspired by a spiritual and ethical sensibility based in Buddhism and the American Transcendentalism of Ralph Waldo Emerson and Henry David Thoreau). Driving both of these programmatic tendencies is the intellectual and political activism of scientists, particularly those based in a utopian iteration of the National Science Foundation—and here Robinson makes his most overt narrative claim for science as an integral element in the global utopian process. Despite appearances, this political trajectory is not one that can result from reform within the present system (not reducible, for example, to the status of a "liberal, democratic manifesto" ascribed to it by Roger Luckhurst); the actions taken demand at the very least a movement toward the transformation of the total world order (Luckhurst 2009: 176). While the overdetermined crises and interventions have a familiar, indeed "realistic," feel to them, Robinson's program does not, contrary to Luckhurst, eschew utopianism; instead, its programmatic maneuver (articulated by the theoretical exchanges between President Phil Chase and his assistant Wade) disrupts the accepted discourse on the present conjuncture and brings readers to the edge of a new reality. In the words of the president, what develops is the "opportunity to remake our relationship with nature, and create a new dispensation ... Seizing the planet's history ... and turning it to the good" (2007a: 6).[15]

The Trilogy therefore adds its own contribution to Robinson's long-term figuration of a radical future for humanity's participation in the totality of Nature Prime. While not fully revolutionary subjects, major characters nevertheless take significant steps toward that horizon as they develop, personally and politically, in the process of addressing the climactic crises. We see it in the leadership exercised by Phil Chase (the fantastic hero who soberly points to what Barack Obama never did) and in the enlightened lives of the Khembali community, the Quibler family, and Frank Vanderwal (the left sociobiologist who not only leads on the scientific front but also pursues a personal quest to live more attentively as part of nature, dwelling in a treehouse and learning new behavior from the baboons who escaped from the Washington DC Zoo during the flooding of the city). In terms of the new subject of nature previously figured in the planet Mars, we see the series open with a short chapter on the Earth itself, as it was before the catastrophes hit; and gradually, we come to know the future primitive environment of Washington's Rock Creek Park (rewilded, to anticipate a later Robinson work, by the catastrophes and inhabited by the feral zoo animals and Frank and his liberated Freegan and Vietnam veteran friends). Consequently, in this exercise in cognitive mapping, Robinson elaborates a scenario that traces a utopian politics growing from material conditions that include the impending climatic crisis as well as the oppositional potential within state and non-state formations. The alternative trajectory that he creates is not one that can result from mere reform of the present system; for the actions needed—in a process of becoming utopian that ranges from the systemic to the personal—demand a total transformation of the world. While the overdetermined crisis and each successive intervention has a familiar feel to it, his vision thoroughly estranges the present and brings us to the edge of a new reality. Thus, instrumental rationality, exploitation, and ecocide are negated by a paradigm shift summed up in the Buddhist inspired phrase "passionate reason," wherein the government becomes the "commons" and acts to make the world better (2004: 245; 2007a: 269). While utopia is not realized in the series, the conditions are established globally for the next significant steps toward it.

In his next two novels, Robinson again leaves Earth, and with it the *immediate* prospect of catastrophic collapse, and considers the ecological and socioeconomic crises in a longer and wider, though no less dire, context; but as he does so, he continues to create what Gerry Canavan has described as a "huge metatextual history of the future, not unlike those sagas imagined by Asimov or Heinlein in the Golden Age of Science Fiction, distributed across overlapping but distinct and mutually irreconcilable texts" (Canavan 2017: online). In *2312,*

Robinson expands the political scope developed in the *Mars Trilogy* throughout the Solar System; while in *Aurora*, he casts his critical and visionary gaze out to the stars, only to spiral back with a sobering lesson for humanity and its future. In both cases, he broadens his imaginative perspective beyond Earth but always with the result of (literally, literarily in *Aurora*) pulling the reader back to the hard times at home. As he details the utopian programs of human societies and communities extending into previously alien environments, Robinson intensifies his investigation into humanity's relationship with the rest of nature in multiple case studies that do not coalesce into a single blueprint for survival but rather remain multiply available as a complex set of warnings and models for the transformative work yet to be done, should we choose to do it.

In *2312*, humans have migrated throughout the Solar System, creating a myriad of social alternatives on terraformed planets and asteroids from Mercury out to Pluto. As Chris Pak notes, this "expansion of environments correlates with an expansion of ideas of the human and opens a space for unprecedented transformations to society and culture" (Pak 505). The novel's historical sweep covers a periodization that runs from 2005 to the year of the novel. It begins with the "wasted years" at the end of the "postmodern" in 2005. It then carries through the period of Crisis from 2016 to 2130 (when "all the bad trends converged in a 'perfect storm'" that ravaged earth and its inhabitants and drove humanity into space) and moves into the Turnaround from 2130 to 2160 (a period of off-planet utopian development of artificial intelligence, terraforming, fusion power, synthetic biology, climate modification technologies, and intensified space propulsion that enabled the social transformations that included the development of radical cooperative systems and a renewed reconfiguration of relations between humanity and the rest of nature, all while Earth still festered poverty and poison) (245). These developments fed the Accelerando of 2116 to 2220 (during which the above technological capacities feed a fresh diaspora into the Solar System and the development of Solar communities, highly diverse but unified in their support for human cooperation and human-nature collaboration). However, during the Ritard, from 2220 to 2270, this progressive development drastically slowed down in the face of faltering technologies, human power struggles, and practical decoherence resulting from accelerating quantum computer use. In the ensuing Balkanization, 2270 to 2320, revived conflicts and disasters prompted by greed and power pressing against further environmental overload and destruction led to the moment of crisis picked up in the year of the novel.

As yet another contribution to Robinson's overarching future history, *2312* deserves a longer discussion to do justice to its extensive critique of the present situation and its expanding collection of utopian thought experiments: the most systemic of which is the author's extrapolation of the Mondragon cooperative in the Basque region of Spain into a relatively successful, if always struggling and endangered, socioeconomic program as it becomes a viable alternative to the totality of the capitalist system (doing what the cooperative movement of the nineteenth century failed to do). But this book's sweeping utopian canvas also includes, on one hand, the narrative of the personal and political relationship between the key protagonists (Swan and Wahram) that winds through the novel and resolves in their alliance of transformative love and action, and, on the other, an exploration of the possibilities of artificial intelligence growing out of quantum computing that leads to a new level of human-AI collaboration. Out of the crises of the Ritard (which stands as an estranged analogue to our contemporary world), Robinson ends his novel with a new stage of utopian resolution, with the Mondragon system unifying much of Earth along with the Solar planets and planetoids and the work of nurturing natural landscapes throughout the areas of human occupation (whether by recreating them on Earth or terraforming them on a variety of extra-terrestrial surfaces). Again, Robinson reminds us that the process of building utopia out of hard times is difficult and ongoing, always facing failures and successes, Thus, the closing sentence of *2312* sums up the novel and the larger project with the appropriate assertion that for the utopian impulse to continue "there is no alternative to continuing to struggle" (553).

For my purposes here I want to limit my comments to those aspects of the novel that, for me, speak most directly to Robinson's ontological and existential embrace of humanity as part of Nature Prime: namely, the practice of terraforming and Swan's intervention in the "reanimation" of Earth. Terraforming has been in Robinson's conceptual and creative toolkit for a very long time, as seen in the Mars books and prefigured in the reclamation ecology and architecture in *Pacific Edge*. Like the conceptual/political unevenness between the scientific and cultural appropriations attributed to the Anthropocene, the same tension applies to the practice of terraforming. As Robinson himself described in the Science in the Capital books, actually existing geoengineering (the more appropriate term for the practice on Earth) is an available technology for the amelioration and repair of the near-terminal damage of our planet. However, like all technology, it also stands available for those projects driven by logics of greed and power, be it material extraction or mega-defense. In earlier sf, terraforming was the opportunistic means for human colonization beyond Earth; yet, in the pages of more recent climate fiction, terraforming not only offers a possible means of environmental refunctioning but, in its underlying science and its sophisticated understanding of feedback relations between human and nonhuman systems, it can also conceptually elucidate what Pak identifies as the "inter-penetrating issues of energy and resource extraction, economics, culture, and society" (Pak 501). In *2312*, as one example of his sense of science as an implicitly utopian praxis, Robinson highlights the *utopian* application of terraforming rather than its greedy dystopian dispensation, as he creates worlds (from the Terminator space on Mercury to the art installations of the Terraria) that accommodate the thriving diversity of human life systems emerging in new controlled and contained environments. Deployed off-planet to facilitate the acceleration of humanity into necessary alternatives beyond their toxic home, terraforming has enabled the "mutual adaptation of human and nonhuman" within novel environments that stand out as utopian nova within the novel (Pak 508). Furthermore, as the crises of the Ritard are confronted, this successful extra-terrestrial re-formation is brought back to the ravaged Earth and redeployed for the purposes of renewal. In *2312*'s treatment of terraforming, I would argue, Robinson comes very close to a position that would appear to favor human technological domination over nature; but, in the larger scope of the narrative, and in an overview that invokes the dynamism of Nature Prime, he pushes against the temptation of an anthropological arrogance through his portrayal of the novel's complex extraterrestrial formations (ranging as they do from his description of the joyful interaction between humans and the solar/planetary ambience of Mercury, achieved by the humility of its terraforming project, to that of the intimate collaboration between human and nonhuman nature facilitated by Swan in her bespoke Terraria across the system).

If terraforming runs throughout the iconic register of the novel, the event of the reanimation of Earth offers a compelling turn of the discrete plot that underscores Robinson's deep affiliation as a sentient being working within nature, not on it. As part of her efforts with Wahram and their allies, the artist/activist Swan brings her talents to the needs of the Earth when she joins the project to rebuild its ecosystem. Already, radical terraforming has enabled landscape restoration, shoreline repair, and coral replanting, but Swan offers another dimension to this utopian intervention as she draws on her experience in populating her Terraria installations with animals. She declares that it's time to move beyond the interim period of off-planet restocking and bring the animals back to Earth. In a narrative description that equals that of restoring the Gulfstream in the Science and the Capital Trilogy, Robinson gives us the sublime image of an Ark-like reversal as thousands of animals are dropped back into Earth in transparent bubbles from large landers:

> Swan looked around, trying to see everywhere at once: sky all strewn with clear seeds, which from any distance were visible only as their contents, so that she drifted eastward and down with thousands of flying wolves, bears, reindeer, mountain lions. There she saw a fox pair; a clutch of rabbits; a bobcat or lynx; a bundle of lemmings; a heron, flying hard inside its bubble. It looked like a dream, but she knew it was real, and the same right now all over Earth: into the seas splashed dolphins and whales, tuna and sharks. Mammals, birds, fish, reptiles, amphibians: all the lost creatures were in the sky at once, in every country, every watershed. Many of the creatures descending had been absent from Earth for two or three centuries. Now all back, all at once. (395)

Initiated by Swan and her comrades, this world-scale delivery and subsequent migration of creatures exceeded the scope of their initial intervention and qualitatively morphed into a global act of Nature Prime. While humans began the reanimation as "the biggest act of civil disobedience ever committed by spacers on earth," the creatures themselves ranged throughout the biome, found new habitat quarters, and established themselves in their new/old home (399). This act of systemic alteration, imitating the purposeful creation of inhabited environments off planet, was catalyzed as "a work of art, shaped by artists"; but understood within the parameters of Robinson's understanding of Nature Prime, the "rewilding" is qualitatively elevated into a project of a dialectically transformed supernature as life once again roamed and ranged across the planet. Swan herself joyfully recognizes this qualitative shift in scale as she declares that "we are part of the family .... the mammal family"—thereby aligning herself with her "horizontal brothers and sisters," for, as she says, we need them, "we need all of them, we are part of them in their part of us" (417). Finally, the third-person quantum/poetic voice of the novel reaffirms this more inclusive ontology of becoming utopian when, after the success of the rewilding, it declares it to be an act of unmistakable "mutualism" (440).[16]

While *2312* carries Robinson's dialectics of ecology into the Solar System, *Aurora* ventures beyond as a generation starship travels to the Tau Ceti system with the purpose of terraforming and settling one of its planetary moons. With a simple plotline that follows the voyage outward, to the event of its arrival, and to the sobering return to the Solar System and Earth, *Aurora* coalesces in a focused meditation on the capacity and the limits of human viability. Not only are the living environment and everyday reality of the ship's crew restricted to the closed environment and system of the starship, but Robinson's own reflection on human potential, and on the capacities of the sf genre itself, is carried out within the strict limits of the novel's tightly structured thought experiment.

Presented from the point of view of Freya (daughter of Devi, the ship's chief engineer and leader), often in conversation with the ship's AI, we learn the history of how the starship project began as part of humanity's plan to move beyond a ravaged Earth and the terraformed settlements of the Solar System. Unexpectedly, the ship's operations begin to falter, and the social system organized around Devi's authoritarian leadership loses its hold over the increasingly endangered crew. This downward spiral continues when the ship arrives to settle the moon that they've named Aurora, and an indigenous alien life form mortally infects the landing party. After vexed, and even violent, debate back on board, the remaining crew concludes that permanent settlement in their new home is impossible. Negotiating amongst themselves and with the ship's increasingly intelligent AI, two factions emerge, with one choosing to attempt reaching the nearby Mars-like planet Iris with the purpose of trying another settlement, and the other group, led by Freya, opting to return to Earth. On the return voyage, the ship's biomes continue to deteriorate as bacteria flourish and crops fail. Freya and the others soon face famine and experiment with an untested form of cryogenic freezing, which is largely successful in its ability to keep them alive until their return to the Solar System. Once back, the Ship's repeated entreaties to Earth for aid are repeatedly refused because of the general sociopolitical strife and the specific anger that many citizens feel about the colonists' "cowardice" in abandoning the human cosmic dream. Eventually, Freya and her remaining crewmates return to Earth, now facing a struggle to be allowed to settle back in. At a space colonization conference, a speaker repeats the optimistic assertion of the techno-capitalists and declares that humanity will continue to send ships into interstellar space no matter how many fail and die; but Freya stands up and denounces him, indeed assaults him. Eventually, she joins a group of home-based terraformers who are attempting to heal the ravaged planet, and the novel closes with Freya swimming and surfing at one of the beaches the Earthfirsters are working to restore.

At all levels, *Aurora* challenges the techno-optimism of the abstract utopian dream of re-producing human society throughout the cosmos, but it does so as a consummate anti-sf novel that negates the genre's long tradition of self-assured and romantic space travel-colonization tales. Against the arrogance of capitalist logic, with its persistent belief in the viability of scientific-technological solutions (ranging from terraforming, or what Pak terms "planet hacking," to colonizing the stars), Robinson offers this thought experiment that exposes human vulnerability and demands human humility (Pak 2018: 508). From page one, the trajectory of the novel follows the path of the failure of human technology to sustain control of the voyage, of the mission, of life itself. With the collapse of this abstract, hypostatized, project of interstellar settlement, Freya and the remaining others, along with the reader, must face the concrete reality that humanity and Earth (with, at most, its Solar analogues) are inextricably linked within a limited set of possibilities. As part of Earth, part of nature, humanity cannot simply indulge in a wish-dream to transcend its context. In his interview with Canavan, Robinson restates this recognition of ontological limits by refusing the fixed teleological assumption that the Earth is simply a "cradle" to accommodate a human infancy that can then be abandoned by a "mature" humanity that can carry out a technological conquest of all of nature, throughout the cosmos. Against this imperialist sf trope, he reasserts human identity as part of Earth, part of Nature Prime: here quoting John Crowley's description of humanity in *Little Big*: "We are bubbles of Earth! Bubbles of Earth!" (quoted in Canavan and Robinson 2014: 254).

From this humbling speculation that pulls humanity off its techno-capitalist pedestal and gently re-positions us back within nature, Robinson returns to near-future political narratives set on Earth, first in *New York 2140* and then in *Red Moon*. In both novels, he has moved from the previous scale of longer-term figurations of myriad utopian visions to more temporally familiar representational descriptions of possible utopian steps that could be taken to realize a utopian program carved out of the tendencies and latencies of our present condition.[17] In these interrelated, but not sequential, narratives, the immediate destruction of nature brought about by rapid climate change moves from a direct target to a persistent background reality (in the iconic register) that always already informs the political and personal plots that develop as the challenge for human togetherness combines with the work of not only surviving ecological and economic destruction but of carving out a new world in spite of it. The approach taken in both books, therefore, is in keeping with that of Donna Haraway's call that we stay "with the trouble" of our era in a concrete engagement involving critique and radical alternatives, rather than capitulating or passively wishing for some magic solution (Haraway 2016).

In *NY 2140*, rapid climate change brings about the financial and social disasters that fill the pages of the novel. In the periodization of this novel, the intensification of global warming in the late 2050s sped up the polar ice melt, and the consequent flooding produced ocean surges that inundated coastal lands around the world. In the First Pulse of the early 2060s, the ocean rose by over 50 feet and, in the setting of the novel, flooded lower Manhattan, turning it into an apocalyptic Venice wherein canals have replaced streets and skyscrapers stand as islands. The continued melting that led to the Second Pulse of flooding exceeded the damage of Hurricane Katrina by 10,000 times, displaced one-eighth of the world's population, destroyed fishing and aquaculture, which accounted for one-third of humanity's food, and wiped out global trade. The combined effect of this two-stage ecological disaster was the rapid halt of neoliberal domination, the creation of millions of refugees, and the rise of an unregulated police state. At this point in the twenty-first century, humanity admitted that it was facing the end of an era: "Apocalyptic, Armageddonesque, pick your adjective of choice. Anthropogenic could be one. Extinctual another. Anthropogenic mass extinction event, the term most often used. End of an era" (144). No longer threatened, as in the *Science in the Capital* books, the natural and social reality of Earth was terminated.

Unlike right-wing evangelical narratives in which the world comes to the End Time under the punishing hand of an authoritarian deity, Robinson's account has more in common with the processual, yet hopeful, apocalyptic timeline developed by Joachim of Fiore in his apocalyptic theology of the twelfth century. Yes, the current world reality is coming to an end, but this durée of destruction also offers the temporal scope for a possible unfolding of a new era (which in the proto-utopian outcome described by Joachim took the form of a human community of love, guided by the Holy Spirit, that will thrive for centuries before the Final Coming). Robinson's approach of course is thoroughly secular (and like the utopian turn itself it is immersed in history), but it does resonate with the dynamic standpoint of hope in the dark that one discovers in Joachim, Haraway, or Rebecca Solnit's eponymous volume.[18] For within these days of destruction, Robinson explores ways in which humans, at existential and systemic levels, can begin to find initial steps to come together again in a more egalitarian and just society, and indeed one that actively collaborates within Nature Prime.

The plot of *NY2140* develops through a series of threads in which several characters (themselves adding up to a representative selection of the city's residents) find their way through this time of crisis and into the nova of emergent conditions that are more promising than what they previously knew. So it is that two young computer hackers, a New York Police Department detective, a hedge fund manager, a social worker and political activist, a social media superstar and campaigner for animal survival, two Dickensian twelve-year-old orphans, and the super of the Met Life building in which all the protagonists live (in an evocative homage to *334*, Thomas Disch's great novel of life in a New York building in the 1970s) wind their way through the plot, and through the city, and join together in a series of political and personal outcomes that may not have turned the tide on the systemic disasters but do appear to mark the first steps against overcoming their immediate causes in the machinations of the neoliberal behemoth and its power arm of finance capital.

A fuller reading of the novel deserves treatment of each of these characters and their plotlines, but in this review, I will focus on the utopian program that arose out of their collective action. In a reflection late in the text, the anonymous "citizen" (who speaks as the collective voice of the City) wonders why the previously compliant citizens did not slide into a fashionably nihilistic resignation, as they wallowed in the "last efflorescence of civilization" and stopped trying to fix things (377). On the contrary, the food crisis in 2074 brought the reality of "hunger, famine, and death" to everyone's door, and climate change became a lived condition rather than a dark abstraction. Prompted by this grassroots awakening arising from an existential and political bottoming-out, world governments changed their approach to agriculture, land use, and technology and adopted the strategic goal of "rapid decarbonization" (378). This radical shift to alternative forms of energy led to the transformation of transportation, reviving the need for a renewed system of social production and reproduction that not only stopped the disaster in its tracks but began the first utopian steps of saving and surviving with what was left of nature and society. Thus, those who suffered were radicalized and chose to act, those who profited began to be brought to justice, and new social forms of living were created in the ashes and the floodwaters: "after the flooding there was a proliferation of cooperatives, neighborhood associations, communes, squats, barter, alternative currencies, gift economies, solar usufruct, fishing village cultures, mantra gardens, unions, Davy's Locker Freemasonries, anarchist blather, and submarine technoculture, including aeration and aquafarming" (209). Lower Manhattan became a "veritable hotbed of theory and practice," working at all levels from the economic infrastructure to social relations and creating an overall "giant collaborative artwork" (209). And so, a utopian program emerged from the utopian impulse of citizens working together not only to survive but to thrive in a new "carbon negative" society (381), though not doing so without continuing resistance. Of course, not everyone agreed. Battle lines were drawn; consequently, the world Robinson describes is a familiar critical utopian scenario that is partially occupied by the apocalyptic hope of this radical new program even as it is fighting for its very life, and indeed for the life of Nature Prime.

In the discrete register of Robinson's narrative, the Met Life protagonists each contribute to this provisional series of steps on the way to a better world. Social worker Charlotte becomes a leader in the organizing campaign for the Householders Union that then led the debt strike wherein ordinary people defaulted on their bank loans, brought the banks to their knees, and forced the nationalization of the banks, with a concomitant change in principles of borrowing and lending based on need rather than profit. From that victory, she successfully runs for Congress and becomes a leader in the national and international progressive movement (uncannily anticipating the 2019 political success of the Democratic Socialist representative from Brooklyn, Alexandra Ocasio-Cortez). Franklin, the self-satisfied hedge fund manager, becomes radicalized through the needs of his fellow building residents and turns his financial knowledge into an oppositional practice of reinvestment that acquires devalued land and housing and makes it available for social rather than investment needs. Amelia, the cloud-based artist, not only leads a successful campaign to save polar bears (in the most direct collaboration with nature in the novel) but also works with her fellow residents in the campaigns carried out by Charlotte and Franklin. The hackers Mutt and Jeff, the orphans Stefan and Roberto, and the wise and canny building supervisor Vlade, each play their role in this spontaneous uprising of city residents who play their role in the overall social revolution that occurs. The Met Life group therefore stands as both a core category of agents and a synecdoche for the entire grassroots revolution taking place in the City.

Fully immersed in the activities of humanity as it fights for its own survival, *NY 2140* consistently brings that human struggle back into the larger perspective of the needs of Nature Prime, and humanity's place within it. Considering his body of work to date, this novel is one of Robinson's most optimistic; for its dénouement includes a victory for both humanity and nature. As the citizen puts it a final entry: "That said, people in this era did do it. Individuals make history, but it's also a collective thing, a wave that people ride in their time, a wave made of individual actions. So ultimately history is another particle/wave duality that no one can pass or understand" (603). However, that human/historical achievement is immediately placed in a larger context in the next paragraph as nature itself is brought into the picture:

> Individuals, groups, civilization, and the planet itself all did these things, in actor networks of all kinds. Remember not to forget, if your head has not already

exploded, the nonhuman actors in these actor networks. Possibly the New York estuary was the prime actor in all that has been told here, or maybe it was bacterial communities, expressing themselves through their own civilizations, what we might call bodies. (603)

Here, Robinson overtly affiliates with the overwhelming force and direction of Nature Prime. Yet, as he does so he admonishes his readers in the last lines of the novel not to be satisfied with this apparently happy ending; for the work is not yet done: "because down there in Antarctica— or in other realms of being far more dangerous— the next buttress of the buttress could go at any time" (604).

Robinson followed *New York 2140* with *Red Moon*. Set a mere thirty years in the future, the novel moves from the iconic text of a flooded metropolis to that of the moon. Rather than being colonized by utopian pilgrims or eco-warriors, the moon has been occupied by the exploitive agents of state interests from around the Earth. However, it is the superpower of China that dominates the occupation, with the other countries (themselves dominated by the counter-power of the United States) relegated to the south polar cap. Again, Robinson foregrounds human political struggle, but the continuing ecological disaster on Earth provides the ground of crisis for all that develops. The larger scope of the plot revolves around a power struggle among the Chinese for leadership of the nation, a struggle played out on Earth and on the Moon. The personal focal point for that plot is Chan Qi, the dissident daughter of one of the leaders in the Chinese Communist Party, and Fred Fredericks, a US quantum communications expert working with China's Lunar Science Foundation who gets caught up in the national and international struggles. Mediating this macro-/micro-dynamic is Ta Shu (the internationally recognized cloud-based travel reporter/poet who first appeared in *Antarctica*).

For the purposes of this overview, I want simply to summarize the threads of Robinson's metatextual utopian program as it runs through the novel along with the indicators of the global destruction of nature, partly exhibited by the description of that destruction and partly by the steps taken, especially by the Chinese government, to rectify the situation. Two utopian strands come together in the author's provisional resolution. The first lies within the Chinese public sphere, as the popular revolution of the millions of dispossessed and disenfranchised Chinese people comes together in an alliance with a progressive leadership that emerges in the power struggle for the next general secretary of the Central Committee of the Communist Party of China (CPC). Qi uses her aristocratic position, and relative freedom, in her leadership role with grassroots

activists, to demand democracy and justice, in the nation and in the Party itself;
while Ta Shu's friend Peng Ling, the most progressive of the candidates for
General Secretary, succeeds in winning the appointment and thereby gaining
the power to grant the demanded reforms. With this united front—informed
by the political wisdom of Confucius, Mao Zedong, and the progressive wing
of the current CPC—strong steps are taken toward forging an uncompromised
socialism with Chinese characteristics (364). The second strand lies in the realm
of the second global superpower, the United States, wherein the "citizens fiscal
revolution" (first presented in *NY 2140*) organized by the Householder Union
had succeeded in delivering a serious blow to the finance and power system:
"markets had crashed, banks had closed to stop depositors from withdrawing
amounts beyond what the banks had on hand, and now most of the biggest
ones were giving themselves over to control by the Federal Reserve to make
them eligible for government bailout" (362). Building on this victory, the US
movement goes on to articulate their utopian demands: "universal basic income,
guaranteed healthcare, free education, and the right to work, all supported by
progressive taxation on both income and capital assets" (432).

The convergence of the two revolutionary movements within the core of
the two superpowers (themselves forming a G2 unit) therefore produces a
geopolitical breakpoint in which the overarching system of global capitalism,
operating by means of distinct national characteristics, is severely shaken. In
this "global peoples revolt," citizens on the streets of Washington DC and Beijing
produced human waves of opposition that broke the existing balance of power
and produced progressive power shifts in both countries even as new leaders took
the beginning steps toward reforms that would vibrate outward in a progressive
call for global governance (410): out of this global "sorting out," in Qi's utopian
phrase, "a better order will come into being" (433). This revolutionary surge on
Earth is replicated on the Moon as the local national powers recognize the new
order back on Earth and as the long-term lunar residents of the "free craters"
continue to consolidate their growing sphere of independence, thus paving the
way for future struggles for democracy and justice on the Moon (see 247, 398).

Again, while not foregrounded in these political struggles, the fight to save the
planet itself is at the core of the global movement, and is particularly pronounced
in China. In summing up the Six Demands that articulate the goals of the
Chinese grassroots revolution, the AI who has increasingly affiliated with the
revolutionary forces makes clear that the imbrication of humanity and nature is
at the core of the utopian program: "What do the people want? The Six Demands
articulate those wants, which in quite a few cases come down to this: they want

what they need. Which is to say many of their desires are basic needs in the Maslovian hierarchy of needs and wants, and therefore nothing can proceed in a successful human history until these needs are met. Food, water, shelter, clothing, healthcare, education: these all need to be adequate for everyone alive before anything else good can happen": but then the AI significantly adds that the "interpenetration of people and planet being so complete as to be determinative of every living thing's shared fate, meeting basic needs for all the living creatures and the shared biosphere is also required to secure the general health and welfare of humanity and its fellow creatures" (405). Here then, Robinson's revolutionary voice becomes the voice of Nature Prime.

At this point, another, ontological, evocation of Nature Prime is brought forth through the voice of Robinson's resident artist. Ta Shu describes his own core practice of feng shui (the art of creating good energy flow by producing harmonizing balance in individuals, society, and the world) as "ecology in action" (126). Looked at in this manner, feng shui emerges as the most radical, utopian, human contribution (located in the larger context of the social revolution) to the ongoing healing and regeneration work of nature itself (see 126). Here then, it seems most appropriate to conclude Robinson's contribution in this work with lines from the eighth-century poet Wang Wei's adaptation of the popular Chinese Peach Blossom Stream poem:

These people were peaceful, calm kind.
The valley was fertile and full of animals.
We stayed until we saw what it was: a good place.
To live here would be fulfilment.
So we said to each other, let's get our families
And bring them back here. Let's move here. (344)

One work remains in this review of Robinson's engagement with our planetary crises and what needs to be done to counter them. In *Shaman*, the author gives us the most radical expression of his ecological/utopian ontology, thereby providing readers with the deep paradigm for his overall political trajectory. The novel tells the tale of humans living close to the Chauvet cave in what is now southern France, about 30,000 years ago, during an ice age. It follows the lives of four members of the Neolithic Wolf Clan: Thorn, the shaman, who teaches those who would follow in his footsteps; Heather, the healer, who holds the clan together; Elga, the outsider and the bringer of change; and the protagonist, Loon, the next shaman, who is searching for his own way in a treacherous and complex world. The plot turns around the coming together of Loon and

Elga, her abduction by a northern tribe, Loon's efforts to rescue her, and the pair's successful escape aided by Thorn and Click, one of the clan elders. At the funeral ritual for Click, Thorn and Loon negotiate a peace settlement with the Northerners. After Thorn's death, because of the early ecological pressure of growing numbers and the strain on the carrying capacity of their territory, the clan decides to split into two; and Loon, now reunited with Elga and their two children, becomes the shaman for both groups. The narrative draws to a close as Loon deepens his relationship with the natural world of which he is a part by way of his painting of horses in the depths of the Chauvet cave and his teaching of his practice to his son, Lucky.

Robinson develops this fable of wandering and wisdom with a mixture of third-person narrative from the point of view of humans and shorter entries from the point of view of others who inhabit Loon's world (the non-human cat and wolverine and an "old one," a Neanderthal). Faithful to the culture of the period, his text is built around forms of storytelling and song, legend and myth. As such, *Shaman* stands out as a formal break from the intricate plot lines of his political narratives, offering us a minimalist tale of personal and social fulfillment set within the iconic fabric of nature that affirms the reality within which all of Robinson's fiction can be situated: namely, Nature Prime, within which humanity grows and contributes as self-conscious agents in that totality.

As Michael Gaffney points out, the underlying creative mechanism that infuses this prehistoric narrative is a "geohistorical imagination" that recognizes not only the primary existence of the nonhuman world but also the historical dynamic that has driven the unfolding of Nature Prime from the beginning of life on Earth to this vexed moment within which we all live (Gaffney 2018: 475). As opposed to the "environmental imagination" that "records the ecosystem," the more dynamic geohistorical imagination enables a human engagement with nature that recognizes its evolution through time, thus making possible human analyses of the stresses and strains produced at particular moments that can lead to a better understanding of how humans have contributed to the situation and how we might responsibly respond as agents within that process (475–6). *Shaman* therefore is an expression of the deep history of the dialectic of Nature-Human-Nature Prime that stresses the "continuity between prehistoric and contemporary humans" (473). Through its long view, Robinson's novel allows us to, as Gaffney puts it, "consider the similarities between the human experience of the ice age and our contemporary encounter with global warming" so as to better understand that we have "always been operating" within this geological history, always responding to "climate transformations" (478). While this ontological perspective allows Robinson to grasp the wider context of our immediate crises and challenges (and to appreciate and respond to the climate fiction that focuses specifically on this present moment), it also takes us beyond the strict confines of our moment and situates us in a more humble position in Earth's overall history as, on one hand, we grasp the relative insignificance of our own (human) place in that history; while, on the other, we also soberly appreciate the contributions we can still make, even as the current crisis transforms and unfolds into a new moment in the history of nature and humankind. Here, then, I come full circle in my discussion, as I return to restating the utopian resonance between Bloch's meta-historical evocation of a supernature that exceeds the human project and Robinson's own ontological paradigm of an all-encompassing Nature Prime, in both its larger ontological sense and its formative role in his exploration of humanity's own efforts to come to terms with the complex relationship of the utopian impulse and this utopian program.

As can be seen throughout his entire body of work, Robinson's sustained meditation on the totalizing utopian impulse of Nature Prime can be read in light of the committed fieldwork and writing of the natural historian, Aldo Leopold, whose *Sand County Almanac*, first published in 1949, was one of the breakthrough works in the new ecological consciousness of the years following the Second World War. In particular, Leopold's articulation of what he termed the "Land Ethic" (1966: 237–64) enlarged our understanding of "community" to include "soils, waters, plants, and animals, or collectively: the land"; consequently, he rejected the alienation of nature that reduced it to the status of either an economic commodity or a religious object to be used or stewarded by a dominant human subject (239). In Leopold's Land Ethic, we encounter a utopian manifesto that is in accord with Robinson's vision of a transformed nature— one that is not simply a matter of an instrumental (be it economic or religious) relationship between humanity and land but rather a sublation of both that resolves into a revolutionary humanity and a liberated land that are part of the larger realm of nature, of supernature, of Nature Prime (N').[19] Like Le Guin's lean, desert environment on Anarres, in his California desert and the so-called dead planet of Mars, Robinson first explored a stripped-down relationship between humanity and the land, one that offered what Jameson has called "a blank slate" that makes possible a radical investigation of the most basic elements in the relationship between utopian process and enclosing instrumentality of present reality. Contrary to their apparent lifelessness, both the high desert and the Martian terrain are vital parts of the natural realm, each with an evolutionary right to exist. These locales—supplemented by the ice continent in Antarctica, the rescued Earth in the *Science in the Capital Trilogy,* and on a much larger scale in the sentient gas giant planets of *Galileo's Dream*—are central, indeed formative, in Robinson's vision and not merely backdrops to a self-interested human story. In each of these works, nature is liberated and celebrated, relative to the conditions of its fictive time.

While it may appear to some readers that Robinson's political narratives often sail close to the standpoint of the Western anthropomorphic domination of an external nature, I argue that his political programs not only stimulate immediate contestation but also, textually and intertextually, pull readers forward with their radical utopian impulse toward a horizon of a holistically better world reality. Writing with the refunctioned specters of Engels and Lenin on one shoulder and Thoreau and Leopold on the other (and perhaps with the first scientist Galileo hovering in between), in both his representational and figurative modes, Robinson reconfigures humanity's stance as one of engaged solidarity *within* and *with* the body of a transformed nature. It is this radical novum coalesced into the overarching reality of Nature Prime that feeds back into and radicalizes the most pragmatic of his political possibilities, even as the break figured by the more poetic impulse is itself made palpable by those immediate maneuvers.[20]

VI

What is at stake in the current moment is not simply a catastrophic (ecological and socioeconomic) breakdown to be addressed by specialists, experts, and leaders. That needs to be done, but this pressing job of work falls to each of us: we all need to see the world differently and then to join in the process of a collective utopian transformation of that world. If we accept that we cannot escape into some primal paleolithic innocence and further admit that the roles of stewardship *over* nature or even partnership *with* nature are neither sufficient nor appropriate, then we need to come to terms with our place *in* and *of* nature, and act accordingly. As a critical and scientific visionary, Robinson (as does Galileo in his eponymous novel) enables us to develop a new habit of mind so we can leave our hegemonic humanity behind and act, with awareness and responsibility, with compassion and cooperation, as part of a healed and revived nature (2009: 35). Robinson's utopian standpoint of the "future primitive" invites us to "cobble together aspects of the postmodern and the paleolithic" so that, as part and parcel of the nature that far surpasses us now and into the deep future, we can, in our time, live lightly on the Earth while we make the best use of the tools of our civilization (including science and the state, philosophy and spirituality) to ensure that we move ahead in a spirit of justice, equality and solidarity with the rest of nature (1997b: 11). As a utopian comrade (who also invokes the radical practice of science fictionality but does so by pulling it through both poetry and science), Haraway echoes Robinson's call to action: she reminds us that we need to work from where we find ourselves, not only to "stir up potent response to devastating events" but to "settle troubled waters and rebuild quiet places …. to address trouble in terms of making an imagined future safe, of stopping something from happening that looms in the future, of clearing away the present in the past in order to make futures for coming generations," and doing so as "moral critters intertwined in myriad unfinished configurations of places, times, matters, meanings" (Haraway 1).

I will close, first, with lines from Robinson's poem, "Canyon Color," that capture his sense of nature transformed, Nature Prime:

> There, on a wet red beach —
> Green moss, green sedge. Green.
> Not nature, not culture: just Mars. (1999: 364)

And then with the first and third stanzas of Gary Snyder's "Tomorrow's Song" (the first entry in Robinson's *Future Primitive* anthology), in which the poet abandons the American dream and embraces a radically transformed future. Still powerful lines, even if his timing was a bit optimistic:

> The USA slowly lost its mandate
> in the middle and later twentieth century
> it never gave the mountains and rivers,
> trees and animals,
> a vote.
> all the people turned away from it
> myths die; even continents are impermanent
>
> …
>
> We look to the future with pleasure
> We need no fossil fuel
> Get power within
> Grow strong on less. (Snyder 1974: 77)

7

On the Utopian Standpoint
of Nonviolence

I

I begin with a poem published by E.E. Cummings in 1931: "I sing of Olaf".[1] It grew out of his service in the US Army in the First World War. Having already seen a fellow recruit abused for refusing to fight during training camp in Massachusetts, while serving on the French front Cummings learned of another soldier heard speaking against the war by his commanding officer, who then oversaw his torture by fellow soldiers and ordered his imprisonment (which for many objectors ended in death). Throughout, the soldier continued to condemn the war and asserted that he would never surrender his principles:

> i sing of Olaf glad and big
> whose warmest heart recoiled at war:
> a conscientious object-or
> his wellbelovéd colonel (trig
> westpointer most succinctly bred)
> took erring Olaf soon in hand;
> but—though an host of overjoyed
> noncoms (first knocking on the head
> him) do through icy waters roll
> that helplessness which others stroke
> with brushes recently employed
> anent this muddy toiletbowl,
> while kindred intellects evoke
> allegiance per blunt instruments—
> Olaf (being to all intents
> a corpse and wanting any rag

upon what God unto him gave)
responds, without getting annoyed
"I will not kiss your fucking flag"
straightway the silver bird looked grave
(departing hurriedly to shave)
but—though all kinds of officers
(a yearning nation's blueeyed pride)
their passive prey did kick and curse
until for wear their clarion
voices and boots were much the worse,
and egged the firstclassprivates on
his rectum wickedly to tease
by means of skilfully applied
bayonets roasted hot with heat—
Olaf (upon what were once knees)
does almost ceaselessly repeat
"there is some shit I will not eat"
our president, being of which
assertions duly notified
threw the yellowsonofabitch
into a dungeon, where he died
Christ (of His mercy infinite)
i pray to see; and Olaf, too
preponderatingly because
unless statistics lie he was
more brave than me: more blond than you.[2]

When I first read of Olaf during my civil rights and anti-war work in the mid-1960s, I saw him as an exemplar of nonviolence.[3] Now, I also recognize him as a utopian subject, one who reached for a better horizon by way of nonviolent resistance, one whose resistance was strengthened and deepened by his aspirations. I will return to the specific American lineage of nonviolence of which this poem is an eloquent part, but first I want to do some binary housecleaning.

I am not conflating utopia with nonviolence or anti-utopia with violence. Nor am I equating nonviolence with a quietest passivity. Too often, those who seek to discredit utopia or nonviolence devalue them as idle dreaming or non-action. Rather than a gesture of standing aside, nonviolence is a self-conscious political force exercised in order radically (the adverb matters) to persuade (with varying degrees of intensity) all parties in a conflict to transform the conditions that are harmful to humans, animals, and environment. Nor am I simply opposing nonviolence and violence. As the social history of nonviolent practice shows, we are not talking here about a polarity but, rather, a field of play. In political movements and in the literary tradition, both violence and nonviolence have been deployed in the service of progressive change (as seen, for example, in the abolition and racial liberation movements in the United States or the freedom movement in South Africa and in the pages of William Morris's *News from Nowhere* or critical utopias such as Ursula K. Le Guin's *The Dispossessed* and Marge Piercy's *Woman on the Edge of Time*). And so I want to highlight the initial negative prefix and then the root of this word: in this light, nonviolence can be seen as a critical engagement with violence, be it dominant and normative or oppositional and revolutionary. While I usually do not draw on a deconstructive problematic, I suggest that nonviolence can be seen as an erasure of violence—or, in theological terms, as a redemption of violence.

At this point, it will be useful to review the basics of nonviolence: whether it proceeds as principled strategy or as contingent tactic, whether it takes the form of direct confrontation or negotiated conflict resolution. Explaining its classic form, the Gandhian philosopher Richard Gregg speaks of how the activist "does not respond to the attacker's violence with counterviolence. Instead ... he states his readiness to prove his sincerity by his own suffering rather than by inflicting suffering on the assailant" (Gregg 1966: 43–4). Gregg describes this exercise of *satyagraha* (holding to truth) as a form of "moral jujitsu" in which a violent attack is redirected by the nonviolent activist, who "not only lets the attacker come, but, as it were, pulls him forward by kindness ... and voluntary suffering, so that the attacker loses his moral balance" (44). This basic standpoint (be it individual or collective) can, then, be expressed as a form of witness, intervention, or a way of life.

Nonviolent witness (in the form of a public affiliation with peace and justice that moves beyond protest and invites others to see the world differently and engage in its transformation in a peaceful manner) includes acts of speaking out or testifying against a social evil in the name of a transformative alternative. These range from speechmaking, letter writing, petitioning, and online campaigns to public demonstrations, picket lines, and marches, as well as unarmed accompaniment or observation in conflict zones. Acting within the legal and cultural norms of society, nonviolent witness "speaks truth to power," as the Quakers put it. Nonviolent intervention moves up a gear with acts that break through business as usual to realize the above-mentioned consciousness of injustice and its alternative. This mode of "marching to the beat of a different drum," as Henry David Thoreau put it, can range from civil disobedience within a legal system to revolutionary actions outside or against that system. These can include non-cooperation (as in the refusal to obey unjust laws or customs, refusal to pay taxes, refusal of conscription or military orders, or refusal to obey prison rules); boycotts of products, goods, and behavior; withdrawal of services (private or public); proscribed marches; sit-ins, blockades, occupations, and other trespasses; personal sacrifices, from prison terms to hunger strikes to self-immolation; sabotage to property; and, more recently, the unauthorized release of electronic information.[4]

Shifting from activism to spatiopolitics, nonviolence can also inform a chosen way of life for members of a community as it brings the expectation of compassionate care to all levels of human relations as well as relations with animals and nature. Mulford Q. Sibley describes a nonviolent society as one that is democratic and egalitarian at all levels, "in which social and political organizations are not used to manipulate for ... glory and gain ... in which conflict ... takes place without resort to violence" (1963: 359–60). In short, the nonviolent way of life asks people to live "as if " (in Hans Vaihinger's phrase) a peaceful world already existed (quoted in Sargent 1994: 23). Again, many readers will know of intentional communities and cooperatives based on nonviolent principles, but here I want to note that political movements have also, at times, achieved a nonviolent way of life: as in the solidarity of workers, the sisterhood of feminists, the "beloved community" of the civil rights movement, or the support networks of draft resisters or eco-activists. Here, I would also include what Hakim Bey has identified as "temporary autonomous zones" such as Greenham Common and the Shannon Peace Park; sanctuaries for battered women and men and for economic and political refugees; cultural festivals such as the Michigan Womyn's Music Festival and the Rainbow Gathering; the self-organization of building, forest, and university occupations; and the assemblies of the Occupy movement and those in the public squares of Madrid, Tunis, Cairo, and elsewhere.[5]

II

Let me now turn to the utopian problematic and look at nonviolence by way of Ruth Levitas's discussion of utopian method: with its archaeological analysis of the contradictions and possibilities in the present situation; its architectural re-visioning that articulates the terms of a transformed society; and its ontological construction of transforming subjects, which, in her words, "entails ... imagining ourselves otherwise and a judgment about what constitutes human flourishing" (2013: 177). In terms of this utopian process, a nonviolent movement can effectuate a transformation from a condition of social harm toward one of peace and justice. This first involves an assessment of the present that judges it to be unacceptable—as in its economic injustice, its lack of freedom, its structural and existential violence, its machinery of war and destruction, or its environmental toxicity—but in that critique, the movement uncovers tendencies available for transformative change. From this, the movement articulates, to a greater or lesser degree, a forward-pulling vision that in almost all our criteria would be regarded as utopian: as in a land of justice and equality, of harmony and nonviolent conflict resolution, or of ecological good behavior in the coevolution of humanity and nature.

In the context of *Becoming Utopian*, however, it is Levitas's ontological mode that has the greatest bearing on my reflections. For this utopian production of our present and potential humanity can be discovered, I believe, in the dynamics of subject formation by which an alienated and angry person becomes a nonviolent activist who usually works collectively with others. This, to me, is an example of how the utopian education of desire can work, as activists literally embody a vision, and a praxis, of a better world as they acquire the anticipatory knowledge and tactical capability to withstand the infliction of pain and the temptation of cooptation. Implicitly present in principled nonviolence and explicitly latent in the exercise of nonviolent tactics, with their powerful interplay of vulnerability and resilience, this new subjectivity acquires the grace and dignity that Levitas ascribes to the existential condition of the utopian subject. In this process, which resembles but is more dialogical than that found in hierarchical monastic or cadre formation, nonviolent activists live and act within the framework of a radically alternative world that implicitly negates and aims to transform the present in which they live. In so doing, they work within what I would call a utopian time slip as they occupy a standpoint that is Not Yet in the now here: as they speak, in a revision of Robert Heinlein's words, as strangers in a familiar land; as they, in Lyman Tower Sargent's words, "choose" utopia and act with a utopian "energy" (Sargent 2007: 306).

In movements based on nonviolent principles, activists exhibit this agency in its strongest form; but it is important to note that even in political movements that do not follow such principles, those committed to nonviolence can bring this education of desire to the politics of the larger movement, as they engage in a Freirean pedagogy with their comrades that is implicitly transformative. In challenging oppositional violence and exemplifying alternative nonviolent maneuvers, they function as a strategic or at least a tactical vanguard, as a utopian sensei or even a utopian "commissar" whose methods are dialogical and not centralist (unlike the political commissar, who served a very different role in Red Army formations). To put it in Fredric Jameson's terms, the practice of nonviolence can bring a strong, and crucially negative, utopian impulse to bear on contingent political programs in order to halt or temper their decline into either reformist strategies or violent adventurism so as to preserve or retrieve their more radical utopian charge.

III

For the rest of this chapter, I will focus on nonviolent subjectivity and practice in the United States—in a strong lineage in its own right but also the one that was personally formative for me. Despite the dominant identity of the United States as an imperialist superpower driven by a military-industrial complex that carries out official violence, from nuclear bombs, to "police actions," to drone strikes and illegal renditions, there has always been a counterhegemonic stream of oppositional politics that invokes the utopian promise of justice, equality, and freedom—and nonviolent activism has been a strong current in that stream from the seventeenth century to the present. The roots of nonviolence in America can be found in the Christian pacifism and democratic tendencies of the radical Reformation (although nonviolent practices were also present in Native American culture). Once settled in America, Quakers such as William Penn and John Woolman engaged in both witness and intervention in their efforts to attain religious freedom and stop the exploitation of Native Americans and the practice of slavery. Later, the Quaker commitment to nonviolence (based in their theological distinction between personal witness and institution building as opposed to coercive rebellion) led to their opposition to what was taken to be the legitimate violence required to overthrow British rule—thus beginning a debate between oppositional nonviolence and violence that was to recur again and again.[6]

As the nineteenth-century abolition campaign intensified, individuals and groups such as the New England Non-resistance Society held firm to nonviolence as the preferred means to end slavery. Speeches and petitions segued into blockades of segregated railways, refusal of taxes, and the aiding and abetting of fugitive slaves. Eventually, however, *counterviolence* became a key element in abolitionist strategy, especially after the Fugitive Slave Law of 1850. This shift is exemplified in the position taken by the abolitionist leader Frederick Douglass, who until 1849 stood firmly in the camp of nonviolent resistance, when he declared that he would welcome a slave insurrection in the South, noting that the peaceful annihilation of slavery was hopeless. Feeding this debate, in 1849, Henry David Thoreau's "Essay on Civil Disobedience" had already eroded the distinction between witness and rebellion and connected the opposing strands in American radicalism in his synthesis of the Christian anarchist advocacy of nonviolent resistance with the oppositional mainstream embrace of radical republican individualism and Jacobin revolution. Implicitly utopian, Thoreau believed in the possibility of a just state: he asked for "not at once no government, but at once a better government," but he also recognized the right of revolution against an unjust state, and here his emphasis was not on witness but on intervention (1981: 90). As an example, he recounts his opposition to slavery, expressed in his refusal to pay the Massachusetts poll tax and his consequent incarceration. But while he advocated noncooperation as the best means to "refuse allegiance to, and to resist, the government, when its tyranny ... [is] great and unendurable," he held that, when such action was insufficient, violence would be necessary—a conclusion exemplified in his support of John Brown's raid at Harper's Ferry (92). While his advocacy of noncooperation is the primary message that comes down to us, it is important to note his acceptance of counterviolence and to recall that Gandhi, who valued this essay, also held that violent resistance was better than none at all if nonviolent options were not viable.

After the Civil War, nonviolent action continued in the labor, suffrage, and peace movements. Less governed by nonviolent principles, the labor movement did, however, adopt the tactic of the strike (an action that is implicitly nonviolent); and the activists of the suffrage movement moved from witness to intervention as they escalated from petitions and marches to illegal confrontations and imprisonment, followed by the refusal of prison work and the choice of some to go on hunger strikes (drawing on its legitimation in ancient Irish law and its use by Irish and Russian political prisoners). As well, the late nineteenth-century industrialization and intensification of military capability and war, now directly impacting on civilian populations, prompted the growth of a modern peace movement, moving from groups such as the Universal Peace Union, begun just after the American Revolution, to the Women's International League for Peace and Freedom, organized in 1915. At the end of the nineteenth century, secular anarchists embraced what in the 1960s came to be known as revolutionary nonviolence as they campaigned for a utopian society that would function without the need of an aggressive state. Against those who opted for bombs and assassinations, many held to the superiority of nonviolent means. While initially committed to the violence required by the propaganda of the deed, for example, Emma Goldman eventually declared in favor of the nonviolence of Gandhi and Tolstoy. Recognizing the necessity for "integrity, self-reliance, and courage" in the nonviolent activist, she called for collective nonviolent direct action in the "defiance of, and resistance to, all laws and restrictions, economic, social, and moral" (2012: 18). Observing its successful use in the antislavery and suffrage movements, she argued that "revolutionary, economic action" (ultimately in the form of the nonviolent general strike) was required in the "battle for industrial liberty" (19). In 1910, William James published a pamphlet for the American Association for International Conciliation that deepened the discourse on nonviolence. Like Thoreau's work, James's essay spoke to its time, but it has also informed the self-understanding of nonviolent practice ever since, influencing individual activists as well as organizations such as the American Friends Service Committee, the Civilian Conservation Corps, and the Peace Corps. James' primary argument in "The Moral Equivalent of War" is that pacifists will never succeed by merely witnessing against war (see 2011). Instead, their task must be to bring a nonviolent energy into the creation of new social forms that replace war. In this productive utopian agenda, he explicitly called for the transformation of the positive elements of warlike impulses into values and practices capable of building a peaceful and just world, and he implicitly challenged individual activists to take on a personal risk comparable to that of military service. Thus, James urged pacifists not to opt out of the society producing war but, rather, to opt in and transform its warlike culture.

In the years following James' essay, anti-war practice intensified in the institutional form of opposition to the machinery of modern war and in the personal form of conscientious objection (as figured, for example, in Cummings's invocation of Olaf). After the war, nonviolence played a key role in the anti-segregation and labor movements of the 1930s, as seen in deliberate violations of segregation laws in the rural South and strikes and occupations in the industrial North. When the fight against fascism was added to these struggles for economic and racial justice, the familiar debate developed within the broad opposition. While many (including pacifists) argued that a war was necessary to defeat fascism, a small but committed number opposed fascism but advocated nonviolent resistance as the proper response. Drawing on the utopian surplus of the American nonviolent tradition—and informed by radical Christianity, Marxism, and Gandhian thought—a multiracial array of activists held firm to their position throughout the war years. Acting in the spirit of Thoreau's noncooperation and James' calculus of risk, those among them who were eligible for military service refused conscription and alternative service, stood trial without defense, and served prison terms— deliberately declaring the terms and conditions of a better world and taking on the suffering that is called for in nonviolent action. Breaking the temporal if not the spatial boundaries of prison, they acted from this utopian standpoint as they opposed wretched conditions in general and segregated facilities in particular by way of work and hunger strikes as well as education and political organizing with their fellow prisoners.

After the war, the seasoned members of this remnant (such as James Farmer, A. J. Muste, Dorothy Day, Bayard Rustin, David Dellinger, and Barbara Deming) emerged as leaders, and teachers, in the movements against segregation and nuclear war in the 1940s and 1950s and in the civil rights, racial liberation, and anti-war/anti-imperialist movements of the 1960s and 1970s. In their actions, they began with expressions of witness but often stepped up to direct interventions, while their values led them to embrace nonviolent principles in all areas of their lives. Leaders such as these helped to articulate a new political culture in which individual resistance led into a collective movement that aimed to be nonhierarchical, decentralized, and oriented toward consensus decision-making. As James's call for a new society and a new subjectivity in 1910 challenged the economic machinery and consumer subjectivity of Fordism, so too did these utopian activists reject the mechanisms of the post–Second World War postfordist economy, with its disciplined subject construction of docile consumers and loyal citizens that eviscerated people's creative and critical capacities. Drawing on the utopian surplus embedded in the figure of the *radical*, they demonstrated the existential capability of each person to act in a free and responsible manner. In so doing, they exemplified an empowered utopian subjectivity that rejected alienation and exploitation through a radical politics of choice that cut through the sutured reality produced by postwar American hegemony rather than settling for the options available in the society as it stood.[7]

As the nonviolent activism of this bridging generation segued into the expansion of nonviolent practice in the civil rights and anti-war/anti-draft movements of the 1960s, the intensification of those struggles (countering the persistence of institutional racism, economic exploitation, and the ongoing war as well as the increasing state suppression of dissent) brought the strategy and tactics of nonviolence to another level. For the rest of this chapter, then, I will focus on three figures who, in the face of these conditions, articulated a more overt stance of revolutionary nonviolence as they directly engaged with those in the larger movements: Bayard Rustin and David Dellinger, who were part of the 1940s generation, and Daniel Berrigan, who became active by the late 1950s. As did the anarchists at the beginning of the century, each in their own way worked from an understanding of nonviolence as an exercise of force that aims radically to transform society as it stands and take it toward the horizon of a better world: once more, nonviolence involved a disruptive and creative action that went beyond the passive stance usually attributed to it.

A communist and a Quaker who early on embraced Gandhian pacifism, Bayard Rustin engaged in anti-segregation direct action before the war and in labor and hunger strikes in prison after his conviction for refusing military service. When the war ended, he played a key role in training new activists in the civil rights and anti-bomb/anti-war movements in the use of nonviolent direct action. A close adviser to Martin Luther King, he was among the more radical architects of the 1963 March for Jobs and Freedom in Washington DC, the occasion of King's "I Have a Dream" speech. What is most striking about Rustin is his commitment to a practice that he regarded as revolutionary right from his early years, as (in the spirit of the 1930s Popular Front) he worked not for piecemeal reforms but, rather, to realize a transformed American society based on freedom, peace, and socialism. Writing to the cautious members of the Fellowship of Reconciliation in 1964, he argued that the fight against segregation had to be deepened to challenge the basic assumptions and institutions of this entire society. In what I would describe as a utopian project for a totalizing transformation that would dismantle capitalism and racism, he worked to reconcile the southern civil rights movement with the northern black liberation movement. While still arguing for the strategic superiority of nonviolence, following Thoreau and Gandhi he declared that

> while we resist and hate violence, we are able to understand how much a man can take and therefore any Negro who resorts to violence will get our moral support, financial support and support in the courts, because it is wrong to turn one's back on people who have been so demoralized and trampled on that they literally have no choice except to fight back.[8]

And, in another article in the *War Resisters League News*, entitled "The Harlem Riot and Nonviolence," he described the way in which Congress of Racial Equality activists worked throughout the four nights of the 1964 riot to temper the angry response with acts of solidarity rather than condemn the mass anger.[9]

Like the others, from the beginning of his activism in the early 1940s, David Dellinger drew on a matrix of radical Christianity, Marxism, and Gandhian nonviolence—although his particular theological base was in the Christian Realism articulated by Reinhold Niebuhr in his earlier work. Active in anti-racist, anti-fascist, and anti-war politics, Dellinger refused conscription in 1941 and was imprisoned along with fellow students of New York's Union Theological Seminary. In prison, he and the others of the "Union Eight" engaged in work and hunger strikes against segregation, while they continued to speak against war and fascism. After the war, he worked for the Peacemakers and the Committee for Nonviolent Action and was one of the founders of the Left magazine *Liberation* and the Pacifica community radio network. He was active in movements against the bomb, for racial liberation, in support of Cuba, and against the Vietnam War and the draft. After A. J. Muste and Dorothy Day brokered the agreement for a broad-based anti-Vietnam War coalition, Dellinger became one of the leaders of that alliance, known as the Mobilization Committee to End the War in Vietnam, and helped to organize actions across the country, especially those in Washington DC in 1967 and Chicago in 1968.

By the later 1960s, the larger movement took on a more revolutionary tenor as the war went on and as the government and its allies struck back (and here it is important to remember the suspicious assassinations of Martin Luther King and Malcolm X and the overt FBI COINTELPRO violence targeted against groups such as the Black Panthers and the Weathermen, as well as the Catholic Left). In turn, the movement was weakened from the inside by sectarian splits as well as by what Dellinger and others saw as the undisciplined lashing out of younger activists.[10] Nevertheless, whereas Rustin's response in the later 1960s led him to work with the liberal center, Dellinger reached out to the radical Left of the Black Panthers, the Youth International Party (Yippies), the Weathermen, and others. Acknowledging that this latest political surge was less informed by the principles and discipline of nonviolence, he strove to restore its integrity by famously urging a "creative synthesis of Gandhi and guerrilla" that could stand up to external repression and internal indiscipline (1967: 5). He therefore worked within the broad Left to escalate a politics of confrontation, and he chided traditional pacifists for their timidity in not participating in the mobilizations, arguing that their experience could contribute a needed discipline and vision. In 1969, Dellinger's networking role became evident when the "leaders" of the 1968 Chicago demonstrations were convicted of conspiracy: once part of the Union Eight, Dellinger was now one of the Chicago Seven, who also included Tom Hayden of the Students for a Democratic Society, Abbie Hoffman and Jerry Rubin of the Yippies, and Bobby Seale of the Black Panthers.

Anticipating these critical tensions in 1965, Dellinger wrote an essay titled "The Future of Nonviolence" as part of his effort to strengthen the larger coalition and redirect the tendency toward violence. To my mind, this is an excellent example of what Kathi Weeks would term a utopian manifesto, in this case one that aims to convince the Left that nonviolence could provide a robust revolutionary vision and method.[11] To support his argument, Dellinger notes the successes of the nonviolent campaigns in India and in the American South; but he also acknowledges the anger and frustration of those who seek change but have little knowledge or training in nonviolence, and (like Rustin and also citing Gandhi) he recognizes the validity of their turn to rioting and to gestures of armed struggle. He therefore challenges the traditional pacifist community to move beyond tactics of passive witness and innovate more interventionist "methods by which [nonviolent action] can be made effective," and he argues against purists who reduce nonviolence to "an act of religious withdrawal and personal perfectionism" (Dellinger 1971: 369). Speaking to a larger and angrier audience, he argues (as a radical humanist) that the strategy of a nonviolent movement "must flow from a sense of the underlying unity of all human beings" as it opposes the power structure by risking well-being and death in actions that are equivalent to the dangers of armed struggle (372). Tapping the utopian surplus of nonviolence and calling for new nonviolent subjects, he closes the essay by saying that the full potential of nonviolent action is yet to be realized and ends in a declaration of hope that accepts the hard work yet to be done.

A half-generation younger, and active in the Occupy movement near the end of his life, Daniel Berrigan was a Jesuit priest and poet who was initially inspired by the French Worker Priest movement and by Dorothy Day, founder of the Catholic Worker. While chaplain at Cornell University, he became involved in civil rights and anti-war work. Like Rustin and Dellinger, he too recognized the shift of the mid-1960s; but instead of their more pedagogical approach of engaged dialogue with the larger movement, Berrigan and others in the Catholic Left opted for a performative response of direct action, undertaken not simply to bear witness but to stop the war machinery. In doing so, they took up Dellinger's challenge to develop innovative nonviolent methods as they worked to help "render the movement less spasmodic and reactive, more on the move, more innovative" in what was seen as a "long patient struggle" (Berrigan 1971: 83).

And so, in May 1968, in an action planned at the Kentucky hermitage of the Trappist monk Thomas Merton, the Catonsville Nine (including Berrigan, his brother who was also a priest, a Christian Brother, and six laypeople who were part of the Catholic Left in Baltimore and Washington DC) chose the path of sabotage against property as a direct means of aiding and abetting draft resisters and disrupting the war effort. Declaring that "some property [such as gas ovens or conscription files] had no right to exist," they broke into Selective Service offices in Maryland, carried several hundred paper files of young men eligible for service into a courtyard, and burned them with napalm. In this pre-electronic age, this was not a symbolic act; for by eliminating the single copies of these documents, they guaranteed that many in this group would not be called for service before the end of their eligibility to serve at age twenty-six. In this act of civil disobedience, they stood by the charred documents and were arrested and convicted. However, while out on bail before incarceration, four of the activists, including Berrigan, escalated their action by going underground with the intention of deflecting the FBI repression of militants and carrying on their own organizing. The Catonsville Nine action prompted others to undertake similar actions. For example, in September 1968, a group of fourteen clergy and laity broke into the Selective Service offices in Milwaukee, Wisconsin, and dragged the registration files into a public square, where they burned them—and in doing so removed another 50,000 subjects from the Selective Service apparatus. Again they stood for arrest, were convicted, and served jail terms. I will not detail the many subsequent actions of this nonviolent tendency—except to note that they included hundreds of Selective Service attacks, blockades of military trains and airplanes, and burglary (including a series of burglaries of church rectories that sought to redistribute Church wealth and the burglary of FBI offices in Media, Pennsylvania, that exposed the reign of suppression led by J. Edgar Hoover).

Berrigan was an articulate agent of this radical intensification. He explained that he and others chose to act directly against the war for its own sake but also as a means of standing in critical solidarity with those advocating armed struggle. By taking on an equivalent risk, they exemplified nonviolent maneuvers that went beyond passive witness. While on the run, Berrigan was given refuge by supporters throughout the United States and Latin America and met with many activists. In the United States, he especially contacted those in the Black Panthers, the Native American Movement, and the Weathermen; while south of the border he met with many revolutionary movements. During this time, he kept a journal, and when he finally gave himself up to serve his sentence, his *Dark Night of Resistance* was published in 1971. In prose and poetry, he meditates on his action and the characteristics of the larger movement in the United States; and he challenges the violent Left to choose a different path, while he also calls on liberals to reject their stance of compromise and co-optation. Directly addressing the Black Panthers, he expresses respect for their reasons for considering violence and then invites them to compare the results of violent and nonviolent action. As he puts it:

> There is a ... lesson here for revolutionaries .... Concentration on the sights of a gun inevitably contracts the bore of the mind. How does one keep the mind open to the full range of action possible to its powers? That range of action includes ... non-violence; even (most of all) in a time totally and officially dedicated to violence. Lives must be defended and protected, yes; but what do we do with our lives? To this question, the gun cannot speak. Can the gunman? (66)

On the other hand, he urges liberals to let go of their compromising respectability and what he calls their "despair, fear, dread of change, dread of loss" (83).

Throughout this volume, Berrigan delivers a moral and political manifesto on nonviolence that speaks not only to its acts of witness and intervention but also to the way of life that it invites. And here, I will end with his account of nonviolent subjectivity—one that I would consider to be a prime account of becoming utopian, as it offers us (in personal and political dimensions) an exemplary form of secular grace that redeems the dark present with the de-alienating and reconciling power of a totalizing vision and incremental action (see Levitas 2013: xiii). In what to me is the familiar utopian maneuver in which the negative is the necessary first step, Berrigan writes that "everything begins with ... no, spoken with the heart's full energies, [with] a suffering and prophetic word" (1971: 5, 2). Yet, from the negation of this negation arises, in his words, "a life worthy of human beings in the darkness," one in which (anticipating Jameson) we are "called to grow new organs ... [to develop new] ways of perceiving, of living in the world ... to give room for others to live at our side" (15).[12] Against the hegemonic rendering of citizens into consumers and patriots, Berrigan offers the radical alternative of a self-aware human being, committed to building a better world—a commitment that has the capability (unlike the pathos of T. S. Eliot's Prufrock) to actually disturb the universe. Or as he puts it: "To live consciously is to sow the whirlwind" (41).

IV

I think that most people would "recoil" at war (as Cummings says of Olaf), and many would abjure social injustice and environmental harm; but nonviolent activists (such as Olaf and those I have discussed here) take the radical next step as they convert that energy of recoil into transformative action. Their nonviolent standpoint locates them at a utopian horizon from which they step back into the struggles of the present: not only to name social evil but to end it, not only to announce a better world but to build it. Revolutionary nonviolence asks for even more. It disallows purist comfort and requires a radical engagement on the broader oppositional field, including a critical dialogue with those who see counterviolence as the only way forward. The effort of these nonviolent and, yes, utopian, subjects has often failed, but in other instances it has tempered counterviolent responses and even redirected them to nonviolent forms of resistance and change.

I will end with the words of Barbara Deming, another radical pacifist of the postwar generation. Initially involved in anti-racist and anti-war movements in the 1950s and 1960s, she then brought her nonviolent stance into the feminist and lesbian/gay rights movements. A critical supporter of the Chinese and Cuban revolutions and of black militancy in the United States, she nevertheless held firm to nonviolent principles as she worked side by side with those who felt that counterviolence was necessary, struggling against the system that produced the present injustices while demonstrating a radical alternative to violence through her own witness, direct action, and entire way of life. In her 1968 essay, "On Revolution and Equilibrium," Deming examines the discipline of revolutionary nonviolence in the context of her engagement in solidarity with Frantz Fanon's discussion of power and violence in *The Wretched of the Earth*, thereby positioning nonviolence as a complementary form of radical activism. She begins with these words:

> It is not possible to act at all and to remain pure; and that is not what I want, when I commit myself to the nonviolent discipline … I stand with all who say of present conditions that they do not allow men and women to be fully human and so they must be changed—all who not only say this but are ready to act. (1)

And she ends with these:

> Yes, the challenge to those who believe in nonviolent struggle is to learn to be aggressive enough. Nonviolence has for too long been connected in people's minds with the notion of passivity … I would substitute another word here— and rename "aggression" "self-assertion." … May those who say that they believe in nonviolence learn to challenge more boldly those institutions of violence that constrict and cripple our humanity. And may those who have questioned nonviolence come to see that one's rights to life and happiness can only be claimed as inalienable if one grants, in action, that they belong to all men. (30–2)

Next Steps: Tracking the Utopian Method

I

Since the turn of this century in the face of the systemic crises that beset our planet, engaged intellectuals have argued for the refunctioning of a utopian process within actually existing politics. Let me offer three quite different examples. In 1999, Russell Jacoby regretted the loss of a transformative utopian spirit, as indicated in the title of his book, *The End of Utopia: Politics and Culture in an Age of Apathy*. Tracing what he saw as the exhaustion of utopian ideals in the last decades of the twentieth century, he argued for their return in the politics of the new century. In 2010, Eric Olin Wright's *Envisioning Real Utopias* and the other books in his Real Utopias series grew out of projects, seminars, and conferences that he organized since the early 1990s. The project, as Wright put it, aimed "to contribute to rebuilding a sense of possibility for emancipatory social change by investigating the feasibility of radically different kinds of institutions and social relations that could potentially advance the democratic egalitarian goals historically associated with the ideals of socialism" (2010: 1).[1] And in *Depression: A Public Feeling*, Ann Cvetkovich drew on feminism, Marxism, and queer theory to attack the medicalization of depression and thus to re-conceptualize it as a cultural and political phenomenon produced by racism, sexism, capitalist exploitation, and commodification. This "public feeling," she argued, can open up to a "utopia of ordinary habit" that while rooted in personal experience can blossom into a socio-political process of transformation (2012: 189).

As seen throughout this book, another critical intellectual who deploys a utopian problematic is David Harvey. Coming from urban geography and deploying *architecture* as a driving metaphor for the process of social transformation, his *Spaces of Hope* argues for a utopianism that is informed by the combination of transformative vision and pragmatic production. He concludes his chapter on "Dialectical Utopianism" with this call to action: "The task is then to define an alternative, not in terms of some static spatial form or even of some perfected emancipatory process. The task is to pull together a spatiotemporal utopianism—a dialectical utopianism—that is rooted in our present possibilities at the same time as it points toward different trajectories for human uneven … developments" (2000: 196). And, as those within the fields of utopian studies and sociology know, Ruth Levitas (who, unlike Wright and Harvey, engages directly with the utopian problematic) has steadily explored utopia as a method of radical change: her monograph *Utopia as Method* offers the most complete articulation of her argument (see 2013).

In this penultimate chapter of *Becoming Utopian*, I want to explore in greater detail the ways in which the utopian impulse can work in the process of radical change. In doing so, I accept the caveats about utopianism's ineffectiveness or cooptation or impossibility (depending on who's making the argument) that are the bedrock of the cold stream of the Marxist tradition (from Marx and Engels to Ernst Bloch to Fredric Jameson) and consequently realize that wishful dreaming or the spinning of castles in the air is not able for the hard work of radical transformation. However, I also (like other utopians of the Left such as Harvey and Levitas) step into the warm stream (as Bloch would have it) of a situated "militant optimism" that seeks to set free "the repressed elements of the new, humanized society" that are available in any set of actually existing conditions (Bloch 1986: 199). I begin my exploration of utopian activism by picking up on my discussion in Chapter 5 and reviewing the dialectical tension of the negative and positive hermeneutics of the utopian method (which I develop by drawing on the approaches of Jameson and Levitas), and I go on to focus on the early stages of becoming utopian: that is, of consciousness-raising in individuals and groups in a utopian process that does not abstractly declare hope but rather concretely educates and activates hope. My theoretical articulation then turns to the specific interventions of critical pedagogy (Paulo Freire) and community organizing (Saul Alinsky) that can inform a praxis that not only produces the preconditions for radical social transformation but also engages people in the initial steps of that transformation.[2]

II

I will return to Levitas's explication of utopian method. Now, I will begin with Jameson's important warning against the *unmediated* conflation of the utopian and the political. As he put it as early as his "Islands and Trenches" essay, Jameson's most challenging argument (with roots in the caveats of Marx, Engels, and Bloch) has been that utopia's "deepest subject" and its "most vibrantly political" intervention are "precisely our inability to conceive it, our incapacity to produce it as a vision" (1977: 21). He has held to this line of thought throughout his work, developing it extensively in *Archaeologies of the Future*, culminating in the last section of his introduction, entitled "The Future as Disruption" (see 2005: 211–37). Since then, he has argued his position ever more forcefully. In *Valences of the Dialectic* (2009), he offers "a reconsideration, if not a supplement" as a response to critiques of *Archaeologies*. Insisting that utopia "is not a representation but an operation calculated to disclose the limits of our own imagination of the future," he nevertheless admits that it would be wrong to say that the representational utopia no longer exists or cannot be effective (Jameson 2009: 413). In support, he cites the utopias of the 1960s and 1970s, Jacques Attali's utopian vision at the time of the French socialist victory in 1981, and the resurgence of anarchist representations in the 1990s. How he values these texts is a different matter. For him, their utopian quality is not in what they propose, but in the fact *that* they propose it; for, as he sees it, their alternatives are caught within the very present against which they react, constituting, as he puts it "replacements of the reigning negative terms by their positive opposites" (427). Instead, he reads these works as "revolutionary idylls" in the tradition of William Morris's "epoch of rest," and he locates their utopian value in their capacity to "destabilize our stereotypes of a future that is the same as our own present" (415).

Having accepted but again contested the representational utopia, Jameson offers his own proposition for a utopian method that proceeds from his importantly negative stance. He begins with his distinction between utopian program and utopian impulse. As I have already discussed, utopian program, achieved by planning and production, is the (however temporary) realization of utopia; it is an act of closure, a totalizing occupation of a space that straddles the boundary between the utopian and the non-utopian (Jameson 2009: 415). On the other hand, utopian impulse, called forth by a hermeneutic exercise, makes available "the Utopian clues and traces in the landscape of the real" (Jameson 2009). Using these categories of transformative realization and acknowledging the force of "allegorical stirrings of a different state of things," he demonstrates the type of utopian analysis that their dialectical synthesis makes available in a discussion of two examples (420). Neither is anything like a typical representational utopia. Rather, they are phenomena embedded in the logic of the global capitalist system, but Jameson teases out the utopian traces in each. In the first, he presents the commercial chain Wal-Mart as "the purest expression of that dynamic of capitalism which devours itself, which abolishes the market by means of the market itself" (421), but he discovers in Wal-Mart's economic structure and political power the possible "shape of the utopian future" that could arise from the negation of this negation, as its productive capacity and channels of power could be refunctioned in a future based on the well-being of humanity and nature (423). In the second, he moves from structure to agency in a reading of the concept of the *multitude*, noting its value as a theorization of collective agency that operates in global spaces that are characterized by the terrible realities of overpopulation, unemployment, and homelessness but which may also be producing new, utopian, forms of everyday life, labor, and political action. Drawing on the work of Paolo Virno, he locates the utopian potential of the multitude in its ability to operate on this horrific ground and to generate a new sense of the public beyond the public sphere, a new experience of the democratic beyond the structures of representational government, and a new terrain of political action that oscillates between civil disobedience and self-organization. In short, his thought experiments do not designate programs but rather expose emergent possibilities that could flourish in a future we do not yet know.

Jameson, however, does not neglect utopian program; rather, he strengthens its potential by inoculating it with the destabilizing power of the utopian impulse. In this sense, he moves beyond both the interpretation of utopian traces so well developed by Bloch and the utopian programs sketched by Marx in the "Civil War in France" and Lenin in *State and Revolution*. Rather than hermeneutic or plan, Jameson identifies his method as *genealogy*: that is, an operation that sets "in place the various logical preconditions for the appearance of a given phenomenon, without in any way implying that they constituted the latter's causes, let alone the latter's antecedents or early stages" (434). With this operation, he refuses reductive political conclusions that might aspire to be revolutionary breakthroughs but in the end remain reformist epicycles in the self-repair of capitalism. He argues that this method is politically effective only in the sense "that it is a contribution to the reawakening of the imagination of possible alternate futures," a revival of "long-dormant parts of the mind, organs of political and historical and social imagination which have virtually atrophied from lack of use, muscles of praxis we have long since ceased exercising, revolutionary gestures we've lost the habit of performing" (Jameson 2009).

Jameson's approach continues in the spirit of his privileging of the utopian impulse as a negative operation, a negation that carries its charge even into imagined representations of a transformed world. He takes this line of thought further in "A New Reading of *Capital*" (2010: online), wherein he addresses the current intellectual and political situation and recognizes the emergence of a "universal multiplicity of others" that privileges "a new and universal equality" and marks the end "of parliamentary or representative democracy, and of that social democratic ideal which the Left has always criticized and condemned" (2010). True to his method, he argues that "newer Left ideals and programs of a direct or a radical democracy" (one can think of the Occupy movement, or the "Spring" uprisings, or mass mobilizations under the banners of Black Lives Matter or Extinction Rebellion) cannot be embraced as actual solutions. Instead, and here his maneuver will be familiar, he re-engineers these options as indicative *symptoms* of the emergent multiplicity, but not as "practical political solutions" (2010).

Admitting that his apparent rejection of radical democracy may be taken as scandalous or reactionary, Jameson goes on to support his maneuver in three moves. First, he argues that Marxism is an economic philosophy and not a political one. Its totalizing objective is to "change and transform capitalism as such" (2010). While this transformation entails politics, such action is contingently embedded in historical structures and is the "affair of an ever-vigilant opportunism" (2010). Returning to the categories of impulse and program, he (perhaps counter-intuitively, but not so in the logic of traditional Marxism) identifies the first with the economic and the second with the political. This distinction allows him to continue his valorization of the negative vocation of the utopian impulse, now directly imbricated with economic condition and potential. In this regard, the economic force of the utopian impulse propels us toward a totality of an entirely different mode of production that includes "personal relations ... possession ... life itself" (2010). Utopian program is therefore positioned in a secondary, yet necessary, position of articulating the "activities of politics and goal-oriented action" (2010). In this category, he includes both utopian texts and revolutions: for example, reading Thomas More's inaugural text not simply as an economic interrogation of emergent capitalism but rather as a political intervention aimed at solving immediate problems (such as the enclosure movement or the growing use of money, or indeed the role of the critical intellectual). Pushing his point further, with provocative language, he describes programmatic utopias as "so many *tinkerings* with possible political schemes in the future, new conceptions of governance, new rules and laws ... in short an endless stream of inventions, sophisticated and naïve alike, calculated to solve problems that exist on the political level" (2010, emphasis mine).

Having made this sharp division, Jameson returns to his prime directive of asserting that utopias "help us to grasp the limits of our images of the future" (2010). Now however he positions his linkage of Marxist analysis and the utopian impulse in a new tension with contemporary Left politics; and he argues, more strenuously than before, that "as the Utopian project comes to seem more realizable and more practical, it turns into a practical political program in our world ... and ceases to be Utopian in any meaningful sense" (2010). Capping his argument, he cites the Marxist distinction of the two stages of revolution: namely, the dictatorship of the proletariat (which he links with social democracy, socialism, and utopian program) and communism (that which is beyond the radical break, that to which the utopian impulse speaks). The first stage occurs within capitalism and is a matter of politics, whereas the second is the "unimaginable fulfillment of a radical alternative that cannot even be dreamt" (2010).

Coming at this time when utopianism is again being seriously invoked, Jameson's hard line is a chastening reminder. His insistence on utopia's inherent impossibility provides a cautionary corrective to scholarship and political action that too eagerly, and uncritically, inflates a certain text or practice as *utopian*, consequently devaluing utopia and emptying it of its transformative potential. His provocative point guards against hermeneutic enthusiasms that try to identify utopian traces everywhere, without engaging in a materialist analysis of the context and consequently missing the centrality of utopia's radical break; and it further guards against premature or misdirected celebrations of political maneuvers that may appear to be radically oppositional but in fact are present-bound reforms that are incapable of eluding capitalism's retrieval mechanisms, thus becoming enclosed in the mechanism of an artificial negativity that reaffirms rather than revolutionizes the present order. However, and this point is central to my argument, there is also a danger here: it lies in the temptation to position Jameson's categories in a binary set wherein the utopian charge falls off in the shift from the radical negativity of impulse to the contingent realization of program. To regard this as an abrupt bifurcation or unmediated relation would be to risk the excision of the utopian from the political, to abandon its transformative energy at the very moment it is most needed. Simply to separate rather than sublate these two moments would either privilege an ultra-radical stance that abandons the terrain of the present struggle (opting for a transcendent rather than an immanent hope of revolution) or condemn political action to the terms and conditions of the present, at best validating a toothless reformism, at worst strengthening capitalism's own cooptive mechanisms. Receiving Jameson's position in this manner would produce a serious misdirection of his powerful dialectical maneuvers, and it would drain the necessary utopian energy from transformative politics. Instead, by maintaining the primary negative force of the utopian impulse and by holding to the holistic goal of economic transformation, his self-identified *scandalous* caveats about politics protect rather than disrupt their radical trajectory.

In what I develop in the following pages, I reaffirm Jameson's argument for utopia's unrealizability and his imperative to focus on the break from the present, and I hold to this as the backbeat to what I say about the persistence of the utopian in the political. But to further support my exploration of how the utopian process can develop in political practice, I want to introduce a third term to the discussion (most effectively detailed by Darko Suvin): for by placing the concept of *horizon* rather than program at the other pole of a continuum that begins with impulse, I think we can more effectively recalibrate impulse and program in a relational manner, rather than letting them slip into binary opposites; and we can consequently account for how impulse and horizon can then frame the middle realm of the overdetermined conditions of political programs.[3]

I want therefore to qualify Jameson's assertion that utopian projects lose their utopian charge as they become "more realizable and more practical" (2010: online); for making that declaration too severely risks missing or suppressing the utopian impulse within ongoing programs. Moving from an orthodox to a more critical and utopian Marxist stance, I would argue that utopia's imbrication with socioeconomic system further requires that the lived political terrain needs to be infused by a utopian energy if the evental break to a new mode of production is to succeed. Utopia's critical and visionary work is required at every step, from impulse *through* program to horizon; for otherwise the structural and ideological lock, the iron cage, of the provincial present will prevail. Treating this triad relationally can help us focus on the morphing of utopia along the contingent continuum of program, that very place where we can trace what Jameson himself calls "the absent first step of renewed praxis" (1994: 71).

I agree with Jameson that literary utopias, from More onward, are primarily concerned with the political; however, I think it's important to note that their concern is not simply with the detail of political *program*, but also with *process*, with the revolutionary steps taken. While More may have focused on political solutions to the specific problems of enclosures or money, his treatment (by way of utopian satire) of these matters is set within the meta-political context of the creation of Utopia itself. He therefore sets the stage for Book Two's utopian alternatives in the conversations of Book One: crucially, with the extended conversation on the importance of critical interventions of princely advisors, since his recognition of this emergent activity (by the likes of himself and Machiavelli) creates the opportunity for establishing the role of the engaged intellectual in the development of both a critique of the present situation and the elaboration of alternative political policies, doing so in what will be increasingly seen in this literary tradition as a never-ending process. Furthermore, he grounds his account of the utopian state in the geographical metaphor of the production of King Utopus's trench, thus capturing the necessary, negative, rupture that establishes but also protects the program of the new commonwealth. On the other hand, while *News from Nowhere* may give us the "epoch of rest" that prefigures a future that Morris's reader does not yet know, the breakthrough narration of revolution in Chapters 17 and 18 ("How the Change Came" and "The Beginning of the New Life") charts a trajectory on what is to be done that sails close to the shore of practical politics and yet never loses the wind of utopia.

As I have argued in this book and elsewhere, the critical utopias of the 1960s and 1970s were especially concerned with the function of the utopian process in pre- and post-revolutionary contexts. In Ursula Le Guin's *The Dispossessed*, readers follow the trajectory of transformation (in everyday life on Anarres as well as in the entire galactic system) as it moves from impulse to program in Shevek's individual radicalization and in the collective organization of the Syndicate of Initiative. However, they also get a provocative replay of the program of revolution on Urras, most dramatically portrayed in that deeply negative moment when a street demonstrator writes, with his own blood, the single word "Down" on the city wall (which is itself inspired by the utopian horizon of Anarres). In Marge Piercy's *Woman on the Edge Time*, readers are treated to the pastoral fulfillment of Mattapoisett, but the driving force of Piercy's text lies in its treatment of the *process* of a revolutionary program that is producing this utopia. Not only do they learn of the political practices informed by the utopian impulse within Mattapoisett itself, but also, and more fundamentally for the narrative structure, they follow Connie's personal trajectory from her initial impulse, through her consciousness-raising, to her participation in the utopian life of Mattapoisett—and most dramatically, as Jameson notes, to her enlistment in the work of realizing that very future in her own present, culminating in that final act of closure, her assassination of the doctors responsible for the repressive hospital policy (Jameson 2005: 233). And, in Kim Stanley Robinson's realized utopias, from *Pacific Edge* onward, readers encounter a prismatic consideration of a range of utopian programs. Indeed, Robinson, more than anyone else in this short list, comes closest to Jameson's limit point wherein the political process has reached a programmatic realization that at times loses its utopian charge, and yet the range of options and the new contradictions of each post-revolutionary equilibrium stimulate the continuity of a utopian impulse that looks toward further revolutionary programs and new utopian horizons.

However important these literary examples are in their own right, my focus here is on the way they invite us to consider the function of the utopian impulse in actual political work. Therefore, I'm especially concerned with the antecedent and early stages of consciousness-raising and organizing that not only produce the logical preconditions for utopian transformation but also constitute the first steps of process. In this regard, I suggest that we can sharpen Jameson's argument by opening up that space in which we can discover the persistence of the utopian impulse in the trajectory from alienation and passivity to radicalization and activism. Without this recalibration, we risk the abandonment of politics to the empirical confines of a present that denies the palpable presence of the future, wherein the word *utopian* is counter-factually deployed to silence and repress the eponymous quality that we need in revolutionary politics.

III

This brings me back to Levitas. As I have already described it in Chapter 5, in her formulation the utopian method is a holistic operation that she terms "the Imaginary Reconstitution of Society" (see Levitas 2013). Her account incorporates a primary mode very like Jameson's genealogical operation, but it then moves to a second mode of *implementation* that carries the utopian energy through to realization. Fundamental to Levitas's sense of method is her definition of utopianism as "the expression of desire for a better way of living" and her consequent argument that utopia is concretely realized through the *education* of desire (2013: 4, see 15). As she earlier put it, the "education of desire is part of the process of allowing the abstract elements of utopia to be gradually replaced by the concrete ... Utopia ... [that] enables people to work toward an understanding of what is necessary for human fulfillment, a broadening, deepening and raising of aspirations in terms quite different from those of their everyday life" (1990: 122). Inspired by Bloch and Morris, she argues that utopia is not simply an expression of hope but also, and necessarily, the organized achievement that proceeds from that initial gesture. Putting this in Jameson's categories, she traces the movement from impulse into program, mapping a series of moves that involves a fundamental break with the present but also produces actualities that open to a transformed horizon.

When Levitas first presented her discussion of the hermeneutics of the utopian method, she elaborated on these two modes: the first of which works to "defamiliarize the familiar"; the second of which creates a space in which we "experience an alternative and [are] called to judgment on it" (2007: 55–6). The first step of "archaeology" requires a hermeneutic exercise, not unlike Jameson's, that seeks to excavate and reconstruct utopian possibilities within existing conditions. However, unlike or more explicitly than Jameson, she extends this work of teasing out utopian "shards" into the realm of political realization; and, in her own scandalous way, she contends that "all political programs ... are ... implicitly utopian" (61). As Jameson adduced the utopian potential within the structural capacity and power of Wal-Mart, Levitas develops her utopian vision of a society based on social inclusion through (for example) her dialectical reading of New Labour's privileging of meritocracy, opening up the Blairite strategy by pitting it against the European Union's policy on developing equal opportunities to compete in an unequal economic system (see 62–3). For Levitas, however much a program may appear to be no longer utopian, there is nevertheless the possibility of discovering and releasing its utopian remnant or surplus. This potential however requires judgment and decision-making to bring it alive: that is, the taking of a political stand that works with the contingencies of the moment but is carried forward by the utopian vision. Step two, "architecture," then puts the flesh of realization on the bones of negation and figuration. While insisting that this step must always be a matter of lived practice and not structural fixity, Levitas nevertheless notes that the achievement of utopia requires the closure of a given program, a given set of transformative structures and practices. Here, she aligns herself with Harvey's dialectical utopianism with its double helix of vision and realization. The second stage, therefore, reiterates in greater detail her long-standing affiliation with the final lines of Morris's *News from Nowhere*, wherein utopia is seen as the achieved vision and not simply the initial dream.

While impulse, program, and horizon can be recognized in these stages, Levitas describes their relationship in a way that captures their braided dynamic. Indeed, it is the second stage—the act of realization requiring judgment and commitment—that pulls the strength of transformative purpose back through the initial negative maneuver. Without this critical movement— be its outcome success or defeat—the potential of the negative gesture or the proffered program could dissipate and come to nothing. In her initial essay on method, Levitas recognizes this danger, and she specifically distances herself from Jameson's position. While valuing his emphasis on impulse, she argues that more is needed to fulfill the requirements of a robust and effective utopian method. As she bluntly puts it: "So what is important for Jameson ... is not *what* we imagine, but *that* we imagine, at the same time exposing the limits of our imagination ... Well, all this openness is a bit much for me. We could do with a bit of closure ... Carried to the extremes of Jameson's argument, this position risks political evasion" (2007: 57). In other words, the utopian method needs both negation and realization, and this dynamic calls forth not only "plausible" alternatives (in the sense of Bloch's tendencies and latencies to be adduced from present conditions and contradictions) but also demands "judgment" as to what is to be done, in this place, at this time (2007). She sums up her position with these words: "The strength of ... the utopian method is precisely that it deals with the concrete instantiation of values, enabling a level of real exploration and judgment. Without a certain element of closure, specificity, commitment and literalism about what would actually be entailed in practice, serious criticism [and, I would add, transformation] is impossible" (2007).

While Jameson's genealogical operation emphasizes utopia's capacity for neutralizing the present and generating the logical preconditions for transformation (thereby protecting against the containment of the utopian impulse within the limits of the present), Levitas's method brings a sharper focus to the fluid functioning of impulse precisely in movements and programs that break through those sutured limits. I therefore argue that this second maneuver—this risky, potentially tainted, incursion into contingent dimensions of action and policy—is necessary if utopia as a totalizing method of transformation is to move successfully against constantly reincorporating capitalist logic. To reprise the activist intellectual Shevek, as I argued in Chapter 5, I think we need to make it difficult and choose both: Jameson's radical negativity and Levitas's radical positivity, wherein each serves as a dialectical challenge to the other.[4]

Reaching back, therefore, to my core concern in this book, there remains a central element to complete this equation, and that is the human person (and by extension human community) who is, or could be, engaged in the process of becoming utopian. For what I am concerned with is not an abstract model or a disembodied study; rather, if utopia is to matter, it has to be regarded as the product not just of structural conditions but of personal and collective knowledge and action, of utopian praxis. While *utopia* is indeed the name for the totalizing transformation of social space and time, the journey it requires inevitably involves agency: a linkage accepted by Jameson himself in his discussion of utopian "mechanism" in *Archaeologies*, and one to be found in the

literary tradition from More's advisers to Morris's revolution to the complex of
alternatives on Robinson's Mars (Jameson 2005: 227). Utopia begins to happen
when, like Connie in Piercy's *Woman on the Edge of Time*, people say "enough"
and choose to enter the struggle for better lives in a better society.

This, then, brings me to the third mode that Levitas adds to her schema in
her 2013 book, *Utopia as Method*: namely, the "ontological," which raises the
"question of what kind of people particular societies develop and encourage"
(2013: 153). Drawing on the work of Andrew Sayer, Roberto Unger, and Martin
Buber, among others, she offers a substantial elaboration of the role of the social
formation of persons in the utopian process, thereby intervening in claims about
"who we are and who we might and should be" (Levitas 2013: 196). As she puts
it: "the ontological mode of the Imaginary Reconstitution of Society, of utopia as
method, is necessary for two reasons. First, any discussion of the good society
must contain, at least implicitly, a claim for a way of being that is posited as
better than our current experience. It entails imagining ourselves otherwise
and a judgment about what constitutes human flourishing" (177). This locus
of person and community is where the education of desire takes hold: in the
existential moment when the lack and the desire in people's experience shift
to another register by way of a critical and reflective praxis, wherein need is
recognized and robust alternatives that are not ameliorations are explored and
designed, wherein action is imagined and executed (179).[5]

Having affirmed the role of the utopian subject, Levitas enlists Raymond
Williams' concept of the structure of feeling in order to describe the productive
context within which the stirrings of the utopian impulse can be developed so
that people can attain what H.G. Wells called "their best selves" (Levitas 2011:
online). Williams originated his concept in order to capture the fluidity of
changing consciousness, for this allowed him to capture cultural developments
that are emergent and potentially counter-hegemonic. Recalling his formulation,
a structure of feeling is social experience "*in solution*, as distinct from other
social semantic formations which have been *precipitated* and are more evidently
and more immediately available" (Williams 1977: 133–4). A structure of feeling
therefore makes available the "specifically active elements of consciousness and
relationships ... thought as felt and feeling as thought: practical consciousness
of the present time, in a living and inter-relating continuity" (132). Williams
further stresses that these embryonic elements are constituted within an
experiential process that is only recognizable at later stages when they are "built
into institutions and formations" (Williams 1977).

It is the "generative immediacy" of the structure of feeling that gives form to the utopian impulse (Williams 1977: 133). While people may rehearse their desire for a better life in abstractions of an entirely new world, they nevertheless embody that desire through the incremental process of moving from passive suffering to active struggle, experiencing thoughts and feelings about their new lives in nascent solution, and thereby garnering the wherewithal to negotiate the difficult steps required to move toward that world. The utopian impulse thus finds its elaboration in structures of feeling wherein quotidian sensibilities are known, felt, and enabled. Utopian scholars might recognize this subjective tendency as it is expressed in the literature of Cockaigne, in "body utopias" as Lyman Tower Sargent has called them, or in Cvetkovich's "utopia of ordinary habit"; but these are expressions that do not stay on the page or in their moment; rather, these are articulations of utopian desire that produce the means to produce their own satisfaction, as they move, in Sargent's terminology, toward a more developed utopian form of social organization, or in Jameson's, a new mode of production (see Sargent 2010: 10–12; Cvetkovich 2012: 154).

Fluid and anticipatory, and available as long as there is the capacity to feel and to think, a structure of feeling imbued with dissatisfaction, anticipation, and hopeful energy names the early stages of the utopian impulse. Through the education of desire, this "solution" of utopian possibility can nurture radicalizing subjects so that they can develop the self-awareness and critical understanding to make the necessary breaks, develop new levels of political consciousness, and engage in actions that can eventually crystallize (in a form of socioeconomic titration) into the formations of a political program. But here is the critical point (and it's one that must be made in the face of both Jameson's and Levitas's accounts): given the insufficiency of any present moment, it is important to acknowledge that the capacity to infuse a utopian impulse within a structure of feeling is always available. In the depths of oppression, dispossession, and outrage, the potential exists for an education of desire that can generate a utopian response. But also, in later moments, down the line of a transformative process, this utopian energy can be reignited in a realized program that has been compromised or defeated, or stymied by non-utopian practicalities.

Understood in this way, considering now the longer continuum from structure of feeling to transformed horizon, both impulse and program can remain utopian along the way, or at least potentially utopian. It is not that a political program ceases to be utopian because of its realization in a particular historical moment, but rather that the utopian surplus within that realization is reduced when no longer sustained by a utopian impulse. As the critical utopias have taught us, the more self-aware and self-critical a utopian political process becomes the more its realized program can be continually re-functioned so that a utopian quality can be re-launched in another turn toward the horizon of the Not Yet. If the utopian impulse is understood as a renewable tendency that can draw on a disruptive and anticipatory structure of feeling and go on to resolve into another programmatic alternative, then the utopian calculus is safeguarded from collapsing into an arithmetic binary of impulse and program. Rather than being regarded as the *more* utopian of Jameson's pair, the utopian impulse can more usefully be seen in terms of its imbrication *within* program, in the way in which it is expedited by structures of feeling that can (re)generate utopian energy at every point of the continuum. And with regard to Levitas's sense of method, especially given her added focus on subjectivity, seeing the process as one in which the early stages of the education of desire enable people to develop utopian structures of feeling that mature into programs provides a comprehensive means of tracking this process and noting those points where political transformation gains traction or falters. Sustained by radical impulse and horizon—and hopefully blossoming under determinate material conditions of development or crisis or both—utopia's practical consciousness can flow through the entire process. In the existential work of becoming utopian, it is the lived element of a process that radicalizes the political even as it moves toward the inconceivable novum. Without maintaining this consciousness in solution, no utopian process can survive the counterattack of the dominant order.

IV

As I conclude this discussion of the process of becoming utopian in the larger project of radical transformation, I want to examine two instances of the ways in which the utopian method can be enlisted to sustain an uncompromising energy along the continuum from impulse to horizon. In Saul Alinsky's community organizing and Paulo Freire's pedagogy of the oppressed, one can identify practices that create utopian subjects capable of fighting for and building that space. Forged in oppositional Left politics as it developed between the 1930s and 1970s, and breaking from the orthodoxies of both liberalism and the Left, both engaged leaders created ways to radically educate desire rather than instrumentally mobilizing it.

Considering both of their projects in the framework of *Poor People's Movements*, the classic study by Frances Fox Piven and Richard Cloward, I argue that both Alinsky and Freire found ways to overcome the binary opposition between grassroots mass defiance and bureaucratic organizations or parties (reconciling Luxembourg and Lenin, if you prefer). With their emphasis on the formation of the reflective consciousness and behavior of every person, both projects protected and expanded the baseline of collective defiance and resisted the privileging of long-term organizational structures and their opportunistic subsumption within the present system. For Alinsky, this involved an *organizing* method based on local leadership and participation; and for Freire, it called for an emphasis on a *dialogic pedagogy* that informed the practice of revolutionary movements. Both projects sought to develop an organized capability for sustained popular defiance rather than reproduce static organizations that would end up protecting their own self-interest and draining the utopian lifeblood from any program.

Over four decades, Saul Alinsky developed a method of grassroots community organizing that still serves as a powerful tool for the dispossessed and disempowered. Born in Chicago in 1909, he was active as an organizer and a writer until his death in 1972. The poverty of the Depression and the terror of Nazism were factors in his own politicization; and while he was friendly with allies in the communist Left—admiring their political commitment, especially in Popular Front days, and standing by them in the repression of the 1950s—he located his own radicalism in the utopian surplus of the American dream, citing a militant lineage that harkened back to Thomas Paine and Thomas Jefferson.

In the 1930s, after earning a sociology degree from the University of Chicago, Alinsky developed his non-elitist approach through organizing the working-class community of Chicago's Back of the Yards neighborhood. From Chicago, he went on to work with communities from New York to California; and by the 1950s, he saw that the deepest contradiction in urban America was festering in the condition of Southern black migrants moving into Northern cities. Just as the postwar utopian demand for racial justice galvanized the Southern civil rights movement, it equally provoked Northern struggles for justice and equality. Responding to this situation, Alinsky helped to organize groups such as The Woodlawn Organization in Chicago and the FIGHT campaign in Rochester, New York.[6] By the mid-1960s, leaders such as Stokely Carmichael and Malcolm X recognized the power of his method, as he went on to play a formative role in the emergent Black Power movement.

As the New Left developed in the 1960s, younger activists shared Alinsky's vision of a radical America. Campaigns such as the anti-poverty/anti-racist project of the Students for a Democratic Society—the Economic Research and Action Project (ERAP)—were informed by Alinsky's method. However, as political conflict intensified in the mid-to-late 1960s, the New Left's strategic focus shifted from organizing to mobilizing, and Alinsky lost patience with the new generation as they failed to develop their structural base through community building, emphasizing instead what he saw as a gestural tactics of confrontation.[7] By the early 1970s, as his health was failing, Alinsky argued that a new front line needed to be developed in organizing the white working and middle classes. Having gotten the message from the Black Power movement that a, at least tactical, separation of organizing efforts was necessary in the face of the realities of white skin privilege and institutional racism, he recognized the job to be done in that part of the population that was increasingly feeling left out of the cultural equation and economically and politically disempowered. This was the sector that would soon be christened the "silent majority," whose conservative cooptation would play a key role in bringing about the turn to the Right at the end of the 1970s. In retrospect, Alinsky was on the mark in his argument that the white working and middle class had to be brought into the larger Left struggle, but his untimely death in 1972 ended the leadership that he could have contributed to that effort.[8]

Alinsky's method is best encapsulated in his two books: *Reveille for Radicals* in 1946 and *Rules for Radicals* in 1971.[9] Published just before the height of anti-communist repression and anticipating the resurgent opposition in the 1960s, *Reveille* offers what he calls a radical realist method for building the free and just society promised by the American dream. Never one to use the word *utopia*, he insisted that an organizer and an organized movement had to work with the world as it was found, and not to indulge in idle dreams. And yet, the driving force behind his irreverent and outrageous tactics is precisely what one can recognize as a utopian impulse. Alinsky's democratic ideal is captured in his celebration of the American radical who aims to restore the values of the progressive American dream as it came down from Jefferson and Paine. In his words, the radical is "that unique person who actually believes what he says … that person to whom the common good is the greatest personal value … [who wants] the creation of a kind of society where all of man's potentialities could be realized; a world where men could live in dignity, security, happiness and peace" (1989a: 15).

The prime objective of Alinsky's method is the creation of a Peoples Organization, a locally based formation that is the product of the people themselves and not of a circle or cadre of privileged leaders. The task of the organization (which, to use New Left terminology of the time, can be understood as a mass intermediate formation working between the street and the party organization) is not the venting of discontent but rather the exercise of political power "that will be controlled and applied for the attainment of a program" (54). Its goal is an "orderly revolution" that produces "the process of people gradually but irrevocably taking their places as citizens of a democracy" (198). Its method of development begins with the work of the organizer, a self-effacing agent who moves into an area, learns the problems, identifies local leaders, educates and catalyzes them as they bring their neighbors and friends together (often with the help of local unions and churches), and grow into a grassroots group that can build from battle to battle to eventually win the war that leads to a better life.[10] The utopian structure of feeling produced by this process is infused with the democratic promise, the belief of ordinary people that they can collectively choose their own way of life, working from their own base and not under the instructions of a vertical leadership or a bureaucratic institution.[11] And yet, for Alinsky, that horizon can only be approached through engagement in an escalating series of conflicts with the power structure, "striking and cutting at the very roots of all the evils which beset the people" (132–3).

As the book comes to a close, Alinsky moves further back in his method, from a focus on confrontation tactics to popular education. He acknowledges that the "very purpose and character of a People's Organization is educational" (155). In the opening stages of a campaign, it is the organizer's mobilization of the volatile mix of anger, democratic hope, and local knowledge that enriches a structure of feeling that supplies a community with a developing sense of community identity and possibility as they see themselves as capable of sustaining the conversations, meetings, demonstrations, confrontations, and victories and losses to come. A key step in this early education is the overcoming of destructive differences among the people being organized—be they based in race, ethnicity, class, or religion—thus creating a commonality of experience that fosters mutual understanding and cooperative action. In this "medium of education," the organizer brings people together and facilitates, but does not design or dictate, their plan of action. It is in this learning curve that new horizons can develop among people who see themselves as having a new sense of identity and power.[12]

Later, in *Rules for Radicals*, Alinsky recapitulated his method in the context of a friendly but firm (and prescient) warning to the New Left (1989b: 184–96, especially). He challenged what he saw as an undisciplined hyper-radicalism that was opting for a politics of confrontation. By emphasizing the role of self-effacing organizers as opposed to dominating leaders, and by valuing the long-term building of activist communities, he critiqued the adventurism that had come to characterize some elements of the movement in the late 1960s. To be sure, there was a good deal of local and national activism that carried on organizing with Alinsky-inspired methods, but the failure to expand those efforts, especially among the white middle and working classes, fed into the reaction of the 1980s. Alinsky believed in the potential of the radical American dream, and he created a method by which ordinary people could organize to achieve that dream. In terms of my argument, his method provides a model that works from a utopian impulse and informs each step into program, as it creates popular structures of feeling and formations that are directly democratic and not simply mass agitations to be coopted by demagoguery.

While Alinsky's grassroots organizing challenged the power structure in urban America, Paulo Freire's pedagogy played a pivotal role from the 1960s onward in revolutionary movements in Central and South America as well as in the radical education movement in the United States. Like Alinsky, Freire grasped the importance of the early stage of organizing, especially as it helped dispossessed and disempowered people develop a renewed sense of themselves and discover ways they could join together to create a better world.

Born in Brazil in 1921 and carrying on his work as a radical educator until his death in 1997, Freire dedicated his life to improving the lives of the poor. After law school, he became part of the movement within radical Catholicism that, informed by liberation theology and organized in base Christian communities, became one of the pillars of revolutionary movements throughout Latin America. His early work in organizing grassroots educational circles was suppressed by the 1964 military coup, and this led to an imprisonment and then exile to Chile, where he worked for the UN Food and Agriculture Organization. He published *Pedagogy of the Oppressed* in Portuguese in 1968, with the English translation following in 1970. Best read as an extension of the decolonizing argument of Franz Fanon's *Wretched of the Earth* (1961), Freire's groundbreaking work led to a visiting professorship at Harvard. Freire's radical pedagogy was adopted in base Christian communities and secular political circles in political movements from Guatemala to Chile, and under his own leadership taking root in Brazil. In addition, his method played a central role in radical pedagogy movement in the United States as it was developed by the likes of Peter McLaren and Henry Giroux and carried on in such long-term interventions as Milwaukee's Rethinking Schools project.[13]

Whether one sees him as a Catholic Marxist or a Marxist Catholic, Freire was committed to revolutionary change, but not to the hierarchical organizing methods of what he called the sectarian Left. Like Alinsky, he valorizes the role of the radical, a subject position strikingly different from that of the instrumental leader too often found in traditional Left parties. For Freire, the radical was "committed to human liberation" developed through a dialogical relationship with people, and not locked into what he called a "circle of certainty" (Freire 1971: 23). As both the producer and product of a pedagogy of the oppressed, the radical learns critically to embrace concrete reality and to commit to the work of revolution in solidarity with people, not in command over them.

As I discussed in Chapters 2 and 3, writing within a left existentialist problematic, Freire introduced dialogic education as a political act, and he described this process of learning as one that aimed to bring every individual— especially the poor, but all who were oppressed by capitalism and imperialism— to a new level of consciousness and collective action. Opposing the "banking concept" of an oppressor education (in which subordinated students are viewed by teachers as empty accounts to be deposited with the static knowledge of the dominant ideology), he called for a "problem-posing" approach that was based in interaction between teachers and students, with the roles flexibly reversed as needed (see 57–75 and 75–119). Throughout his work, it is clear that the method Freire advocates is meant to be an ongoing activity, one that initiates the politicization process, or the education of desire, as it informs the revolutionary movement but then goes on to sustain it in a post-revolutionary, liberated society. At no point does this radicalizing pedagogy cease to play a dynamic role in the work of political transformation. Freire terms this a process of *conscientización*, one that he describes as a "prophetic" unfolding that leads to the production of a "revolutionary futurity" (Freire 1971: 72). As an open process, it works by means of a hermeneutic spiral in which oppressed individuals begin with the moment of the problem, the "present, existential, concrete situation" (85). They move into a suspicious interrogation of that reality in light of its failure to meet their needs and aspirations, and then develop a radical re-interpretation of that reality. Stirred by this awareness and with a new sense of self-dignity, they resolve the contradiction of the oppressor and oppressed by taking on a new form of humanity engaged in "the process of liberation" (42). As their radical subjectivity develops, they are able to enter into incremental acts of rebellion, casting off their "disheartened, fearful, and beaten" character and transforming society (51). This ontological and historical trajectory produces the "awakening of critical consciousness" that sustains the liberated, or liberating, people and takes them from *conscientización* to *praxis*, that Freire describes as the dialectic unity of "*reflection* and *action* directed at the structures to be transformed" (20, 120). For Freire, as for Alinsky, reflection is crucial to the process, for it "leads to action [and when] the situation calls for action, that action will constitute an authentic praxis only if its consequences become the object of critical reflection" (52–3).[14] It was essential for Freire that praxis be openly embraced by every individual in the movement, that it not be the result of an imposition of a party line by an aloof leadership upon a malleable membership. Carried out in open dialogue, the process "constantly expands and renews itself" as each situation and state of struggle is studied and then acted upon (101). Freire especially argues that the "earlier dialogue begins, the more truly revolutionary" the movement will be (122); for in those first steps a deeper transformation can take place in the humanization of each individual, thus providing them with the understanding and the will to join with others in changing the condition of their existence. Working along the entire political continuum, this pedagogy makes possible the production of a liberated structure of feeling that can inform the transformative process at each stage, motivated by a radical sense of horizon, flowing into program, and thus being empowered by it but never subordinated to it.

While Freire himself never wrote of his method as *utopian*, one of the most radical of the liberation theologians, Gustavo Gutiérrez, did. Gutiérrez recognizes that Freire's aim is not the production of a once-off revolutionary moment but rather "a permanent effort" to exercise humanity's "creative potential" and responsibilities at each historical stage (Gutiérrez 1973: 92). As I earlier outlined, in the closing section of *Theology of Liberation*, entitled "Faith, Utopia, and Political Action," Gutiérrez recalls Freire's hermeneutic stages of a denunciation of the existing order opening into an annunciation of "a different order of things, a new society" (233). Between these two stages is the time "for building, [for] the historical *praxis*" (234). Breaking from what has been denounced and inspired by the annunciation of the new world, the process that Gutierrez's specifically names as *utopian* "postulates, enriches, and supplies new goals for political action, while at the same time it is verified by this action" (234). Embodied in the pedagogical structure of feeling that nurtures dialogical reflection and action, the revolutionary movement can progress from impulse into program, opening each stage to the further horizon of liberation.

V

Alinsky's organizing and Freire's pedagogy are two iterations of the early steps that can be taken in the unfolding of a materially grounded utopian politics that grows out of a continual process of becoming utopian. Resisting the limit cases of both utopian impossibility in the present moment and a realized program of a compromised or collapsed utopian vision, these distinct but complementary approaches succeeded in creating structures of feeling and formations that motivated people to grow from apathy to action, from alienation to solidarity. Starting with the early education of desire and staying with the radical project as it unfolds, they keep the utopian charge alive at each step toward the (ongoing) realization of program and the building of a post-revolutionary society.

However, if we were to go back to Jameson's "scandalous" hesitation about the relationship between the utopian and the political, we might well hesitate. For do not both of these overtly political undertakings occasion the very sort of opportunism and tinkering that prompts Jameson to question the utopian potential of political interventions? Do they not fall into the trap of articulating a desired future in the terms of the present, getting caught in symptomatic reversals rather than concrete transformations? To be sure, as they have been coopted by reformist political forces within the prevailing system, their deployment within the confines of a liberal focus on immediate electoral gain or on a non-transformative Christian approach to spirituality and education certainly meets the conditions of Jameson's warning. And yet, the original projects (and later applications that have remained integrally radical) kept to their insistence on a radical standpoint and horizon and on grassroots organizing structures as they refused to restrict their reach and impact to either the opportunism of instrumental application or the abstractions of revolutionary idylls. For while Alinsky and Freire require an intervention in the actually existing world, it is their very strategic decision to work with that everyday reality that afforded them the wherewithal to develop (in benighted neighborhoods, impoverished favelas, suffocating suburbs, or stultifying schools) the critical consciousness that can lead to the utopian break required for a radical praxis. It's therefore not a matter of the consciousness of utopia abstractly preceding the material conditions, but rather of the material conditions as revealed in all of their horrific contradictions producing radical consciousness and action. Whether in a meeting in the back of a local tavern or a study circle in a base community or a free school, organizers and teachers aim to create conditions in which people heretofore disempowered can gain a new sense of self, individually and collectively, that finds meaning in struggle and victory.

In terms of Jameson's approach, it is, to be sure, the figures of hope that enrich the emergent structures of feeling experienced by such newly radicalized subjects. However, between negative denunciation and anticipatory annunciation, it is precisely the continuum of lived, embodied, space for building a new society, as identified by Gutiérrez, that stands available as the site for horizon-bearing confrontations and programs. Certainly, Alinsky and Freire embrace the figure of Jameson's second stage of *revolution* (the moment of communism beyond the eventful break), but their work is firmly located in the hard tasks inherent to his first stage of political *engagement*. Their concerns are with what is to be done and how the change can come, and yet their holistic horizon (that for both is socialist and democratic) keeps them breaking beyond each achieved step, reflecting on the gains and limitations, and moving on to the next.

In Levitas's terms, both can be seen in this utopian light as working at the second stage of her schema: implementing the education of desire in the complex realities of personal/political existence and producing an adjudged and planned execution of utopian program in a given context, at a given time. To be sure, Alinsky's organizing tactics often took him to the brink of an opportunism evacuated of its utopian potential; yet time and again, he surprised his coworkers and his opponents by taking the battle to the next step, reaching again toward the horizon of the radical American dream. Freire's pedagogical maneuvers, in their conceptualization and execution, more clearly held their utopian charge, and they especially ensured that this would be the case in the early stages of consciousness-raising.

Both projects fulfill the utopian terms of Jameson's problematic of negation and figuration, on one hand, and Levitas's engaged method, on the other. Both projects locate themselves on the dangerous terrain of the political, struggling through the dark woods of a contemporary dystopia, avoiding its briars of opportunism and co-optation, and moving forward with the hope of one day reaching the pastoral commons. With their bi-focal perspective, both Alinsky and Freire keep their eyes on the long-distance prize of what Bloch terms the utopian *Totum* even as their close focus is on the step-by-step journey with and through the tendencies and latencies of existing conditions as new human subjects engaged in transformative praxis move toward that radical realization.

Yet, however reconfigured within the context of existing conditions, the revolutionary attainment of a communist mode of production and a liberated mode of everyday life that engenders fully realized human and natural subjects and creates a renewed socio-ecological reality must always be the fundamental aim of a Left utopian project. In all its diverse situations and practices, humanity must hope and fight for that goal; but in the meantime, in these mean times, once denunciation is proclaimed and the figuration of the new society is announced, the everyday movement along the way needs to get on with it. The challenge today is no longer a matter of securing utopian enclaves, of holding out in oppositional mountains. Rather—in the spirit of the grassroots activism that stimulated and was stimulated by the organizing work of groups such as the IWW (International Workers of the World), Communist Popular Front, New Left, and national/racial/gender liberation movements—it's a matter of continuing the long march, of getting over mournful losses and getting up again to organize. It is a matter, in Bloch's words, of realizing that the revolutionary utopian subject is always on the way, *immer unterwegs,* always becoming. Whether in Alinsky's or Freire's versions, what the utopian method has to offer is an exemplary means for all who work to realize utopia, even as they then must confront the next set of contradictions and struggles that emerge.

Coda: '68 and the Critical Utopian Imagination

Hugh O'Connell interview with Tom Moylan

TM: In 1969, in *Long March, Short Spring: The Student Uprising at Home and Abroad*, Barbara and John Ehrenreich reported on the May '68 student mobilizations in New York and Europe. What the authors delivered was an account of young people undergoing a radical, utopian gestalt shift from an unexamined life within the normative ideological system into a self-conscious/self-reflective process of becoming radical human beings committed to building a better society. As one of that cohort, my '68 took place in Milwaukee, Wisconsin. I'm grateful to Hugh O'Connell for creating this opportunity to reflect on the continuing legacy of the Long Sixties within the context of my own life and work and the overall argument of this book. Today, I'm still doing what I can to carry on the utopian energy of that metonymic year, one of the concrete utopian moments in modern history (Bloch 1986: 142–7).[1]

Activism and Academe

HOC: You were an activist before you were an academic. How did you get involved in activism?

TM: I hear you on the distinction between "activist" and "academic," but I'd add that for me these are abstract names for specific dimensions of personal existence: of intellectual activity (with its un-alienated sense of vocation, and its alienated structure of paid work) and political activity (as an existential commitment, sometimes as a job). As I tell it in my first chapter, "Strong Thought," my personal journey began in the 1950s on Chicago's North Side where I lived between my immigrant family home and the postwar society of American promise. Irish Catholic, I learned values that stood against the new consumerist culture; working class, I developed a class solidarity as I saw my father and aunt demeaned by their wealth-flaunting employers and deeply felt a situated solidarity with the people of Ireland. While this ethnic, class, and religious formation gave me a secure, and happy, sense of self and belonging, I nevertheless sought out the sensibilities and experiences of the new secular society. Yet, even with this outward pull there was the stability of that healthy base, and so early on I realized that each of my worlds opened up the other for me in a process that broke through the apparent binary difference and shaped a new structure of feeling (as I would now term it) that encompassed and superseded both dimensions in a fresh existential dynamism.

This structure of feeling gradually became confrontational. The sense of committed difference that Catholicism gave me, the class anger I developed, and the more distant sense of being of a people whose history was one of dispossession morphed into a more direct standpoint of assertion and contestation as I ventured out to the streets as a "teenager." Moving beyond family into a youth culture that refused 1950s conformism, my friends and I stood for each other and against those who tried to tell us what to do. In the new popular culture, inflected by the shadow of nuclear destruction, I negotiated that synergy of old and new worlds with an undeveloped sense of "existential" freedom. Folded into this was the contradictory appeal of mainstream American culture, that offered a disciplinary call for loyalty and commitment (inspired by the twinned ideological hooks of anti-communism and consumerism) and a call to heroism (as enacted in re-run war movies, TV spy dramas and Westerns, and advertising that sang the ideals of democracy and liberty). Out of this formative mix, a promise of unalienated/undisciplined existence enhanced my Catholic call to take a moral stand in a valueless world and led into the development of my social, if not yet political, consciousness. By the end of high school, I was a member of the Young Christian Students (YCS) movement (whose college-age organizers had moved to the Left through their engagement with the Southern civil rights movement, thus flipping the politics of the organization from anti-communism into the anti-racism work of Chicago's Catholic Interracial Council). What I would now call my "activism" began with CIC's campaign against racism, my writing on such matters for the citywide YCS newspaper, and my own confrontation with white skin privilege.

HOC: What kinds of issues were you fighting for/against? How was your activism situated in and influenced by the larger issues driving the Long '68? Were you focused on mainly local and national struggles or did your activism connect to any of the global movements of the period?

TM: Just to note that as I speak to your questions, for me the Long Sixties run from the late 1950s into the early 1980s; but yes, the year 1968 was a punctal Event in this trajectory. Imbued with that nascent sense of religious vocation and street solidarity, I entered college in 1961 with an intellectual curiosity that was intensified by my desire to make the world a better place. That intellectual and (at that time) moral formation prepared me for direct political work. I joined the St. Mary's (Winona, Minnesota) chapter of YCS; and by second year, I and others had organized a Students for a Democratic Society (SDS) chapter. Our early activity moved in two directions. Developing our existential politics of freedom, we challenged the *in loco parentis* rule that the Christian Brothers administration had imposed on our college life; but also, drawing on the progressive teaching of Vatican II, we called for more attention in the curriculum and in college policy to questions of social justice. This local campaign segued into our work in the larger civil rights movement; and, as part of national SDS, we also confronted the economic injustice of American society. While working on the West Side of Chicago in the summer of 1963 with the SDS ERAP (Economic Research Action Project), I learned more about the escalating US involvement in Vietnam. Soon after, as a young male who had to make a pressing decision in what I came to call "choice" or "body politics," I became active in the anti-war/anti-draft movement (campaigning against the war, filing in 1966 as a conscientious objector, and working as a draft counselor to help others make their own service choices, that ranged from entering the military to various forms of legal and extra-legal resistance to it). And at individual level of the politics of choice, driven by the dynamics of my married relationship, I began the long project of confronting my own male privilege as well as strengthening my solidarity with women's liberation. From then on, in all dimensions of my personal and political life, I affiliated with the politics of the New Left and socialist-feminism, joining with others who had come to embrace activism as core to their lives.

Moving to Milwaukee in 1965, I began graduate study in English at the University of Wisconsin-Milwaukee (paradoxically on a National Defense Education Fellowship) even as I remained active in what had become a larger Movement in which the separate struggles against racism, poverty, and war came together in a larger fight against the capitalist economy, the imperial state, institutional and structural racism, and, increasingly, against sexism and homophobia and for the liberation of all who were oppressed. By 1966, I was involved with the Open Housing Movement led by Father James Groppi and the NAACP Youth Council Commandoes in a year-long campaign comprised of legal challenges to the city's segregated housing policies, daily marches, and civil disobedience. Still affiliated with the Catholic Left, I also helped to organize the Milwaukee chapter of the Catholic Worker, and our small group worked with the open housing campaign and an array of anti-war and anti-draft activities. By 1967, I additionally worked with the Milwaukee Communist Party's Milwaukee Organizing Committee in campaigns for draft counseling in schools and in several (unsuccessful) attempts to disrupt the Selective Service system by way of bus blockades and SS office occupations.

In terms of global politics, in a more self-aware embrace of international solidarity, as I saw it we were not simply opposing the various forms of oppression but standing with all who experienced it: thus, with liberation movements within the United States (African American, Hispanic, Asian, Native American) and globally (with the Vietnamese, and then spreading outward to the peoples of Central and South America, South Africa, and onward). I also began to support the struggle for Irish freedom. While my father had been involved in the Irish War of Independence, like many immigrants he downplayed his past as he moved on to make a living for his family in the US (a country that he never fully embraced). As that afore-mentioned first-generation immigrant kid, I had only given an unformed allegiance to Ireland's history and the culture. My gestalt shift in this regard began with my love of early 1960s folk music as I discovered its Irish dimension, beginning with the Clancy Brothers and moving onto the likes of Luke Kelly, Christy Moore, Dolores Keane, and Planxty. Subsequently, through our shared love of this music, I connected my political world with my father's; and, from the early 1970s, I did support work for the Irish republican socialist politics of the Official IRA and the Workers Party.

With the Event of 1968, I experienced a larger gestalt shift. In Alain Badiou's terms, I severed my fidelity with the US state and affiliated fully with the movements for a just and equal society—in a break that is figured in the Ralahine Edition of *Demand the Impossible*'s cover image of the famous Black Power salute at the 1968 Olympics (Badiou 2003: 2010). After completing my English MA in 1967, I chose to give up my PhD studies because I would no longer accept monies from (nor sign the loyalty oath required by) the National Defense system. Instead, I moved into a life of political activism, community organizing, and teaching (and by the 1970s co-parenting my two daughters). Looking ahead, I developed a plan to do an MA in Urban Studies at UW-M, but first to frame it by way of a year of study of post-Vatican II political theology at Marquette University (with both preparing me to eventually do a PhD in Literature and Theology at the University of Chicago Divinity School). In 1967–1968, however, these personal, political, and intellectual threads intertwined and transformed through a series of breaks, wherein each transformed the overall pattern of my life and work.[2]

From the beginning of 1968 with the Tet Offensive, our collective sense in the Movement was that US power was being successfully countered by the people of Vietnam, and the intensity of our support for them and against the US state escalated. The history of the various uprisings throughout that year is well-known; but in Milwaukee in May, motivated by the campaign for desegregated open housing, Marquette students (of which I was then one) took their Jesuit administration to task for its institutional racist exclusion of students of color and its expansion into the city that denied affordable housing in favor of student accommodation and for its complicity with the US war machine by way of its official Naval Reserve Officers Training Corps (NROTC) program.

At the peak of the campaign, three hundred of us occupied the student union, ending when we (reluctantly) agreed to a negotiated settlement with our demands (one that ultimately led to a retrenchment by the university administration). At that point, I decided it was time to abandon my immediate plans for further graduate study and settle in Milwaukee (only resuming PhD work at UW-M on a part-time basis in the 1970s with Jack Zipes and other faculty affiliated with the journal *New German Critique* and the Center for Twentieth Century Studies). By September, I had taken a teaching job at the two-year campus of the University of Wisconsin-Waukesha. Continuing my political work, I helped in the preplanning for the Milwaukee 14 civil disobedience raid (by priests, brothers, nuns, and laypeople) that successfully napalmed 50,000 personal files in the downtown Selective Service office, and I joined in several disruptive interventions during Catholic masses, calling on the institutional Church to condemn the war and support draft resistance. From the end of 1968, I balanced a life of caring for my daughters, teaching, and being politically active: moving from the Catholic Left into the secular Left (though severing my ties with the CP after the post-Stalinist Prague tanks in August betrayed what I valued as the spirit of the Popular Front) and a sequence of affiliations with the Wisconsin Alliance, the New American Movement, and the Democratic Socialists of America (being especially active in the community schools movement and grassroots urban renewal, as well as being a member of our local socialist-feminist men's group).

Here, I want to emphasize a key issue of this time, and that is the question of the political *process* itself. By 1968, many of us already felt that traditional revolutionary politics were not effective in the West (though still succeeding in many liberation movements globally), nor was social democratic liberalism overcoming its fatal temptation to white male privilege and class accommodation, but it was also evident that the growing spontaneous movements around the world required leadership and direction (especially in need of becoming grounded in the economic and the structural and not simply the realm of the cultural). I, like many others, struggled with these questions. In terms of my own trajectory at the time, I simply want to say what is probably by now obvious: that through all my political work I was primarily a foot soldier, one of many comrades. At times I took on leadership roles and wasn't afraid to do so, but I never was moved to embrace the class or cadre privilege of being a front-line leader. This was due, I'm sure, to my personal formation but also to my intellectual and political sense of the importance of grassroots politics, of the need for collective action taken in solidarity. Here, my understanding and practice were also informed by the approach to questions of process and power as they were developed in the struggles of feminism. Nevertheless, I was not simply an anarchist. I believed that non-authoritarian leadership was needed, that a party formation of some form was needed; and, throughout the 1970s, as I discuss in my Introduction, I found a viable political vehicle in the Wisconsin Alliance's mass socialist organization (that interim formation that worked between grassroots action and more orthodox party structures). How and where such a democratic party leadership structure can develop at any given time is always up for examination, debate, and hard work. In any context, however, I've always stressed the constant need to be critical and inclusive, to be spontaneous and disciplined, in personal life and society but also in the Movement.

HOC: In terms of '68 politics, Debord was often critical of academics and their role in defanging radical politics. How did you move from activism to academia? Did you see the two as related? If so, in what ways?

TM: I'll begin again by qualifying the term "academia." While by my college years I was comfortable with seeing myself as an "activist," I have never been comfortable with regarding myself as an "academic." At the most personal level, I suppose it's a matter of class: although I've always been comfortable with the identity and labor of being a *teacher*, I've never been fully comfortable with regarding myself as a professionalized *academic* (although I have become socially located as one, and have benefitted from its middle-class lifestyle and privilege, I've never been eager to embrace its full degree of cultural capital).

I'm therefore in sympathy with Debord: too often, secure "academics" have (often unintentionally) compromised or tamed a campaign. Just one example that has shaped my behavior ever since: when the three hundred of us had occupied the Marquette Student union and were edging the university president toward negotiation, two professors (leading theologians who were at the core of a very progressive program) offered to mediate with the administration and thus to fight for our demands and indeed to put their own jobs on the line. The outcome was all too familiar: at the professors' urging (significantly as "mediators" and not allied participants), we ended the occupation and trusted in the proffered meeting. An agreement was reached, and we appeared to have "won." A few changes were achieved, including an African American Studies program and targeted recruitment amongst Milwaukee's non-white populations. However, the building program slowly moved along, and the NROTC/military affiliation continues to this day. Had there been a fully committed student-faculty alliance and had we all held out and forced the moment to its crisis, I believe that much more could have been achieved. A common story, and in keeping with Debord's critique of the role of "respectable" academics.

For me, therefore, the movement from activism to academia was neither binary nor unidirectional. Reading, wondering about the world, wondering about how to be a good person in the world were always core to my life, and this would later be formed into an intellectual understanding and practice in my everyday life (including politics) and in the workplace (which for me happens to be the university, my own location in the "long march through the institutions"). In this regard, active political life was primary, though always in a dialectical relationship with my teaching and research, and indeed my personal life. This political structure of feeling for me was especially shaped by two phenomena. First, the overwhelming presence in the 1950s of what Joseph Nuttall later called "bomb culture" led me, paradoxically, not to existential nihilism but in the spirit of the progressive theology of the time to a stubborn hope for a peaceful and better world.[3] Second, the *embodied* politics of the civil rights/racial liberation, anti-war/anti-draft, and anti-sexism/women's liberation movements (literally, putting one's body on the line at lunch counters, in front of buses, inside buildings; and maintaining autonomy over the access to, control over, and experience of individual bodies) especially as they were enhanced by the politics of *choice* (for men, in terms of their decision to submit their bodies to the military machine; for women, in terms of their decision to take back control of their own bodies). This strong activism from the end of high school shaped the way I thought about and acted in the world. It informed my life as a student, and later fed my work as a teacher, researcher, writer, parent, and citizen. I will speak further on of my move into self-declared utopianism, but its roots can be found here in the triple sense of how we can live in the world by means of a commitment to understand the *totality* of the world system, to *transgress* as much as possible to change its unjust and unfree structures, and to *transform* reality into a better place for all humanity and all of nature.

HOC: How did/does your activist work shape your academic identity? How has activism influenced the kind of work that you have pursued in your academic career? Has it impacted your writing style or any other decisions you've made about your career?

TM: In terms of the direct influence of my activism on my university work, there are several dimensions. First and foremost, I've always considered my primary role to be that of a teacher (with research and writing necessary for good teaching) and not that of an alienated "academic." I consider teaching to be a matter of imparting knowledge in the context of facilitating with compassion a learning process that helps each individual break with their normative development and come to see the world freshly in order to develop a responsible sense of their place and path in that world.[4]

Good teaching, however, requires interpersonal sensitivity as well as the rigor of intellectual analysis and creative vision. And here, I want to affirm the role that, especially nonorthodox, Marxist thought and critical theory played in the mix of my political, pedagogical, and academic work from the 1970s but to add that this intellectual development germinated more in the world of radical politics than within the walls of the university: I therefore learned my theory primarily in Communist Party and Wisconsin Alliance study groups, my socialist-feminist men's consciousness-raising group, the New German Critique editorial collective, science-fiction fan conventions such as Wiscon in Madison, and longer-term gatherings such as the Marxist Literary Group's Summer Institute in Culture and Society, and only secondarily in university seminars such as those taught by faculty linked with *New German Critique* or the Center for Twentieth Century Studies. One of the great tragedies of the Left and the political victories of the Right by the 1980s was the successful cooptation of the organic use of critical theory by the instrumentalizing machinery of mainstream academia, as a wide range of political and intellectual work was leveraged into the "disciplinary" realm of anointed experts.[5] I'm not saying that good work didn't, or doesn't, occur within the university, but it was, and is, too often done in spite of, against the grain of, the managerial and consumerist knowledge industry (increasingly so in these days of the neoliberal precarious regime).

Of course, my political work influenced the subjects I taught. Every English course that I taught included the historical, economic, political, cultural context and somehow focused on the history of progressive struggles. Also, from the initial sf course that I developed in Wisconsin in the late 1960s (among the first in the state, developed with the urging of my student Jeanne Gomoll, one of the founders of Wiscon, the feminist fan convention), the core of my teaching and research was in speculative and utopian fiction. However, I also brought my political consciousness to my teaching of college writing (for twenty-two years I taught three sections of composition each semester at Waukesha). What some would have regarded as drudgery was for me, as for many writing teachers, the good work of helping to develop a complex literacy, based on writing skills but always extending into a critical and creative sense of the world. And, there was my direct work with students: especially listening to and suggesting possibilities. During the Vietnam War, I was a faculty adviser for a student activist group opposing the war (significantly after 1968 urging them to step back from the siren call of armed struggle and to continue the hard work of grassroots organizing). I also worked with the college's counselling center to provide nondirective guidance on the range of options available to draft-age men and to help returned veterans struggling to cope with their post-service condition and feelings. And I was privileged to do cultural work with students, such as helping to develop and sustain a student-run radio station on the Waukesha campus and offering a program of Irish culture and music on the Milwaukee Public Schools station.

As part of my political and intellectual standpoint, I embraced Herbert Marcuse's "great refusal" over loyalty to any hegemonic system, universities included; I have always valued what Gary Snyder calls the "real work" over instrumentalized knowledge or discipline (Snyder 1974).[6] When I became a Professor at the University of Limerick, my administrators wanted me to become a Dean; I chose instead to develop a research center. Whenever I could, I worked with colleagues to develop such units of interdisciplinary research and pedagogy around specific themes: at Waukesha in the late 1970s, several of us founded Wilderness University, one of the first ecological studies centers; at George Mason University in the 1990s, I helped change the American Studies Program into the Center for the Study of the Americas (which delivered programming on veterans and the Vietnam War, the misogynistic violence of the Montréal Massacre, the prison-industrial complex, and the workshop that founded the

Latin American Subaltern Studies Group); and most recently in Limerick, the Ralahine Centre for Utopian Studies.

As for your question regarding the impact of my politics on my writing style, I believe I have always tried to make my expression accessible yet rigorous and informative (I'm no fan of density or obscurity). However, my political standpoint is always evident in what I write. While others may call this trenchant or presumptive, I think that I try to write about what I see and what I believe can be done, and should be done (I'm no believer in detached or objective expression). As I get older (hopefully reflective, not boringly nostalgic), I find my writing is becoming more personal, but I hope that it works more in the spirit of memoir as practiced by Ann Cvetkovich and others.

SF, Utopianism, and 1968

HOC: *Demand the Impossible* takes its title from a Situationist slogan from '68. How does the project of this book relate to the philosophy and politics of this period? The year '68 was driven by critiques of consumer capitalism and Soviet-style communism, anti-party, anti-authoritarianism, spontaneity and autogestion, sexual liberation, and anti-colonialism. How do these concepts operate in *Demand the Impossible* and its theorization of the critical utopia?

TM: *Demand the Impossible* is deeply rooted in the political spirit of the 1960s and 1970s. There is no question that your list of '68's critical issues constitutes a substantial part of the bad old worlds (and bad old politics) portrayed in each of the critical utopias; but while such portrayals inform these texts (in their iconic register), it is crucial to note that the driving narrative in each (in the discrete register) expresses and explores a revolutionary/transformative political process that occurs at both a personal and a collective level. Here especially, the 1960s feminist and New Left emphasis on self-reflexive and self-critical movement, as opposed to authoritarian/fixed blueprints based on a fixed telos, is at the core of each narrative. However, I also want to emphasize (as I did in my 2014 introduction to the Ralahine Classic Edition of *Demand*) that it wasn't just the subject matter of my study that was based in '68; for my research and writing itself occurred *within* this lived moment. While the publication date of *Demand* is 1986 (within the long period of reaction), the work on the book grew out of my life and study all through the 1970s. Since I was working in a community college that did not require a PhD of its faculty, I felt no compulsion to earn further qualifications or to submit myself to further professional formation.

Consequently, working on this material was an organic part of my everyday life, and I was fortunate to be able to do this in a PhD program that facilitated such independent work (itself a product of the radical pedagogy movement of the 1960s).

Demand therefore was written within the structure of oppositional, indeed utopian, feeling that not only led to the critical and creative fictions of which I wrote but also shaped the lives of those of us who were active in the Movement. For me, several key elements were central to this context. First, there was the growing deployment of critical theory (Marxist, structuralist, cultural studies, feminist) as not only a second-order reflection but as a dialectically engaged component: such a theoretical sensibility runs through the critical utopias, shaping not only the societal critique but also debating, criticizing, and redirecting the utopian process itself. Second, there was the new writing that had been emerging in the sf of the 1960s (sometimes under the term New Wave): this writing worked with, yet distanced itself from, the Golden Age of postwar sf, and much of it was also influenced by postmodern fiction. But what (for me, and others such as Peter Fitting, Bülent Somay, Fran Borkowski, and Angelika Bammer) catalyzed a deeper change in this already politically attuned and critical genre was its unabashed embrace of the utopian imagination. Here the critical capacity of sf to portray the contradictions and problems of existing society was opened up to bold creations of possible alternatives. Several of us then felt that these new works (by the likes of Ursula Le Guin, Samuel Delany, Joanna Russ, Marge Piercy, Ernest Callenbach, Suzy McKee Charnas) constituted a significant shift in both the science fictional and political imagination and accordingly deserved careful attention. Crucially, the way in which each of these works focused on protagonists who became critically aware of their situation and decided to do something about it spoke to the radical potential that was seething in what Ernst Bloch would call the tendencies and latencies within contemporary society. These works therefore spoke to the pressing question of radical political responsibility, of what is to be done; and in this regard, they offered their readers (fans and activists) thought experiments, social maquettes, working models of how political alternatives could come about and could continue.

HOC: More specifically, how do your concepts of critical utopias and the function of the utopian imagination operate in relation to the politics and philosophy of 1968? What ideas do they take up from this period?

TM: I'll first say more about my general turn to the utopian problematic and then segue into what you're asking about the critical utopian imagination. As

I said above, moving from high school through graduate school, my sense of being in the world developed from a moral to a political commitment, and from '68 onward I began to call that desire and work *utopian*. As it happens, one of the first steps in this paradigmatic shift occurred during that year of theological study at Marquette in 1968 (although I was already attuned to the thematic of utopia through a special issue of *Daedalus* in 1965). In a seminar on political theology, I first read Bloch's work by way of his reception by political theologians such as Jűrgen Moltmann and Johannes Metz. I came to value his hermeneutic retrieval of the principle of hope and his political mobilization of utopian proclivity. The second, minor, moment in this turn occurred in 1973 after I had begun part-time PhD classes at UWM: my emergent interest in utopia led me to write my first seminar paper on Thomas More's treatment of just war theory, thus linking my activist focus with my emerging intellectual project.

This theoretical embrace of utopianism gradually intersected with the love of sf that had been with me since I took that Robert Heinlein novel off the library shelf in 1953. My embraiding of sf and politics was significantly moved along in 1972 by Darko Suvin's "On the Poetics of the Science Fiction Genre" (the heavily annotated *College English* original still sits on my bookshelf). Suvin's articulation of sf's capacity for cognitive estrangement gave historical and theoretical substance to my own experience of this subversive genre. His work reinforced my decision to resume graduate study where I was fortunate to work with Jack Zipes, who not only was breaking new ground in his studies of fairy tales by way of Bloch's utopian hermeneutic but who also was bringing the work of the Frankfurt School to Anglophone readers in *New German Critique*. With Jack (ever since a lifetime friend and comrade, as is Suvin), I was able to begin the long journey of my dissertation: learning from his work in children's literature, I pursued my own in sf. And most fundamentally, I was influenced, and shaped, by the deeply feminist nature of the fiction (see below) and criticism of the time: here I was personally challenged and changed by the critical work of Mary Kenny Badami, Samuel R. Delany, Teresa De Lauretis, Catherine McClenahan, and Jan Bogstad and Jeanne Gomoll (the organizers of Wiscon: the Feminist Fan convention)—as well as learning from the writings of Pamela Annas, Elaine Baruch, Marilyn Hacker, Nadia Khouri, Joanna Russ, and Shulamith Firestone.

By the mid-1970s, my utopian shift took hold. Agreeing with Suvin's controversial argument that we can usefully regard the utopia as a subgenre of the sf imaginary, I found in these cognitively estranged narratives of better worlds a compelling object of study that conjoined my scholarly and political interests (see Suvin 1973). This focus was locked in with the timely publication of Le Guin's *The Dispossessed* in 1974. As I'm sure it was for many, Le Guin's work brought the full capacity of sf's thought experiments into an exploration of the sociopolitical and existential struggles of the time. *The Dispossessed* crystallized my sense that sf's utopian potential could be articulated in a powerful new way, influenced by and subsequently influencing the oppositional political culture. Then came the other books that touched me deeply: Russ's *The Female Man* (1975; but written in 1968) and Piercy's *Woman on the Edge of Time* and Delany's *Triton* (1976; the US bicentennial year).

I began to see these works not only as a revival of the traditional form of utopian writing but also as a historical refunctioning within the sf mode. Taking a lead from the Frankfurt School sense of *critique*, I began to think of them as *critical utopias*—a formulation also used by Peter Fitting (another life-long friend and fellow utopian who I first met at the Marxist Literary Group Summer Institutes in the mid-1970s).[7] Both the form and content of these works articulated a utopian imagination that held utopia itself open to history's contradictions and struggles; and importantly, they focused on the process not just of building the new society but also the individual trajectory of consciousness-raising, radicalization, and action required for that collective effort. As I read them, these tales of awakening and action offered the mediation between the political process and individual agency that is needed to take radical social change forward, to become utopian.

So not only did the critical utopian period of writing grow out of and contribute to the struggles of the 1960s and 1970s, it also challenged and changed the literary utopia itself: namely, by morphing it into a form that drew on both the eutopian evocation of a new spatial reality and the temporal, dystopian, account of personal suffering, systemic discovery, and radical transformation. This formulation allowed me to speak about the way in which this utopian variation facilitated one of the key insights of the oppositional imagination of '68: that the personal is political and vice versa. Furthermore, in their examination of a revolutionary process that requires democratic leadership and systemic change as well as cultural transformation, the critical utopias reinforced the radical political strand of '68 and spoke against the valorization of individual freedom that the countercultural strand of '68 left available for neoliberal opportunists. The critical utopia is therefore an outcome of the cultural logic of an emergent *alter-modernity* that privileges a self-aware agency capable of producing new systems and then continues the process of critiquing and renewing them.

HOC: In his early writings on delimiting the poetics of science fiction, Darko Suvin presented it as a necessarily subversive genre with clear implications for political activism. This relationship can be seen as indebted in certain ways to the spirit and atmosphere of 1968 given the historical position of his initial writings from within this period. Do/did you agree with Suvin?

TM: Yes. As I note above, Suvin's work has been core to my engagement with sf and utopianism. With minor caveats and debates always occurring between us, to this day I find his approach compatible with my own, indeed often pulling me back to ground or challenging me to new directions. And yes, I see his contribution as very much a part of the spirit of 1968. While those of us who read his work at the time were well aware of his political affiliation, all one need do is look at his recent memoirs based in the history and politics of Yugoslavia to see evidence of the *longue durée* of his political formation. To catch the flavor of his own structure of feeling, see my discussion in Chapter 4 of his utopian poem, "Growing Old Without Yugoslavia," written in 1993, and published as Yugoslavia verged on the despair of its destruction (1994a: 124–6).

Most importantly, there was the "Poetics" essay, with its fresh approach to sf. While the essay was published in 1972, it grew out of Suvin's earlier work at McGill University in comparative literature (especially his studies on Brecht) and before that in his political and scholarly (and fan) contributions at home in Yugoslavia. This essay shifted sf scholarship beyond the limiting tendencies of New Criticism and canonical literary studies, enabling us to regard the genre more clearly as a didactic literary form with its own history (however debated that would come to be) and its own formal operations. If "Poetics" shaped my study of sf, Suvin's next essay, "Defining the Literary Genre of Utopia" (in 1973) addressed utopian writing, formally and politically. And in 1977, his paper on "Science Fiction and the Novum" (delivered in a seminar I organized during my stint as a Research Fellow at UWM's Center for Twentieth Century Studies) deepened my understanding of the creative and intellectual work of the utopian form, and especially its capacity to produce a totalizing analysis and alternative vision (see Suvin 1980). In my view, as I argue in Chapter 4, Suvin's work on the novum has constituted one of his most significant contributions, especially in its evocation of the productivity of the concept of *totalization*; but this has also been more ignored and indeed resisted, especially in the anti-communist maneuvers of an academic poststructuralism that has rejected this deployment of totality by way of an invidious conflation of that category with totalitarianism. This is not the place to review the entire body of Suvin's contributions, so for now I refer you to two re-publications that evince my own, and others, estimation of his work (both in Ralahine Utopian Studies volumes): *Defined by a Hollow: Essays on Utopia, Science Fiction and Political Epistemology* (2010) and *Metamorphoses of Science Fiction: On the Poetics and History of a Literary Genre* (2016); I also refer you to the introductions in each volume that contextualize and evaluate Suvin's work by Phil Wegner and Gerry Canavan respectively.

To be sure, as history and the sf genre have continued to develop, there have been useful critiques of Suvin's arguments. The questioning of his taxonomic approach, with its tendency to valorize individual titles over a reading of the entire genre, has been useful, as has the important intervention by China Miéville that addressed Suvin's dismissal of fantasy. In fairness, Suvin has responded in productive ways to both critical engagements, and his work and ours are all the better for it. Unfortunately, another direction of liberal, indeed anti-communist, responses to his work has tended to dismiss rather than critique it. I fear much of this line of attack is the output of "academics" (including those in sf and utopian studies) who have, since the 1980s, settled into the comfort of the university system's encapsulation of theory in the civilized amber of an apolitical discourse that is much more suited to the requirements of disciplinary neoliberalism.

HOC: Relatedly, many Marxist critics—your work included—have looked at the explicit formal, aesthetic, and political relationships between sf and utopianism. Are sf and utopianism indelibly linked? If it was once possible to posit sf in such a way, does this still hold today (especially as more critics align the sf imagination with imperialism than radical utopianism)? How do you understand the relationship between politics, economics, and science fiction today? Do you think that contemporary sf production and the sf imagination is still indebted to 1968 in any way? How do you see the genre functioning in relation to 1968 in the years following the movements; or more broadly, how has the sociopolitical function of the genre shifted over the last fifty years?

TM: The direct answer is yes. Working from a historical materialist sense of science and utopian fiction as modes of estranged writing, I locate their deepest commonality in their formal structure: namely, the nonnarrative, spatial capacity to imagine and describe a totalized account of a social reality (from the economic to the personal to the material world). The quality of that systemic imaginary (be it an extrapolated version of a given reality or an analogous re-vision or anticipation) rests on the depth of thought and detail that an author puts into the creative process of worldbuilding; but in all cases, the generic form privileges this production of an "other world" that then stands in an estranged relationship to the author's (and the author's readers). A second commonality is that of the historical and programmatic roots of both genres in the cognitive and formal mechanisms of early modernity. This development, however, must be understood within the greater context of the global ubiquity of the utopian impulse across history and in diverse cultures (as seen in hermeneutic and bibliographic research by Bloch and Sargent and taken further in newer scholarship); here, long-overdue attention to independent strands of estranged writing before and beyond the "West" has catalyzed a sense of the history, narrative technology, reception, and reading protocols of both genres that is more critical, expansive, and nuanced (see Wegner 2020: 277, n. 70). A third commonality emerges at the end of the nineteenth century as science and utopian fiction begin not only to portray better worlds but also to describe the political process of producing them (as seen in William Morris's *News from Nowhere*).

I would hold that this strong linkage between sf and utopian writing continues today (working in both eutopian and dystopian modes), working in both and in doing so still indebted to the long historical tether of '68. Recognition of this continuation can be seen in the contributions of critics such as Wegner, Canavan, Eric Smith, Mark Bould, Sherryl Vint, and indeed yourself. Therefore, I'd argue that the above commonalities continue. First, the form has not substantially changed. Second, while the critical openness to fantasy and the expanded global location and production of sf and utopian writing has strengthened an overall understanding of the political and aesthetic capacity of these genres, the contextualization of these estranged forms of writing still holds (and has been further elaborated on in Phil Wegner's recent work and the work on Afrofuturism and decolonial and indigenous futurism). Importantly, the capacity of this expanding generic output to address the process of revolutionary change has not diminished – and indeed has been well represented in the writing of the aforementioned Miéville and Robinson, but also in the work of Iain M. Banks and Octavia Butler. However, and additionally, given the rich expansion beyond its Western, predominantly white, tradition, the form and substance of these interrelated genres has morphed in many directions: a richer spatial imagination has taken us beyond instrumentally rational Western systems; a vibrant cultural diversity has taken us to a wider range of consciousness and interaction with the world and a set of creative narratives that has expanded rather than destroyed the available estranged and utopian imaginaries (in sf itself, let me point to writers such as Nnedi Okorafor, Nalo Hopkinson, N. K. Jemisin, and Tade Thompson).

Therefore, we need to value the new manifestations of critical dystopian and eutopian writing that is occurring *within* this moment of darkness, seeking ways to work through the tendencies and latencies at the end of the

Anthropocene rather than simply reaching back to a previous utopian age or into mere capitulation. Here, Donna Haraway's *Staying with the Trouble* (2016) argues that we should work *within* the darkness toward transformation.[8] And, for but one example, Margaret Atwood's *The Testaments* (2019), set in the dystopian world of her earlier *Handmaid's Tale* (1985), offers a recent response in a critical dystopian mode that is not only oppositional but transformational in its depiction of the overthrow of the Republic of Gilead by an alliance of the international activists in the external Mayday resistance and the alienated and angry Aunts working within the Gilead infrastructure (in a process of change that is especially interesting in the way in which Atwood intertwines the power of writing, with its mobilization of archive and narrative, with that of overt organizing and resistance).[9] And, of course, the many young adult dystopias (with wide variation) offer further examples of how the utopian imagination can survive, and speak effectively, within the terms and conditions of our apparently hopeless present.

However, I say all this in the context of the intensified commodification of the sf (especially dystopian) imaginary that has pulled it into the core of the market by way of capitalism's capability to (re)capture all elements of life. I think we can all recognize the hypoglycemic production and consumption of this profitable sf form (visual and print) that challenges no universe, estranges no one. As critics, I suggest that we need to examine more closely the way in which publishing trends (for example, endless series offering little more than repetitive plots), media mechanisms (such as action-adventure films that reproduce the neoliberal structure of feeling in their superheroes), as well as opportunistic academic studies (caught up in professional achievement rather than intellectual engagement) reinforce consumptive passivity at the expense of sf's capacity for complex iconic worlds and challenging discrete narratives. I therefore think we need to register how much this mobilization of a dystopian structure of feeling by market forces has, against the critical grain of the sf imaginary, produced a strain of moral and political inoculation and indulgence that leads to a passive, sometimes nihilist, acceptance of the status quo at the end of the Anthropocene—even as oppositional and transformative creative, intellectual, and sociopolitical work continues to emerge and push against such an absorptive sphere.

HOC: Critics like Nancy Fraser, Luc Boltanski, and Eve Chiapello, among others, have argued that the intellectual work of 1968 has come to function as the generative conditions for contemporary neoliberalism. To what degree do you agree or disagree with this leftist autocritique? Do we need a reconceptualization of the utopian politics and strategies of the '68 period in light of this right-wing individualist economic turn? As a related question, in *Scraps of the Untainted Sky* you explore the shift from critical utopias to critical dystopias. Do you see this shift related to the waning of the spirit of '68, to what Michael Gardiner describes as its recuperation in "Hip Capitalism" through the eclipse of the sociopolitical ends of 1968 by the aesthetic ends?

TM: It's important that such left autocritiques take place, and I agree with this general direction. However, I regard this engagement more as part of the dialectical retrieval of the spirit of '68 that continues in a strong left tradition rather than a component of the liberal and right-wing reaction that began in the 1970s and 1980s. Having said that, I think we must continue to recognize two strands (at least) that were operative in the Long Sixties: the countercultural movement and the organized politics of the New Left (and its Old Left supporters). As I said above, in the political and the intellectual Left that carried on from the 1970s the "real work" of '68 continues, and autocritiques by Fraser and others help sustain its strength by way of a self-critical apprehension of what happened then and what can happen now. On the other hand, the counterculture's valorization of individual freedom and generation of new forms of social/economic production (what Boltanski, Chiapello, Gardiner, and several others have rightly identified as "hip capitalism") fed into the rising neoliberal mechanism from the late 1970s.[10] It is important therefore that such historical and analytical distinctions be made, and that the strands of '68 that led to compromising co-optation rather than the ongoing march and struggle be identified and superseded in the contemporary fight against the neoliberal order and environmental destruction.

Yes, we do live in darker, entropic times, and this turn began in the counter-revolution of the 1980s and the rise of neoliberalism. Here then, *Scraps of the Untainted Sky* addressed not so much the waning of the radicalism of the Long Sixties (though there was that, for reasons we need to better understand) but more so its pushback, its defeat, by well-organized tendencies on the Right (the economic rise of neoliberalism, the Reagan-Thatcher-Kohl political shift, and the cultural cooptation of Left thought and practice by the religious and secular Right). In the darkness of these times, however, I argue that the progressive capacity of utopian sf continued, this time by going underground and re-emerging in what Raffaella Baccolini and I termed the critical dystopias of the 1990s. In the work of Marge Piercy, Butler, Le Guin, Robinson, and others, we discovered a formal and political maneuver analogous to but different from that of the critical utopia. Such works took seriously the terrible times and exposed that new order in a dystopian mode, but they did so in ways that exposed the limits of the traditional dystopia, especially its tendency to lapse into anti-utopian resignation and even complicity. As a result, they helped to save dystopia from its own anti-utopian tendencies and to hold it available for radical utopian expression and intervention. As I said in the previous section, I would argue that this critical dystopian sensibility has influenced the stubborn hopefulness emerging in the aforementioned theory and narratives that are "staying with the trouble."

Further, in the political sphere itself, the strategic options explored in the 1990s critical dystopias (especially a global/local intersectional political bloc that supersedes the limitations of micro-politics and new social movements) have continued to offer valuable thought experiments and political scenarios for the contemporary progressive political imagination.[11]

HOC: Your own work argues that critical utopia and critical dystopia are historical, even periodizing concepts. Critics like Kathi Weeks, however, have argued that they have utility outside of their own periods. How do you understand the function of critical utopias and dystopias today? How has the function of these concepts changed given the shifts in politics and economics over the last fifty years? In a related fashion, one of the most pressing concerns of the present is the issue of the Anthropocene with its dystopian insistence on impending, unalterable apocalypse. In this light, the Anthropocene seems like a vexing issue for utopian thought. What challenges does this provide for the utopian method? What might the utopian method bring to the problem of the Anthropocene missing from contemporary theoretical and sociopolitical approaches?

TM: As I described above, I've consistently asked that the critical utopias be understood as a distinct formal maneuver that emerged within the historical conditions of 1970s. However, as I said in my Introduction to the Ralahine Classic edition of *Demand*, I have learned from the work of several people who have identified a critical utopian problematic in works published before the 1960s and in those that have continued into our own time. In this regard, while I think it's important to understand and value the historical determinations of the 1970s texts (and, in *their* own time, those of the 1990s), I have welcomed contributions that elaborate the ongoing use value of the critical utopia as an interpretive problematic or protocol. In particular, I appreciated Kathi Weeks's response in "Reflections on *Demand*" section in the Ralahine edition. I was touched by the care of her reading and thinking, especially the way in which she identifies the "untimely" value of what she calls my "meditations about the relationship between utopian systems and utopian desires, between blueprints and processes" as they have continued to be available. I value the way in which she enlists the very strategy of the critical utopia (its capacity for self-critique and for refunctioning the utopian impulse in new conditions) in her appraisal of the potential for its mobilization in cultural and political work yet to be done. As she puts it so well, the critical utopia "travels beyond" its historical frame: "The text's past may be fixed, but its future remains open" (Weeks 2014: 250).[12]

I would therefore fully agree with the argument for the continuing viability of the critical utopian (and critical dystopian) imaginary and methodology in creative work and in politics. Certainly, we need the capacity for a critical utopian vision and method to sustain us and to pull us forward as we struggle within the current historical conditions of a pervasive neoliberalism and a world-destroying environmental toxicity. As I've said above, Robinson's persistent utopian contributions exemplify the continuation of the critical utopian problematic, and the work of Haraway and Atwood that refuses to give up the utopian project within our time of trouble draws on the related continuation of the critical dystopian sensibility.

As ever, we can fruitfully reach back to Bloch and draw on his understanding of the way in which earlier historical moments can generate a *utopian surplus* that can be tapped by later generations long after the specific time of hope and defeat that generated the initial utopian impulse. Knowing our history, knowing the value of earlier utopian contributions (such as that of the critical utopia and dystopia, and indeed the radical utopianism of the late nineteenth century) and re-functioning them as concrete utopian elements within our own present (not imposing or dismissing such utopian capacity as a simple abstraction) is, I believe, one of the most important lessons that the utopian method brings to us today.

HOC: Your most recent work has shifted away from literary studies to more practical utopian politics and the idea of the utopian method more broadly. What precipitated this turn? To what extent is this related to the problems of recuperation by the neutralization of the sociopolitical aspects of 1968 by the aesthetic ends? By the waning of the utopian impulse in late capitalist cultural production? How do you understand the role of utopian thought and method in contemporary activist politics? Do you feel you've come full circle in your academic work as you return to your early activist impulses?

TM: This shift or turn began shortly after I arrived at the University of Limerick in 2002. One of the first things I did on arrival was to launch the Ralahine Centre for Utopian Studies. My aim was not only to foster international research in utopianism but to bring a better understanding of the utopian problematic to Irish audiences: this double purpose called for a meta-theoretical and pedagogical focus in my own work and in the Centre's programming. To that end, we began with a two-year seminar ("Utopia Method Vision") in which twelve international utopian scholars gave presentations on the utopian method as they understood it, and spoke to its impact on their personal and professional lives. Their papers were published as the first volume in our book series, and further led to Ruth Levitas's groundbreaking *Utopia as Method*. Although I have taken on a few literary projects since then, I have primarily aimed to disseminate a better understanding and articulation of the utopian problematic. In doing this, I began with Levitas's sense of method, then regarded it as a form of what I call strong thought, and from there worked with Jameson's distinction between impulse and program. I therefore came to look at the way in which the utopian proclivity is mobilized in direct political work along a continuum that runs from the initial impulse through programs but then reaches beyond toward the ever available utopian horizon. I moved steadily into this last area of writing after my official retirement from the university in 2009, with studies of the utopian capacity in environmental thought and practice, radical pedagogy, community organizing, and revolutionary nonviolence, all understood within a framing understanding of the way in which normatively constructed persons can attain a utopian gestalt shift and become active utopian subjects.

In all this work, and now in *Becoming Utopian*, my aim has been to speak against those reactionary/managerial tendencies in the wider social discourse and academia that repress intellectual intervention that goes against the persistent drive of our neoliberal society. So it should be clear that I agree with what you refer to as the (attempted) neutralization of the sociopolitical aspects of '68, especially as we see this playing out in the normative and "respectable" aestheticization of cultural studies and critical theory (and here sf and utopian studies must be included); for in this atmosphere of commodification and managerial discipline, the oppositional work of creating, critiquing, teaching, and organizing is increasingly endangered. I want to therefore negate neoliberal hegemony by reaffirming the utopian process as a legitimate mode of *radicalization* and the utopian subject as a *radical*. My hope is to help reclaim the progressive legacy of these categories in the face of the moral panic generated by those who conflate radicalization with the work of "terrorists." In valorizing this quality, I am (in a critical utopian spirit) privileging a pedagogical practice that is, in Paulo Freire's sense, dialogical: open and self-critical, but also affiliated and committed, while being fully imbricated within the transformative/revolutionary work of building a radically better future, not simply reproducing a reformed or accommodated present (Freire 1971).

Moving to the current, personal dimension for this turn, I think it's a matter of where I find myself in this late(r) period of my life, perhaps aging but certainly not yet finished, for the "real work" is never complete. Especially since legally mandated institutional retirement, I've wanted to draw on what I've done in order to think through what utopianism has to offer as we humans work together to make a better world. And so, you're right to say that this new time brings me closer to my former activist life insofar as I'm now involved in trying to make a more social, less institutional, contribution to changing the world and not simply understanding it: as Levitas puts it in her Foreword, this has partly involved going "back to what we were thinking about before we were interrupted by the need to earn a living." However, this move is not a circle but a spiral; for now my interventions are more reflective, happening more often in gatherings and writing than on the street. But in whatever mode, I do feel a resonance with that earlier time when I worked as an organizer and a teacher, now perhaps more directly as a person reaching out to others, in society at large and not only in the academy. While no longer building socialism by going to meetings every night (in the spirit of Oscar Wilde's call in *The Soul of Man under Socialism*), I am still committed to the vocation of co-creating a better world for all of humanity, carrying on with the standpoint and choice I made long ago. Now however, I do my part by researching and writing as well as teaching and mentoring, as and when I can. Also, from my location in Ireland, I support and join in campaigns against capitalism (now in this neoliberal moment); against militarism and all forms of organized violence; against sexism, racism, and all forms of xenophobia and hatred; and against the deepening destruction of nature—even as I endeavor to practice positive social and personal relations that are compassionate and cooperative, nurturing and facilitating, in the process of building that better world, existentially and sociopolitically.

But yes, in these dark times the utopian impulse does *appear* to have waned. Jameson, reaching back to Marcuse, has described this collapse as a weakening of utopian muscularity, and I agree. All one has to do is try teaching this material to appreciate this loss (I still conduct a final-year seminar on utopianism at

Limerick's architecture school; and while the students are concerned about this nasty world, their capacity to develop their dissatisfaction into a sustained transformative project is hampered by the shrinking of their university experience into narrow economic mandates). I think however that the utopian impulse only *appears* to have waned; for if we who are teachers listen closely to students and if we all look at the many struggles across the world, indeed if in all cases we listen deeply to each other, it is clear that there is still a persistent desire to stop what's going on and to create a better way of being. It's this ongoing project that gives me hope, and that inspires me to speak and write about the utopian problematic, the utopian process, and the utopian creation of radical new subjects. It's what I think we in the "party of utopia" need to do: to educate desire, to teach the history of how progressive struggles have been informed by utopian hope, to help with the formation of utopian agents, and to live *as utopians*. In doing this, very much in the spirit of '68, my hope is that, together, we can more productively nurture the "use value" of the utopian method in the sphere of actually existing politics—in political organizing, radical pedagogy, design and planning, artistic creation, in the implementation of local and global policies from the economic to the ecological—as well as in the daily practice of our everyday lives. Through mobilizing utopia as hermeneutic and intervention, I believe we as utopians can help articulate ways in which humanity can work together, in intersectional solidarity, to develop a totalizing project of transgression and transformation that aims to exorcize the specter of global apocalypse and actually achieve the end of capitalism.

I want to thank you, Hugh, for this opportunity to engage with your thoughtful and challenging questions. These are indeed terrible times. It is therefore all the more important that we respond—as citizens, as intellectuals and artists, as persons—with all our capacities, by calling up the strength and solidarity implicit in the utopian persuasion in order to critique and transform this world into one that enhances all of nature and humanity.

Annacotty, Ireland
March, 2020

Afterword: For Those Who Come Before

At the very heart of Tom Moylan's new book stands the question of how we become utopian in all aspects of our lives—not only as readers, scholars, and critics, but as teachers, organizers, activists, and even in our everyday interactions. If utopia is method—a notion developed by Ruth Levitas and which is so important for Moylan throughout *Becoming Utopian*—it is a method not only for reading but for making and living in the world.[1]

Moylan reminds us that utopia is always a becoming, something we must, as in Stanley Cavell's utopian concept of remarriage, renew and reinvent together, every day and in every moment.[2] What makes the work of this volume so exemplary is the way Moylan enacts a becoming utopian not only in the content but in the very form of his project. This book thus stands, as I noted in my comments on the occasion of the republication of Moylan's most influential book, *Demand the Impossible: Science Fiction and the Utopian Imagination* (1986 and 2014), "not only as a testimony to the possibility of doing things in new ways, it offers in its content and form an education of the desire to do so" (2014a: 282). In these chapters—worked on over the course of the three decades succeeding *Demand the Impossible*—Moylan makes a singular contribution both to the studies of science fiction and utopian literature (a contribution for which he is most well known, as Levitas reminds us in her generous opening remarks to this volume) and to a reinvigoration for our dark times of Marxism, dialectical theory, and utopianism more generally.

A crucial aspect of such a process of becoming utopian involves recognizing that our intellectual and political stances are deeply rooted in our concrete individual and collective histories and experiences: we become utopian, but we don't become utopian in conditions of our own choosing. In this spirit then, I would like to open with a personal anecdote. As I was beginning to work on this Afterword and re-reading Moylan's chapters—which in their earlier manifestations had a profound impact on my development as a scholar and teacher—I gave a series of talks at Kyungpook National University in Daegu, South Korea. (For the invitation to do so, allow me here to express my profound gratitude to Jin-Ho Kang.) The final presentation was a keynote lecture for a conference in honor of the sixtieth anniversary of the founding of The British and American Language and Literature Association of Korea. Preceding my talk, a former president of the Association, Joong-Eun Ahn, offered an overview of its founding and subsequent history. Although the talk was in Korean—a language I do not understand, something I regret given the vital literature, film, and scholarship being produced in Korea today—the speaker effectively conveyed through his slides and the response of his audience his profound gratitude to those who had come before and made possible the organization's current flourishing. At one especially touching moment, he showed a slide of himself as a young man at his wedding proudly standing alongside some of his teachers and the founder of the Association, Kyu-Dong Lee.

What moved me in this presentation was its ample generosity and expression of a deep sense of a shared collective project. Such a stance could not but strike a visitor such as myself as a way of being utopian, as it brushes against the grain of what Kathleen Fitzpatrick identifies as the "competitive individualism" that defines too many of our activities in the contemporary North American and European universities (Fitzpatrick 2019: 26). Fitzpatrick maintains,

> This individualistic, competitive requirement is inseparable from the privatization that [Christopher] Newfield describes as the political unconscious of the contemporary university. Competition and the race for individual distinction structure the growing conviction that not only the benefits of higher education but also all of our categories of success (both in educational outcomes and in intellectual achievement) can only ever be personal, private, individual rather than social.(28)

In response to recent arguments for a movement beyond critique—of which she notes "the critique of critique *is still critique*" and "is too often driven either by a disdain for difficulty or by a rejection of the political in scholarly work" (31)— Fitzpatrick further argues,

> rather than critical thinking … that which has in fact created an imbalance in scholarly work—and not just in the humanities, but across the curriculum— is *competitive* thinking, thinking that is compelled by what sociologist and economist Thorstein Veblen called "invidious comparison," or what [Winifred] Fluck refers to as the "race for professional distinction." It is the competitive that has undermined the capacity for community-building, both within our campuses and the broader public.(33)

In the face of such a dire situation, Fitzpatrick posits the utopian alternative of what she terms "generous thinking," which is "first and foremost a willingness to think *with* someone" and which "is grounded in a deceptively simple practice: listening" (55, 72). Fitzpatrick suggests that such a "connection with others that is grounded in listening may lie at the heart of what's required of all of us in order to ensure the future of all of our fields, including the humanities, the liberal arts more broadly, and in fact the university as we have known it" (73). It is just such a model of generosity and deep listening that is amply on display in *Becoming Utopian*.

Anyone who has worked with Tom Moylan will readily attest to his immense generosity as a mentor and a leader in the development of utopian studies. I have known and worked closely with Tom since the mid-1990s and without his unwavering support—expressed in his enthusiastic response to my earliest essays, advice on future writings, ongoing dialogue, press reviews and endorsements of my books, invitations to speak, and various letters of recommendation—I would not be in the position I am in today. Similarly, Moylan's work as the founding director of the Ralahine Centre for Utopian Studies has contributed in numerous ways to the growth of the inter-, trans-, and post-disciplinary spaces of utopian studies, fostering a greater sense of community and conversation across traditional disciplinary and national borders.

The same can be said for the Ralahine Utopian Studies book series, which Moylan played a central role in establishing. A purview of the volumes published in the series shows the breath and range of work—in political theory, literary and cultural studies, philosophy, architecture and urban planning, communal studies, and anthropology—that engages in a serious and sustained fashion with the problematic of utopia. One of the unique aspects of the series, alongside its original monographs, edited collections, and readers, is to be found in the Ralahine Classics: republications of groundbreaking studies, many of which are engaged with in some detail in the preceding chapters of this book, including Levitas's *The Concept of Utopia*, Darko Suvin's *Metamorphoses of Science Fiction: On the Poetics and History of a Literary Genre*, Barbara Goodwin and Keith Taylor's *The Politics of Utopia: A Study in Theory and Practice*, Vincent Geoghegan's *Utopianism and Marxism*, Robert C. Elliott's *The Shape of Utopia: Studies in a Literary Genre*, Angelika Bammer's *Partial Visions: Feminism and Utopianism in the 1970s*, and Moylan's own *Demand the Impossible*. These volumes, which also regularly include new material and collective meditations on the influence of the original, at once honor the sometimes-overlooked work of those who have come before, make it available to a younger generations of readers, and, most importantly, forge a sense of a multi-disciplinary and multi-generational community of those participating in the party of utopia.

A similar generosity and readiness to honor the work of those who have come before mark all of the chapters in this volume. Throughout, Moylan listens deeply to an extraordinary range of thinkers and puts their lessons to work in productive fashion. The opening chapters reveal the depth of Moylan's engagement with work of Ernst Bloch and liberation theology, especially for the latter in the landmark writings of Gustavo Gutiérrez. Indeed, one of the consequences of these first chapters is Moylan's establishment of the year 1971 as an especially momentous one for the development of utopian thought and action, as that year witnessed the publication of two works which introduced Bloch's immense and fecund thought to a wider audience—Fredric Jameson's *Marxism and Form: Twentieth-Century Dialectical Theories of Literature* and Gutiérrez's *Teología de la liberación: Perspectivas* (translated in 1973 under the title of *A Theology of Liberation: History, Politics, and Theology*)—and whose deep influence on his own becoming utopian Moylan readily acknowledges. Later chapters make evident the ongoing influence of the work and example of scholars such as Jameson and Suvin as well as activists including Bayard Rustin, David Dellinger, Daniel Berrigan, Saul Alinsky, and Paulo Freire. An equally generous mobilization takes place in these pages of the work of many contemporary and younger thinkers—Levitas, Geoghegan, Lyman Tower Sargent, Peter Fitting, Raffaella Baccolini, Lucy Sargisson, Kathleen Spencer, Søren Baggesen, Kathi Weeks, myself, and many others—as well as such more recent utopian fiction writers as Ken MacLeod, China Miéville, Philip Pullman, and Kim Stanley Robinson. There is even a generosity and invitation to collective dialogue expressed in the very design of this book, which includes both Levitas's Foreword and my Afterword, as well as poetry by Suvin, Robinson, and E.E. Cummings, and a marvelous contribution by the Irish cover artist, Sarah Browne.

In no way does Moylan's reading practice preclude critique. However, this is not the "pugilistic forms of critique" that Fitzpatrick identifies as a manifestation of the competitive ethos of the contemporary university and which are deployed "not only to demonstrate our dominance over the materials that we study and the ways that those who've gone before us have studied them, but also to establish and maintain our standing within the academic marketplace" (129–30). Rather, Moylan thinks with these works to underscore what he identifies as potential limits in them. Moreover, his first and most generous impulse is to focus on what he finds most productive about each of these projects and then build upon their potentialities by placing them in conversation with one another. A marvelous encapsulation of this practice of reading is to be found in Moylan's discussion of radical theology's own generous deployment of Bloch:

> Unlike Bloch, however, the most progressive of them did not inhibit their thinking with an ideological hypostatization of their own theology. Instead, they turned Bloch's critical utopian Marxism against his limitations as well as

their own and thereby generated a radical method that apprehends the signs of
the times and constantly looks beyond them to newly emergent possibilities in
human society.

Similarly, Moylan strenuously resists the temptation of the ethical binary, which
Jameson characterizes as "the root form of all ideology," as, for example, when
he argues that "we need to choose both (the vision of program and impulse, the
material of representation and figuration) so that we can approach these political
and formal modes in a dialectical fashion, thereby seeing how each opens up and
transforms the other" (2009: 408). The result is flexible and infinitely mobile
practices of reading, writing, and thinking that become utopian in the ways they
forge original intellectual assemblages and call into being a collectivity bound
together by a common project.

The roots of this exemplary practice of scholarly generosity lie in Moylan's
formative experiences. In both the autobiographical section of the book's
opening chapter and the concluding interview with Hugh O'Connell, Moylan
discusses his early years in Chicago as the son of working-class Irish Catholic
immigrants, his father having participated in the early twentieth-century
struggles for Irish independence. Moylan crucially notes, "Roman Catholic, in an
Irish immigrant way, I found a set of values and discipline (and repression) that
gave me an alternative to an increasingly consumerist culture, even as that larger
sphere offered enticements not allowed by my parochial life." His earliest political
activism was similarly shaped by his religious upbringing, first in the Young
Christian Students movement and then in the anti-racist activities of Chicago's
Catholic Interracial Council. This strand continued into his undergraduate years
at St. Mary's College in Winona, Minnesota, when he and his fellow activists drew
upon the "progressive teaching of Vatican II" in order to call "for more attention
in the curriculum and in college policy to questions of social justice," as well
as during his early years as a graduate student in Milwaukee, where he helped
organize the local chapter of the Catholic Worker. These activities ultimately
would lead him to his activist-based encounter with Marxism and critical theory.

These early experiences, coupled with his later deep reading and radical
political commitments, account for what I find to be one of the most important
contributions of this volume: namely, its underscoring of the theological
dimension of utopian thought and action—what Bloch memorably names
in the title of his most significant work *das Prinzip Hoffnung*, the principle
of hope. Indeed, one of the supplementary benefits of Moylan's work is the
renewed attention he brings to Bloch's discussion of religion, "Growing
Human Commitment to Religious Mystery, to Astral Myth, Exodus, Kingdom:

Atheism and the Utopia of the Kingdom," found in the third volume of *The Principle of Hope* (1183–311). First encountering Bloch in the radical theology of the 1950s, Moylan recognizes the deep roots of Bloch's concept of utopia in Western and even global religious traditions. If Marxism offers a scientific analysis—rigorous and axiom-based—of the capitalist mode of production, as well as its immanent tendencies toward crisis and expansion, then utopia provides Marxism with a vital ideological complement.[3] Walter Benjamin suggests something similar in the first of his theses "On the Concept of History," also invoked by Moylan at the openings of both Chapters 2 and 3 and elsewhere, where he maintains that Marxist historical materialism "can easily be a match for anyone if it enlists the services of theology, which today, as we know it, is small and ugly and has to keep out of sight" (2003: 389). In the spirit of Benjamin, Bloch, the liberation theologians, and others, Moylan strives to bring this aspect of the problematics of both Marxist and utopia into full view again.

Let me underscore that in no way do I mean ideology in the narrow sense of false consciousness, expressed in Marx's early condemnation of religion as "the opium of the masses" (1975b: 244). Rather, I have in mind something like Louis Althusser's still vital reformulation of ideology as the horizon of beliefs, values, and commitments that both constrain and enable our actions. For Althusser, there is no outside of ideology, and so the goal of any revolutionary commitment has to be the production of new ideology as much as the material conditions of existence. It is this latter sense of ideology that underlies what Marx refers to as the people's "demand for their *real* happiness" (1975b: 244). Such a notion of the "real" is not one that comes naturally, but rather is cultivated through a variety of mechanisms, what Althusser refers to as "ideological state apparatuses" (ISAs), such as the church, school, media, and other related institutions, representations, and practices. Moylan too suggests as much in his emphasis, in *Demand* and in these chapters, on the didactic elements of utopia: utopia as the "education of desire," a notion first developed by Miguel Abensour, and further expanded upon in productive ways by E.P. Thompson, Raymond Williams, Levitas, and others. In a beautiful evocation of this process that occurs near the conclusion of Chapter 5, Moylan writes:

> In this regard, the pedagogical opportunity of utopian sf works like the "subtle knife" in Philip Pullman's *Dark Materials Trilogy*: as a device that enables us, as it did for Will and Lyra, to cut through the boundaries of provincial reality and open a "gap in mid-air through which they could see another world" and, hopefully, learn that life in this world can be radically better. (Pullman 1998: 194)

For Moylan then, a vital resource for the cultivation of utopia is to be found in the traditions of radical theology (primarily Christian, but he also explores Judaic and Buddhist sources), extending from the twelfth-century medieval Renaissance writings of Joachim of Fiore up through Bloch and Benjamin and into liberation theology. I would also want to underscore the important contributions made by the early Christian mystic thinkers such as Origen and Gregory of Nyssa.[4] Bloch himself refers to the former, when he notes, "The more gentle as well as complete solution of Origen, apocatastasis or the bringing of all things, even of hell, into paradise, is rejected by Augustine, undoubtedly influenced by Persian dualism" (1248). Indeed, Origen's utopian doctrine of *apocatastasis* is also central to Jo Walton's brilliant recent historical and fantasy novel, *Lent* (2019).

These diverse and wide-ranging resources account for three fundamental aspects of the notion of utopia formulated over the course of Moylan's book: its universality, its totalizing nature, and its experiential dimensions. That is, utopia, as Moylan uses it, must be open to all people—to paraphrase John Sayle's extraordinary and still timely vision of radical labor organizing, *Matewan* (1987), any utopia that keeps this man out ain't a utopia, it's a club. And as Moylan's superb overview in Chapter 6 of Robinson's oeuvre indicates, it also now needs to take into account such non-human actors as the environment and planet. Second, utopia involves a radical break with the whole of what currently exists. However, this break is not a destination, but rather always open-ended and emerging, resisting premature closure and drawing us forward beyond the finitude of what is into the infinity of what might become. Finally, utopia in its fullness can only ever be experienced in itself, and hence utopia continuously draws attention to the challenges and limits of efforts to represent it directly. These axioms of utopia also suggest productive resonances with the recent thought of Alain Badiou concerning the ontological dialectic of being and event, and it thus comes as no surprise that in his introduction to this book Moylan also generously invokes Badiou.

It is his unwavering and confident fidelity to such a notion of utopia that enables Moylan at once to model a utopian generosity in his own writing and consistently counter both a conservative anti-utopianism (with its ideological privileging of our world as the least worst of all possible worlds) and so-called realistic utopias (grounded in anthropological myths evoking immutable laws of human nature and thus positing limits beyond which we dare not go). It is these last two ideologies that serve in our neoliberal moment as especially potent opiates of the people. With these principles, however, in no way does

Moylan dispense with the necessity of an engagement with the content of utopian visions, nor does he take any less seriously concrete and local political programs and experiences that might fall short of a true evental horizon. As he emphasizes throughout, and especially in the chapters making up the latter section of the book, utopia "not only negates the present but also generates the opportunity for a cognitive encounter with what might be and with what might be done to get there: for the present is not just made impossible by the invocation of utopia's horizon but also by the steps taken on the way (*unterwegs*) to it." Content and local action thus play indispensable roles in the pedagogies of hope, in the becoming utopian of any particular subject. As Moylan puts it: "While the representations of such possibilities will always be trapped within the limits of the present (dependent as they are on the ideological matrix of the time in which they are imagined), their utopian surplus (with its models or scenarios) can nevertheless deliver a pedagogical effect that stimulates debate, subverts capitulation, and provokes steps toward a transformative praxis."

Here then we arrive at one of the most important dimensions of Moylan's happily ongoing project. In his penultimate chapter, Moylan writes, "while utopia is indeed the name for the totalizing transformation of social space and time, the journey it requires inevitably involves agency ... Utopia begins to happen when, like Connie in Piercy's *Woman on the Edge of Time*, people say 'enough' and choose to enter the struggle for better lives in a better society." In short, utopia is always already the process of becoming utopian: it is fully imbricated in the education of every subject to demand *real* happiness—that is, to demand that which seems, especially in our current dark times, impossible. As Moylan stresses throughout his book, such an education is at once a matter of content and form, of theory and practice. In the book's concluding interview, Moylan states, "I've always considered my primary role to be that of a teacher (with research and writing necessary for good teaching)." In all of its multiple dimensions—in its generosity and call to community that brush against the grain of dominant institutional practices, in its underscoring of the inseparability of the experiential and the intellectual dimensions of all of our work, and in its revitalization of both the practical and theological dimensions of utopia— Moylan's book contributes so much to our own education in becoming utopian. He has become utopian before us, and his is a path that we would all benefit from following as best we can.

Phillip E. Wegner
Gainesville, 2019

Appendix: Sarah Browne, "Report to an Academy"

Author's Note

The artwork for the cover of *Becoming Utopian* grew out of a collaboration between the Irish artist Sarah Browne and myself as we discussed the process of radical utopian transformation. Both of us explore this process that involves a break from the normative order of the global system and the generation of a radical new way of being, not just individually but collectively, for all of humanity and all of nature. In our conversations, we agreed that any contribution from Sarah would not be a simple representation of my theme or argument but rather an expression of her own meditation on the utopian process.

The image of the octopus is a still taken from Browne's 2016 film essay, "Report to an Academy." As Browne describes it, her project appropriates and inverts the Franz Kafka story of the same title, where a captured ape delivers an address to an assembled academy of experts, pleading for mercy on the basis of how he has acquired speech and entered the community of human beings. In Browne's reformulation, the central character is one of the lecturers of the academy who has transformed herself from human material into an octopus. Struggling with the dysfunction of managerial language in the neoliberal university, she outlines the difficulties of solidarity, the constraints of academic freedom, and describes her search of new forms of articulacy and agility in an effort to "train the whole body as a tongue." The narrator's voice becomes feminine (a computerized feminine, since the octopus has surrendered speech), with a Glaswegian accent. This simulated voice is native to Apple Mac OSX, tool of choice of the creative industries and indicative of new kinds of prestigious and precarious work.

Certainly, both Kafka and Browne speak to the destructive alienation of modernity in general and academic life in particular (more so in the neoliberal/managerial university of our present time), yet both express a new voice and a new way of being. What I see and hear in Browne's creation is an even more radical figuration of a transformed subject: even less anthropomorphic than the primate, fluid in its watery world, yet expressive in its eye and mouth and the undulations of its tentacles. I find it a compelling and resonant expression of becoming utopian.

I am deeply grateful to Sarah for her wonderful contribution to this collaboration.

The transcript of its narrative follows below. The film can be viewed on request by contacting the artist: hello@sarahbrowne.info. I recommend doing so in order to appreciate the work's full power.

Credits

Written, directed and edited by Sarah Browne
   Voice: Fiona for Apple OSX 10.10.5
   Composition: Alma Kelliher
   Camera: Colum O'Dwyer, Sarah Browne
   Movement in collaboration with performers Saoirse Wall and Liv O'Donoghue
   Report to an Academy was commissioned for Manual Labours: The Complaining Body, the second stage of the practice-based research project Manual Labours initiated by Sophie Hope and Jenny Richards that explores people's physical relationships to work. Manual Labours: The Complaining Body is developed in partnership with The Showroom, London; In Certain Places, Preston and Movement and Division of Labour, Worcester. Manual Labours: The Complaining Body is supported by Arts Council England's Grants for the Arts, The Elephant Trust, The Birkbeck/Wellcome Trust Institutional Strategic Support Fund and Birkbeck University Widening Access.

Sarah Browne, "Report to an Academy"

Dear members of the Academy,

Thank you for the invitation to speak here today. It's an honour to be called upon to submit a report to the Academy concerning my previous life. Your inability to listen to, or to hear, my complaints when within the Academy was the primary reason I withdrew and made this leap into another existence, this choice to become an octopus. So, I must ask that you listen very carefully now when you did not before.

One night I had a dream that I was a bell that had the tongue taken out. In a way this was strange, but it was probably just caused by a typical day at work.

Though my mouth would fill up with words, repeatedly when I tried to speak up, usually in the Meetings, I could never seem to be heard. It was very perplexing. I began to think that there was perhaps a physical problem that was affecting my voice. Maybe my voice sounded too flat? Too weak or quiet? Maybe there was too much hiss? Was I speaking at the incorrect pace, or maybe without realizing it, I was speaking "through my nose" too much? Could it have seemed too croaky or high-pitched? I had a soft jaw you see, and a weak singing voice.

This was the main difficulty I had as a worker in the Academy: the persistent fight between verbal, or more severely, written language and material fact. The building itself was weeping—rebellious plumbing, wet walls—but this could never be acknowledged. Language beat down experience at every turn, forcing the impossible. It was entirely strange.

Confusedly reading draft documents, shyly searching out companionship, warily attempting to speak when anyone came near—these were the first occupations in my new role. I supposed that my apparent vocal ineptitude was my own fault, and that I would have to do something about it. Introduce training exercises, work with what body I had: tongue, larynx, vocal chords. So I began to carry out a series of physical exercises, particularly working on developing the muscular strength of my tongue, to correct these deficiencies. I tried flexibility, mobility and strength work; daily tutorials and exercises, a change in diet. I thought of this as an exercise in self-improvement, as if my body was a kind of capital that could be augmented through investment and continued attention. Internally, I became my own manager. But I felt alone in this apparently inadequate body that I needed to perform better, but seemed to keep failing me. The effort was producing a debt rather than a profitable return. I wondered was this also how the Students in the Academy experienced aspects of learning? Eventually I felt a searing, skinless shame with my poor performance, and nothing in my relations with the Managers had seemed to really change either. So I changed tactic and began to observe these Managers who would lead the Meetings. I wanted to investigate why they couldn't seem to hear.

I knew that different creatures have different kinds of hearing ability, depending on what the hearing sense is primarily used for. What is audible to a given species depends on a number of things, particularly the size of the body: the bigger the animal's body, the lower the frequency range. That's why animals smaller than humans, such as dogs, can hear much higher tones. Hearing is used to locate the presence of another, whether for mating or for prey. The hearing ability is usually sharpest in identifying the calls and vocalizations of others of the same species—so humans will hear the human voice most clearly, there will be a kind of a focussed pull towards sounds in that range.

Imagine being a toad, hearing sound underwater, where it travels four times faster … with flat discs for ears and sound waves distributed through your body, absorbed by your lungs, so that your outrageously loud mating calls can be safely absorbed without harming you. Imagine being in a body where the vocalised force of your desires would cause that body to explode? More predatory animals tend to be quiet, keeping an ear out for the movements of prey. I noticed in the Academy that we seemed to treat Managers as though they were predators, but they are actually rather verbose for that, and also often seem to have quite poor hearing. I looked at the men in the Meetings, going back and forth, always the same faces, the same movements. Often it seemed to me as if there was only one man. So the man or these men went undisturbed. No one promised me that I could become like them, should I want to. These men in themselves were nothing that attracted me very much. I would certainly have preferred the expanse of the ocean to the way out displayed in the dull gaze of these men. But in any case, I observed them for a long time before I even thought about such things.

In discussions after the Meetings, I noticed that the word "Kafkaesque" occurred very frequently with my colleagues—much more often than I'd expect when discussing daily working life rather than analysing literature.

Kafkaesque
Kafkaesque
Kafkaesque
Kafkaesque
Kafkaesque

I began to consider, what is that word really being used to describe? What does *Kafkaesque* feel like? What are some of the instances of the *Kafkaesque*?

I collected a number of examples:

Meetings are taken up with dates of planning for the next Meeting.

Phrases become solidified into forms that aren't understood clearly but are relied on as structural elements of conversation, leaving it with shaky foundations.

By this I mean phrases such as

spatial considerations
period of unprecedented cuts in resourcing and challenge
creating change makers
change management
consolidate the level of change
Was this striving metamorphosis the *Kafkaesque* bit?

Other phrases included

sectoral reform
educational landscape

doing more with less
academic offer
silo model of practitioner and related silo learning
institutional status quo
known employment but also employment not yet known

During a Meeting, a colleague's leave of absence due to illness, breast cancer, was described euphemistically as "the next challenge." It wasn't clear if this was a challenge to the workings of the Academy (her absence) or to her body (the presence of the cancer).

Because of the recent accounting scandal in the Academy, expenditure at every level needed to be examined closely. One eventual result was that a purchase order for soap could not be fulfilled. For a time, Students had to wash their hands with coffee grinds.[1]

Throughout the Meetings, there was a sensation of being underwater, that the atmosphere had thickened, become salty and viscous. I watched the mouths of my colleagues around me, noticing how they opened and closed in disbelief, like little fishes. I would sometimes spend time in the toilets afterwards, overwhelmed, listening to the institution gurgling around me and wondering how I could possibly survive it.

You might ask, what did the Students have to say about all this?

To my relief, and others too I'm sure, the Students protested and produced a list of demands. These demands were focused on material facts, such as the overcrowding, the need for more space for them to work in and the dilapidated state of both equipment and financial practices. New chairs were ordered that had strange little hinged attachments; micro-desks that reduced the need for table space. They were made of cheap plastic and frequently snapped. The Students drew attention to specific costs that affected them in monetary and bodily ways: new supplementary fees had been introduced, without evidence of how the money was being spent, and there was a new charge for them to visit the doctor, which previously had been free.[2]

The Students articulated the difficulties of ideas like *freedom* and *cost* in the Academy. We were all constrained by debts of various kinds. Sometimes I sorrowfully thought of that as our common bond. And our freedoms, like freedom of speech or expression, didn't seem to be symmetrical either.[3]

Complaints manifested privately too, unofficially, addressed to an uncertain audience. Inside the women's bathrooms in the Students' social area was a stall with one side covered by graffiti. The wall accommodated a variety of expression. There were declarations of love and lust:

Small, neat and emphatic: *I [heart] Fiona O'Neill*
Tall letters, exuberant: *I [heart] Jakey*
There was philosophizing and agony aunt-ing:
Do what you want, don't wait for approval (except rape)
Do boys actually have feelings like girls do?

There were discussions about the relative merits of various academic courses. And there were what might be called anonymous cries for help:

Loopy lettering, up high on the wall: *Help me please, I'm giving up rather quickly*

Concise capital letters: I'M SO LONELY FUCK RADIOHEAD

I had never seen so many diverse representations of penises and vulva, styled both cartoonishly and with a veiny, hairy, enthusiastic attention to realism. And among the drawings of cocks and cunts, where women sat to take a piss or a shit, blunt frustration with the Academy loomed too.

Frustrated cursive in black marker: *Why is this place so under-funded? What the fuck?!*

Doodling, leisurely, elaborated letters: *This college is a kip.*

Terse capitals, eye-level when sitting on the toilet: *This college has been destroyed by bad management. It is shameful.*

I was not frightened of the Students. I didn't fear complaints from them and I didn't worry that I would be accused of being insensitive toward their feelings. I didn't think of them like customers wielding the power of the complaints line, and I didn't feel that my rights to do as I wished were being curtailed by them, though it seemed others did. But speaking with them freely was not straightforward either. Legislation has been introduced recently that requires educators at all levels to keep watch for Students who are vulnerable, at risk of radicalisation, and makes the reporting of that student mandatory.[4] What critically-minded, political student could safely or wisely speak without fear of repercussions? What happens to the values of open, critical engagement and fearless speech in the Academy then?

I was not afraid to talk to them; but I feared for them talking to me. It seemed we needed a new physical language altogether, some kind of way out of all this. I realized that rather than speaking with them I might be have to model a way out.

I had started to understand that *Kafkaesque* was being used by my colleagues to describe the watery sense of unreality I'd been experiencing, the separation between language and sense that bordered on violence, and the atmosphere of looming, uncertain threat. It clearly affected the Students too, even if we had different modes of describing and responding to it. This kind of language had certain spatial peculiarities, spatial politics even. It was mainly the language of the Managers, quite forceful in its written expression, flooding into all available gaps and squeezing out any bubbles of difference or disagreement. It performed tricks with matter, pressuring new realities into existence through macabre documents, press releases and spreadsheets. More students needed to be accommodated in less space. Teaching needed to be accelerated, somehow. Apparently from nowhere and through dint of its sheer insistence this language formed an invisible but impermeable force.

By this point, I had learned that the existence of a policy can change what is possible, even if that policy is not explicitly acted on. I learned that speech itself can cause harm, and that the Academy always wants to limit damage to itself. I learned that continual talking about change, whether how to implement or "manage" it, mainly produced stasis and inhibited movement.

The Meetings had also begun to give me minor pain, but pain I couldn't prove, because the pain obliterated language even as it had to be described inside it.

[Jumping, Flashing, Shooting, Pricking, Boring, Drilling, Stabbing, Sharp, Cutting, Lacerating, Pinching, Pressing, Gnawing, Cramping, Crushing, Tugging, Pulling, Wrenching, Hot, Burning, Scalding, Searing, Tingling, Itchy, Smarting, Stinging, Dull, Sore, Hurting, Aching, Heavy, Tender, Taut (tight), Rasping, Splitting, Tiring, Exhausting, Sickening, Suffocating, Fearful, Frightful, Terrifying, Punishing, Grueling, Cruel, Vicious, Killing, Wretched, Blinding, Annoying, Troublesome, Miserable, Intense, Unbearable]

So, I began to devise a plan. I realised that speaking was not the way to find a way out in the Academy. I began a new series of practical exercises, leaving the linguistic to one side and instead focusing on the physical. Previously, I had been trying to train my tongue inside my body to perform better, which was the wrong approach: I realized that what I needed to do was train my whole body as a tongue.

Initially I had to learn by imitation, and as an educator, imitation was not something that pleased me. I imitated because I was looking for a way out, for no other reason.

The first things I had to learn were –
How to smell and taste with my entire body, through my skin
How to feel my brain dispersed through my arms rather than my head
How to become agile enough to tie a knot in my arm
How to locate my mouth in my armpit
How to move using jet propulsion
How to squirt ink

How to flow into holes and tiny crevices
How to change the colour and texture of my surface
How to become boneless

It was extremely difficult, as a vertebrate, to learn how to behave otherwise. Not to scream or shout or cry in frustration when I remained attached to my skeletal imaginary. It was infuriating—I'd decided to be a formless bag of protein, why couldn't I do it! But instead of that, and because I couldn't do anything else, because my senses were roaring, I'd sometimes cry out, HELLO! HELLO! breaking out into human sounds.

And with this cry I sprang back into the community of human beings, and I felt its echo like a kiss on my entire sweat-soaked body. All too often, the lesson went that way.

However, I learned, as one has to. One learns when one wants a way out. One learns ruthlessly. There was an urgency to all this: there wasn't much time left in my contract.

I'm concerned that you might not understand precisely what I mean by a way out. I use the expression in its most common and fullest sense. I am deliberately not saying freedom. I do not mean this great feeling of freedom on all sides. As far as I am concerned, I did not demand freedom either then or today. People all too often deceived by ideas of freedom, and I didn't want that. Only a way out—to the right or left or anywhere at all. To move on further! Sucking, tasting, holding, grabbing, releasing.

To master the training of an escape artist, I needed to recognise and interpret my environment. The only properly dry substance in the Academy was the chalk, and I recognised that even that was composed of million-years-old sea creatures. How could I deal with this place that declared itself to be dry, but felt watery? I started to eat more fish, moving from cooked, to raw, to still alive. I developed an appetite for crab, greedily enjoying the sensation of crunching up their shells and sucking out the flesh inside. I realised that I needed to produce more lubrication to move through the Academy: literally, I needed to produce a kind of slime. Slime could help me move through the institution without drag. It would help me slip from the catch of predators and squeeze through constricted spaces. It would keep my skin fresh and healthy and deliver me nutrition. Slime feels really good, and it doesn't wreck or damage anything: the only problem is that some people find it disgusting. I realized that if I could overcome my personal shame, I would discover a new power in my state of abjection at the Academy. So I would practice after hours by sitting in my office or the first floor toilets, willing myself to get wet, for my body to leak outside itself.

Everything I could want to learn about the labour politics of the Academy could be found in those toilets. I overheard the Cleaners describing how two of their colleagues, longstanding workers in the Academy, had recently lost their jobs when the contract changed. Something similar had happened in the 1980s, and after the cleaners had gone on strike they were surprised to come in one Saturday to see very senior Academics, wearing jeans and overalls, crossing the picket to clean the bins and the toilets.[5] It was one of the Cleaners who interrupted my training one day too as I sat in the toilet stall—I must have forgotten to lock the door in my enthusiasm. The shock of discovery made me drench myself suddenly in fright, and as the dense blackness of the ink squirted over the white ceramic and tiles in the stall, I realized my transition was complete. I saw the Cleaner's face curdle in shock, and then wonder, before he carefully gathered up my slimy arms, placed me in a bucket and brought me to the Academics. This is how I come to be delivering this report now.

Learning in captivity, my accomplishments are limited. But if I review my development and its goal up to this point, I do not complain.

I know that opinion thinks badly, or not at all. I have no opinions for you, those ideas that come before effort. I have only the sensations of my new body, and the knowledge that each body distributes in its own special way.

I now know how to see almost in complete darkness, dilating my pupils as if newly in love:

> Where before everything seemed beige, now my skin can see, and produce so many colours.
>
> My body is nearly completely silent, but my insides know unheard-of songs.
>
> I can taste many things that I couldn't before: I can even taste the difference between tears of irritation and happiness. I know that being deaf to others, whether Students, women, or Eskimos, amounts to the same thing as being deaf to other forms of knowledge. This exclusion will protect the structure, even if the structure is empty. I am here to tell you that it isn't worth it.

I know that on the whole, I have achieved what I wished to achieve, and I will keep working with what time I have left. Given that my solitary nature is now softening and turning towards companionship, I can tell the end is close. In any case, I don't want any judgment. I only want to expand knowledge. I simply report.

Given that I have tried my hardest to withdraw from speaking, this may be my last one.

Notes

Introduction

1   In the same "Symposium," P. Murphy challenges sf and sf studies to address the fatalism of "what-if" stories and to champion "if-then" stories that reject the compensations of resignation or techno-fixes and explore radical alternatives (2018).

2   See R. Williams, "Structures of Feeling," *Marxism and Literature* (1977: 128–36).

3   Levitas develops her critique of the limits of a "utopianism" that is expressed singularly as an "open" process rather than as a critical openness dialectically imbricated in the holistic movement toward and achievement of revolutionary transformation; see R. Levitas, *The Concept of Utopia* (1990: 156–200). In many ways, *Becoming Utopia* is an extended reflection on her critique.

4   The phrase "concrete dystopia" was coined by M. Varsam in "Concrete Dystopia: Slavery and Its Others," *Dark Horizons* (2003a). Varsam drew on Ernst Bloch's concept of "concrete utopia" as she inverted his evocation of a realistically utopian possibility within the existing world as a form of anticipation that can transform human imagination and activity (as opposed to his category of "abstract utopia" which offers idealized wishful dreams that are compensatory in so far as they deflect the desire for radical change into the realm of the never attainable). For Varsam, the practice of slavery, historically and in the present, is brought down to earth as darkly and totally real. As she puts it: "What concrete utopia shares with concrete dystopia is an emphasis on the real, material conditions of society that manifest themselves as a result of humanity's desire for a better world. For both, reality is not fixed but fluid, pregnant with both positive and negative potential for the future ... concrete utopia brings together the past and present, creating thus a continuum in time whereby historical reality is dystopian, possibly punctuated by utopian ruptures in the form of literature, art, and other cultural manifestations" (208). On concrete utopia, see E. Bloch, *The Principle of Hope* (1986: *passim*) and *On Karl Marx* (1971a: 159–73); see also the commentary by R. Levitas in *The Concept of Utopia* (1990: 83–106).

5   See U. Le Guin's description of the General Temporal Theory developed in her utopian society of Anarres, which achieves a unitary physics of sequence and simultaneity, of the diachronic and the synchronic (Le Guin 1974: 195–7), also expressed in Shevek's declaration that he prefers to make things difficult

by choosing "both" (see 197). G. Gutiérrez draws on Marx's "Third Thesis on Feuerbach," which argues that the revolutionary task includes both transforming consciousness and altering conditions (1973: 265–72). In this articulation, Gutiérrez draws on the denunciation/annunciation formulation used in the radical pedagogy of Paulo Freire as he develops his argument that utopia is "revolutionary and not reformist" (1973: 233). For more on Gutiérrez and Freire, see Chapter 3, "Denunciation/Annunciation" and Chapter 8, "Next Steps," respectively.

6 Bloch's *Principle of Hope* helped to produce a renewed engagement with utopianism in the development of post–Second World War critical Marxist theory and politics, especially after the publication of English translations from the 1960s. For more, see Chapter 2, "Bloch Against Bloch," and Chapter 3, "Denunciation/Annunciation."

7 I am grateful to Jack Zipes for reminding me that "Hope for a Better World" was the original title for *Principle of Hope*.

8 See F. Jameson, "Utopia as Replication," *Valences of the Dialectic* (2009: 410–35).

9 In developing this line of thought regarding the formation and activity of the flourishing utopian subject, I'm grateful to Kathleen Eull for our ongoing conversations in which our particular standpoints and approaches (hers, broadly but not exclusively Buddhist and meditative; mine, broadly but not exclusively Marxist and activist) continue to embraid and unfold as we explore the nature of reality, subjectivity, and, most basically, being in the world.

10 See E. Bloch, "Upright Carriage, Concrete Utopia" (1971b: 159–73); and V. Geoghegan, *Ernst Bloch* (1996: 40–1). In the final section of his astute study, Geoghegan discusses Bloch's "radical materialism" and his belief in the "dynamic element in nature" and locates humanity *within* the unfolding potentialities of nature (153). In an extension of Friedrich Engels' dialectics of nature, Bloch positions humans as thoroughly embedded in nature independent of their consciousness yet capable of acting self-consciously within this totality. He thereby establishes the framework for an understanding of a "natural subject" that is unfinished and incomplete, "with its genesis at the end and at the beginning" (155). Bloch's cosmic utopian perspective therefore enables Geoghegan to situate the human subject as part of a much larger utopian reality. I locate my own discussion of the human continuum of impulse, practice, and horizon within this larger perspective; and in this regard, I develop my understanding of the utopian subject as both ontological and political (see Chapter 6, "N-H-N'").

11 On *habitus*, see P. Bourdieu (1977).

12 For more on my approach to the relationship between the utopian and the ideological, see T. Moylan, "The Utopian Imagination," *Demand the Impossible* (1986: 15–29).

13 See H. Marcuse, *One-Dimensional Man* (1964). This resonance is particularly evident in Book Two of *Gestalt Therapy* (1951: 400–1, especially). Of course,

Marcuse can be read more fruitfully within the context of the larger Frankfurt School project, including the works of Eric Fromm, Theodore Adorno, and Max Horkheimer. I also recognize that this line of analysis resonates (in its negative diagnosis but not in its radical response) with Michel Foucault's work on the disciplinary society.

14 In *Gestalt Therapy*, the description of the compliant subject of advanced Western industrial society suggests the poetic anticipation in W. H. Auden's poem of 1939, "The Unknown Citizen," which ends with the following lines: "Was he free? Was he happy? The question is absurd: / Had anything been wrong, we should certainly have heard": see W. H. Auden (1940: 85).

15 See, for example, the discussion in Book Two, *Gestalt Therapy* (1951: 358–71).

16 On the Event and the break, see A. Badiou, *Being and Event* (2005). For the most developed statement of Badiou's communist standpoint, see *The Communist Hypothesis* (2010). For a still timely presentation of the ways in which people who are "subject to social abjection" throw off their dehumanization through the process of struggle and revolt, see I. Tyler, *Revolting Subjects* (2013: 39).

17 See also A. Badiou (2001).

18 In *Utopia as Method*, Levitas also draws on the existential quality of "grace" as she describes the utopian engagement of being human as, for example, "the longing for [the utopian horizon of] Heimat and for the fulfilled moment can also be understood as the quest for a (sometimes) secular form of grace … [which is] the root of gracefulness and graciousness" (2013: 11–12).

19 For one example of Badiou's concept of fidelity to an Event, see his discussion of the Paris Commune in *Communist Hypothesis* (2010: 168–229). Here, I note the resonance between Badiou's examples of the Event and that of Bloch's list of concrete utopian moments (with many overlaps, including the Commune), and between Badiou's mobilizing sense of fidelity and that of Bloch's description of the ability to tap the "utopian surplus" within concrete utopian moments in the service of inspiring and informing subsequent revolutionary conditions.

20 My metaphor of titration comes from quantitative chemistry, wherein it names the process in which a measured volume of a solution is slowly added (drop-by-drop via a burette) into another solution in a flask until the observable solution markedly changes (typically, in color). For me, the drop-by-drop quantitative process resulting in a qualitative transformation has always captured the dialectical nature of long-term political organizing and social revolution rather than the metaphor of, say, a nuclear explosion.

21 See E. P. Thompson, *William Morris* (1977); R. Williams, "Utopia and Science Fiction" (1978).

22 Continuing this thread from Thompson, Levitas draws on the work of George Steiner and offers his question to capture the core of this educative process: "what do you feel, what do you think of the possibilities of life, of the alternative shapes

of being which are explicit in your experience of me, in our encounter" (quoted in Levitas 2013: 15). As she puts it, "just as the education of desire aims implicitly or explicitly at social transformation and the instauration of concrete utopia, so Steiner asserts that this interrogation intends change, at least in our encounter with human others" (Levitas 2013: 15).

23 See Badiou's discussion of this collective trajectory in his provocative discussion of the Chinese Cultural Revolution in *The Communist Hypothesis* (2010: 112–13, especially).

24 An extended exploration of the role of change agents (such as teachers, therapists, artists, organizers) in the formation of utopian subjects must wait for another time. However, I will offer a few indications of the direction in which such a discussion could go. Certainly, the praxis of Perls, Hefferline, and Goodman offers an example of the type of radical therapy that can generate a utopian gestalt shift. In terms of the literal education of desire, the practice of radical pedagogy offers the type of utopian development of desire implied in the work of Thompson, Williams, and Levitas. Here, of course, Freire (1971) is the primary text, but also see the wider body of work on radical pedagogy, especially in the Northern Hemisphere, by Henry Giroux and Ira Shor, and most recently Darren Webb. On the nature and techniques of political organizing, the literature is extensive; for me, the primers for effective organizing of newly radicalized individuals into a collective movement are those by S. Alinsky *Reveille for Radicals* (1989a) and *Rules for Radicals* (1989b); and for an exemplary filmic narrative that explores the role of the organizer and the organizing process, see J. Sayles, *Matewan* (1987). Again, the impact of art and artistic practice in the development of radical subjects is extensive, but one of the key works is H. Marcuse, *Eros and Civilization* (1955). See also Levitas' caveat on the relationship between art and the development of utopian subjectivity and practice in *Utopia as Method* (2013: 10–19). For more on Alinsky and Freire, see Chapter 8, "Next Steps."

25 See K. Weeks, "The Future Is Now: Utopian Demands and the Temporalities of Hope," *The Problem with Work* (2011: 175–227).

26 For a thoughtful account of *L'Organisation Politique* (OP) and Badiou's role as an activist intellectual within it, see A. Robinson, "Alain Badiou: Political Action and the *Organisation Politique*" (2015).

27 I refer to the importance of the Wisconsin Alliance in my Coda, "'68 and the Critical Utopian Imagination." How this model can be recognized and worked with in contemporary political formations (such as *Organisation Politique* in France, the Zapatistas (EZLN) in Mexico, the Indignados in Spain, Momentum in the UK, or Black Lives Matter and the Democratic Socialists of America in the United States, to name but a few examples) is of course a matter of pressing importance. For an additional way of interpreting the forcefulness and effectivity of such formations,

see P. McLean, *Culture in Networks* (2017); and for an insightful analysis of the "soft politics" of republican, feminist, socialist consciousness and action enabled by the network of the radical salon culture of the late nineteenth and early twentieth centuries, see C. Ní Bheacháin and A. Mitchell, "Alice Stopford Green and Vernon Lee: Salon Culture and Intellectual Exchange" (2019).

28 I am grateful to Laurence Davis for his thoughtful gloss on my refusal to be held back by an instrumental realism trapped within the amber of the present as opposed to the radical realism of which utopian transformation is capable. As Davis put it in a private email: "I particularly like Zygmunt Bauman's early formulation of the relationship between utopianism and realism in his book *Socialism: The Active Utopia* (1976). As Bauman aptly observes, it is precisely the unnuanced boldness of utopian insight, its ability to cut loose and be impractical, that sets the stage for a genuinely realistic politics that takes stock of all opportunities in the present. By exposing the partiality of current empirical reality, by scanning the field of the possible in which the presently real occupies merely a tiny plot, utopianism paves the way for a transformative critical attitude and activity. Or, as Ruth Levitas notes more concisely, what is needed now more than ever is a transformative utopian realism that recognizes (in drawing on Roberto Unger) that we must be visionaries to become realists. In short, let's not concede the political terrain of realism to the fantasists who insist that capitalism and liberal democracy are the be all and end all of history."

Chapter 1

1 On the discrete and iconic registers of the sf/utopian text, their relationship in critical utopias, and critical utopianism as a radical form of utopian method, see T. Moylan, *Demand the Impossible*, Ralahine Classic Edition (2014a): this edition includes the original text but also a new introduction by me and critical reflections on the critical utopia by a number of contemporary scholars.

2 In *Archaeologies*, Jameson recalls Perry Anderson's assertion that the utopias of the 1960s (Anderson focuses on Piercy) "were somehow the last traditional ones," even as they themselves were a move away from earlier utopian forms (2005: 216). Moving forward to the 1980s, the break achieved by neoliberalism and neoconservatism and the crisis of socialism called forth yet another creative moment, one in which we see not only the negativities of cyberpunk and the critical dystopia but also a "new formal tendency" that, as in Robinson's work for example, does not represent utopia as such but rather registers a "conflict of all possible utopias, and the arguments about the nature and desirability of utopia as such" (216). While I agree with Jameson's recognition of this historical and formal

development, for me the critical utopias did not so much end the older tradition as begin this new set of tendencies, indeed leading to utopian writing that Robinson and others have developed from the late 1980s to the present. Working from the utopian surplus of that critical utopian impulse, and against such setbacks, the *eutopian* imaginary is still stubbornly, and creatively, at work; see also the work of R. Kabo on "commons utopias," for a more contemporary example (2020).

3   See *Archaeologies,* in which Jameson discusses dystopia (including the critical dystopia) and recognizes the difference between the critical dystopia that carries utopian hope and classical dystopias (such as Orwell's) that tend toward the anti-utopian ("Journey into Fear"). Rather than stressing this difference as indicative of an epistemological, formal, political break, it can be useful to read these relative textual positions along the continuum proffered in *Scraps of the Untainted Sky* wherein the dystopian genre can be seen as working within a militant, utopian pessimism to those adopting a resigned, anti-utopian pessimism (see *Scraps,* Chapters 5 and 6) and my discussion in Chapter 4, "Look into the Dark."

4   Jameson's use of the term "enclave" in *Archaeologies* operates at a different register than the textual analysis of the enclave as a formal element in the critical dystopia that Baccolini and I develop; however, there is a direct relationship between the two. As Jameson puts it, utopian space "is an imaginary enclave within real social space," and its "possibility is dependent on the momentary formation of a kind of eddy or self-contained backwater within the general differentiation process and its seemingly irreversible forward momentum" (2005: 15). This description of utopian space as a productive holding mechanism or counter-hegemonic zone within the apparently unstoppable drive of history can stand as a referent for the very textual signifier of the utopian enclave found in the critical dystopias (see also Kabo 2020).

5   As Jameson puts it, the utopian calling comes "to us as barely audible messages from a future that may never come into being" (2004: 54).

6   On "utopian energy," see L. T. Sargent, "Choosing Utopia: Utopianism as an Essential Element in Political Thought and Action," *Utopia Method Vision* (2007: 301–19).

7   The utopian function of forward-looking memory is brought to life in Robinson's alternative history, K. S. Robinson, *The Years of Rice and Salt* (2002). In this counter-epic, three characters (I, K, and B) reappear in historical episodes from the eighth century up to present day, revolutionary China. As they live, die, and are resurrected (in Robinson's materialist version of this process), the three take control of history by finding a way to retain their memories (and hence their power to know and revolt) that are always erased by the gods after each lifetime. This process enters its critical stage when one of the three, Iagogeh, draws on a text she had written in an earlier life in her efforts to retain a political memory and articulates their revolutionary strategy of refusing to drink "the vial of forgetting" (Robinson

2002: 333). Following her plan, the three spit out the gods' liquid of forgetting and reach the shore of their new lives with memories intact. Iagogeh then reminds them that in this new life they can remember, and "make something new" (335).

Chapter 2

1   This encounter between Christianity and Marxism can be helpfully understood in terms of the work of E. Laclau and C. Mouffe that describes the way in which a "sutured" or closed discourse can be opened to new possibilities of analysis and action through a process of "interruption" or subversion by an external discourse. As they argue, "it is only in terms of a different discursive formation" that the "positivity" of the categories of a given discourse can be challenged and changed. In other words, what is needed is a "discursive 'exterior' from which the discourse in question can be interrupted" (1985: 154).

2   D. Kellner and H. O'Hara in "Utopia and Marxism in Ernst Bloch" (1976) rightly resist a simple cooptation of Bloch by theologians of any stripe and point out the important break with institutional Christianity that Bloch's work represents. However, I fear they fall into an orthodox Marxist trap of rejecting all revolutionary potential in the religious sphere and miss the subtleties of Bloch's refunctioning of religious space. As G. Raulet notes, "Bloch's thought rediscovers the meaning of Marx's statement that the critique of religion is the precondition of all critique" (Raulet 1976: 84).

3   For Bloch, Feuerbach represents the point at which "the final history of Christianity begins" (1986: 1286). Feuerbach "brought religious content ... back to man, so that man is not made in the image of God but God in the image of man ... As a result God as the creator of the world disappears completely, but a gigantic creative region in man is gained, into which—with fantastic illusion, with fantastic richness at the same time—the divine as a hypostatized human wishful image of the highest order is incorporated" (1284–5). The limitation of Feuerbach, however, is that he "knows man ... only in the form of existence in which he has so far appeared, an abstractly stable form of existence, that of the so-called species of man.., above all man's uncompletedness is missing here" (1285). Bloch therefore breaks with Feuerbach's mechanical materialism: "There is least place of all in Feuerbach's statically existent subject for status-shattering images of religion" (1285). In Bloch's analysis, "religion as inheritance (meta-religion) becomes ... the act of transcending without any heavenly transcendence but with an understanding of it; as a hypostatized anticipation of being-for-itself" (1288).

4   As A. Rabinbach puts it in "Ernst Bloch's *Heritage of Our Times* and the Theory of Fascism," Bloch "rejects the view accepted by Marxism, if not by Marx himself,

that religion is merely a compensation for an unpalatable and painful existence. The paradox of the rationalized world is that it cannot contain the powerful forces within human beings which not only created belief and affirmation in the past, but also constantly emerge to challenge it in the present. Religion is not merely the expression of conditions which demand illusion, but a human potential that nourishes itself with illusion only insofar as it cannot fully find expressions in reality" (1977: 9).

5   An analysis of Bloch's treatment of religions other than Judaism and Christianity must wait for another time, but a consideration of Bloch's work from the perspective of Edward Said's critique of orientalism, along with all the work following from this, would be an enlightening project. One important development in this direction (even though he does not directly reference Bloch) is Thomas Merton's exploration of the intersections among Catholic, Buddhist, and Marxist thought and practice. Undertaken by this monk/theologian/poet late in his life, this work is best seen in T. Merton, *Asian Journal* (1975).

6   For more on messianism and its creatively destructive power by Bloch and Benjamin, see A. Rabinbach, "Between Enlightenment and Apocalypse" (1983).

7   For more on the implicit atheism of Judaism and Christianity, see E. Bloch, "Religious Truth" (1971c); and T. Moylan, "Rereading Religion: Ernst Bloch, Gustavo Guttiérez and the Post-Modern Strategy of Liberation Theology" (1988).

8   My summary, and critique, of Moltmann and Metz draws on their own work and on Gutiérrez's assessments. See J. Moltmann (1967), J. Metz (1969), and G. Gutiérrez (1973).

9   The influence of liberation theology can also be seen in those areas of (in the terminology of the time) the "First World" that functioned as "Third World" sectors of the economic and social machinery of global capitalism. These included, for example, Ireland, Spain, and the predominantly Hispanic areas of the Southwestern United States (especially in Los Angeles and along the US-Mexican border).

10 For histories of liberation theology, see P. Berryman (1987), P. Kirby (1981), and P. Lernoux (1982). For my early discussions of Guttiérez, see T. Moylan, "Rereading Religion" (1988) and "Mission Impossible: Liberation Theology and Utopian Praxis" (1990).

11 On the metaphor of the "upright gait," see E. Bloch, "Upright Carriage, Concrete Utopia" (1971b: 168–75, especially).

12 I would further argue that Joachim of Fiore's apocalyptic theology, developed in the tumultuous twelfth century at the onset of not yet recognizable Western modernity, offers a proto-political (indeed proto-utopian) dialectical sublation of the Old Testament God of law and the New Testament God of redemption in his account of a new gospel of the Holy Spirit, which then serves as the guide for a transformed human community of love in apocalyptic times (thus working as a figurative sign

and narrative of hope in the Franciscan monk's own time and available now as a utopian surplus for humanity today in this apocalyptic moment); perhaps the radical mass politics implicated in the figure of Thomas Műntzer is also equally timely. For useful discussions of Joachim, see M. Reeves (1969 and 1976), M. Reeves and W. Gould (1987), and B. McGinn (1979).

13 See E. Bloch, "A Jubilee for Renegades" (1975) for Bloch's defense of his support for the Moscow trials. For a historical perspective on Bloch's position, see O. Negt (1975) and D. Gross (1988). For a sobering critique of Bloch, see T. Eagleton (2015); although for a contrapuntal critique of Eagleton's approach to Bloch, see J. Zipes (2019), 178–9.

14 Bloch's criticism of the immersive oppression perpetrated by US capitalism is not addressed in this chapter. As Jan Bloch suggests, the elder Bloch did not develop an adequate dialectical reading of US society that identified the progressive potential as well as the exploitative dangers of the emerging consumer society. Nevertheless, Bloch did anticipate the social failures of the postwar affluent society. In the light of his insights into the false promises of the "American utopia," Bloch's uncritical support of the Soviet Union (as also happened with so many members of the US Communist Party, and Popular Front fellow travelers, who also looked through red-tinted glasses from a distance) is perhaps more understandable, but this is a matter for a much longer treatment that deals with the tensions between engaged activism and sustaining ideology.

15 On Bloch's later repudiation of Stalinism, see E. Bloch, "Upright Carriage, Concrete Utopia" (1971b).

16 I would be tempted to characterize the two strands running through Bloch's work as "anarchist" and "Marxist" if those words were not themselves subject to far too much ideological fixation. Bloch's early political outlook is still largely unexamined (as A. Rabinbach asserts in "Between Enlightenment and Apocalypse," 109; but see V. Geoghegan 1996); that said, Bloch's combination of anarchist, pacifist, expressionist, messianic, apocalyptic positions was radically unorthodox and appears to have generated a deep aleatory strain that constitutes one strand of his dialogic tension. Indeed, his later move into Marxism seems to have been prevented from becoming fully orthodox by this early sensibility. Contrary to J. Zipes's speculation that Bloch's early positions appear "to have prevented him from seeing reality," it may well have been the opposite case that this radical base was the key factor that informed his revelatory method of reading utopia against the ideological grain and therefore the source of the attitude that kept him from totally adhering to the orthodox strand of his work (Zipes 1988: 6).

17 Here, see Jameson's discussion of the imbrication of the utopian and the ideological (even in discourses such as fascism) in *The Political Unconscious* (1981: 281–301, especially).

18   For two examples of the critical post-Western discourse emerging from the indigenous cultures of Central America as they have been influenced by the intersection of Marxism and Christianity in liberation theology, see the essays of T. Borge, *Christianity and Revolution* (1987) and the *testimonio* of Rigoberta Menchú (1983). For more on Menchú, see J. Beverley (1989) and G. Yúdice (1983).

Chapter 3

1   W. Benjamin: "The story is told of an automaton constructed in such a way that it could play a winning game of chess, answering each move of an opponent with a countermove. A puppet in Turkish attire and with a hookah in its mouth sat before a chessboard placed on a large table. A system of mirrors created the illusion that this table was transparent from all sides. Actually, a little hunchback who was an expert chess player sat inside and guided the puppet's hand by means of strings. One can imagine a philosophical counterpart to this device. The puppet called 'historical materialism' is to win all the time. It can easily be a match for anyone if it enlists the services of theology, which today, as we know, is wizened and has to keep out of sight" (1969: 253).

2   Among those who have responded to what Lamb calls the "theological challenges" are S. Aronowitz (1981), J. Kovel (1986), and C. West (1982).

3   Two points: first, this chapter focuses on liberation theology as it has developed in Roman Catholic discourse. The Protestant tradition of "freedom of judgment, reliability, pioneering and enterprising spirit, and moral seriousness" also contributes an important emphasis on "activity, culture, and life as opposed to ritualism, idle speculation, and the next world" (Míguez Bonino 1975: 10). Jewish thought has also developed in this direction (see Ellis 1987), and there are African, Asian, and other liberation theologies—as well as black and feminist theologies in North America. Second, this essay is itself a "misreading" that occurs on the terrain of North American scholarly discourse; however, from within this terrain, I also oppose the distortions of the academy (driven by its imbrication with dominant power and discourse) from a position of political solidarity with those in the liberation constellation.

4   For a description, see P. Lernoux (1982). For additional summaries of the theology, see P. Berryman (1987) and J. Míguez Bonino (1975). On the roots of liberation theology, see R. Chopp (1986), A. Fierro (1977), and M. Lamb (1982).

5   For a summary, see Fierro (1977). For a discussion of a more dialectical appropriation of the same tradition, especially the work of Karl Rahner and Bernard Lonergan, see M. Lamb (1982).

6   For important titles that evince this development, see, for example, R. Garaudy's *From Anathema to Dialogue* (1966), T. Eagleton's *The New Left Church* (1965),

"*Slant Manifesto*" (1966), A. Rabinbach's "Between Enlightenment and Apocalypse: Benjamin, Bloch and Modern Jewish Messianism" (1983), and M. H. Ellis's *Towards a Jewish Theology of Liberation* (1987).

7   In the United States, a Catholic Left developed through the anarcho-communist and pacifist influence of the theologically conservative but politically left Catholic Worker movement. Influenced by the politics of nonviolent civil disobedience practiced in the post–Second World War antinuclear movement and in the growing Southern civil rights movement, US Catholic radicalism stimulated an inspirational intensity of active resistance that its European counterparts did not achieve.

8   For a journalistic account of the communities, see P. Lernoux (1982); for a theoretical account, see L. Boff (1986); for a record of one of the most activist communities in Nicaragua, see E. Cardenal (1982).

9   The work of the base community leaders can be further understood in terms of Antonio Gramsci's concept of "organic intellectuals." Gramsci distinguished between those ecclesiastical and political intellectuals who maintain the historical continuity of a dominant structure and those who, as members of a subaltern class, work as "constructor, organizer, permanent persuader" in the counterhegemonic movement (1971: 5–23).

10   For a North American commentary, see M. Lamb (1982: 1–13, 116–42). See J. Brenkman (1987: 228–35) for a discussion of the operation in the secular sphere of a socially critical negative and reconstructive hermeneutic.

11   The method benefits from the contemporary understanding of the function of language, the operation of ideology, and the importance of cultural practices in the production and reproduction of the social. See M. Lamb (1982) on liberation theology's rejection of innocence and S. Welch (1985) on the conflict between traditional theology and feminist theology in terms of Foucault.

12   For a useful analysis of Bloch's category of nonsynchronicity, by the author and in discussion with others, see A. Bammer, *Partial Visions*, Ralahine Classic Edition (2015).

Chapter 4

1   I dedicate this chapter to Darko Suvin and Raffaella Baccolini. I'm grateful to both of them for the conversations and collaborations that I've shared with each of them since our first meetings (Darko at an MLA convention in the 1970s, Raffaella at an SUS meeting in the 1990s).

2   In the Preface to *Positions,* Suvin contests "on one hand the academic elitism wrinkling its none too perfect nose at the sight of popular literature and art and, on the other hand, the fannish shoreless ocean of indiscriminately happy passages to continents full of masterpieces miraculously emerging year upon year" (1988c: xi).

3   Suvin's initial presentation of these taxonomic definitions and distinctions, along
     with his discussion of extrapolative and analogic models of sf, appeared in D.
     Suvin, "SF and the Genological Jungle" (1972), and reappeared as Chapter 2 in
     Metamorphoses (1979b). He made a different, but nevertheless key, contribution to
     sf and utopian studies when he joined Dale Mullen as co-editor of *Science-Fiction
     Studies* in 1973; *SFS* subsequently became one of the journals in the critical Left
     constellation of the 1970s. For a valuable source for fleshing out the nature of the
     "early" forms of estranged writing in terms of the relations and tensions between
     emergent "scientific" and "literary" discourses in the Renaissance, see D. Albanese,
     New Science, New World (1996). In regard to the further elaboration of these
     distinctions and positions, see the very productive debate on the estrangement
     function of sf and fantasy that grew from C. Miéville's critique of Suvin and Suvin's
     response: see D. Suvin, "Science Fiction and Utopian Fiction: Degrees of Kinship,"
     Positions and Presuppositions in Science Fiction (1988e: 33–43); C. Miéville,
     "Editorial Introduction: Symposium on Marxism and Fantasy," *Historical
     Materialism* (2002b: 47–8); D. Suvin, "Considering the Sense of 'Fantasy' or
     'Fantastic Fiction': An Effusion," *Extrapolation* (2000: 209–47).

4   For additional commentary on the important contribution of *Metamorphoses*, see
     the Ralahine Classic Edition (2016), especially the Introduction by G. Canavan and
     Suvin's additional essays. A useful collection of other Suvin essays, including several
     cited here, is D. Suvin, *Defined by a Hollow* (2010).

5   A shorter version of Suvin's keynote address (entitled "Where Are We? Or How Did
     We Get Here? Is There Any Way Out?: Or, News from the Novum") was published
     as "Novum Is as Novum Does" (1997b).

6   See C. McGuirk's 1994 essay and Suvin's and McGuirk's response in 1995. A
     study of the related issue of the "science question" in Suvin's work might begin
     with his 1976 "'Utopian' and 'Scientific'" essay and work through to his 1997
     Foundation essay wherein he reaffirms his "quite conscious" founding decision in
     Metamorphoses, dating from a silent debate with Brecht in the 1950s, to use the
     nomination of "cognition" instead of "science" (1997b: 39). Such a study might
     then consider the connections and differences between his position and that of
     D. Haraway in "Situated Knowledges" (1988).

7   For another critique in this vein, see T. Eagleton's *Illusions* (1996).

8   The groundbreaking essay here is M. Angenot's "Absent Paradigm" (1979), but see
     also P. Fitting, "Positioning and Closure" (1987), and K. Spencer, "The Red Sun"
     (1983).

9   My discussion of the dystopian genre in this essay was further developed as the
     central argument of my *Scraps of the Untainted Sky*, also published in 2000 but
     fully written after this essay; see Chapters 4, 5, 6, especially my elaboration on the
     dynamics of dystopian form, the relationship between dystopia to the spectrum of
     utopia and anti-utopia, and the critical dystopia (see 2000c: 147–99).

10 This is the place to recall Suvin's own account of the shift in utopian writing in the 1960s, in a contribution that was influential to my own work on the critical utopia. In "Not Only But Also" (written in 1979), the two authors note how new utopian work envisaged "the pros and cons of a dynamic, provisional ... utopia" (1988g: 58). And, in D. Suvin, "The SF Novel as Epic Narration" (written in 1982) he notes that "utopia ... turned from anatomy to novel, and its voyage-of-discovery plot was enriched by a doubly new consciousness" (1988f: 83). In the interest of settling accounts, this is also the place to apologize for not citing, and benefiting from, these essays in my own work in *Demand the Impossible,* even though both were in print before I completed the book.

11 Jameson's point that dystopia is narrative and utopias are mostly "non-narrative" (however much I disagree with its extreme opposition) does clarify how "dystopias" privilege the plot elements of the discrete register of the text (closer to the spirit, perhaps, of Marx's political analysis in *Eighteenth Brumaire)* and how "utopias" work from the iconic register (more in keeping with Marx's "camera obscura" metaphor of ideological analysis) wherein what is significant about the alternative utopian world is not so much what it describes but rather what it does not, what it has negated in the author's social environment. See T. Moylan, "Dare to struggle" (2000a) and *Demand the Impossible* (1986: 29–59).

12 Although Jameson, Adorno, Benjamin, and others have treated this utopian quality in terms of the Jewish *Bilderswerbot* (though Protestant iconoclasm is also relevant), another metaphor emerges from the Roman Catholic definition of a sacrament, wherein the material form of the rite stands as the "outward sign of an inward grace" (see *Baltimore Catechism*). Indeed, the metaphor of transubstantiation is also helpful, for it names a sign (the bread and wine) that means both its own materiality and the transcendent presence of the divinity. Utopia comes to us, perhaps, not by *no* name, but by *a* name: one not reducible to itself, yet with its own force of meaning in the provisional moment on the way to salvation or spiritual transcendence, revolution or material transcendence. Utopian content, indeed even narrative, is perhaps of more significance than Jameson and others usually recognize. See Chapter 5, "On the Vocation of Utopian Science Fiction" and T. Eagleton (1997).

13 P. Fitting suggests that a distinguishing approach might be to regard "dystopias" as fictions that privilege setting and "anti-utopias" as those that work with plot (1995: 281). Although I hold with Jameson that dystopias are overall more concerned with narrative (see note 11), Fitting's point is apt if considered within the spectrum of "dystopian" and what I term "pseudo-dystopian" narratives.

14 For a related argument, see R. Williams on "willed transformation" in "Utopia and Science Fiction" (1978).

15 Although I take Suvin's point, I think that care must be taken to heed feminist critiques of the epic tradition's privileging of the male hero. However, if indeed the

sf novum is that which exceeds the social, and formal, limits of the present, then it has the potential to transcend the ideological limits of the epic tradition even as it makes use of the epical form. Of course, the best commentary on the power of sf to shatter existing gender structures and power relations can be found in the critical essays of J. Russ. See especially J. Russ, "What Can a Heroine Do?" (1972).

16   I part with Suvin's argument that utopia, anti-utopia, and dystopia are sub-genres of sf, for I think sf is more accurately a product of modernity (where *that* begins is another matter); and in this regard, see also P. E. Wegner, "The Modernisms of Science Fiction: Toward a Periodizing History," *Shockwaves of Possibility* (2014c: 1–65). Since the roots of all these forms precede modernity, I prefer the term "estranged writing" to name their overall provenance. Nevertheless, I agree that—in the twentieth century, or at least the second half—all three sub-genres were usually conceived, written, and certainly marketed, within the generic sphere of sf. See also T. Eagleton (1997: 7).

17   I take C. Penley's point that "critical dystopia" could name (filmic) texts that "suggest causes rather than merely reveal symptoms" (1989: 122). For a good analysis of an earlier dystopia negotiating utopia/anti-utopia, see P. E. Wegner's chapter "On Zamyatin's *We*" in *Imaginary Communities* (2002: 147–83); and for a useful analysis of the "auto-critical impulse" in dystopia, see G. McKay's "Metapropaganda" (1994).

18   One specific study was my monograph, *Scraps of the Untainted Sky*, published the following year; another was the collection edited by R. Baccolini and myself, *Dark Horizons*, published in 2003.

19   "Growing Old Without Yugoslavia, Part 2" (1994a). In an e-mail exchange, Suvin reported that he had sent Part 2 to *SFS* editor Dale Mullen in 1992, who agreed to place it in the back-matter of a future issue; by the time he also submitted the first part to be added to that publication, Mullen replied that he had room only for Part 2. Since the *SFS* text is the published version (and the one that struck me when I read it), it is the text I worked with in the initial draft of this chapter. While my commentary, also published here, was based on that *SFS* version, I nevertheless quote the entire poem, as taken from the author's website, with his permission: see https://darkosuvin.com/poetry-short-prose/poems–1993–1995 (accessed 1 December 2019).

20   The best elucidation of these opposing types of memory is V. Geoghegan, "Remembering the Future," *Not Yet* (1997). For studies of the place of memory and imagination in dystopia, see R. Baccolini "It's Not in the Womb the Damage Is Done" (1995a) and "Journeying through the Dystopian Genre" (1995b).

21   Another example of this dual stance (i.e., critique/denunciation and hope/ annunciation), though developed in a different context, is D. Suvin, "Revelation vs. Conflict" (1994b).

Chapter 5

1   On "cognitive estrangement," see D. Suvin, "Estrangement and Cognition," *Metamorphoses* (2016: 15–29). I cite the Ralahine Classics Edition (2014) so that readers can avail of the added material in this volume, including the new Introduction by Gerry Canavan and additional essays by Suvin.

2   For more on the historical materialist basis of this formal shift, see P. E. Wegner's study of the cultural productions of the 1990s (with the rise of neoliberalism and a new world order): *Life between Two Deaths* (2009).

3   See S. Budgen, S. Kouvelakis, and S. Žižek (2007). As the authors put it: "liberal-democratic Germany is sustained by a kind of unwritten *Denkverbot* (thought prohibition) similar to the infamous *Berufsverbot* (banning the employment of leftists by any state institution) of the late 1960s in Germany. The moment one shows a minimal sign of engaging in political projects that aim at seriously challenging the existing order, he or she receives the following immediate answer: "Benevolent as it is, this will necessarily end in a new Gulag!" (1).

4   For an insightful study of that late nineteenth-century utopian visionary energy and politics, see M. Robertson, *The Last Utopians* (2018).

5   See also Jameson's eutopian presentation, *An American Utopia* (2016), in which he retrieves the traces of utopian impulse and program in the existing social formation of the US military.

6   For more on actually existing radical alternatives to capitalist structures and practices, see E. O. Wright, *Envisioning Real Utopias* (2010).

7   For an account of sf's imbrication with popular science discourse and publishing, see G. Westfahl, *The Mechanics of Wonder* (1998).

8   Working onward from Jameson, P. E. Wegner further develops our understanding of sf's formal development within the systemic realities of modernity in *Imaginary Communities* (2002), *Periodizing Jameson* (2014b), and *Shockwaves of Possibility* (2014c).

9   In *The Modernist Papers*, Jameson develops his own argument for the importance of content, especially when seen as "a defamiliarization that asks us to imagine what a real political proposal or program, one that had real content, might be" (2007a: xvii). Indeed, he posits the persistence of utopian content, in its figuration of such "real" possibilities, as a negation of the aesthetic privileging of pure form (xix). See also M. Morris, "Banality in Cultural Studies" (1988).

10 Or, as L. Sargisson put in on the web page for a research project on "Practical Utopias and Utopian Practices," "the term 'utopia' may evoke images of perfect worlds and escapist fantasies but utopias have a very real function in the political and social world. Utopian discontent and desire lie at the heart of much radical

politics and politics of resistance" (see http://www.nottingham.ac.uk/politics/Utopia/, accessed 1 December 2019).

11 See L. T. Sargent, "Ideology and Utopia: Karl Mannheim and Paul Ricoeur" (2008: 263–73); V. Geoghegan, "Ideology and Utopia" (2004: 123–38); and S. McManus, *Fictive Theories* (2005).

12 On the revolutionary political vision of each author, see W. J. Burling, "The Theoretical Foundation of Utopian Radical Democracy in Kim Stanley Robinson's *Blue Mars*" (2005) and C. Freedman, "To the Perdido Street Station: The Representation of Revolution in China Miéville's *Iron Council*" (2005).

13 I offer my evocation of "slowness" in resonance with the insightful study of the practice of slow violence in the environmental exploitation of the poor as developed by R. Nixon in *Slow Violence and the Environmentalism of the Poor* (2013).

14 Suvin's initial critique of the fantasy genre appeared in "On the Poetics of the Science Fiction Genre" (1972). For his developing approach, see D. Suvin, "Considering the Sense of 'Fantasy' or 'Fantastic Fiction': An Effusion" (2000) and his brief response to Miéville in his introductory remarks to the reprint of that essay in the Ralahine Edition of *Metamorphoses* (2016: 382).

15 One of Bloomsbury's anonymous reviewers suggested a further development of this comparison that would include the work of Margaret Atwood. Indeed, beyond the brief references I make to Atwood's work throughout this book, such a comparative analysis would be very helpful, in assessing both the relative positions and impact of all three writers—especially concerning their positions on estranged narrative forms (sf and fantasy) and the politics of form, and their related but differing responses (critical and transformative) to the current global reality. This discussion would most certainly involve an exploration of Atwood's initial dismissive position regarding the value of sf as well as an appreciation of her more recent positive embrace of the sf imaginary and the impact of that embrace on her work (which, as I note in the Coda, results in a more effective mobilization of sf form in a sharper political standpoint). However, I'm afraid that all I can offer at this stage (of final revisions) is my agreement on the value of such a three-way comparison and my intention to put it on my list of work to be done once *Becoming Utopian* is published. In this regard, such an analysis would fit effectively into my proposed essay, entitled "Apocalypse and Hope," which I mention in Coda, note 11.

16 E-mail message, June 20, 2007.

Chapter 6

1 See also the updated presentation: J. Hansen, "Climate Change in a Nutshell: The Gathering Storm" (2018).

2   For a powerful treatment of the pervasive destructiveness of capitalism in all
    dimensions of life (including race, gender and sexuality, and nature itself) in a
    radical utopian feminist manifesto, see C. Arruzza, T. Bhattacharya, and N. Fraser,
    Feminism for the 99 Percent: A Manifesto (2019).

3   See T. Luke, "Culture and Politics in the Age of Artificial Negativity" (1978);
    P. Piccone, "The Changing Function of Critical Theory" (1977), and "The Crisis
    of One-Dimensionality" (1978).

4   Increasingly, we all are learning from the guiding militancy of children and young
    people. See the work of the grassroots activist formation Extinction Rebellion and
    the speeches and actions of G. Thunberg as she works with students organizing
    around the globe: see, for example, her UN speech, "How dare you!" (2019). For a
    groundbreaking study of children, political agency, and the process of becoming
    utopian, see M. Cummings, *Children's Voices in Politics* (2020).

5   For an earlier and more extensive discussion of science fictionality, see I. Csicsery-
    Ronay, *The Seven Beauties of Science Fiction*, in which the author speaks of the "kind
    of awareness we might call science-fictionality, a mode of response that frames and
    tests experiences as if they were aspects of a work of science fiction" (2008: 2).

6   On the distinction between concrete and abstract utopia, see E. Bloch, *The Principle
    of Hope* (1986), and *On Karl Marx* (1971: 159–73). See also the commentary by
    R. Levitas (1990: 83–106).

7   In this regard, Robinson's position resonates with A. Dobson's description of
    ecologism, that, as he puts it, "envisages a post-industrial future quite distinct from
    that with which we are most generally acquainted … [in which] the Good Life will
    involve more work and fewer material objects" (2007: 190, 189).

8   For reasons of focus, and space, I do not discuss the intriguing and insightful
    alternative history novels, *The Years of Rice and Salt* (2002) and *Galileo's Dream*
    (2009); however, Robinson's exploration of post-death, post-human agency in *Years*
    and of planetary non-human agency in *Galileo* is worthy of a study in their own right.

9   For a valuable treatment of the imbrication of radical politics and spirituality
    that resonates with Robinson's thought experiment, see Rev. A. K. Williams et al.,
    Radical Dharma (2016).

10 This debate is consistently deepened by Robinson's regard for science as an overtly
    utopian project and not merely a tool of capitalism. As he puts it in *Galileo's Dream*:
    "Science was broke and so it got bought. Science was scared and so did what it was
    told"; but then, in his utopian vision, humanity manages to "shift history into a new
    channel" and thus keeps "the promise of science" (2009: 575–6).

11 On the utopian surplus of death, see E. Bloch, "Self and Grave-Lamp or Images of
    Hope against the Power of the Strongest Non-Utopia: Death," (1986: 1103–82).

12 As described by R. Markley, the process that occurred on Mars can be understood
    as a "relationship that is transforming humans as humans transform the land"
    (2009: 141).

13 See E. Yanarella, who summarizes Robinson's position in the *Mars Trilogy* as "an act of human hubris and only the latest directing myth of an imperialistic science of the dawning millennium" (2001: 303).

14 Robinson's original three volumes were reworked, condensed by 300 pages, and republished in a single volume, entitled *Green Earth* (2015b).

15 As G. Prettyman puts it, Robinson approaches the break "from our current ideological state of mind" and offers models for revolutionary disruptions that are both discursive and scientific (2009: 199).

16 This entire narrative vision resonates strongly with the argument for a transformed level of human-nature utopian agency developed in D. Haraway's *Staying with the Trouble* (2016).

17 As Robinson acknowledged in an interview with Canavan, the writing of a viable post-catastrophe utopia "really … should be set much closer to now," and in light of this observation I believe we can read both of these novels as preparatory thought experiments for a fuller near future, post-Anthropocene, utopia (Canavan and Robinson 2014: 246).

18 See R. Solnit, *Hope in the Dark* (2016).

19 For more on the form and function of the utopian manifesto, see K. Weeks (2011: 175–227).

20 In this light, I suggest that Jameson's conclusion that utopia "as a form is not the representation of radical alternatives" but "simply the imperative to imagine them" might be more usefully recast not as a binary opposition but a dialectically imbricated relationship (Jameson 2000: 231).

Chapter 7

1 I dedicate this chapter to Hoda Zaki, long-standing friend and utopian co-conspirator. I'm grateful for our ongoing conversations, especially concerning the substance and state of transformative activism within the racist society of the United States. In regard to this current study, I learned from her insights on the early years of the postwar civil rights movement (particularly regarding Bayard Rustin and Rosa Parks) and the links between that period and the prewar struggle against racism and segregation, including the important contribution of the Black self-defense movement. For more on Black self-defense (e.g., in groups such as the Deacons for Defense and Justice and the Black Panther Party, and in the personal standpoint of Rosa Parks), see R. F. Williams, *Negroes With Guns* (1962).

2 E. E. Cummings, "I Sing of Olaf," *E. E. Cummings Complete Poems: 1904–1962* (1994: 340).

3 For the complementary prose narrative, see Cummings' anti-war novel, *The Enormous Room* (1928).

4   A random list of examples of nonviolent witness and intervention would include the feminist lineage from the sex strike in *Lysistrata* to the performative activism of Pussy Riot; the nonviolent resistance to Nazi occupation in Norway and Denmark; the nonviolent campaigns of farmworkers, miners, and others; the post-1968 resistance in Prague; the standoff in Tiananmen Square; the Israeli draft resistance movement; the Palestinian Intifada; the Timorese Resistance; the Mass Action for Peace organized by Liberian women; and the interventions of Greenpeace. For an analysis of more than fifty recent anti-regime, anti-occupation, and self-determination campaigns, see E. Chenoweth and M. Stefan, *Why Civil Resistance Works* (2011).

5   H. Bey, *T.A.Z.: The Temporary Autonomous Zone* (1985).

6   On the Quaker distinction between witness and rebellion, see *Quaker Faith and Practice* (1995: 24.12 ff.).

7   For an incisive assessment of this generation, see J. Tracy, *Direct Action* (1966).

8   B. Rustin, quoted in Staughton Lynd, *Nonviolence in America* (1966: 494).

9   As a self-criticism, I want to note my neglect in this present work of the important contribution of Rosa Parks. Too often limited to the role of the brave woman who once sat on a bus and refused to move (thus catalyzing the Montgomery Bus Boycott), Parks was a dynamic and influential leader in the long civil rights movement from her early years in the South to her latter days in Detroit. In terms of this chapter, although she was not one of the Second World War cohort upon which I focus, I regret that I did not consider the impact of her influential position regarding the relative appropriateness and effectivity of both nonviolent and counterviolent (self-defense) action. For more on Parks, I strongly recommend the work of Jeanne Theoharris, who has done so much to restore her to the center of the history of the US struggle against racism and for liberation, see Theoharris (2013).

10 For more on the FBI COINTELPRO, see W. Churchill and J. Vander Wall, *The COINTELPRO Papers* (1990).

11 See K. Weeks (2011: 213–22). Describing the manifesto as a utopian form that "speaks from and within the effective register of what Bloch calls militant optimism," Weeks characterizes it as a "literature of provocation, a species of utopian writing that challenges its readers to think the future and—more overtly and insistently than the traditional and critical utopias—bring it into being"; she goes on to argue that if "utopian writing is eager to have an effect on the world, the manifesto goes a step further" as it "bridges the divide between writing and acting" (214).

12 In *Valences of the Dialectic* (2009), in words that resonate with Berrigan's, Jameson argues that the utopian method is politically effective in the sense "that it is a contribution to the reawakening of the imagination of possible alternate futures," a revival of "long-dormant parts of the mind, organs of political and historical

and social imagination which have virtually atrophied from lack of use, muscles of praxis we have long since ceased exercising, revolutionary gestures we've lost the habit of performing" (434).

Chapter 8

1   See also the volume edited by M. D. Gordin, H. Tilley, and G. Prakash (2010).
2   Here, I want to gratefully acknowledge and appreciate the ongoing conversations and collaborations I've had with Phillip E. Wegner over several decades, as we both have explored the radical potential of utopian hope and action. In this regard, I'm happy to add that his own insightful monograph on such matters (*Invoking Hope: Theory and Utopia in Dark Times*) has also been published in 2020; see P. E. Wegner (2020).
3   I am especially indebted to D. Suvin's "Locus, Horizon, and Orientation: The Concept of Possible Worlds as a Key to Utopian Studies" (1997a).
4   I want to acknowledge the history of this developing line of thought. While Levitas's assertion of the need for closure is a critical response to Jameson's work, it appears to me, even though he makes no direct reference, that his later essay on utopian impulse and program is itself a response to Levitas, as well as other commentators on *Archaeologies*.
5   In an expansion of the ontological dimension that enriches the specific realm of the political (one that opens up to another and broader discussion), Levitas deepens the sense of a holistic formation of the utopian subject by acknowledging the roles of spirituality and the "transcendent human spirit in art, music, literature and responses to (evolved) nature" in the broader de-alienation of self and community made possible by the utopian process (Levitas 2013: 195). Citing S. McManus, she brings to the fore the "wonder" that infuses the overall utopian experience—thus blending the cold stream of the critical work of utopianism with the warm stream of its existential fullness (see Levitas 2013: 195). For a good essay on "materialist spirituality," see J. Kovel (1986).
6   Other community activists inspired by his approach went on to organize groups as various as the West Central Organization in Detroit, that was affiliated with the League of Revolutionary Black Workers; the Chicago Developing Communities Project (DCP) of the Calumet Community Religious Conference (CCRC) (where Barack Obama briefly worked in the mid-1980s); the radical rural project, ACORN (Association of Community Organizations for Reform); the Center for Third World Organizing; the East London Communities Organisation; or the Sydney Alliance. For historical commentaries on Alinsky-influenced organizing, see E. Chambers (2008), D. Georgakas and M. Surkin (1998), S.D. Horwitt (1989), A. Schutz and M. Miller (2015), and N. Von Hoffman (2010).

7 Years later, Tom Hayden, one of the SDS leaders who favored Alinsky's strategy, admitted that this tactical shift represented a "missed opportunity, the road tragically not taken" (quoted in Horwitt 1989: 526).

8 Since then, the educational institute that Alinsky founded, the Industrial Areas Foundation, has continued to play a major role in training grassroots organizers and in developing new organizing campaigns, with successful projects in San Antonio, Los Angeles, New York, and Chicago, but also in the rural organizing of the group, ACORN. At its best, the work of the IAF remains a significant part of a left populist agenda, often linked with the liberation theology informed radicalism of some Catholic and Protestant congregations; but, at its worst, it has become a tool in the hands of a more restrained and reformist liberal and Catholic leadership. Famously, Alinsky's methods attracted the attention of Hillary Clinton in her postgraduate thesis, and we have all heard about Barack Obama's stint as a community organizer in an Alinsky-style Chicago organization. Both seem to have left the radicalism of Alinsky's praxis behind, with Obama abjuring the community organizing base centered around Reverend Jeremiah Wright's church. Most bizarrely, in its campaigning surge, the reactionary Tea Party movement issued its own expurgated edition of Alinsky's writing, advocating the method but framing it within its own right-wing agenda. As with any utopian movement or method, the tools are there to be used or abused.

9 For an additional understanding of Alinsky's admiration for the CIO and the organizing techniques of its long-serving president, John L. Lewis, see his biography of Lewis (1949).

10 An indicative portrayal of an organizer's work, both structurally and in the experience of everyday life, can be seen in J. Sayles' *Matewan* (1987).

11 The problem in American society, as Alinsky saw it, was the "general surrender of everyday democratic rights and responsibilities of the people" (Alinsky 1989a: 192). Whatever the specific battle engaged in by a local organization, the horizon was always the successful restoration of the "active desires of a democratically minded citizenry" (Alinsky 1989a: 193).

12 Alinsky sums up his commentary on education with these words: "In a People's Organization popular education is an exciting and dramatic process. Education instead of being distant and academic becomes a direct and intimate part of the personal lives, experiences, and activities of the people … Knowledge then becomes an arsenal of weapons in the battle against injustice and degradation. It is no longer learning for learning sake, but learning for a real reason, a purpose. It ceases to be a luxury or something known under the vague, refined name of culture and becomes as essential as money in the bank, good health, good housing, or regular employment" (Alinsky 1989a: 173).

13 For more on the ongoing work of this exemplary, ongoing, radical project, see http://www.rethinkingschools.org/index.shtml (accessed 1 December 2019).

14 While it is clearly a subject for another time, I think it's helpful to note the emphasis on critical reflection as it took shape in the number of movements during the time of Alinsky's and Freire's work. I'm thinking here of manifestations as varied as Maoism's criticism self-criticism, Second Wave feminism's consciousness-raising, the New Left's emphasis on consensus decisions, and indeed the Frankfurt School's theoretical understanding of critique and the truly critical core of deconstruction.

Coda

1 Some passages in this interview are taken from Chapter 1, "Strong Thought," and "Introduction to the Classics Edition" in T. Moylan, *Demand the Impossible* (2014b: ix–xxvi). Here, I want to thank Lyman Tower Sargent for his own bibliographic and critical contributions and his support of my work since the 1980s. His engagement has always been appreciative and critical, challenging me to look farther, to do better.

2 A later component of that personal and political break came in 2007 after I had settled in Ireland. After opposing US military incursions throughout the world since the Vietnam War, I felt that I had to make a (final) moral and political stand against the second US war against Iraq, launched by President George W. Bush in 2003. As a citizen of Ireland and the European Union (thanks to my mother's birthright), I made the very painful decision to sever my fidelity to the US state. And so, whereas decades ago I handed in my draft card as part of my opposition to conscription in the US war in Vietnam, I now turned in my US passport, thereby renouncing my citizenship, even as I continued to stand in international solidarity with the US opposition. In what I feel was a deeply *utopian* decision, I chose instead to live in fidelity with the small nation of Ireland (with its, at least declared, political neutrality) and the larger entity of the European Union (with its strong roots in social democracy and democratic socialism, despite its more contemporary neoliberal tendencies). This was a hard step in my long journey, but one that felt necessary and proper, and one that I have never regretted.

3 J. Nuttall, *Bomb Culture* (1970).

4 My understanding and appreciation of the value and power of this pedagogical break are especially due to my most influential university teacher: Basil O'Leary. A Christian Brother at St. Mary's College (Winona, Minnesota), Basil taught philosophy and theology (and occasionally economics and English), while also serving as the faculty adviser to the Young Christian Students student group and as the organizer of the annual student symposium that critiqued local and global issues, both religious and secular. He always said that his vocation as a teacher was to help students break through all they had previously learned and spend their remaining years seeing the world anew, critically and hopefully.

He left the Christian Brothers in 1968 and joined in the Milwaukee 14 civil disobedience action of napalming 50,000 draft files, for which he served two years in federal prison. He spent the rest of his life as a lay researcher and teacher at the Institute for Nonviolence at the University of Notre Dame. Basil was a formative influence on me, and a dear friend. I remember and honor him whenever I can.

5   In this regard, I found G. Spivak's *Death of a Discipline* to be a helpful critique of contemporary academia and a strong declaration of an engaged intellectual project (2003). See too, the Kafka-inspired text of Sarah Browne's "Report to an Academy," that appears at the end of this volume.

6   As G. Snyder puts it in the last lines of "I Went into the Maverick Bar" (1974: 9):

> We left—onto the freeway shoulders—
> under the tough old stars—
> In the shadow of bluffs
> I came back to myself,
> To the real work, to
> "What is to be done."

7   As P. Fitting put it in "The Modern Anglo-American SF Novel: Utopian Longing and Capitalist Co-optation": "within SF's generic ability to provide a place for imagining utopian alternatives, the critique of capitalism and specifically of sexism has produced some of the most significant SF at the last 10 years as exemplified by the work of Ursula K. Le Guin and Joanna Russ …. [Thus] the 1960s … generated a SF which was, at its best, both critical and utopian" (1979: 70, 72). My first published use of "critical utopia" was in 1980 (although I presented my own version of the concept in UW-Milwaukee seminar papers with Ihab Hassan and Jack Zipes in 1974): I apologize to Peter for not citing him in 1980, but I simply wasn't aware of his essay at the time.

8   See D. Haraway (2016).

9   For an interesting (and still useful) exploration of the revolutionary political power of creative and critical writing based in the paradigm of Marxist criticism in the face of the turn to "high" or "meta" literary and cultural theory that emerged in the late 1960s, see the collection edited by N. Rudich: *Weapons of Criticism: Marxism in America and the Literary Tradition* (1976). Indeed, the epigram for the volume speaks to my point about the political effectivity of Atwood's portrayal of writing as a productive form of opposition/transformation in *The Testaments*: "The weapon of criticism obviously cannot replace the criticism of weapons. Material force must be overthrown by material force. But theory [and here add art] also becomes a material force once it has gripped the masses" (Karl Marx, "Toward the Critique of Hegel's Philosophy of Law: Introduction"). The volume includes essays by leading thinkers in the Marxist tradition (F. Jameson, S. Finkelstein, G. LeRoy, D. Stratman,

L. Baxandall, L. Robinson, E. San Juan Jr., P. Siegel, S. Delany, F. Whitehead, L. Rudich, L. Harap, H. B. Franklin, A. Rubinstein, S. Zelnick, D. Suvin, H. and N. Fuyet and G. and M. Levilan, and Rudich). For a review, see D. Peck (1977).

10 See also D. Spencer, who argues that the counterculture enabled neoliberalism as it was driven by its "efforts to escape existing power structures rather than to contest them directly" and therefore the "possibilities of a new contract between nature, man and technology explored by the counterculture and its communes, promoted and serviced by Stewart Brand and his *Whole Earth Catalogue*, cultivated a cybernetically oriented and entrepreneurial culture that spawned figures such as Steve Jobs" (2016: 34, 6–7).

11 For more on my recent engagement with the theoretical and creative work resonating with the contemporary dystopian structure of feeling, its neoliberal cooptation, and the possibilities for a refunctioned utopianism (taking the form of an "apocalyptic utopianism"), see my 2020 essay, "The Necessity of Hope in Dystopian Times: A Critical Reflection," and watch for a follow-up essay, tentatively entitled "Apocalypse and Hope."

12 One of the most interesting recent contributions addressing the recent apocalyptic imaginary by engaging with the problematic of the critical utopia can be found in R. Kabo's 2020 PhD dissertation, entitled "Imagining the End of Capitalism: Utopia and the Commons in Contemporary Literature." Working with and beyond the framework of my discussion of the critical utopia (with its own historical situatedness), Kabo argues for the emergence of a new corpus of utopian texts in the second decade of the twenty-first century: namely, *That Winter the Wolf Came* by Juliana Spahr (2015), *Exit West* by Mohsin Hamid (2017), *New York 2140* by Kim Stanley Robinson (2017), *The Book of Joan* by Lidia Yuknavitch (2017), and *Walkaway* by Cory Doctorow (2017). Identifying these texts as "commons utopias," he argues that they "build on the forms of earlier utopian literature, particularly the 'critical utopias' of the 1960s-70s; actively oppose contemporary capitalism; depict the crises of the present alongside the utopian spaces which emerge within it; and make use of a *commons poetics*, a toolkit of literary techniques which captures the politics, subjectivities, and spatialities of oppositional utopian commons"; thus, these texts are "chiefly concerned with depicting the process of creating and inhabiting utopian spaces as an opposition to the capitalist present— often through anti-capitalist strategies of spatial production, namely commoning" (2020: 3, 17).

Afterword

1 The title of this Afterword comes from Bertolt Brecht's poem, "An die Nachgeborenen" (1939), specifically recalling the line: "Gedenkt unsrer Mit Nachsicht" [Should think upon us/With leniency].

2 I discuss Cavell's comedy of remarriage in *Shockwaves of Possibility* (2014c: chapter 2) and *Invoking Hope* (2202: chapter 6).

3 See D. Suvin (1976), discussed by Moylan in Chapter 5; F. Jameson (1983); P. E. Wegner (2014b: chapter 4).

4 For a useful introduction, see Merton (2017).

Appendix

1 Amidst the related funding crisis, the institution hired a PR company. The Students criticized this apparent prioritizing of the public image of the Academy over their needs.

2 See http://papervisualart.com/?p=10941 (accessed April 2015).

3 Many complaints were made by Students when a stylized image of a naked woman was used to advertise a Student event. Those who objected were subjected to verbal and written abuse by their peers, accused of being overly sensitive, of not getting the joke, and promoting excessive "political correctness." The Academy made no intervention.

Some time later, a Student made a diptych of paintings, depicting himself and the Director of the Academy as solo nude portraits. In this case, the Academy sought legal advice and a Manager met with the Student to encourage him to consider the consequences of making the painting public, in the context of the Academy's Dignity and Respect in the Workplace Policy and its duty of care to all employees. While the Academy has the right to request that any work of art that breaches the policy be taken down, it chose not to exercise this right on this occasion, leaving the decision of whether or not to exhibit the work with the Student. He chose not to exhibit the paintings publicly, afterwards describing the pressure he felt. See http://www.irishtimes.com/news/education/ncad-rejects-censor-claim-over-withdrawal-of-nude-from-show-1.2246448 (accessed June 2015). These contrasting incidents proved to me firstly that visual depictions and speech acts could cause harm, but also that the handling of such incidents would be different, depending on whether they were directed at Students or Managers.

4 In 2015, the UK government introduced the Counter Terrorism and Security Act, 2015, which includes the Prevent Strategy. This introduces a statutory requirement for educators from pre-school to university to report students "at risk of radicalisation" or not acting in accordance with "fundamental British values." Many university staff and community representatives have claimed that PREVENT tends toward racism and Islamophobia in its targeting and definition of potential "extremism"; that "radicalisation" is not sufficiently defined; and that ultimately there will be a chilling effect on open debate, free speech and political dissent in educational contexts.

For more see www.educatorsnotinformants.wordpresscom; www.togetheragainstprevent.org; http://www.nusconnect.org.uk/articles/why-i-won-t-be-working-with-prevent-and-how-you-can-avoid-it-too; http://www.communitycare.co.uk/2016/07/20/wording-boys-t-shirt-prompts-radicalisation-referral-social-workers/; http://www.aljazeera.com/indepth/features/2015/10/uk-keyword-warning-software-schools-raises-red-flag-151004081940435.html (accessed March 2016).

5   See http://su40.ucd.ie/the-ucd-cleaners-strike/ (accessed April 2015).

References

Adorno, T. (1994), *Negative Dialectics*, New York: Continuum.

Ahmed, S. (2017), *Living a Feminist Life*, Durham and London: Duke University Press.

Albanese, D. (1996), *New Science, New World*, Durham and London: Duke University Press.

Alinsky, S. (1949), *John L. Lewis: An Unauthorised Biography*, New York: Cornwall Press.

Alinsky, S. (1989a), *Reveille for Radicals* (1946), New York: Vintage.

Alinsky, S. (1989b), *Rules for Radicals: A Pragmatic Primer for Realistic Radicals* (1971), New York: Vintage.

Amis, K. (1969), *New Maps of Hell: A Survey of Science Fiction*, New York: Harcourt Brace.

Angenot, M. (1979), "The Absent Paradigm: An Introduction to the Semiotics of Science Fiction," *Science-Fiction Studies* 6: 9–20.

Annas, P. (1977), "New Worlds, New Words: Androgyny in Feminist Science Fiction," *Science-Fiction Studies* 15: 143–56.

Aronowitz, S. (1981), *The Crisis in Historical Materialism: Class, Politics and Culture in Marxist Theory*, New York: Praeger.

Atwood, M. (1985), *The Handmaid's Tale*, Toronto: McClelland and Stewart.

Atwood, M. (2003–2013), *Oryx and Crake*, London: Bloomsbury.

Atwood, M. (2009), *The Year of the Flood*, London: Bloomsbury.

Atwood, M. (2013), *MaddAddam*, London: Bloomsbury.

Atwood, M. (2019), *The Testaments*, London: Chatto and Windhus.

Auden, W. H. (1940), "The Unknown Citizen," in *Another Time*, 83–5, New York: Random House.

Baccolini, R. (1995a), "'It's not in the womb the damage is done': Memory, Desire and the Construction of Gender in Katherine Burdekin's *Swastika Night*," in E. Siciliani, A. Cecere, V. Intoni, and A. Sportelli (eds.), *Le trasformazione del narrare*, 293–309, Fasano: Schena.

Baccolini, R. (1995b), "Journeying through the Dystopian Genre: Memory and Imagination in Burdekin, Orwell, Atwood, and Piercy," in R. Baccolini, V. Fortunati, and N. Minerva (eds.), *Viaggi in utopia*, 343–57, Ravenna: Longo.

Baccolini, R. (2000), "Gender and Genre in the Feminist Critical Dystopias of Katharine Burdekin, Margaret Atwood, and Octavia Butler," in M. S. Barr (ed.), *Future Females, The Next Generation: New Voices and Velocities in Feminist Science Fiction Criticism*, 13–34, Lanham: Rowman & Littlefield.

Baccolini, R. (2003), "'A useful knowledge of the present is rooted in the past': Memory and Historical Reconciliation in Ursula K. Le Guin's *The Telling*," in R. Baccolini and T. Moylan (eds.), *Dark Horizons: Science Fiction and the Dystopian Imagination*, 113–34, New York and London: Routledge.

Baccolini, R. and T. Moylan, eds. (2003a), *Dark Horizons: Science Fiction and the Dystopian Imagination*, New York and London: Routledge.

Baccolini, R. and T. Moylan (2003b), "Introduction: Dystopia and Histories," in R. Baccolini and T. Moylan (eds.), *Dark Horizons: Science Fiction and the Dystopian Imagination*, 1–13, New York and London: Routledge.

Badami, M. K. (1976), "A Feminist Critique of Science Fiction," *Extrapolation* 18 (1): 6–19.

Badiou, A. (2001), *Ethics: An Essay on the Understanding of Evil*, trans. P. Hallward, London and New York: Verso.

Badiou, A. (2003), *Saint Paul: The Foundation of Universalism*, trans. R. Brassier, Stanford: Stanford University Press,

Badiou, A. (2005), *Being and Event*, trans. O. Feltham, London/New York: Continuum.

Badiou, A. (2010), *The Communist Hypothesis*, trans. D. Macey and S. Corcoran, London and New York: Verso.

Baggesen, S. (1987), "Utopian and Dystopian Pessimism: Le Guin's *The Word for World Is Forest* and Tiptree's 'We Who Stole the Dream,'" *Science-Fiction Studies* 14: 34–43.

Baltimore Catechism (2005), Boston-Catholic-Journal.com.

Bammer, A. (2015), *Partial Visions: Feminism and Utopianism in the 1970s*, Ralahine Classic Edition, Oxford and Berne: Peter Lang.

Baruch, E. (1979), "A Natural and Necessary Monster: Women in Utopia," *Alternative Futures* 2 (1): 29–49.

Benjamin, W. (1969), "Theses on the Philosophy of History," in Hannah Arendt (ed.), *Illuminations*, trans. Harry Zohn, 253–64, New York: Schocken.

Benjamin, W. (2003), "On the Concept of History," in *Selected Writings, Volume 4: 1938–1940*, trans. E. Jephcott et al., Cambridge, Mass.: Harvard University Press.

Benton, Ted., ed. (1996), The Greening of Marxism, New York and London: Guildford.

Berardi, F. (2019), *Futurability: The Age of Impotence and the Horizon of Possibility*, London and New York: Verso.

Berrigan, D. (1971), *The Dark Night of Resistance*, New York: Bantam.

Berryman, P. (1987), *Liberation Theology: Essential Facts about the Revolutionary Movement in Latin America and Beyond*, New York: Pantheon.

Betto, F. (1987), *Fidel and Religion: Castro Talks on Revolution and Religion with Frei Betto*, trans. Cuban Center for Translation and Interpretation, New York: Simon and Schuster.

Beverley, J. (1989), "The Margin at the Center, On *Testimonio* (Testimonial Narrative)," *Modern Fiction Studies* 35 (1): 3–11.

Bey, H. (1985), *T.A.Z.: The Temporary Autonomous Zone, Ontological Anarchy, Poetic Terrorism*, Brooklyn: Autonomedia.

Bloch, E. (1971a), *On Karl Marx*, trans. J. Maxwell, New York: Herder and Herder, 1971.

Bloch, E. (1971b), "Upright Carriage, Concrete Utopia," in J. Maxwell (ed. and trans.), *On Karl Marx*, 168–75, New York: Herder and Herder.

Bloch, E. (1971c), "Religious Truth," in *Man on His Own: Essays in the Philosophy of Religion*, trans. E. B. Ashton, 111–18, New York: Herder and Herder.

Bloch, E. (1975), "A Jubilee for Renegades," *New German Critique* 4: 17–26.

Bloch, E. (1986), *The Principle of Hope*, 3 vols., trans. N. Plaice, S. Plaice, and P. Knight, Cambridge, Mass.: MIT Press.

Bloch, E. (1991), *Heritage of Our Times*, trans. N. Plaice and S. Plaice, Berkeley: University of California Press.

Bloch, J. R. (1988), "How Can We Understand the Bends in the Upright Gait," *New German Critique* 45: 9–41.

Boff, L. (1986), *Ecclesiogenesis: The Base Communities Reinvent the Church*, trans. R. R. Barr, Ossining, NY: Orbis.

Bookchin, M. (1996), *Urbanization without Cities: The Rise and Decline of Citizenship*, Montreal: Black Rose Books.

Bourdieu, P. (1977), *Outline of a Theory of Practice*, Cambridge: Cambridge University Press.

Brecht, B. (1939), "An die Nachgeborenen," available online: https://www.lyrikline.org/de/gedichte/die-nachgeborenen-740, (accessed April 10, 2020).

Brecht, B. (1957), "A Short Organum for the Theatre," in J. Willett (ed.), *Brecht on Theatre: The Development of an Aesthetic*, 179–209, New York: Hill and Wang.

Brenkman, J. (1987), *Culture and Domination*, Ithaca: Cornell University Press.

Buchanan, I. (2006), "Live Jameson Interview," in *Fredric Jameson: Live Theory*, 120–33, London: Continuum.

Budgen, S., S. Kouvelakis and S. Žižek (2007), "Introduction: Repeating Learning," in S. Budgen, S. Kouvelakis, and S. Žižek (eds.), *Lenin Reloaded: Toward a Politics of Truth*, 1–6, Durham and London: Duke University Press.

Burling, W. J. (2005), "The Theoretical Foundation of Utopian Radical Democracy in Kim Stanley Robinson's *Blue Mars*," *Utopian Studies* 16 (1): 75–97.

Butler, O. E. (1991), *The Parable of the Sower*, New York: Four Walls Eight Windows, 1991.

Callenbach, E. (1975), *Ecotopia*, Berkeley: Bantam.

Canavan, G. (2016), "Introduction," in Gerry Canavan (ed.), *Metamorphoses of Science Fiction: On the Poetics and History of a Literary Genre*, Ralahine Classic Edition, xi–xxxvii, Oxford and Bern: Peter Lang, 2016.

Canavan, G. (2017), "Utopia in the Time of Trump," *Los Angeles Review of Books*, available online: https://lareviewofbooks,org/article/utopia-in-the-time-of-trump/#, (accessed January 30, 2019).

Canavan, G. and K. S. Robinson (2014), "Afterword: Still, I'm Reluctant to Call This Pessimism," in G. Canavan and K. S. Robinson (eds.), *Green Planets: Ecology and Science Fiction*, 243–61, Middletown: Wesleyan University Press.

Cardenal, E. (1982), *The Gospel in Solentiname*, Vol. 1, trans. D. D. Walsh, Maryknoll, NY: Orbis.

Chambers, E. T. (2008), *Routes for Radicals: Organising for Power, Action, and Justice*, New York and London: Continuum.

Chenoweth, E., and M. Stephan (2011), *Why Civil Resistance Works: The Strategic Logic of Nonviolent Conflict*, New York: Columbia University Press.

Chopp, R. S. (1986), *The Praxis of Suffering: An Interpretation of Liberation and Political Theologies*, Maryknoll, NY: Orbis.

Churchill, W., and J. Vander Wall (1990), *The COINTELPRO Papers: Documents from the FBI's Secret Wars Against Dissent in the United States*, Boston: South End Press.

Coleman, N. (2005), *Utopia and Architecture*, London and New York: Routledge.

Cox, H. (1968), "Ernst Bloch and 'The Pull of the Future,'" in M. Marty and D. G. Peerman (eds.), *New Theology* 5, 191–204, New York: Macmillan.

Csiscery-Ronay, I. (2008), *The Seven Beauties of Science Fiction*, Middletown: Wesleyan University Press.

Cummings, E. E. (1928), *The Enormous Room*, London: Jonathon Cape.

Cummings, E. E. (1994), "I Sing of Olaf," in George James Firmage (ed.), *E. E. Cummings Complete Poems: 1904–1962*, 340, New York: Liveright.

Cummings, M. (2020), *Children's Voices in Politics*, Oxford and Bern: Peter Lang.

Cunningham, A., T. Eagleton, B. Wicker, M. Redfern, and L. Bright, eds. (1966), *"Slant Manifesto": Catholics and the Left*, London and Melbourne: Sheed and Ward.

Cvetkovich, A. (2012), *Depression: A Public Feeling*, Durham and London: Duke University Press.

Daniel, J. O., and T. Moylan, eds. (1997), *Not Yet: Reconsidering Ernst Bloch*, London and New York: Verso.

Davis, M. (1998), *The Ecology of Fear: Los Angeles and the Imagination of Disaster*, New York: Holt.

Dean, J. (2019), *Comrade: An Essay on Political Belonging*, London and New York: Verso.

De Lauretis, T. (1984), *Alice Doesn't: Feminism, Semiotics, Cinema*, London: Macmillan.

Delany, S. R. (1976), *Triton*, New York: Bantam.

Delany, S. R. (1991), "Reading Modern American Science Fiction," in D. Kostelanetz (ed.), *American Writing Today*, 517–28, Troy: Whitson.

Dellinger, D. (1967), "Resistance: Vietnam and America," *Liberation* 12 (8): 5–6.

Dellinger, D. (1971), "The Future of Nonviolence," in *Revolutionary Nonviolence: Essays by Dave Dellinger*, 368–81, New York: Anchor.

Deming, B. (undated), "On Revolution and Equilibrium," in Nat Hentoff (ed.), *A. J. Muste Essay Series*, 2, New York: War Resisters League.

Dobson, A. (2007), *Green Political Thought*, London and New York, Routledge.

Doctorow, C. (2017), *Walkaway*, London: Head of Zeus.

Dussel, E. (1985), *Philosophy of Liberation*, trans. A. Martinez and C. Morkovsky, Maryknoll, NY: Orbis.

Eagleton, T. (1965), *The New Left Church*, Baltimore: Helicon.

Eagleton, T. (1996), *The Illusions of Postmodernism*, London: Wiley-Blackwell.

Eagleton, T. (1997), "Pretty Much Like Ourselves: Review of *Modern British Utopias 1700–1850* by G. Claeys," *London Review of Books* 19 (17): 6–7.

Eagleton, T. (2015), *Hope Without Optimism*, New Haven and London: Yale University Press.

Eckersley, R. (1992), "Divining Evolution: The Ecological Ethics of Murray Bookchin," *Society and Nature* 2: 120–43

Ehrenreich, B., and J. Ehrenreich (1969), *Long March, Short Spring: The Student Uprising at Home and Abroad*, New York and London: Modern Reader.

Ellis, M. H. (1987), *Toward a Jewish Theology of Liberation*, Maryknoll, NY: Orbis.

Else, L. and S. Žižek (2010), "Wake Up and Smell the Apocalypse: Interview," *New Scientist* 2775: 28–9.

Engels, Frederick (1940), *Dialectics of Nature*, London: Lawrence and Wishart.

Evans, R. (2018), "Nomenclature, Narrative, and Novum: The 'Anthropocene' and/ as Science Fiction," "Symposium on the Climate Crisis," *Science Fiction Studies* 45: 284–500.

Fierro, A. (1977), *The Militant Gospel: A Critical Introduction to Political Theologies*, trans. J. Drury, Maryknoll, NY: Orbis.

Firestone, S. (1970), *The Dialectic of Sex*, New York: Bantam.

Fisher, M. (2009), *Capitalist Realism: Is There No Alternative?* Winchester: Zero Books.

Fitting, P. (1979), "The Modern Anglo-American SF Novel: Utopian Longing and Capitalist Co-optation," *Science-Fiction Studies* 6: 59–76.

Fitting, P. (1987), "Positioning and Closure: On the 'Reading Effect' of Contemporary Utopian Fiction," in G. Beauchamp, K. M. Roemer, and N. D. Smith (eds.), *Utopian Studies I*, 23–36, Lanham, MD: University Press of America.

Fitting, P. (1995), "Impulse or Genre or Neither?" *Science-Fiction Studies* 22: 272–81.

Fitting, P. (1998), "The Concept of Utopia in the Work of Fredric Jameson," *Utopian Studies* 9 (2): 8–18.

Fitzpatrick, K. (2019), *Generous Thinking: A Radical Approach to Saving the University*, Baltimore: Johns Hopkins University Press.

Foote, I. F. [Bud] (2009), "A Conversation with Kim Stanley Robinson," in W. J. Burling and K. S. Robinson (eds.), *Kim Stanley Robinson Maps the Unimaginable: Critical Essays*, 277–92, Jefferson: McFarland and Company.

Foster, J. (2000), *Marx's Ecology: Materialism and Nature*, New York: Monthly Review Press.

Freedman, C. (2005), "To the Perdido Street Station: the Representation of Revolution in China Miéville's *Iron Council*," *Extrapolation* 46 (2): 235–49.

Freire, P. (1971), *Pedagogy of the Oppressed*, trans. M. B. Ramos, New York: Herder and Herder.

Gaffney, M. (2018), "Dark Ice Age and Us: Imagining Geohistory in Kim Stanley Robinson's *Shaman*," *Science Fiction Studies* 45: 469–83.

Garaudy, R. (1966), *From Anathema to Dialogue: A Marxist Challenge to the Christian Churches*, trans. Luke O'Neill, New York: Herder and Herder.

Gardiner, M. E. (2009), "The Grandchildren of Marx and Coca-Cola: Lefebvre, Utopia, and the Recuperation of Everyday Life," in P. Hayden and C. el-Ojeili (eds.), *Globalisation and Utopia: Critical Essays*, 220–37, Basingstoke: Palgrave-Macmillan.

Garforth, L. (2018), *Green Utopias: Environmental Hope Before and After Nature*, Cambridge and Medford: Polity.

Geoghegan, V. (1996), *Ernst Bloch*, London and New York: Routledge.

Geoghegan, V. (1997), "Remembering the Future," in J. O. Daniel and T. Moylan (eds.), *Not Yet: Reconsidering Ernst Bloch*, 15–31, New York: Verso.

Geoghegan, V. (2004), "Ideology and Utopia," *Journal of Political Ideologies* 9 (2): 123–38.

Georgakas, D. and M. Surkin (1998), *Detroit: I Do Mind Dying*, Boston: South End Press.

Goldman, E. (2012), "Anarchism: What It Really Stands For," in *Anarchism and Other Essays*, 13–19, London: Emereo.

Gordin, M. D., H. Tilley, and G. Prakash, eds. (2010), *Utopia/Dystopia: Conditions of Historical Possibility*, Princeton and Oxford: Princeton University Press.

Gramsci, A. (1971), *Selections from the Prison Notebooks*, ed. and trans. Q. Hoare and G. N. Smith, New York: International.

Green, R. M. (1969), "Ernst Bloch's Revision of Atheism," *Journal of Religion* 49: 128–35.

Gregg, R. (1966), *The Power of Nonviolence*, New York: Schocken Books.

Gross, D. (1988), "Bloch's Philosophy of Hope," *Telos* 75: 189–98.

Gutiérrez, G. (1973), *A Theology of Liberation: History, Politics, Salvation*, trans. C. Inda and J. Eagleson, Maryknoll, NY: Orbis.

Hacker, Marilyn (1977), "Science Fiction and Feminism: The Work of Joanna Russ," *Chrysalis* 4: 67–79.

Hall, S. (1990), "The Emergence of Cultural Studies and the Crisis of the Humanities," *October* 53: 11–23.

Hansen, J. (2009), *Storms of My Grandchildren*, New York: Bloomsbury.

Hansen, J. (2018), "Climate Change in a Nutshell: The Gathering Storm," The Nutshell Document, available online: http://www.columbia.edu/~jeh1/mailings/2018/20181206_Nutshell.pdf, (accessed November 20, 2019).

Haraway, D. (1988), "Situated Knowledges: The Science Question in Feminism and the Privilege of Partial Perspective," *Feminist Studies* 14 (3): 575–99.

Haraway, D. (2016), *Staying with the Trouble: Making Kin in the Chthulucene*, Durham and London: Duke University Press.

Hardt, M. (1996), "Introduction: Laboratory Italy," in P. Virno and M. Hardt (eds.), *Radical Thought in Italy: A Potential Politics*, 1–10, Minneapolis and London: University of Minnesota Press.

Hardt, M., and A. Negri (2000), *Empire*, Cambridge, Mass., and London: Harvard University Press.

Hardt, M., and A. Negri (2004), *Multitude*, New York: Penguin.

Hardt, M., and A. Negri (2009), *Commonwealth*, Cambridge, Mass.: Harvard University Press.

Harvey, D. (2000), *Spaces of Hope*, Berkeley: University of California Press.

Heinitz, K. (1968), "The Theology of Hope according to Ernst Bloch," *Dialog* 7: 34–41.

Higgins, D. M. and H. C. O'Connell, eds. (2019), "Special Issue on Speculative Finance/Speculative Fiction," *New Centennial Review* 19 (1).

Higgins, M. D. (2017), *When Ideas Matter*, London: Head of Zeus.

Hinkelammert, F. J. (1986), *The Ideological Weapons of Death: A Theological Critique of Capitalism*, trans. P. Berryman, Maryknoll, NY: Orbis.

Horwitt, S. D. (1989), *Let Them Call Me Rebel: Saul Alinsky – His Life and Legacy*, New York: Knopf.

Huston, S. (2009), "Murray Bookchin on the Production of Mars! The Production of Nature in the Mars Trilogy," in W. J. Burling and K. S. Robinson (eds.), *Kim Stanley Robinson Maps the Unimaginable: Critical Essays*, 231–42, Jefferson: McFarland and Company.

Jacoby, R. (1999), *The End of Utopia: Politics and Culture in an Age of Apathy*, New York: Basic Books.

James, W. (2011), "The Moral Equivalent of War," pamphlet, Milton Keynes: Read Books.

Jameson, F. (1971), *Marxism and Form*, Princeton: Princeton University Press.

Jameson, F. (1975), "World-Reduction in Le Guin: The Emergence of Utopian Narrative," *Science Fiction Studies* 2: 221–30.

Jameson, F. (1976), "Introduction/Prospectus: To Reconsider the Relationship of Marxism to Utopian Thought," Special Supplement on "Marxism and Utopia," *the minnesota review* 6: 53–9.

Jameson, F. (1977), "Of Islands and Trenches: Neutralization and the Production of Utopian Discourse," *diacritics* 7 (2): 2–21.

Jameson, F. (1981), *The Political Unconscious: Narrative as a Socially Symbolic Act*, Ithaca: Cornell UP.

Jameson, F. (1982), "Progress Versus Utopia; Or, Can We Imagine the Future?" *Science-Fiction Studies* 27: 147–59.

Jameson, F. (1983), "Science Versus Ideology," *Humanities in Society* 6 (2): 283–302.

Jameson, F. (1988), "Cognitive Mapping," in C. Nelson and L. Grossberg (eds.), *Marxism and the Interpretation of Culture*, 347–57, Urbana and Chicago: University of Illinois Press.

Jameson, F. (1994), *The Seeds of Time*, New York: Columbia University Press.

Jameson, F. (2000), "'If I find one good city I will spare the man': Realism and Utopia in Kim Stanley Robinson's Mars Trilogy', in P. Parrinder (ed.), *Learning From Other Worlds: Estrangement, Cognition and the Politics of Science Fiction and Utopia*, 208–32, Liverpool and Durham: Liverpool University Press and Duke University Press.

Jameson, F. (2002), "Radical Fantasy," *Historical Materialism* 10 (4): 273–80.

Jameson, F. (2004), "The Politics of Utopia," *New Left Review* 25: 35–56.

Jameson, F. (2005), *Archaeologies of the Future: The Desire Called Utopia and Other Science Fictions*, London: Verso.

Jameson, F. (2007a), *The Modernist Papers*, London: Verso.

Jameson, F. (2007b), "Lenin and Revisionism," in S. Budgen, S. Kouvelakis, and S. Žižek (eds.), *Lenin Reloaded: Toward a Politics of Truth*, 59–74, Durham and London: Duke University Press.

Jameson, F. (2009), *Valences of the Dialectic*, London and New York: Verso.

Jameson, F. (2010), "A New Reading of Capital," *Mediations* 25, available online: http://www.mediationsjournal.org/articles/a-new-reading-of-capital, (accessed December 14, 2019).

Jameson, F. (2016), "An American Utopia," in S. Žižek (ed.), *An American Utopia: Dual Power and the Universal Army*, 1–97, London and New York: Verso.

Kabo, R. (2020), "Imagining End of Capitalism: Utopia and the Commons in Contemporary Literature," Ph.D. Dissertation, Birkbeck, University of London.

Kellner, D. and H. O'Hara (1976), "Utopia and Marxism in Ernst Bloch," *New German Critique* 9: 11–35.

Khouri, N. (1980), "The Dialectics of Power: Utopia in the Science Fiction of Le Guin, Jeuty, and Piercy," *Science-Fiction Studies* 7: 49–61.

Kirby, P. (1981), *Lessons in Liberation: The Church in Latin America*, Dominican Publications.

Kovel, J. (1986), "Cryptic Notes on Revolution and the Spirit," *Old Westbury Review* 2: 23–35.

Kovel, J. (2007), *The Enemy of Nature: The End of Capitalism or the End of the World*, London and New York: Zed.

Laclau, E. and C. Mouffe (1985), *Hegemony and Socialist Strategy: Towards a Radical Democratic Politics*, trans. W. Moore and P. Cammack, London: Verso.

Lamb, M. (1982), *Solidarity with Victims: Toward a Theology of Social Transformation*, New York: Crossroad.

Le Guin, U. K. (1974), *The Dispossessed*, New York: Harper.

Leopold, A. (1966), *A Sand County Almanac*, New York: Ballantine Books.

Lernoux, P. (1982), *Cry of the People: The Struggle for Human Rights in Latin America – The Catholic Church in Conflict with U.S. Policy*, Harmondsworth: Penguin.

Levitas, R. (1990), *The Concept of Utopia*, Syracuse: Syracuse University Press.

Levitas, R. (1997), "Educated Hope: Ernst Bloch on Abstract and Concrete Utopia," in J. O. Daniel and T. Moylan (eds.), *Not Yet: Reconsidering Ernst Bloch*, 65–80, London and New York: Verso.

Levitas, R. (2007), "The Imaginary Reconstitution of Society: Utopia as Method," in T. Moylan and R. Baccolini (eds.), *Utopia Method Vision: The Use Value of Social Dreaming*, 47–69, Oxford and Berne: Peter Lang.

Levitas, R. (2013), *Utopia as Method*, New York and London: Palgrave Macmillan.

Luckhurst, R. (2009), "The Politics of the Network: The Science in the Capital Trilogy," in W. J. Burling and K. S. Robinson (eds.), *Kim Stanley Robinson Maps the Unimaginable: Critical Essays*, 170–81, Jefferson: McFarland and Company.

Luke, T. (1978), "Culture and Politics in the Age of Artificial Negativity," *Telos* 35: 55–73.

Lynd, S., ed. (1966), *Nonviolence in America: A Documentary History*, Indianapolis: Bobbs-Merrill.

MacLeod, K. (2005), *Learning the World: A Novel of First Contact*, London: Orbit.

Marcos, Subcomandante [R. S. G. Vicente] (2001), "The Way," in *Zapatista Stories*, trans. D. Livingstone, 116–20, London: Katabasis.

Marcuse, H. (1955), *Eros and Civilization*, Boston: Beacon Press.

Marcuse, H. (1964), *One-Dimensional Man: Studies in the Ideology of Advanced Industrial Society*, Boston: Beacon Press.

Markley, R. (2009), "Falling into Theory: Simulation, Terraformation and Eco-Economics in the Mars Trilogy," in W. J. Burling and K. S. Robinson (eds.), *Kim Stanley Robinson Maps the Unimaginable: Critical Essays*, 122–44, Jefferson: McFarland and Company.

Marx, K. (1975a), "Letter from Marx to Arnold Ruge, February 10, 1842," in *Marx Engels Collected Works*, Vol. 1, 381–2, New York: International Publishers.

Marx, K. (1975b), *Early Writings*, trans. R. Livingstone and G. Benton, New York: Vintage.

"Marxism and Utopia" (1976), Special Supplement, *the minnesota review* 6.

Matewan (1987), dir. J. Sayles, US: Cinecom.

Matrix, The (1999), dir. L. Wachowski and L. Wachowski, US and Australia: Warner Brothers.

McClean, Paul. 2017, *Culture in Networks*, Cambridge, MA: Polity.

McClenahan, C. (1982), "Textual Politics: The Uses of the Imagination in Joanna Russ's *The Female Man*," *Transactions of the Wisconsin Academy of Sciences, Arts, and Letters*, 7: 114–25.

McGinn, B., ed. (1979), *Apocalyptic Spirituality*, trans. B. McGinn, New York and Toronto: Paulist Press.

McGuirk, C. (1994), "No Where Man: Towards a Poetics of Post-Utopian Characterisation," *Science-Fiction Studies* 21: 141–55.

McGuirk, C. (1995), "On Darko Suvin's Good-natured Critique," *Science-Fiction Studies* 22: 138–40.

McKay, G. (1994), "Metapropaganda: Self-Reading Dystopian Fiction: Burdekin's *Swastika Night* and Orwell's *Nineteen Eighty-Four*," *Science-Fiction Studies* 21: 302–15.

McManus, S. (2003), "Fabricating the Future: Becoming Bloch's Utopians," *Utopian Studies* 14 (2): 1–22.

McManus, S. (2005), *Fictive Theories: Towards a Deconstructive and Utopian Political Imagination*, New York and Basingstoke: Palgrave.

McRobbie, A. (1982), "The Politics of Feminist Research: Between Talk, Text and Action," *Feminist Review* 12: 46–57.

Menchú, R. (1984), *I, Rigoberta Menchú*, ed. E. Burgos-Debray, trans. A. Wright, London and New York: Verso.

Merton, T. (1975), *Asian Journal*, New York: New Directions.

Merton, T. (2017), *A Course in Christian Mysticism*, ed. J. Sweeney, Collegeville: Liturgical Press.

Metz, J. B. (1969), *Theology of the World*, trans. W. Glen-Doepel, New York: Herder and Herder.

Metz, J. B. (1980), *Faith in History and Society: Toward a Practical Fundamental Theology*, trans. D. Smith, New York: Seabury.

Miéville, C. (2000), *Perdido Street Station*, London: Macmillan.

Miéville, C. (2002a), *The Scar*, London: Macmillan.

Miéville, C. (2002b), "Editorial Introduction: Symposium on Marxism and Fantasy," *Historical Materialism* 10 (4): 39–51.

Miéville, C. (2004), *The Iron Council*, London: Macmillan.

Míguez Bonino, J. (1975), *Doing Theology in a Revolutionary Situation*, Philadelphia: Fortress.

Moltmann, J. (1967), *The Theology of Hope*, trans. J. Leitch, New York and Evanson: Harper and Row.

Moltmann, J. (1968), "Hope and Confidence: A Conversation with Ernst Bloch," *Dialog* 7: 42–55.

Moore, J. (2015), *Capitalism in the Web of Life: Ecology and the Accumulation of Capital*, London and New York: Verso.

Morris, M. (1988), "Banality in Cultural Studies," *Discourse* 10: 3–29.

Moylan, T. (1980), "Beyond Negation: The Critical Utopias of Ursula K. Le Guin and Samuel R, Delany," *Extrapolation* 21 (3): 236–54.

Moylan, T. (1986), *Demand the Impossible: Science Fiction and the Utopian Imagination*, London and New York: Methuen.

Moylan, T. (1988), "Rereading Religion: Ernst Bloch, Gustavo Gutiérrez and the Post-Modern Strategy of Liberation Theology," *Center for Twentieth Century Studies Working Papers* 2: 1–26.

Moylan, T. (1989), "Anticipatory Fiction: *Bread and Wine* and Liberation Theology," *Modern Fiction Studies* 35 (1): 103–21.

Moylan, T. (1990), "Mission Impossible: Liberation Theology and Utopian Praxis," in M. Cummings and N. D. Smith (eds.), *Utopian Studies III*, 20–30, Lanham, MD: University Press of America.

Moylan, T. (1991), "Denunciation/Annunciation: The Radical Methodology of Liberation Theology," *Cultural Critique* 20: 33–64.

Moylan, T. (1997), "Bloch against Bloch: The Theological Reception of *Das Prinzip Hoffnung* and the Liberation of the Utopian Function," in J. O. Daniel and T. Moylan (eds.), *Not Yet: Reconsidering Ernst Bloch*, 96–121, New York: Verso.

Moylan, T. (2000a), "'Dare to struggle, dare to win': On Science Fiction, Totality, and Agency in the Nineties," in Karen Sayer and John Moore (eds.), *Science Fiction: Critical Frontiers*, 48–69, New York and Oxford: Macmillan.

Moylan, T. (2000b), "'Look into the dark': On Dystopia and the Novum," in Patrick Parrinder (ed.), *Learning from Other Worlds: Estrangement, Cognition and the Politics of Science Fiction and Utopia*, 51–72, Liverpool: Liverpool University Press.

Moylan, T. (2000c), *Scraps of the Untainted Sky: Science Fiction, Utopia, Dystopia*, Boulder and Oxford: Westview.

Moylan, T. (2004), "Report on Scenario Building in Millennium Ecosystem Project," *Millennium Ecosystem Assessment*, World Resources Institute.

Moylan, T. (2007), "Realizing Better Futures: Strong Thought for Hard Times," in T. Moylan and R. Baccolini (eds.), *Utopia Method Vision: The Use Value of Social Dreaming*, 191–223, Oxford and Bern: Peter Lang.

Moylan, T. (2008), "Making the Present Impossible: On the Vocation of Utopian Science Fiction," *Arena* 31: 79–109.

Moylan, T. (2011), "N-H-N': Kim Stanley Robinson's Dialectics of Ecology," *Arena* 35 (36): 22–44.

Moylan, T. (2014a), *Demand the Impossible: Science Fiction and the Utopian Imagination*, Ralahine Classic Edition, ed. R. Baccolini, Oxford and Bern: Peter Lang.

Moylan, T. (2014b), "Introduction to the Classic Edition," in R. Baccolini (ed.), *Demand the Impossible: Science Fiction and the Utopian Imagination*, ix–xxix, Oxford and Bern: Peter Lang.

Moylan, T. (2015), "'To live consciously is to sow the whirlwind': Reflections on the Utopian Standpoint of Nonviolence," *Utopian Studies* 26 (1): 184–202.

Moylan, T. (2016), "Steps of Renewed Praxis: Tracking the Utopian Method," *the minnesota review* 86: 101–22.

Moylan, T. (2020), "The Necessity of Hope in Dystopian Times: A Critical Reflection," *Utopian Studies* 31 (1): 164–93.

Moylan, T., and R. Baccolini, eds. (2007), *Utopia Method Vision: The Use Value of Social Dreaming*, Oxford and Bern: Peter Lang.

Murphy, P. D. (2000), *Farther Afield in the Study of Nature-oriented Literature*, Charlottesville: University Press of Virginia.

Murphy, P. D. (2018), "SF and Anthropogenic Climate Change," "Symposium on the Climate Crisis," *Science Fiction Studies* 45: 423–24.

Negt, O., and J. Zipes (1975), "Ernst Bloch—The German Philosopher of the October Revolution," *New German Critique* 4: 3–16.

Ní Bheacháin, C. and A. Mitchell (2019), "Alice Stopford Green and Vernon Lee: Salon Culture and Intellectual Exchange," *Journal of Victorian Culture*, vcz053, available online: https://doi.org/10.1093/jvcult/vcz053, (accessed March 15, 2020).

Nixon, R. (2013), *Slow Violence and the Environmentalism of the Poor*, Cambridge, MA, and London: Harvard University Press.

Nuttall, J. (1970), *Bomb Culture*, New York: Harper.

Otto, E. (2009), "The Mars Trilogy and the Leopoldian Land Ethic," in W. J. Burling and K. S. Robinson (eds.), *Kim Stanley Robinson Maps the Unimaginable: Critical Essays*, 242–57, Jefferson: McFarland and Company.

Pak, C. (2018), "Terraforming and Geo-engineering in *Luna: New Moon*, *2312*, and *Aurora*," *Science Fiction Studies* 45: 500–14.

Parrinder, P., ed. (2000), *Learning from Other Worlds: Estrangement, Cognition and the Politics of Science Fiction and Utopia*, Liverpool: Liverpool University Press.

Peck, D. (1977), "*Weapons of Criticism: Marxism in America and the Literary Tradition: Review*," *the minnesota review* 8: 153–6.

Penley, C. (1989), *The Future of an Illusion: Film, Feminism and Psychoanalysis*, Minneapolis: University of Minnesota Press.

Perls, F. S., R. F. Hefferline, and P. Goodman (1951), *Gestalt Therapy: Excitement and Growth in the Human Personality*, New York: Penguin.

Peterson, B. (1975), "Mass Socialist Organizations: What They Are, Why We Must Build Them, and How They Relate to the Current Tasks of the Movement," pamphlet, Milwaukee: Wisconsin Alliance.

Piccone, P. (1977), "The Changing Function of Critical Theory," *New German Critique* 12: 24–38.

Piccone, P. (1978), "The Crisis of One-Dimensionality," *Telos* 35: 43–55.

Piercy, M. (1976), *Woman on the Edge of Time*, New York: Knopf.

Piercy, M. (1991), *He, She and It*, New York: Knopf.

Piven, F. F. and R. A. Cloward (1979), *Poor People's Movements: Why They Succeed, How They Fail*, New York: Vintage Books.

Prettyman, G. (2009) "Living Thought: Genes, Genres and Utopia in the Science in the Capital Trilogy," in W. J. Burling and K. S. Robinson (eds.), *Kim Stanley Robinson Maps the Unimaginable: Critical Essays*, 181–204, Jefferson: McFarland and Company.

Pullman, P. (1998), *The Subtle Knife*, New York: Scholastic Point.

Quaker Faith and Practice (1995), London: Religious Society of Friends in Britain.

Rabinbach, A. (1977), "Ernst Bloch's *Heritage of Our Times* and the Theory of Fascism," *New German Critique* 1: 5–21.

Rabinbach, A. (1983), "Between Enlightenment and Apocalypse: Benjamin, Bloch and Modern Jewish Messianism," *New German Critique* 34: 78–125.

"Radioactive Half-Life" (2005), February 12, available online: http//hyperphysics.phy-astr.gsu.edu/hbase/nuclear/halfi.html, (accessed February 12, 2005).

Raulet, G. (1976), "Critique of Religion and Religion as Critique: The Secularized Hope of Ernst Bloch," *New German Critique* 9: 71–85.

Reding, A., ed. (1987), *Christianity and Revolution: Tomás Borge's Theology of Life*, trans. A. Reding, Ossining, NY: Orbis Books.

Reeves, M. (1969), *The Influence of Prophecy in the Later Middle Ages: A Study in Joachimism*, Notre Dame and London: University of Notre Dame Press.

Reeves, M. (1976), *Joachim of Fiore and the Prophetic Future*, London: SPCK Press.

Reeves, M. and W. Gould (1987), *Joachim of Fiore and the Myth of the Eternal Evangel in the 19th Century*, Oxford: Clarendon Press.

Reuther, R. R. (1983), *Sexism and God-Talk: Toward a Feminist Theology*, Boston: Beacon Press.

Richard, P., and R. Alves (1986), "Introduction," in F. J. Hinkelammert, *The Ideological Weapons of Death*, trans, P. Berryman, xi–xxi, Maryknoll, NY: Orbis.

Robertson, M. (2018), *The Last Utopians: Four Late Nineteenth Century Visionaries and their Legacy*, Princeton and Oxford: Princeton University Press.

Robinson, A. (2015), "Alain Badiou: Political Action and the Organisation Politique," *Ceasefire*, available online: https://ceasefiremagazine.co.uk/alain-badiou-political-action-organisation-politique/, (accessed March 30, 2015).

Robinson, K. S. (1990), *Pacific Edge*, New York: Unwin Hyman.

Robinson, K. S. (1992), *Red Mars*, New York: HarperCollins.

Robinson, K. S. (1993), *Green Mars*, New York: HarperCollins.

Robinson, K. S. (1994) "Introduction," in K. S. Robinson (ed.), *Future Primitive: The New Ecotopias*, 9–13, New York: Tor Books.

Robinson, K. S. (1996), *Blue Mars*, New York: HarperCollins.

Robinson, K. S. (1997) *Antarctica*, New York: HarperCollins.

Robinson, K. S. (1999), *The Martians*, London: HarperCollins.

Robinson, K. S. (2002), *The Years of Rice and Salt*, London: HarperCollins.

Robinson, K. S. (2004), *Forty Signs of Rain*, New York: Bantam.

Robinson, K. S. (2005), *Fifty Degrees Below*, New York: Bantam.

Robinson, K. S. (2007a), *Sixty Days and Counting*, New York: Bantam.

Robinson, K. S. (2007b), "Imagining Abrupt Climate Change: Terraforming Earth, an Amazon Short," available online: http://www.amazon.com/Imagining-Abrupt-Climate-Change-Terraforming, (accessed August 22, 2007).

Robinson, K. S. (2009), *Galileo's Dream*, London: Harper.

Robinson, K. S. (2012), *2312*, London: Orbit.

Robinson, K. S. (2013), *Shaman*, London: Orbit.

Robinson, K. S. (2015a), *Aurora*, London: Orbit.

Robinson, K. S. (2015b), *Green Earth*, New York: Del Rey.

Robinson, K. S. (2016), "Remarks on Utopia in the Age of Climate Change," *Utopian Studies* 27 (1): 2–16.

Robinson, K. S. (2017), *New York 2140*, New York: Orbit.

Robinson, K. S. (2018), "Story Spaces of Climate Change," "Symposium on the Climate Crisis," *Science Fiction Studies* 45: 426–7.

Rowbotham, S. (1979), "The Women's Movement and Organizing for Socialism," in S. Rowbotham, L. Segal, and H. Wainwright (eds.), *Beyond the Fragments: Feminism and the Making of Socialism*, 21–57, Boston: Alyson.

Rudich, N., ed. (1976), *Weapons of Criticism: Marxism in America and the Literary Tradition*, Palo Alto: Ramparts Press.

Russ, J. (1972), "What Can a Heroine Do? Or Why Women Can't to Write," in S. Kopelman Cornillon (ed.), *Images of Women in Fiction: Feminist Perspectives*, 79–93, Bowling Green: Bowling Green University Popular Press.

Russ, J. (1975), *The Female Man*, New York: Bantam.

Sargent, L. T. (1994), "Three Faces of Utopianism Revisited," *Utopian Studies* 5 (1): 1–38.

Sargent, L. T. (2007), "Choosing Utopia: Utopianism as an Essential Element in Political Thought and Action," in T. Moylan and R. Baccolini (eds.), *Utopia Method Vision: The Use Value of Social Dreaming*, 301–19, Oxford and Berne: Peter Lang.

Sargent, L. T. (2008), "Ideology and Utopia: Karl Mannheim and Paul Ricoeur," *Journal of Political Ideologies* 13 (3): 263–73.

Sargent, L. T. (2010), *Utopianism: A Very Short Introduction*, Oxford: Oxford University Press.

Sargent, L. T (2016), *Utopian Literature in English: An Annotated Bibliography from 1516 to the Present*, University Park, PA: Penn State Libraries Open Publishing, doi:10.18113/P8WC77.77

Sargisson, L. (2007), "The Curious Relationship between Politics and Utopia," in T. Moylan and R. Baccolini (eds.), *Utopia Method Vision: The Use Value of Social Dreaming*, 25–47, Oxford and Berne: Peter Lang.

Segundo, J. L. (1973), *The Liberation of Theology*, trans. J. Drury, Maryknoll, NY: Orbis.

Sibley, M. Q., ed. (1963), *The Quiet Battle: Writings on the Theory and Practice of Nonviolent Resistance*, Chicago: Quadrangle Books.

Singh, V. (2018), "What Is to Be Done about Climate Change? Some Thoughts as a Writer," "Symposium on the Climate Crisis," *Science Fiction Studies* 45: 429–30.

Smith, P. (1997), *Millennial Dreams: Contemporary Culture and Capital in the North*, London and New York: Verso.

Snyder, G. (1974), "I Went into the Maverick Bar," in *Turtle Island*, 9, New York: New Directions.

Solnit, R. (2009), *A Paradise Built in Hell: There Are Extraordinary Communities That Arise in Disaster*, New York: Penguin.

Solnit, R. (2016), *Hope in the Dark: Untold Histories, Wild Possibilities*, Edinburgh and London: Canongate.

Soper, Kate (1995), *What Is Nature?* London: Blackwell.

Spahr, J. (2015), *That Winter the Wolf Came*, Oakland: Commune Editions.

Spencer, D. (2016), "The Spatial Construction of the Neoliberal Subject," in *The Architecture of Neoliberalism: How Contemporary Architecture Became an Instrument of Control and Compliance*, 25–47, London: Bloomsbury.

Spencer, K. (1983), "'The Red Sun Is High, the Blue Low': Towards a Stylistic Description of Science Fiction," *Science-Fiction Studies* 10: 35–50.

Spivak, G. (2003), *Death of a Discipline*, New York: Columbia University Press.

Suvin, D. (1972), "On the Poetics of the Science Fiction Genre," *College English* 34 (3): 372–83.

Suvin, D. (1973), "Defining the Literary Genre of Utopia: Some Historical Semantics, Some Genology, a Proposal, and a Plea," *Studies in the Literary Imagination* 2 (1973): 121–45.

Suvin, D. (1976), "'Utopian' and 'Scientific': Two Attributes for Socialism from Engels," Special Supplement on "Marxism and Utopia," *the minnesota review* 6: 59–76.

Suvin, D. (1979a), "Defining the Literary Genre of Utopia," in *Metamorphoses of Science Fiction: On the Poetics and History of a Literary Genre*, 37–63, New Haven: Yale University Press.

Suvin, D. (1979b), "SF and the Genological Jungle" in *Metamorphoses of Science Fiction: On the Poetics and History of a Literary Genre*, 16–37, New Haven: Yale University Press.

Suvin, D. (1979c), "SF and the Novum," in *Metamorphoses of Science Fiction: On the Poetics and History of a Literary Genre*, 63–87, New Haven: Yale University Press.

Suvin, D. (1980), "Science Fiction and the Novum," in T. de Lauretis, A. Huyssen, and K. Woodward (eds.), *The Technological Imagination: Theories and Fictions*, 141–59, Madison: Coda.

Suvin, D. (1988a), "For a 'Social' Theory of Literature and Paraliterature: Some Programmatic Reflections," in *Positions and Presuppositions in Science Fiction*, 3–22, Kent: Kent State University Press.

Suvin, D. (1988b), "Narrative Logic, Ideological Domination, and the Range of SF: A Hypothesis with a Historical Text," in *Positions and Presuppositions in Science Fiction*, 61–73, Kent: Kent State University Press.

Suvin, D. (1988c), "Preface," in *Positions and Presuppositions in Science Fiction*, ix–xvii, Kent: Kent State University Press.

Suvin, D. (1988d), "SF as Metaphor, Parable and Chronotope (with the Bad Conscience of Reaganism)," in *Positions and Presuppositions in Science Fiction*, 185–214, Kent: Kent State University Press.

Suvin, D. (1988e), "Science Fiction and Utopian Fiction: Degrees of Kinship," in *Positions and Presuppositions in Science Fiction*, 33–43, Kent: Kent State University Press.

Suvin, D. (1988f), "The SF Novel as Epic Narration: For a Fusion of 'Formal' and 'Sociological' Analysis," in *Positions and Presuppositions in Science Fiction*, 74–86, Kent: Kent State University Press.

Suvin, D., with M. Angenot (1988g), "Not Only But Also: On Cognition and Ideology in SF and SF Criticism," in *Positions and Presuppositions in Science Fiction*, 44–61, Kent: Kent State University Press.

Suvin, D. (1994a), "Growing Old Without Yugoslavia," *Science Fiction Studies* 21: 124–6.

Suvin, D. (1994b), "Revelation vs. Conflict: A Lesson from Nô Plays for a Comparative Dramaturgy," *Theatre Journal* 46 (4): 523–38.

Suvin, D. (1995), "For the 'Quirks & Quarks' (Moods and Facts?) Dept," *Science-Fiction Studies* 22: 137–8.

Suvin, D. (1997a), "Locus, Horizon, and Orientation: The Concept of Possible Worlds as a Key to Utopian Studies," in J. O. Daniel and T. Moylan (eds.), *Not Yet: Reconsidering Ernst Bloch*, 122–37, New York: Verso.

Suvin, D. (1997b), "Novum Is as Novum Does," *Foundation: The Review of Science Fiction* 69: 26–43.

Suvin, D. (2000), "Considering the Sense of 'Fantasy' or 'Fantastic Fiction': An Effusion," *Extrapolation* 41 (3): 209–47.

Suvin, D. (2010), *Defined by a Hollow: Essays on Utopia, Science Fiction, and Political Epistemology*, Ralahine Reader, Oxford and Berne: Peter Lang.

Suvin, D. (2016), *Metamorphoses of Science Fiction: On the Poetics and History of a Literary Genre*, Ralahine Classic Edition, ed. Gerry Canavan, Oxford and Berne: Peter Lang.

Taussig, M. T. (1987), *Shamanism, Colonialism, and the Wild Man: A Study in Terror and Healing*, Chicago: University of Chicago Press.

Theoharris, J. (2013), *The Rebellious Life of Mrs. Rosa Parks*, Boston: Beacon Press.

Thompson, E. P. (1977), *William Morris: Romantic to Revolutionary*, London: Merlin.

Thoreau, H. D. (1981), "Essay on Civil Disobedience," in Joseph Wood Krutch (ed.), *Walden and Other Writings*, 89–111, New York: Bantam.

Thunberg, G. (2019), "How Dare You!" UN Speech, available online: https://www.youtube.com/watch?v=rYxt0BeTrT8, (accessed September 24, 2019).

"Titration" (2006), March 15, available online: https://www.britannica.com/science/titration, (accessed 15 March 2006).

Tracy, J. (1966), *Direct Action: Radical Pacifism from the Union Eight to the Chicago Seven*, Chicago: University of Chicago Press.

Tyler, I. (2013), *Revolting Subjects: Social Abjection and Resistance in Neoliberal Britain*, London and New York: Zed Books.

Unger, R. (2005), *What Should the Left Propose?* London: Verso.

"Utopia," Special Issue, 1965, *Daedalus* (Spring).

Varsam, M. (2003), "Concrete Dystopia: Slavery and Its Others," in R. Baccolini and T. Moylan (eds.), *Dark Horizons: Science Fiction and the Dystopian Imagination*, 203–25, New York and London: Routledge.

Vattimo, G. (1992), *The End of Modernity*, trans. J. R., Snyder, Cambridge: Polity.

Vint, S. and M. Bould (2009), "Dead Penguins in Immigrant Pilchard Scandal: Telling Stories about 'the Environment' in *Antarctica*" in W. J. Burling and K. S. Robinson (eds.), *Kim Stanley Robinson Maps the Unimaginable: Critical Essays*, 257–77, Jefferson: McFarland and Company.

Virno, P. (1996), "The Ambivalence of Disenchantment," in P. Virno and M. Hardt (eds.), *Radical Thought in Italy: A Potential Politics*, 13–37, Minneapolis and London: University of Minnesota Press.

Von Hoffman, N. (2010), *Radical: A Portrait of Saul Alinsky*, New York: Nation Books.

Walton, J. (2019), *Lent*, New York: Tor.

Webb, D. (2016), "Educational Studies and the Domestication of Utopia," *British Journal of Educational Studies* 64 (4): 431–8.

Webb, D. (2020), *Utopian Subjectivities: Education, Hope and the Radical Imagination*, Oxford and Berne: Peter Lang.

Weeks, K. (2011), *The Problem with Work: Feminism, Antiwork Politics, and Postwork Imaginaries*, Durham: Duke University Press.

Weeks, K. (2014), "Timely and Untimely Utopianism," in R. Baccolini (ed.), *Demand the Impossible: Science Fiction and the Utopian Imagination*, Ralahine Classic edition, 248–50, Oxford and Berne: Peter Lang.

Wegner, P. E. (1998), "Horizons, Figures, and Machines: The Dialectic of Utopia in the Work of Fredric Jameson," *Utopian Studies* 9 (2): 58–74.

Wegner, P. E. (2002), *Imaginary Communities: Utopia, the Nation, and the Spatial Histories of Modernity*, Berkeley: University of California Press.

Wegner, P. E. (2009), *Life between Two Deaths, 1989–2001: U. S. Culture in the Long Nineties*, Durham and London: Duke University Press.

Wegner, P. E. (2014a), "Musings from a Veteran of the Culture Wars; or, Hope Today," in R. Baccolini (ed.), *Demand the Impossible: Science Fiction and the Utopian Imagination*, 275–82, Oxford and Bern: Peter Lang.

Wegner, P. E. (2014b), *Periodizing Jameson: Dialectics, the University, and the Desire for Narrative*, Evanston: Northwestern University Press.

Wegner, P. E. (2014c), *Shockwaves of Possibility: Essays on Science Fiction, Globalization, and Utopia*, Oxford and Bern: Peter Lang.

Wegner, P. E. (2020), *Invoking Hope: Theory and Utopia in Dark Times*, Minneapolis: University of Minnesota Press.

Welch, S. D. (1985), *Communities of Resistance and Solidarity: A Feminist Theology of Liberation*, Maryknoll, NY: Orbis.

West, C. (1982), *Prophesy Deliverance! An Afro-American Revolutionary Theology*, Philadelphia: Westminster.

Westfahl, G. (1998), *The Mechanics of Wonder: The Creation of the Idea of Science Fiction*, Liverpool, Liverpool University Press.

Wilde, O. (2003), *The Soul of Man under Socialism*, London: Collins.

Williams, Rev A. K., and Lama R. Owens, with J. Syedullah (2016), *Radical Dharma: Talking Race, Love, and Liberation*, Berkeley: North Atlantic Books.

Williams, R. (1977), *Marxism and Literature*, Oxford and New York: Oxford University Press.

Williams, R. (1978), "Utopia and Science Fiction," *Science-Fiction Studies* 5: 203–14.

Williams, R. F. (1962), *Negroes with Guns*, New York: Marzani & Munsell.

Wright, E. O. (2010), *Envisioning Real Utopias*, London and New York: Verso.

Yanarella, E. J. (2001), *The Cross, the Plow and the Skyline: Contemporary Science Fiction and the Ecological Imaginationi*, Parkland: Universal Publishers.

Yúdice, G. (1983), "Marginality and the Ethics of Survival," in Andrew Ross (ed.), *Universal Abandon? The Politics of Postmodernism*, 214–57, Minneapolis: University of Minnesota Press.

Yuknavitch, J. (2017), *The Book of Joan*, Edinburgh: Canongate.

Zaki, H. M (1990), "Utopia, Dystopia and Ideology in the Science Fiction of Octavia Butler," *Science-Fiction Studies* 17: 239–51.

Zipes, J. (1988), "Introduction: Ernst Bloch and the Obscenity of Hope," *New German Critique* 45: 3–8.

Zipes, J. (2019), *Ernst Bloch: The Pugnacious Philosopher of Hope*, Cham, Switzerland: Palgrave Macmillan.

Index